PUBLIC SECTOR MANAGEMENT

Theory, Critique and Practice

edited by

David McKevitt and Alan Lawton
at The Open Business School

in association with
The Open University

SAGE Publications
London · Thousand Oaks · New Delhi

Selection and editorial material © The Open University 1994

Chapter 6 © Leonard Wrigley and David McKevitt 1994

First published 1994

SAGE Publications Ltd
6 Bonhill Street
London EC2A 4PU

SAGE Publications Inc
2455 Teller Road
Thousand Oaks, California 91320

SAGE Publications India Pvt Ltd
32, M-Block Market
Greater Kailash - I
New Delhi 110 048

British Library Cataloguing in Publication data

Public Sector Management:Theory, Critique and
Practice
 I. McKevitt, David II. Lawton, Alan
 354.4107

 ISBN 0–8039–7712–3
 ISBN 0–8039–7713–1 (pbk)

Library of Congress catalog card number 93–087485

Typeset by Type Study, Scarborough
Printed in Great Britain by The Cromwell Press Ltd,
Broughton Gifford, Melksham, Wiltshire

Contents

Preface

This book forms part of the Open Business School's MBA course, Managing Public Services. This course began in 1991 and has been studied by some 600 managers up to 1993. The Reader is intended to provide managers and the interested public with an overview of the purposes, tasks and responsibilities of the public manager.

Throughout the 1980s a key issue for managers was the distinctiveness, or otherwise, of the public sector compared to the private sector. The debate often took on an ideological fervour with an assumption that private sector management, by definition, was good and public sector management, by definition, was inefficient and ineffective. Very little evidence was produced to support this contention. We believe that drawing such battle lines does little to capture the complexity of managing in the public sector. In the 1990s the boundaries of the public sector are being redrawn with purchaser–provider splits, agencies, partnerships and so on. Not only that, but it is increasingly difficult to characterize a generic public sector manager: the image of the 'faceless bureaucrat' bears no relation to reality, if indeed it ever did. Managers are increasingly developing new skills of networking, negotiating, managing budgets and people, developing strategy and taking on leadership roles.

This Reader addresses the political, economic and social context within which managers operate and examines the content of what managers do and the processes through which they do it. In selecting the articles for this Reader we were influenced by the requirement of reflecting some of the current debates on managing in the public services such as those concerned with measuring performance, being responsive to the citizens and managing across organizational boundaries; at the same time we wanted to return to some of the classical debates concerning the role of government, the relationship between the state and the citizen and the economic, moral and social purposes which underpin the role of the manager in the public services. We believe that the issues raised by Oakeshott, Foucault and Simon are crucial in locating theorizing about the public services manager within a wider tradition of theorizing about the role of government. In the concern with markets, competition, privatization and so on hard questions about an appropriate role for government have rarely been asked.

We were also concerned to address that mode of thinking which presupposes that technical or rational solutions can be found for complex social and moral problems. The politicians' search for certainty and the attempt to impose private sector solutions on the 'foreign soul' of the public sector was a feature of the 1980s and its legacy continues to be found in the advocacy of markets and privatization.

The choice of readings is necessarily personal and eclectic, but we believe we have captured the complexity of the management task in the public services and have provided a distinctive collection of readings that will support managers in that task.

The readings are divided into three parts. Part 1 is concerned with the external context of economic, social and moral purposes within which public sector organizations operate. Part 2 addresses some of the internal issues associated with operations and control and Part 3 examines how public service managers can respond to external stakeholders.

Acknowledgements

The editors and publishers wish to thank the following for permission to use copyright material.

Blackwell Publishers for material from Jenny Potter, 'Consumerism and the public sector: how well does the coat fit?', *Public Administration*, Vol. 66, Summer (1988) pp. 149–64; Andrew Dunsire, Keith Hartley and David Parker, 'Organizational status and performance: summary of the findings', *Public Administration*, Vol. 69, Spring (1991) pp. 21–40; and John Stewart and Stewart Ranson, 'Management in the public domain', *Public Money and Management*, Spring/Summer (1988); Cambridge University Press for material from Richard Rose, 'Charges as contested signals', *Journal of Public Policy*, Vol. 9, 3, pp. 261–86; and Challis *et al.*, 'Investigating policy coordination: issues and hypotheses', in *Joint Approaches to Social Policy* (1988) pp. 24–44; Neil Carter for material from his 'Performance indicators: "backseat driving" or "hands off" control?', *Policy and Politics*, Vol. 17, 2, pp. 131–38; The Free Press, a Division of Macmillan, Inc for material from Herbert A. Simon, *Administrative Behavior*, 3rd edn, pp. 172–97. Copyright © 1945, 1947, 1957, 1976 by Herbert A. Simon; Harvester Wheatsheaf and The University of Chicago Press for material from Michel Foucault, 'Governmentality' in *The Foucault Effect*, eds G. Burchell, C. Gordon and P. Miller (1991) pp. 87–104; The Institute of Economic Affairs for material from John Gray, *Limited Government: A Positive Agenda* (1989) pp. 20–36; V. Lynn Meek for material from 'Organizational culture: origins and weaknesses', *Organization Studies*, 9/4 (1988) pp. 453–73; Pergamon Press Ltd for material from Vicki Eaton Baier, James G. March and Harald Sætren, 'Implementation and ambiguity', *Scandinavian Journal of Management*, May (1986) pp. 179–212; Prentice Hall International for material from Anthony Hopwood, 'Accounting and the pursuit of efficiency' in *Issues in Public Sector Accounting*, eds A. G. Hopwood and C. Tomkins, pp. 167–87; Routledge for material from M. Oakeshott, *Rationalism and Politics and Other Essays*, pp. 1–12, Methuen & Co.; and P. Day and R. Klein, *Accountability*, (1957) pp. 227–50, Tavistock Publications. Sage Publications Ltd for material from Margareta Bertilsson, 'The welfare state, the professions and citizens' in *The Formation of Professions: Knowledge, State and Strategy*, eds R. Torstendahl and M. Burrage (1990) pp. 114–33; and Hans Weggemans, 'Personnel and public management' in *Managing Public Organizations*, eds J. Kooiman and K. A. Eliassen (1987) pp. 158–72; Sweet & Maxwell Ltd for material from Joseph M. Jacob, 'Lawyers go to hospital', *Law*, Summer (1991) pp. 255–81; Yale University Press for material from

Rosemary Moss Kanter and David Summers, 'Doing well while doing good: dilemmas of performance measurement in nonprofit organizations and the need for a multiple-constituency approach', *The Non-profit Sector: A Research Handbook*, ed. W. W. Powell, pp. 98–110.

PART 1
THE CONTEXT OF IDEAS

Introduction

The selection of readings has been driven by the requirement to present arguments for the existence of the public sector which do not rest on ideologies of political purposes but rather on economic, social and moral grounds. That is, the value placed on public services is conditioned by historical and cultural tradition as much as it is constrained by current economic and political considerations. The reform of the delivery of public services expressed in such initiatives as the Next Steps agencies and the creation of the internal market in the NHS rest on quite deep and often unstated assumptions concerning the relationship between the state and the citizen. Current political thinking in the UK on public service management is expressed by way of Citizen's Charters in services as diverse in function and purpose as tax collection, education, health care and transport. Leaving aside the issue of what, if any, similarities these diverse functions have in common the question then becomes the nature of the service or transaction that characterizes the relationship between citizen and the state. More exactly, what is the nature of the relationship between the citizen and the managers and professionals who deliver public services in a complex social and economic environment?

The readings in Part 3 address this question in more detail and explore the nature of the citizen–public service manager relationship. Rabbi Hillel expressed the complexities and paradoxes in relations between the individual and his action in a social context: 'If I am not for myself, then who is for me? And if I am not for others, then who am I? And if not now, then when?' The public service manager is one important part of the complex transactions that characterize the relationship between the citizen and the state. This is a role of sovereign importance which can bear heavily on managers as they seek to allocate and ration resources for services to the citizen. Such managers require assistance and support: the Open University MBA course, Managing Public Services, seeks to address their needs.

The problems faced by public service managers are important: do you spend more money on services for 16-year-olds in education as against the allocation of resources to pre-school children in the inner cities? The general nature of political policies finds concrete expression in the work of managers who seek to juggle limited resources in a context of legitimate and competing demands.

The public sector accounts for some 40 per cent of Gross National Product (GNP), some 20 per cent of total employment and, perhaps, some 30 per cent of professional-level employment. Such a large sector requires effective management so that society's resources are properly expended: the current dominant thinking on what constitutes effective public management requires it to be as close to private sector management as possible. The plethora of political reforms in the public sector share a common trait – a remorseless drive to mimic market conditions with devices such as Compulsory Competitive Tendering, Local Management of Schools, and the purchaser–provider split in the 'new NHS market'. It is as if there was one best way, in a technical sense, to manage relationships between the citizen and the state. Michael Oakeshott in the first chapter cautions against the search for universal solutions to political and social problems, a search he sees expressed in the cult of rationality (in this he prefigures the popular airport management books on 'How to Succeed in Business'), the application of technical solutions to complex social and moral issues. He writes that 'if the rational solution for one of the problems of society has been determined, to permit any relevant part of the society to escape from the solution is, *ex hypothesi*, to countenance irrationality. There can be no place for preference that is not rational preference, and all rational preferences necessarily coincide. Political activity is recognized as the imposition of a uniform condition of perfection upon human activity.'

The political search for salvation in mimicking market conditions in the public sector is one such search for a 'uniform condition of perfection'. Michel Foucault's chapter traces the growth of government in Europe; he also identifies this passion for technical solutions to society's problems and associates the rational with the growth of governments' scope and functions. He too is sceptical of the claims for technical solutions to social problems and he asserts that the growth of government has, perforce, crowded out other legitimate social arrangements: 'maybe what is really important for our modernity – that is, for our present – is not so much the étatization of society, as the "governmentalization" of the state'. John Gray's chapter provides the third companion piece in this reflection on the scope and purposes of government. He cautions that 'theories of the minimum state . . . are worse than uninformative – they are virtually empty of content. Even if we grant them a rough-and-ready sense, they are unrealizable. Government in Britain has never, even at its smallest, been the minimum state of classical liberal doctrine'.

Public management shares quite a deal of commonalty in tasks with its private sector counterparts: every manager has to allocate resources, decide on priorities, review progress and plan for future needs. In Chapter 5 Stewart and Ranson argue that the purposes of public management go beyond these tasks: indeed, they assert that public management is primarily concerned with the creation and realization of collective values. The public manager responds to need, not consumer demand; citizen voice is a condition of public management, where consumer exit is a feature of the private market. Stewart and Ranson's chapter is primarily didactic in that they do not provide operational guidance for the public manager as to how desired outcomes can be achieved. Simon provides such operational guidance in his focus on efficiency in Chapter 4: his concept of efficiency specifically includes the realization of community values, a definition much wider than the usual microeconomic-based definitions. In this sense Simon gives us a powerful reminder that values are *endemic* in public management and any attempt to filter out such considerations leads to an impoverished concept of public management. In Chapter 6 Wrigley and McKevitt argue that the grounds for public sector management can be found in terms of professional codes of ethics, differential information and the agenda of government. The articles in Part 1 support and justify a social and moral purpose for the role of the public sector manager.

The readings in Part 1 provide a foundation for examining, in a historical and comparative context, the role and purposes of public management. Their primary value lies in the fact that they demonstrate and explicate the role and functions of public managers in a manner supportive of their tasks: the objective of this Reader is to critically support and evaluate that task. In a very real sense this Reader is directed at *managers*; it is not concerned with treating the role of managing in an abstract or ideological way. There are many treatments of the latter type available; while some may be written from a supportive perspective, we consider that many such texts are driven by less kind motives. The objectives of public managers include the answering of Rabbi Hillel's question 'If I am not for others, then who am I?' It is our wish to support public managers in this social and moral objective: this Reader is part of the broader MBA course objective of providing operational support for this important task.

1

Rationalism in Politics

Michael Oakeshott

1

The object of this chapter is to consider the character and pedigree of the most remarkable intellectual fashion of post-Renaissance Europe. The Rationalism with which I am concerned is modern Rationalism. No doubt its surface reflects the light of rationalisms of a more distant past, but in its depth there is a quality exclusively its own, and it is this quality that I propose to consider, and to consider mainly in its impact upon European politics. What I call Rationalism in politics is not, of course, the only (and it is certainly not the most fruitful) fashion in modern European political thinking. But it is a strong and a lively manner of thinking which, finding support in its filiation with so much else that is strong in the intellectual composition of contemporary Europe, has come to colour the ideas, not merely of one, but of all political persuasions, and to flow over every party line. By one road or another, by conviction, by its supposed inevitability, by its alleged success, or even quite unreflectively, almost all politics today have become Rationalist or near-Rationalist.

The general character and disposition of the Rationalist are, I think, not difficult to identify. At bottom he stands (he always *stands*) for independence of mind on all occasions, for thought free from obligation to any authority save the authority of 'reason'. His circumstances in the modern world have made him contentious: he is the *enemy* of authority, of prejudice, of the merely traditional, customary or habitual. His mental attitude is at once sceptical and optimistic: sceptical, because there is no opinion, no habit, no belief, nothing so firmly rooted or so widely held that he hesitates to question it and to judge it by what he calls his 'reason'; optimistic, because the Rationalist never doubts the power of his 'reason' (when properly applied) to determine the worth of a thing, the truth of an opinion or the propriety of an action. Moreover, he is fortified by a belief in a 'reason' common to all mankind, a common power of rational consideration, which is the ground and inspiration of argument: set up on his door is the precept of Parmenides – judge by rational argument. But besides this, which gives the

From *Rationalism in Politics and Other Essays*, London: Methuen, 1962 (abridged).

Rationalist a touch of intellectual equalitarianism, he is also something of an individualist, finding it difficult to believe that anyone who can think honestly and clearly will think differently from himself.

But it is an error to attribute to him an excessive concern with *a priori* argument. He docs not neglect experience, but he often appears to do so because he insists always upon it being his own experience [. . .] and because of the rapidity with which he reduces the tangle and variety of experience to a set of principles which he will then attack or defend only upon rational grounds. He has no sense of the cumulation of experience, only of the readiness of experience when it has been converted into a formula: the past is significant to him only as an encumbrance. He has none of that *negative capability* [. . .] – the power of accepting the mysteries and uncertainties of experience without any irritable search for order and distinctness – only the capability of subjugating experience; he has no aptitude for that close and detailed appreciation of what actually presents itself [. . .] but only the power of recognizing the large outline which a general theory imposes upon events. [. . .] There are some minds which give us the sense that they have passed through an elaborate education which was designed to initiate them into the traditions and achievements of their civilization; the immediate impression we have of them is an impression of cultivation, of the enjoyment of an inheritance. But this is not so with the mind of the Rationalist, which impresses us as, at best, a finely tempered, neutral instrument, as a well-trained rather than as an educated mind. Intellectually, his ambition is not so much to share the experience of the race as to be demonstrably a self-made man. [. . .] His mind has no atmosphere, no changes of season and temperature; his intellectual processes, so far as possible, are insulated from all external influence and go on in the void. And having cut himself off from the traditional knowledge of his society, and denied the value of any education more extensive than a training in a technique of analysis, he is apt to attribute to mankind a necessary inexperience in all the critical moments of life, and if he were more self-critical he might begin to wonder how the race had ever succeeded in surviving. With an almost poetic fancy, he strives to live each day as if it were his first, and he believes that to form a habit is to fail. And if, with as yet no thought of analysis, we glance below the surface, we may, perhaps, see in the temperament, if not in the character, of the Rationalist, a deep distrust of time, an impatient hunger for eternity and an irritable nervousness in the face of everything topical and transitory. [. . .]

To the Rationalist, nothing is of value merely because it exists (and certainly not because it has existed for many generations), familiarity has no worth, and nothing is to be left standing for want of scrutiny. And his disposition makes both destruction and creation easier for him to under-stand and engage in, than acceptance or reform. To patch up, to repair (that is, to do anything which requires a patient knowledge of the material), he regards as waste of time; and he always prefers the invention of a new device to making use of a current and well-tried expedient. He does not recognize change unless it is a self-consciously induced change, and consequently he falls easily into the error of identifying the customary and the traditional with the changeless. This is aptly illustrated by the rationalist attitude towards a tradition of ideas. There is, of course, no question either of retaining or improving such a tradition, for both these involve an attitude of submission. It must be destroyed. And to fill its place the Rationalist puts something of his own making – an ideology, the formalized abridgment of the supposed substratum of rational truth contained in the tradition.

The conduct of affairs, for the Rationalist, is a matter of solving problems, and in this no man can hope to be successful whose reason has become inflexible by surrender to habit or is clouded by the fumes of tradition. In this activity the character which the Rationalist claims for himself is the character of the engineer, whose mind (it is supposed) is controlled throughout by the appropriate technique and whose first step is to dismiss from his attention everything not directly related to his specific intentions. This assimilation of politics to engineering is, indeed, what may be called the myth of rationalist politics. And it is, of course, a recurring theme in the literature of Rationalism. The politics it inspires may be called the politics of the felt need; for the Rationalist, politics are always charged with the feeling of the moment. He waits upon circumstance to provide him with his problems, but rejects its aid in their solution. That anything should be allowed to stand between a society and the satisfaction of the felt needs of each moment in its history must appear to the Rationalist a piece of mysticism and nonsense. And his politics are, in fact, the rational solution of those practical conundrums which the recognition of the sovereignty of the felt need perpetually creates in the life of a society. Thus, political life is resolved into a succession of crises, each to be surmounted by the application of 'reason'. Each generation, indeed, each administration, should see unrolled before it the blank sheet of infinite possibility. [. . .]

Two other general characteristics of rationalist politics may be observed. They are the politics of perfection, and they are the politics of uniformity. Either of these characteristics without the other denotes a different style of politics; the essence of rationalism is their combination. The evanescence of imperfection may be said to be the first item of the creed of the Rationalist. He is not devoid of humility; he can imagine a problem which would remain impervious to the onslaught of his own reason. But what he cannot imagine is politics which do not consist in solving problems, or a political problem of which there is no 'rational' solution at all. Such a problem must be counterfeit. And the 'rational' solution of any problem is, in its nature, the perfect solution. There is no place in his scheme for a 'best in the circumstances', only a place for 'the best'; because the function of reason is precisely to surmount circumstances. Of course, the Rationalist is not always a perfectionist in general, his mind governed in each occasion by a comprehensive Utopia; but invariably he is a perfectionist in detail. And from this politics of perfection springs the politics of uniformity; a scheme which does not recognize circumstance can have no place for variety. 'There must in the nature of things be one best form of government which all intellects, sufficiently roused from the slumber of savage ignorance, will be irresistibly incited to approve', writes Godwin. This intrepid Rationalist states in general what a more modest believer might prefer to assert only in detail; but the principle holds – there may not be one universal remedy for all political ills, but the remedy for any particular ill is as universal in its application as it is rational in its conception. If the rational solution for one of the problems of a society has been determined, to permit any relevant part of the society to escape from the solution is, *ex hypothesi*, to countenance irrationality. There can be no place for preference that is not rational preference, and all rational preferences necessarily coincide. Political activity is recognized as the imposition of a uniform condition of perfection upon human conduct. [. . .]

2

Every science, every art, every practical activity requiring skill of any sort, indeed every human activity whatsoever, involves knowledge. And, universally, this knowledge is of two sorts, both of which are always involved in any actual activity. It is not, I think, making too much of it to call them two sorts of knowledge, because (though in fact they do not exist separately) there are certain important differences between them. The first sort of knowledge I will call technical knowledge or knowledge of technique. In every art and science, and in every practical activity, a technique is involved. In many activities this technical knowledge is formulated into rules which are, or may be, deliberately learned, remembered and, as we say, put into practice; but whether or not it is, or has been, precisely formulated, its chief characteristic is that it is susceptible of precise formulation, although special skill and insight may be required to give it that formulation. The technique (or part of it) of driving a motor car on English roads is to be found in the Highway Code, the technique of cookery is contained in the cookery book, and the technique of discovery in natural science or in history is in their rules of research, of observation and verification. The second sort of knowledge I will call practical, because it exists only in use, is not reflective and (unlike technique) cannot be formulated in rules. This does not mean, however, that it is an esoteric sort of knowledge. It means only that the method by which it may be shared and becomes common knowledge is not the method of formulated doctrine. And if we consider it from this point of view, it would not, I think, be misleading to speak of it as traditional knowledge. In every activity this sort of knowledge is also involved; the mastery of any skill, the pursuit of any concrete activity is impossible without it.

These two sorts of knowledge, then, distinguishable but inseparable, are the twin components of the knowledge involved in every concrete human activity. In a practical art, such as cookery, nobody supposes that the knowledge that belongs to the good cook is confined to what is or may be written down in the cookery book; technique and what I have called practical knowledge combine to make skill in cookery wherever it exists. And the same is true of the fine arts, of painting, of music, of poetry; a high degree of technical knowledge, even where it is both subtle and ready, is one thing; the ability to create a work of art, the ability to compose something with real musical qualities, the ability to write a great sonnet, is another, and requires, in addition to technique, this other sort of knowledge. Again, these two sorts of knowledge are involved in any genuinely scientific activity. The natural scientist will certainly make use of the rules of observation and verification that belong to his technique, but these rules remain only one of the components of his knowledge; advance in scientific discovery was never achieved merely by following the rules. The same situation may be observed also in religion. It would, I think, be excessively liberal to call a man a Christian who was wholly ignorant of the technical side of Christianity, who knew nothing of creed or formulary, but it would be even more absurd to maintain that even the readiest knowledge of creed and catechism ever constituted the whole of the knowledge that belongs to a Christian. And what is true of cookery, of painting, of natural science and of religion, is no less true of politics: the knowledge involved in political activity is both technical and practical. Indeed, as in all arts which have men as their plastic material, arts such as medicine, industrial management, diplomacy, and the art of military command, the knowledge involved in political activity is pre-eminently of this dual character. Nor, in these arts, is it correct to say that whereas technique will tell a man (for example, a doctor) *what* to do, it is practice which tells him *how* to do it – the 'bedside manner', the appreciation of the individual with whom he has to deal. Even in the *what*, and above all in diagnosis, there lies already this dualism of technique and practice: there is no knowledge which is not 'know how'. Nor, again, does the distinction between technical and practical knowledge coincide with the distinction between a knowledge of means and a knowledge of ends, though on occasion it may appear to do so. In short, nowhere, and pre-eminently not in political activity, can technical knowledge be separated from practical knowledge, and nowhere can they be considered identical with one another or able to take the place of one another.

Now, what concerns us are the differences between these two sorts of knowledge; and the important differences are those which manifest themselves in the divergent ways in which these sorts of knowledge can be expressed and in the divergent ways in which they can be learned or acquired.

Technical knowledge, we have seen, is susceptible of formulation in rules, principles, directions, maxims – comprehensively, in propositions. It is possible to write down technical knowledge in a book. Consequently, it does not surprise us that when an artist writes about his art, he writes only about the technique of his art. This is so, not because he is ignorant of what may be called the aesthetic element, or thinks it unimportant, but because what he has to say about *that* he has said already (if he is a painter) in his pictures, and he knows no other way of saying it. And the same is true when a religious man writes about his religion or a cook about cookery. And it may be observed that this character of being susceptible of precise formulation gives to technical knowledge at least the appearance of certainty: it appears to be possible to be certain about a technique. On the other hand, it is a characteristic of practical knowledge that it is not susceptible of formulation of this kind. Its normal expression is in a customary or traditional way of doing things, or, simply, in practice. And this gives it the appearance of imprecision and consequently of uncertainty, of being a matter of opinion, of probability rather than truth. It is, indeed, a knowledge that is expressed in taste or connoisseurship, lacking rigidity and ready for the impress of the mind of the learner.

Technical knowledge can be learned from a book; it can be learned in a correspondence course. Moreover, much of it can be learned by heart, repeated by rote, and applied mechanically: the logic of the syllogism is a technique of this kind. Technical knowledge, in short, can be both taught and learned in the simplest meanings of these words. On the other hand, practical knowledge can neither be taught nor learned, but only imparted and acquired. It exists only in practice, and the only way to acquire it is by apprenticeship to a master – not because the master can teach it (he cannot), but because it can be acquired only by continuous contact with one who is perpetually practising it. In the arts and in natural science what normally happens is that the pupil, in being taught and in learning the technique from his master, discovers himself to have acquired also another sort of knowledge than merely technical knowledge, without it ever having been precisely imparted and often without being able to say precisely what it is. Thus a pianist acquires artistry as well as technique, a chess-player style and insight into the game as well as a knowledge of the moves, and a scientist acquires (among other things) the sort of judgement which tells him when his technique is leading him astray and the connoisseurship which enables him to distinguish the profitable from the unprofitable directions to explore.

Now, as I understand it, Rationalism is the assertion that what I have called practical knowledge is not knowledge at all, the assertion that, properly speaking, there is no knowledge which is not technical knowledge. The Rationalist holds that the only element of *knowledge* involved in any human activity is technical knowledge, and that what I have called practical knowledge is really only a sort of nescience which would be negligible if it were not positively mischievous. The sovereignty of 'reason', for the Rationalist, means the sovereignty of technique.

The heart of the matter is the preoccupation of the Rationalist with certainty. Technique and certainty are, for him, inseparably joined because certain knowledge is, for him, knowledge which does not require to look beyond itself for its certainty; knowledge, that is, which not only ends with certainty but begins with certainty and is certain throughout. And this is precisely what technical knowledge appears to be. It seems to be a self-complete sort of knowledge because it seems to range between an identifiable initial point (where it breaks in upon sheer ignorance) and an identifiable terminal point, where it is complete, as in learning the rules of a new game. It has the aspect of knowledge that can be contained wholly between the two covers of a book, whose application is, as nearly as possible, purely mechanical, and which does not assume a knowledge not itself provided in the technique. For example, the superiority of an ideology over a tradition of thought lies in its appearance of being self-contained. It can be taught best to those whose minds are empty; and if it is to be taught to one who already believes something, the first step of the teacher must be to administer a purge, to make certain that all prejudices and preconceptions are removed, to lay his foundation upon the unshakeable rock of absolute ignorance. In short, technical knowledge appears to be the only kind of knowledge that satisfies the standard of certainty which the Rationalist has chosen.

Now, I have suggested that the knowledge involved in every concrete activity is never solely technical knowledge. If this is true, it would appear that the error of the Rationalist is of a simple sort – the error of mistaking a part for the whole, of endowing a part with the qualities of the whole. But the error of the Rationalist does not stop there. If his great illusion is the sovereignty of technique, he is no less deceived by the apparent certainty of technical knowledge. The superiority of technical knowledge lay in its appearance of springing from pure ignorance and ending in certain and complete knowledge, its appearance of both beginning and ending with certainty. But, in fact, this is an illusion. As with every other sort of knowledge, learning a technique does not consist in getting rid of pure ignorance, but in reforming knowledge which is already there. Nothing, not even the most nearly self-contained technique (the rules of a game), can in fact be imparted to an empty mind; and what is imparted is nourished by what is already there. A man who knows the rules of one game will, on this account, rapidly learn the rules of another game; and a man altogether unfamiliar with 'rules' of any kind (if such can be imagined) would be a most unpromising pupil. And just as the self-made man is never literally *self*-made, but depends upon a certain kind of society and upon a large unrecognized inheritance, so technical knowledge is never, in fact, self-complete, and can be made to appear so only if we forget the hypotheses with which it begins. And if its self-completeness is illusory, the certainty which was attributed to it on account of its self-completeness is also an illusion. [. . .]

2

Governmentality

Michel Foucault

[. . .] Throughout the Middle Ages and classical antiquity, we find a multitude of treatises presented as 'advice to the prince', concerning his proper conduct, the exercise of power, the means of securing the acceptance and respect of his subjects, the love of God and obedience to him, the application of divine law to the cities of men, etc. But a more striking fact is that, from the middle of the sixteenth century to the end of the eighteenth, there develops and flourishes a notable series of political treatises that are no longer exactly 'advice to the prince', and not yet treatises of political science, but are instead presented as works on the 'art of government'. Government as a general problem seems to me to explode in the sixteenth century, posed by discussions of quite diverse questions. One has, for example, the question of the government of oneself, that ritualization of the problem of personal conduct which is characteristic of the sixteenth century Stoic revival. There is the problem too of the government of souls and lives, the entire theme of Catholic and Protestant pastoral doctrine. There is government of children and the great problematic of pedagogy which emerges and develops during the sixteenth century. And, perhaps only as the last of these questions to be taken up, there is the government of the state by the prince. How to govern oneself, how to be governed, how to govern others, by whom the people will accept being governed, how to become the best possible governor – all these problems, in their multiplicity and intensity, seem to me to be characteristic of the sixteenth century, which lies, to put it schematically, at the crossroads of two processes: the one which, shattering the structures of feudalism, leads to the establishment of the great territorial, administrative and colonial states; and that totally different movement which, with the Reformation and Counter-Reformation, raises the issue of how one must be spiritually ruled and led on this earth in order to achieve eternal salvation. [. . .]

Out of all this immense and monotonous literature on government which extends to the end of the eighteenth century, with the transformations which I will try to identify in a moment, I would like to underline some points that are worthy of notice because they relate to the actual definition of what is meant by the government of the state, of what we would today call the

From G. Burchell, C. Gordon and P. Miller (eds), *The Foucault Effect*, Hemel Hempstead: Harvester Wheatsheaf, 1991, pp. 87–104 (abridged).

political form of government. The simplest way of doing this is to compare all of this literature with a single text which from the sixteenth to the eighteenth century never ceased to function as the object of explicit or implicit opposition and rejection, and relative to which the whole literature on government established its standpoint: Machiavelli's *The Prince*. It would be interesting to trace the relationship of this text to all those works that succeeded, criticized and rebutted it.

We must first of all remember that Machiavelli's *The Prince* was not immediately made an object of execration, but on the contrary was honoured by its immediate contemporaries and immediate successors, and also later at the end of the eighteenth century (or perhaps rather at the very beginning of the nineteenth century), at the very moment when all of this literature on the art of government was about to come to an end. *The Prince* re-emerges at the beginning of the nineteenth century, especially in Germany. [. . .] It makes its appearance in a context which is worth analysing, one which is partly Napoleonic, but also partly created by the Revolution and the problems of revolution in the United States, of how and under what conditions a ruler's sovereignty over the state can be maintained; but this is also the context in which there emerges, with Clausewitz, the problem [. . .] of the relationship between politics and strategy, and the problem of relations of force and the calculation of these relations as a principle of intelligibility and rationalization in international relations; and lastly, in addition, it connects with the problem of Italian and German territorial unity, since Machiavelli had been one of those who tried to define the conditions under which Italian territorial unity could be restored. [. . .]

This whole debate should not be viewed solely in terms of its relation to Machiavelli's text and what were felt to be its scandalous or radically unacceptable aspects. It needs to be seen in terms of something which it was trying to define in its specificity, namely an art of government. Some authors rejected the idea of a new art of government centred on the state and reason of state, which they stigmatized with the name of Machiavellianism; others rejected Machiavelli by showing that there existed an art of government which was both rational and legitimate, and of which Machiavelli's *The Prince* was only an imperfect approximation or caricature; finally, there were others who, in order to prove the legitimacy of a particular art of government, were willing to justify some at least of Machiavelli's writings. [. . .]

The essential thing is that they attempted to articulate a kind of rationality which was intrinsic to the art of government, without subordinating it to the problematic of the prince and of his relationship to the principality of which he is lord and master.

The art of government is therefore defined in a manner differentiating it from a certain capacity of the prince, which some think they can find expounded in Machiavelli's writings, which others are unable to find; while others again will criticize this art of government as a new form of Machiavellianism.

This politics of *The Prince*, fictitious or otherwise, from which people sought to distance themselves, was characterized by one principle: for Machiavelli, it was alleged, the prince stood in a relation of singularity and externality, and thus of transcendence, to his principality. The prince acquires his principality by inheritance or conquest, but in any case he does not form part of it, he remains external to it. The link that binds him to his principality may have been established through violence, through family heritage or by treaty, with the complicity or the alliance of other princes; this makes no difference, the link in any event remains a purely synthetic one and there is no fundamental, essential, natural and juridical connection between the prince and his principality. [. . .] Finally, this principle and its corollary lead to a conclusion, deduced as an imperative: that the objective of the exercise of power is to reinforce, strengthen and protect the principality, but with this last understood to mean not the objective ensemble of its subjects and the territory, but rather the prince's relation with what he owns, with the territory he has inherited or acquired, and with his subjects. This fragile link is what the art of governing or of being prince espoused by Machiavelli has as its object. As a consequence of this the mode of analysis of Machiavelli's text will be twofold: to identify dangers (where they come from, what they consist in, their severity: which are the greater, which the slighter), and, secondly, to develop the art of manipulating relations of force that will allow the prince to ensure the protection of his principality, understood as the link that binds him to his territory and his subjects.

Schematically, one can say that Machiavelli's *The Prince*, as profiled in all these implicitly or explicitly anti-Machiavellian treatises, is essentially a treatise about the prince's ability to keep his principality. And it is this *savoir-faire* that the anti-Machiavellian literature wants to replace by something else and new, namely the art of government. Having the ability to retain one's principality is not at all the same thing as possessing the art of governing. But what does this latter ability comprise? To get a view of this problem, which is still at a raw and early stage, let us consider one of the earliest texts of this great anti-Machiavellian literature: Guillaume de La Perrière's *Miroir Politique*.

This text, disappointingly thin in comparison with Machiavelli, prefigures a number of important ideas. First of all, what does La Perrière mean by 'to govern' and 'governor': what definition does he give of these terms? On page 24 of his text he writes: 'governor can signify monarch, emperor, king, prince, lord, magistrate, prelate, judge and the like'. Like La Perrière, others who write on the art of government constantly recall that one speaks also of 'governing' a household, souls, children, a province, a convent, a religious order, a family.

These points of simple vocabulary actually have important political implications: Machiavelli's prince, at least as these authors interpret him, is by definition unique in his principality and occupies a position of externality and transcendence. We have seen, however, that practices of government are, on the one hand, multifarious and concern many kinds of people: the head of a family, the superior of a convent, the teacher or tutor of a child or pupil; so that there are several forms of government among which the prince's relation to his state is only one particular mode; while, on the other hand, all these other kinds of government are internal to the state or society. It is within the state that the father will rule the family, the superior the convent, etc. Thus we find at once a plurality of forms of government and their immanence to the state: the multiplicity and immanence of these activities distinguishes them radically from the transcendent singularity of Machiavelli's prince.

To be sure, among all these forms of government which interweave within the state and society, there remains one special and precise form: there is the question of defining the particular form of governing which can be applied to the state as a whole. [. . .]

This means that, whereas the doctrine of the prince and the juridical theory of sovereignty are constantly attempting to draw the line between the power of the prince and any other form of power, because its task is to explain and justify this essential discontinuity between them, in the art of government the task is to establish a continuity, in both an upwards and a downwards direction.

Upwards continuity means that a person who wishes to govern the state well must first learn how to govern himself, his goods and his patrimony, after which he will be successful in governing the state. [. . .] It is the pedagogical formation of the prince, then, that will assure this upwards continuity. On the other hand, we also have a downwards continuity in the sense that, when a state is well run, the head of the family will know how to look after his family, his goods and his patrimony, which means that individuals will, in turn, behave as they should. This downwards line, which transmits to individual behaviour and the running of the family the same principles as the good government of the state, is just at this time beginning to be called *police*. The prince's pedagogical formation ensures the upwards continuity of the forms of government, and police the downwards one. The central term of this continuity is the government of the family, termed *economy*.

The art of government [. . .] is essentially concerned with answering the question of how to introduce economy – that is to say, the correct manner of managing individuals, goods and wealth within the family (which a good father is expected to do in relation to his wife, children and servants) and of making the family fortunes prosper – how to introduce this meticulous attention of the father towards his family into the management of the state.

This, I believe, is the essential issue in the establishment of the art of government: introduction of economy into political practice. And if this is the case in the sixteenth century, it remains so in the eighteenth. In Rousseau's *Encyclopaedia* article on 'Political economy' the problem is still posed in the same terms. What he says here, roughly, is that the word 'economy' can only properly be used to signify the wise government of the family for the common welfare of all, and this is its actual original use; the problem, writes Rousseau, is how to introduce it, *mutatis mutandis*, and with all the discontinuities that we will observe below, into the general running of the state. To govern a state will therefore mean to apply economy, to set up an economy at the level of the entire state, which means exercising towards its inhabitants, and the wealth and behaviour of each and all, a form of surveillance and control as attentive as that of the head of a family over his household and his goods.

An expression which was important in the eighteenth century captures this very well: Quesnay speaks of good government as 'economic government'. This latter notion becomes tautological, given that the art of government is just the art of exercising power in the form and according to the model of the economy. But the reason why Quesnay speaks of 'economic government' is that the word 'economy', for reasons that I will explain later, is in the process of acquiring a modern meaning, and it is at this moment becoming apparent that the very essence of government – that is, the art of exercising power in the form of economy – is to have as its main objective that which we are today accustomed to call 'the economy'.

The word 'economy', which in the sixteenth century signified a form of government, comes in the eighteenth century to designate a level of reality, a field of intervention, through a series of complex processes that I regard as absolutely fundamental to our history.

[. . .] Government is the right disposition of things. I would like to pause over this word 'things', because if we consider what characterizes the ensemble of objects of the prince's power in Machiavelli, we will see that for Machiavelli the object and, in a sense, the target of power are two things, on the one hand the territory, and on the other its inhabitants. In this respect, Machiavelli simply adapted to his particular aims a juridical principle which from the Middle Ages to the sixteenth century defined sovereignty in public law: sovereignty is not exercised on things, but above all on a territory and consequently on the subjects who inhabit it. In this sense we can say that the territory is the fundamental element both in Machiavellian principality and in juridical sovereignty as defined by the theoreticians and philosophers of right. Obviously enough, these territories can be fertile or not, the population dense or sparse, the inhabitants rich or poor, active or lazy, but all these elements are mere variables by comparison with territory itself, which is the very foundation of principality and sovereignty. [. . .] One governs things. But what does this mean? I do not think this is a matter of opposing things to men, but rather of showing that what government has to do with is not territory but rather a sort of complex composed of men and things. The things with which in this sense government is to be concerned are in fact men, but men in their relations, their links, their imbrication with those other things which are wealth, resources, means of subsistence, the territory with its specific qualities, climate, irrigation, fertility, etc.; men in their relation to that other kind of things, customs, habits, ways of acting and thinking, etc.; lastly, men in their relation to that other kind of things, accidents and misfortunes such as famine, epidemics, death, etc. The fact that government concerns things understood in this way, this imbrication of men and things, is I believe readily confirmed by the metaphor which is inevitably invoked in these treatises on government, namely that of the ship. What does it mean to govern a ship? It means clearly to take charge of the sailors, but also of the boat and its cargo; to take care of a ship means also to reckon with winds, rocks and storms; and it consists in that activity of establishing a relation between the sailors who are to be taken care of and the ship which is to be taken care of, and the cargo which is to be brought safely to port, and all those eventualities like winds, rocks, storms and so on; this is what characterizes the government of a ship. The same goes for the running of a household. Governing a household, a family, does not essentially mean safeguarding the family property; what concerns it is the individuals that compose the family, their wealth and prosperity. It means to reckon with all the possible events that may intervene, such as births and deaths, and with all the things that can be done, such as possible alliances with other families; it is this general form of management that is character-istic of government; by comparison, the question of landed property for the family, and the question of the acquisition of sovereignty over a territory for a prince, are only relatively secondary matters. What counts essentially is this complex of men and things; property and territory are merely one of its variables.

This theme of the government of things [. . .] can also be met with in the seventeenth and eighteenth centuries. Frederick the Great has some notable pages on it in his *Anti-Machiavel*. He says, for instance, let us compare Holland with Russia: Russia may have the largest territory of any European state, but it is mostly made up of swamps, forests and deserts, and is inhabited by miserable groups of people totally destitute of activity and industry; if one takes Holland, on the other hand, with its tiny territory, again mostly marshland, we find that it nevertheless possesses such a population, such wealth, such commercial activity and such a fleet as to make it an important European state, something that Russia is only just beginning to become.

To govern, then, means to govern things. Let us consider once more the sentence I quoted earlier [. . .]: 'government is the right disposition of things, arranged so as to lead to a convenient end'. Government, that is to say, has a finality of its own, and in this respect again I believe it can be clearly distinguished from sovereignty. I do not of course mean that sovereignty is presented in philosophical and juridical texts as a pure and simple right; no jurist or, *a fortiori*, theologian ever said that the legitimate sovereign is purely and simply entitled to exercise his power regardless of its ends. The sovereign must always, if he is to be a good sovereign, have as his aim, 'the common welfare and the salvation of all'. [. . .] The ruler may not have consideration for anything advantageous for himself, unless it also be so for the state. What does this common good or general salvation consist of, which the jurists talk about as being the end of sovereignty? If we look closely at the real content that jurists and theologians give to it, we can see that 'the common good' refers to a state of affairs where all the subjects without exception obey the laws, accomplish the tasks expected of them, practise the trade to which they are assigned, and respect the established order so far as this order conforms to the laws imposed by God on nature and men: in other words, 'the common good' means essentially obedience to the law, either that of their earthly sovereign or that of God, the absolute sovereign. In every case, what characterizes the end of sovereignty, this common and general good, is in sum nothing other than submission to sovereignty. This means that the end of sovereignty is circular: the end of sovereignty is the exercise of sovereignty. The good is obedience to the law, hence the good for sovereignty is that people should obey it. This is an essential circularity which, whatever its theoretical structure, moral justification or practical effects, comes very close to what Machiavelli said when he stated that the primary aim of the prince was to retain his principality. We always come back to this self-referring circularity of sovereignty or principality.

[. . .] Government is defined as a right manner of disposing things so as to lead not to the form of the common good, as the jurists' texts would have said, but to an end which is 'convenient' for each of the things that are to be governed. This implies a plurality of specific aims: for instance, government will have to ensure that the greatest possible quantity of wealth is produced, that the people are provided with sufficient means of subsistence, that the population is enabled to multiply, etc. There is a whole series of specific finalities, then, which become the objective of government as such. In order to achieve these various finalities, things must be disposed – and this term, *dispose*, is important because with sovereignty the instrument that allowed it to achieve its aim – that is to say, obedience to the laws – was the law itself; law and sovereignty were absolutely inseparable. On the contrary, with government it is a question not of imposing law on men, but of disposing things: that is to say, of employing tactics rather than laws, and even of using laws themselves as tactics – to arrange things in such a way that, through a certain number of means, such and such ends may be achieved.

I believe we are at an important turning point here: whereas the end of sovereignty is internal to itself and possesses its own intrinsic instruments in the shape of its laws, the finality of government resides in the things it manages and in the pursuit of the perfection and intensification of the processes which it directs; and the instruments of government, instead of being laws, now come to be a range of multiform tactics. Within the perspective of government, law is not what is important: this is a frequent theme throughout the seventeenth century, and it is made explicit in the eighteenth-century texts of the Physiocrats which explain that it is not through law that the aims of government are to be reached. [. . .]

This schematic presentation of the notion and theory of the art of government did not remain a purely abstract question in the sixteenth century, and it was not of concern only to political theoreticians. I think we can identify its connections with political reality. The theory of the art of government was linked, from the sixteenth century, to the whole development of the administrative apparatus of the territorial monarchies, the emergence of governmental apparatuses; it was also connected to a set of analyses and forms of knowledge which began to develop in the late sixteenth century and grew in importance during the seventeenth, and which were essentially to do with knowledge of the state, in all its different elements, dimensions and factors of power, questions which were termed precisely 'statistics', meaning the science of the state; finally, as a third vector of connections, I do not think one can fail to relate this search for an art of government to mercantilism and the Cameralists' science of police.

To put it very schematically, in the late sixteenth century and early seventeenth century, the art of government finds its first form of crystallization, organized around the theme of reason of state, understood not in the negative and pejorative sense we give to it today (as that which infringes on the principles of law, equity and humanity in the sole interests of the state), but in a full and positive sense: the state is governed according to rational principles which are intrinsic to it and which cannot be derived solely from natural or divine laws or the principles of wisdom and prudence; the state, like nature, has its own proper form of rationality, albeit of a different sort. Conversely, the art of government, instead of seeking to found itself in transcendental rules, a cosmological model or a philosophico-moral ideal, must find the principles of its rationality in that which constitutes the specific reality of the state. [. . .] But we can say here that, right until the early eighteenth century, this form of 'reason of state' acted as a sort of obstacle to the development of the art of government.

This is for a number of reasons. Firstly, there are the strictly historical ones, the series of great crises of the seventeenth century: first the Thirty Years War with its ruin and devastation; then in the mid-century the peasant and urban rebellions; and finally the financial crisis, the crisis of revenues which affected all Western monarchies at the end of the century. The art of government could only spread and develop in subtlety in an age of expansion, free from the great military, political and economic tensions which afflicted the seventeenth century from beginning to end. Massive and elementary historical causes thus blocked the propagation of the art of government. I think also that the doctrine formulated during the sixteenth century was impeded in the seventeenth by a series of other factors which I might term, to use expressions which I do not much care for, mental and institutional structures. The pre-eminence of the problem of the exercise of sovereignty, both as a theoretical question and as a principle of political organization, was the fundamental factor here so long as sovereignty remained the central question. So long as the institutions of sovereignty were the basic political institutions and the exercise of power was conceived as an exercise of sovereignty, the art of government could not be developed in a specific and autonomous manner. [. . .] Mercantilism is the first rationalization of the exercise of power as a practice of government; for the first time with mercantilism we see the development of a *savoir* of state that can be used as a tactic of government. All this may be true, but mercantilism was blocked and arrested, I believe, precisely by the fact that it took as its essential objective the might of the sovereign; it sought a way not so much to increase the wealth of the country as to allow the ruler to accumulate wealth, build up his treasury and create the army with which he could carry out his policies. And the instruments mercantilism used were laws, decrees, regulations: that is to say, the traditional weapons of sovereignty. The objective was sovereign's might, the instruments those of sovereignty: mercantilism sought to reinsert the possibilities opened up by a consciously conceived art of government within a mental and institutional structure, that of sovereignty, which by its very nature stifled them.

Thus, throughout the seventeenth century up to the liquidation of the themes of mercantilism at the beginning of the eighteenth, the art of government remained in a certain sense immobilized. It was trapped within the inordinately vast, abstract, rigid framework of the problem and institution of sovereignty. This art of government tried, so to speak, to reconcile itself with the theory of sovereignty by attempting to derive the ruling principles of an art of government from a renewed version of the theory of sovereignty. [. . .] Contract theory enables the founding contract, the mutual pledge of ruler and subjects, to function as a sort of theoretical matrix for deriving the general principles of an art of government. But although contract theory, with its reflection on the relationship between ruler and subjects, played a very important role in theories of public law, in practice [. . .] it remained at the stage of the formulation of general principles of public law.

On the one hand, there was this framework of sovereignty which was too large, too abstract and too rigid; and on the other, the theory of government suffered from its reliance on a model which was too thin, too weak and too insubstantial, that of the family: an economy of enrichment still based on a model of the family was unlikely to be able to respond adequately to the importance of territorial possessions and royal finance.

How then was the art of government able to outflank these obstacles? Here again a number of general processes played their part: the demographic expansion of the eighteenth century, connected with an increasing abundance of money, which in turn was linked to the expansion of agricultural production through a series of circular processes with which the historians are familiar. If this is the general picture, then we can say more precisely that the art of government found fresh outlets through the emergence of the problem of population; or let us say rather that there occurred a subtle process, which we must seek to reconstruct in its particulars, through which the science of government, the recentring of the theme of economy on a different plane from that of the family, and the problem of population are all interconnected.

It was through the development of the science of government that the notion of economy came to be recentred on to that different plane of reality which we characterize today as the 'economic', and it was also through this science that it became possible to identify problems specific to the population; but conversely we can say as well that it was thanks to the perception of the specific problems of the population, and thanks to the isolation of that area of reality that we call the economy, that the problem of government finally came to be thought, reflected and calculated outside of the juridical framework of sovereignty. And that 'statistics' which, in mercantilist tradition, only ever worked within and for the benefit of a monarchical administration that functioned according to the form of sovereignty, now becomes the major technical factor, or one of the major technical factors, of this new technology.

In what way did the problem of population make possible the derestriction of the art of government? The perspective of population, the reality accorded to specific phenomena of population, render possible the final elimination of the model of the family and the recentring of the notion of economy. Whereas statistics had previously worked within the administrative frame and thus in terms of the functioning of sovereignty, it now gradually reveals that population has its own regularities, its own rate of deaths and diseases, its cycles of scarcity, etc.; statistics shows also that the domain of population involves a range of intrinsic, aggregate effects, phenomena that are irreducible to those of the family, such as epidemics, endemic levels of mortality, ascending spirals of labour and wealth; lastly it shows that, through its shifts, customs, activities, etc., population has specific economic effects: statistics, by making it possible to quantify these specific phenomena of population, also shows that this specificity is irreducible to the dimension of the family. The latter now disappears as the model of government, except for a certain number of residual themes of a religious or moral nature. What, on the other hand, now emerges into prominence is the family considered as an element internal to population, and as a fundamental instrument in its government.

In other words, prior to the emergence of population, it was impossible to conceive the art of government except on the model of the family, in terms of economy conceived as the management of a family; from the moment when, on the contrary, population appears absolutely irreducible to the family, the latter becomes of secondary importance compared to population, as an element internal to population: no longer, that is to say, a model, but a segment. Nevertheless it remains a privileged segment, because whenever information is required concerning the population (sexual behaviour, demography, consumption, etc.), it has to be obtained through the family. But the family becomes an instrument rather than a model: the privileged instrument for the government of the population and not the chimerical model of good government. This shift from the level of the model to that of an instrument is, I believe, absolutely fundamental, and it is from the middle of the eighteenth century that the family appears in this dimension of instrumentality relative to the population, with the institution of campaigns to reduce mortality, and to promote marriages, vaccinations, etc. Thus, what makes it possible for the theme of population to unblock the field of the art of government is this elimination of the family as model.

In the second place, population comes to appear above all else as the ultimate end of government. In contrast to sovereignty, government has as its purpose not the act of government itself, but the welfare of the population, the improvement of its condition, the increase of its wealth, longevity, health, etc.; and the means that the government uses to attain these ends are themselves all in some sense immanent to the population; it is the population itself on which government will act either directly through large-scale campaigns, or indirectly through techniques that will make possible, without the full awareness of the people, the stimulation of birth rates, the directing of the flow of population into certain regions or activities, etc. The population now represents more the end of government than the power of the sovereign; the population is the subject of needs, of aspirations, but it is also the object in the hands of the government, aware, *vis-à-vis* the government, of what it wants, but ignorant of what is being done to it. Interest at the level of the consciousness of each individual who goes to make up the population, and interest considered as the interest of the population regardless of what the particular interests and aspirations may be of the individuals who compose it, this is the new target and the fundamental instrument of the government of population: the birth of a new art, or at any rate of a range of absolutely new tactics and techniques.

Lastly, population is the point around which is organized what in sixteenth-century texts came to be called the patience of the sovereign, in the sense that the population is the object that government must take into account in all its observations and *savoir*, in order to be able to govern effectively in a rational and conscious manner. The constitution of a *savoir* of government is absolutely inseparable from that of a knowledge of all the processes related to population in its larger sense: that is to say, what we now call the economy. [. . .] In other words, the transition which takes place in the eighteenth century from an art of government to a political science, from a regime dominated by structures of sovereignty to one ruled by techniques of government, turns on the theme of population and hence also on the birth of political economy.

This is not to say that sovereignty ceases to play a role from the moment when the art of government begins to become a political science; I would say that, on the contrary, the problem of sovereignty was never posed with greater force than at this time, because it no longer involved, as it did in the sixteenth and seventeenth centuries, an attempt to derive an art of government from a theory of sovereignty, but instead, given that such an art now existed and was spreading, involved an attempt to see what juridical and institutional form, what foundation in the law, could be given to the sovereignty that characterizes a state. It suffices to read in chronological succession two different texts by Rousseau. In his *Encyclopaedia* article on 'Political economy', we can see the way in which Rousseau sets up the problem of the art of government by pointing out (and the text is very characteristic from this point of view) that the word 'economy' essentially signifies the management of family property by the father, but that this model can no longer be accepted, even if it had been valid in the past; today we know, says Rousseau, that political economy is not the economy of the family [. . .]. Later he writes *The Social Contract*, where he poses the problem of how it is possible, using concepts like nature, contract and general will, to provide a general principle of government which allows room both for a juridical principle of sovereignty and for the elements through which an art of government can be defined and characterized. Consequently, sovereignty is far from being eliminated by the emergence of a new art of government, even by one which has passed the threshold of political science; on the contrary, the problem of sovereignty is made more acute than ever.

As for discipline, this is not eliminated either; clearly its modes of organization, all the institutions within which it had developed in the seventeenth and eighteenth centuries – schools, manufactories, armies, etc. – all this can only be understood on the basis of the development of the great administrative monarchies, but nevertheless, discipline was never more important or more valorized than at the moment when it became important to manage a population; the managing of a population not only concerns the collective mass of phenomena, the level of its aggregate effects, it also implies the management of population in its depths and its details. The notion of a government of population renders all the more acute the problem of the foundation of sovereignty (consider Rousseau) and all the more acute equally the necessity for the development of discipline (consider all the history of the disciplines, which I have attempted to analyse elsewhere). [. . .]

In conclusion I would like to say that on second thoughts the more exact title I would like to have given [to the course of lectures which I have begun this year] is not the one I originally chose, 'Security, territory and population': what I would like to undertake is something which I would term a history of 'governmentality'. By this word I mean three things:

1 The ensemble formed by the institutions, procedures, analyses and reflections, the calculations and tactics that allow the exercise of this very specific albeit complex form of power, which has as its target population, as its principal form of knowledge political economy, and as its essential technical means apparatuses of security.
2 The tendency which, over a long period and throughout the West, has steadily led towards the pre-eminence over all other forms (sovereignty, discipline, etc.) of this type of power which may be termed government, resulting, on the one hand, in the formation of a whole series of specific governmental apparatuses, and, on the other, in the development of a whole complex of *savoirs*.
3 The process, or rather the result of the process, through which the state of justice of the Middle Ages, transformed into the administrative state

during the fifteenth and sixteenth centuries, gradually becomes 'governmentalized'.

We all know the fascination which the love, or horror, of the state exercises today; we know how much attention is paid to the genesis of the state, its history, its advance, its power and abuses, etc. The excessive value attributed to the problem of the state is expressed, basically, in two ways: the one form, immediate, affective and tragic, is the lyricism of the *monstre froid* we see confronting us; but there is a second way of overvaluing the problem of the state, one which is paradoxical because apparently reductionist: it is the form of analysis that consists in reducing the state to a certain number of functions, such as the development of productive forces and the reproduction of relations of production, and yet this reductionist vision of the relative importance of the state's role nevertheless invariably renders it absolutely essential as a target needing to be attacked and a privileged position needing to be occupied. But the state, no more probably today than at any other time in its history, does not have this unity, this individuality, this rigorous functionality, nor, to speak frankly, this importance; maybe, after all, the state is no more than a composite reality and a mythicized abstraction, whose importance is a lot more limited than many of us think. Maybe what is really important for our modernity – that is, for our present – is not so much the *étatisation* of society, as the 'governmentalization' of the state.

We live in the era of a 'governmentality' first discovered in the eighteenth century. This governmentalization of the state is a singularly paradoxical phenomenon, since if in fact the problems of govermentality and the techniques of government have become the only political issue, the only real space for political struggle and contestation, this is because the governmentalization of the state is at the same time what has permitted the state to survive, and it is possible to suppose that if the state is what it is today, this is so precisely thanks to this governmentality, which is at once internal and external to the state, since it is the tactics of government which make possible the continual definition and redefinition of what is within the competence of the state and what is not, the public versus the private, and so on; thus the state can only be understood in its survival and its limits on the basis of the general tactics of governmentality.

And maybe we could even, albeit in a very global, rough and inexact fashion, reconstruct in this manner the great forms and economies of power in the West. First of all, the state of justice, born in the feudal type of territorial regime which corresponds to a society of laws – either customs or written laws – involving a whole reciprocal play of obligation and litigation; second, the administrative state, born in the territoriality of national boundaries in the fifteenth and sixteenth centuries and corresponding to a society of regulation and discipline; and finally a governmental state, essentially defined no longer in terms of its territoriality, of its surface area, but in terms of the mass of its population with its volume and density, and indeed also with the territory over which it is distributed, although this figures here only as one among its component elements. This state of government which bears essentially on population and both refers itself to and makes use of the instrumentation of economic *savoir* could be seen as corresponding to a type of society controlled by apparatuses of security. [. . .]

3

Limited Government

John Gray

Freedom, like a recipe for game pie, is not a bright idea; it is not a 'human right' to be deduced from some speculative concept of human nature. The freedom which we enjoy is nothing more than arrangements, procedures of a certain kind. . . . And the freedom which we wish to enjoy is not an 'ideal' which we premeditate independently of our political experience, it is what is already intimated in that experience. (Michael Oakeshott, *Rationalism in Politics and Other Essays*. London: Methuen, 1962, p. 120)

The Fallacy of the Minimum State and the Mirage of *Laissez-Faire*

The scope and limits of government cannot be determined *a priori*. Time, place and historical circumstance are of crucial importance in determining the range and character of intervention by the state in civil society. To assert this necessary indeterminacy in the functions of government is to go against a powerful tradition in classical liberal thought, which has sought to specify the proper activities of government by a universal doctrine. The simplest (and least compelling) of these is the doctrine of the minimum state, which asserts that the sphere of government action is exhausted by the protection of negative rights. This is the doctrine espoused by von Humboldt, by Herbert Spencer and, in our own day, by Robert Nozick. It has many difficulties, some of them fatal to it.

Most fundamentally, there is the difficulty generated by the vagueness of those negative rights which it is claimed the state has the duty to protect. Is there only one such right – to liberty, say – and, if so, how is it to be defined? (How are conflicts between one man's liberty and another's – between a sphere of privacy and the liberty of expression or information, for example – to be adjudicated?) If there are many such rights, how is practical competition among them to be resolved? The history of judicial review in the United States, which is founded on the supposition that such rights exist and

From John Gray, *Limited Government: A Positive Agenda*, London: Institute of Economic Affairs, 1989, ch. 2, 'Theory', pp. 20–36 (abridged).

have a definite and ascertainable content, is a history of endemic and intractable conflict about them. [. . .]

Classical liberal conceptions of the role of the state that are spelt out in terms of a principle of *laissez-faire* suffer from the disability that that principle is itself practically vacuous. In civil society, the sphere of independence is constituted by a most complex structure of legal immunities, forms of property, and personal and economic liberties – a structure whose specification is given us by no general theory. The contours of the sphere of independence are not natural truths, but instead artefacts of law and convention, subject to the need for recurrent redefinition and sometimes expressing a balance between competing interests and values. The ideal of *laissez-faire* is only a mirage, since it distracts us from the task of assessing our historical inheritance of laws and procedures and reforming it so as to promote the diffusion of power and initiative and thus to enhance the liberty and dignity of individuals.

The Idea of the Minimum State: An Empty Theory

Theories of the minimum state, then, are worse than uninformative – they are virtually empty of content. Even if we grant them a rough-and-ready sense, they are unrealizable. Government in Britain has never, even at its smallest, been the minimum state of classical liberal doctrine. We may regard the severely limited government that prevailed in the late eighteenth and early nineteenth centuries in England as embodying in many respects an ideal worthy of restoration. Nevertheless, present policy cannot be governed simply by the goal of restoring an earlier phase of more limited government. A century and more of interventionism has built up needs and expectations which must be addressed, and it is a mistake to suppose that every move from the status quo in the direction of earlier forms of limited government represents an unequivocal improvement. Again developments wholly external to the growth of government – exogenous changes such as technological innovation and the emergence of a truly global market – render the project of returning to the limited state of early nineteenth-century England an exercise in anachronism.

We are on firmer ground if instead we take the status quo as our point of departure, and ask how government may best be constrained, given the history of the last 200 years. This involves asking what might be the positive responsibilities of government. In the British tradition [. . .] the primordial obligation of government is to make and keep peace, where this encompasses forging and maintaining in good repair the institutions of civil society whereby persons and communities with different and incompatible values and perspectives may co-exist without destructive conflict. It is evident that discharging this duty will commit government to activities that go well beyond the provision of the public goods of national defence and law and order. It may [. . .] entail government supplying families and communities with the means whereby their distinctive values and ways of life may be affirmed and renewed across the generations.

Again, the legal framework of a limited government cannot be (as it might be, if theories of the minimum state were credible) fixed and unalterable. As technology develops and social conditions change, the rules, conventions and practices which make up civil society – which specify the terms of contractual liberty, the character of property rights and the forms of market competition – are bound to require amendment and alteration.

Yet again, the renewal of civil society demands more from government than patient attention to the rules of the game of the market. It requires concern for the health of the autonomous and intermediary institutions which stand between the individual and the state – trade unions, universities, professional organizations and the like. Wise legislators (if such we had) would have the responsibility of maintaining what Burke called 'a balanced constitution' by at once ensuring that none of these autonomous institutions becomes inordinate in its demands and at the same time assuring them all a protected sphere of independence under the rule of law.

Finally, the conception of the minimum state neglects the crucial questions of membership and allegiance. Who is to be a subject of the minimum state, and how is its jurisdiction to be demarcated? And how could a minimum state command the loyalty of its subjects in time of war? These are questions which classical liberal thought passes over or suppresses, but which are salient to any defensible conception of the modern state.

The Limits of Constitutionalism

The insufficiency of the minimum state is patent. Far less obvious is the danger of relying primarily on constitutionalism as a panacea for our ills. I do not mean by this that we cannot benefit by devising new constitutional conventions. On the contrary, I shall suggest, there are indeed new constitutional devices which we might profitably adopt. The danger to which I refer is rather in supposing that we can at a single stroke cut government down to size by removing personal liberty, and especially the economic dimensions of personal liberty, from the realm of political contestation and embedding it in constitutional law. The ideal of curbing the political domain and enhancing the scope of law, in the belief that individual liberty might thereby be better secured, is a captivating one that has charmed many liberal thinkers. It is nevertheless a snare and a delusion for anyone who seeks to diminish the threat to liberty in Britain today.

That constitutional law, in and of itself, gives insubstantial protection to individual liberty, and fails when it is most needed, is clear enough when we consider recent history. The Constitution of the USSR must be one of the most impressive ever to be conceived, but it counts for little or nothing in the

Soviet Union because of the lack of an independent judiciary and the overwhelming concentration of power in the Communist Party. The Soviet example should teach us that, more than upon the terms or provisions of any constitution, individual liberty depends on the dispersion of power through autonomous institutions and society at large.

The Soviet example is, of course, an extreme one in that it instances a totalitarian state which from its inception has been animated by the project of destroying or repressing the institutions of civil society. In Latin America, and in post-colonial Africa, however, where totalitarian regimes are not yet firmly established, there is many an example of an admirable constitution whose lifespan is limited by the brevity of the regime which gave it birth. This should teach us a second lesson – that the efficacy of a constitution depends critically on the stability of the distribution of power which undergirds it. And that suggests a final, and more comprehensive, observation – that the efficacy of a constitution in protecting individual liberty depends not only on the distribution of economic and political power, but also on the political culture of the people it is meant to safeguard. No constitution will thrive, or even take root, if the soil in which it is planted is that of a tyrannous or barbarous political culture.

Limitations of Constitutional Safeguards

In fact, we need not leave the English-speaking world to see the delusiveness of relying on constitutional provisions as the principal guardians of individual liberty. The paradigm case of the United States is deeply instructive in this regard. The American Constitution was deliberately designed to fragment governmental power, restrain majoritarian democracy and protect the necessary conditions of freedom and enterprise. Its early framers and theorists generated constitutionalist insights, which remain valuable today – above all, those of James Madison, who saw that no Bill of Rights could enumerate exhaustively the liberties of the individual (an insight embodied in the Ninth Amendment). Further, the Constitution provided an indispensable framework within which a country of immigrants could develop a national political culture. Its achievements in limiting government over a century and a half in America should never be underestimated. Over the past 50 years, however, it has proved a poor protection against inordinacy in government. For, despite the manifest intentions of its framers, the American Constitution has in many important areas allowed worse invasions of individual liberty than have occurred in many other Western states. We need only think of antitrust legislation, of the over-regulation of industry, especially of banking, finance and pharmaceuticals, of occupational licensure, of environmentalist legislation, of many decades of protectionism, of the far-reaching powers of the Internal Revenue Service and of the myriad attempts made by government, at both federal and state level, to enforce paternalist and moralist laws (of which

Prohibition is only the most obvious instance) to see that the Constitution has not prevented legislators from making greater inroads into individual liberty in the United States than in many other Western countries.

The case is in practice worse than this. For in the United States, issues – such as abortion, the interests of ethnic and cultural minorities and of women – which elsewhere are resolved by ordinary political reasoning, by mutual accommodation and the political arts, are treated as issues of constitutional law and of basic rights. The result of this process has not been the containment of the political realm but instead the politicization of law. In consequence, questionable and often plainly unjustified politics of affirmative action, for example, which in other states are matters of legislation whose content is open to political debate, have in the United States become embedded in law at its highest and least alterable levels.

Finally, the separation of powers, which is a cornerstone of the American Constitution, has progressively enfeebled the office of the Presidency and goes far to account for the limitations of the Reagan administration, in which the need to bargain with a refractory and fragmented legislature inhibited the making of hard choices in many areas of policy, and, above all, in respect of the federal deficit. The economic pre-eminence of the United States in the post-war world is owed not to its Constitution, but to the entrepreneurial genius of its people and to the individualist character of its culture. There are, doubtless, important reforms in the US Constitution which might be hoped to return it to the intentions of its framers, but such reforms have little relevance in Britain. In general, the experience of the United States gives small comfort to those in Britain who imagine that the adoption of a written constitution is the best answer to the dilemmas generated by an over-mighty government.

The Failure of the Canadian Constitution and the Treaty of Rome

If there were any reasonable doubt as to this conclusion, it would be dissipated by the evidence of the recent Canadian constitution, in which many of the fads and fallacies of our time – such as the elevation of minority interests to entrenched legal privileges and all the apparatus of affirmative action – have been carved in stone in the tablets of constitutional law. This is indeed the inexorable result of any uncritical recourse to constitutionalism at the present time – that it will freeze for perpetuity our current confusions. Nor is it at all likely that economic liberties – supposing them to be written into a new constitution, which given the current intellectual and political climate is inherently implausible – would be effectively protected by a written constitution.

Doubt as to the efficacy of constitutionalism as the principal guarantor of liberty is turned into certainty when we consider the results of the Treaty of

Rome, whose manifest intent of protecting economic freedom has been subverted in practice at many crucial points. If an economic Bill of Rights were enacted in Britain which entrenched liberties of enterprise, contract, trade and property, it would survive only so long as it was not challenged by a majority in parliament. A conflict between the Commons, say, and whichever body interpreted or adjudicated the terms of an economic Bill of Rights, could only trigger a constitutional crisis in which the constitution as a whole, and thereby the stability of the entire political system, would be likely to be weakened, and our existing liberties endangered.

All this is on the supposition that we are in a position to specify the personal and economic liberties which the Constitution seeks to protect, which is far from being evident. Many issues of personal liberty – such as those raised by the legal control of immigration, of pornography and narcotics – are matters of legitimate disagreement among reasonable people who are concerned with individual liberty. They are appropriately dealt with in detailed legislation which expresses a compromise between conflicting interests and values rather than by judicial interpretation of a fixed constitution.

Again, many proposals for an economic Bill of Rights presuppose a liberal world order which no longer exists and which will not be recreated in any foreseeable future. Proposals to entrench a constitutional right to free trade, for example, neglect the vital fact that trade between free economies and totalitarian states, although it may carry with it the classical economic benefits of free trade, nevertheless, by strengthening the economies of the communist states, may harm the cause of liberty. Thus, in terms of domestic political life, in which powerful socialist and interventionist movements would relentlessly contest it, and also in international terms where it would need to be severely qualified in virtue of the rise of totalitarian states, an economic Bill of Rights is a non-starter. And in the absence of these conditions it is probably unnecessary. [. . .]

The Importance of the Constitutional Outlook

Nothing in my criticism of constitutionalist illusion is intended to deny that there are significant constitutional measures which would serve the cause of individual liberty in Britain today. Several examples could be cited, but I will confine myself to four. An amendment requiring that tax allowances be raised in line with inflation [. . .] has an important role in inhibiting the process whereby government pre-empts by stealth an ever greater pro-portion of the national income.

Again, but more radically, we might envisage a legislative measure which would require government to balance its budget. [. . .]

A third measure is yet more radical – one requiring that government preserve a stable value in the currency. [. . .]

A fourth measure might be the incorporation into British law of the European Convention on Human Rights (to which we are, of course, already signatories) – a measure supported by the fact that the rights protected in the Convention are substantially those of classical liberal thought and practice and have proved helpful in curbing the over-mighty powers of trade unions and government bureaucracies.

I am far from underestimating the practical and the potential difficulties of implementing such constitutional measures in Britain. Nor do I intend to comment on the detailed content of such measures – a task beyond the author's competence. At this point, I stress only that measures of a 'constitutional' sort – constitutional in the sense that they aim to institute a framework of rules, conventions or procedures by which the policies of governments of any party are to be constrained – are not only a desirable, but even an indispensable condition of reviving the project of limited government in Britain. No party at present is committed, clearly and unequivocally, to long-term policies of fiscal conservatism and monetary stability. [. . .] We have therefore no alternative to pressing on with the task of persuading the major parties that, whereas a fixed constitution or economic Bill of Rights has little or nothing to offer us, we all stand to benefit by forging and adhering to constitutional conventions which restrain the discretionary authority of government economic policy. In other words, we must persuade the major parties of the importance of adopting what James Buchanan has called *a constitutional mentality* in respect of economic policy.

The New Hobbesian Dilemma

I do not seek to disguise the magnitude of the transformation in existing political attitudes, policies and practices presupposed by the adoption of constitutional conventions of the sort I have sketched. It involves a metamorphosis in the character of the modern state as it is found in Britain today that is little short of revolutionary. For consider the stark contrast between the state as Hobbes conceived of it and a modern state such as ours. The state as Hobbes conceived of it had no resources of its own. Its duty in respect of property was exhausted when it had specified the rules for its acquisition and transfer and instituted procedures for arbitrating disputes about it. The Hobbesian state was not (as we have seen) a minimum state of the doctrinaire sort [. . .] and its tasks were not to protect an imaginary set of abstract (and contentless) natural rights. It had tasks above and beyond the provision of law and national defence, including charitable works and an early version of workfare, but its interventions in economic life were strictly limited. Certainly the Hobbesian state is not conceived of as being itself an economic enterprise.

The contrast with a modern state such as ours could not be clearer. The modern British state, like practically every other modern state, owns vast assets (notwithstanding recent exercises in privatization). At present levels of taxation and expenditure, something between a third and a half of national income is pre-empted by government. Furthermore, the modern British state, again like virtually every other modern state, operates a colossal apparatus of income transfers via progressive taxation, welfare payments, and a welter of tariffs and subsidies. As a result of its tremendous economic power, the modern British state continues to exercise an invasive influence on social life of a sort only comparable to that of the absolutist monarchies of early modern Europe. It is perhaps worth remarking that, by virtue of the current burden of taxation, government in Britain today expropriates more of the income and wealth of its subjects than did the lords of feudal times (who were often restricted to command over only one in three of their serfs' labour). And it is worth repeating the point that, on most measures, *the burden of taxation in Britain has increased after a decade of Thatcherism, while the proportion of national income pre-empted by government has not significantly decreased.*

The consequences of the growth of the state as an owner and controller of great assets with a stake in every aspect of enterprise are large indeed. In a context of mass democracy, it will almost invariably be in the interest of political elites to confer resources on existing and nascent interest groups rather than to reduce or do away with subsidies to them, since the loss to concentrated and collusive groups will always be more politically significant than corresponding benefits to groups that are dispersed. In the modern British state, accordingly, government tends overwhelmingly to service private interests rather than to protect the common good. Contrary to the classical (and Hobbesian) theory of the state as the provider of public goods, *the modern British state is first and foremost a supplier of private goods.* Whereas in the Hobbesian conception, government exists to supply the public good of civil peace, the modern British state exists primarily to satisfy the private preferences of collusive interest groups. A prime example is that of agricultural policy, in which farmers have for decades colluded with civil servants to mould policy according to their interests as producers, but many other instances could be adduced of the transformation of government from a provider of public goods into an engine for the promotion of private interests. In suffering this metamorphosis, government has defaulted on its classical functions of defending the realm, keeping the peace and renewing and repairing the institutions of civil society.

The Waning of Civil Society

As government has waxed, so civil society has waned. This is the mutation in our circumstances identified in Hayek's *The Road to Serfdom*. The result in contemporary Britain of the erosion of civil society by an expansionist state has been the eruption of a *political struggle for resources*. From being an umpire which enforces the rules of the game of civil association, the *British state has become the most powerful weapon in an incessant competition for resources*. Its power is sought by every interest and enterprise, partly because of the huge assets it already owns or controls, but also because no private or corporate asset is safe from invasion or confiscatory taxation. From being a contrivance whereby the peaceful co-existence of civil association is assured, the state has itself become an instrument of predation, whereby a political war of all against all is fought. Civil life soon comes to resemble the Hobbesian state of nature from which it was meant to deliver us. [. . .]

In the modern British state this order of things has been reversed. Individuals and enterprises are constrained to organize collusively so as to capture or colonize the interventionist state. As a result, productive energies are distracted into the struggle for influence in government. So is generated *the new Hobbesian dilemma*, in which subjects are constrained, often solely in self-defence, to expend their energies in capturing or colonizing government institutions, in seeking influence over government policy, in order to protect or promote their interests against others – typically other producer groups – who are similarly constrained. [. . .]

The nemesis of this process, which we are mercifully far from confronting at present, can only be an impoverishment of civil society and the recreation of the state of nature by political means. [. . .] In Britain, we need think only of the later years of the last Labour government to see that it would be complacency to suppose that we are immune to this new Hobbesian dilemma. Indeed, it is the burden of my argument that, contrary to its professed intentions, the present government is abandoning the project of a limited state, and in arrogating to itself ever more discretionary powers, is creating the machinery through which a new political struggle for resources is bound to be fought. What is to be done?

Public Goods and Market Competition

The first and most essential step is the recognition that government activity should be confined to the production of public goods. In a Hobbesian perspective, the greatest of these is peace, but the pursuit of peace involves government in the provision of goods that go well beyond those comprehended in the maintenance of law and order. [. . .] The concern by government for a civil society that is free from destructive conflict should lead it to a concern with the distribution (and not just the efficient production) of wealth, since a society with a substantial propertyless underclass cannot reasonably be expected to be stable when the resentments of those with nothing are open to exploitation by radical movements. In addition to such involvements by government as are imposed upon it by its task of keeping the peace and superintending civil society, government may legitimately act to provide a variety of other public goods. Here I do not intend to specify as public only those goods which in the strict economic theory of the subject are indivisible and non-excludable, so that they are either produced by government or not at all, but instead any good which has weighty positive 'externalities'.

Universal literacy, for example, whatever disadvantages it may have, is a benefit to everyone in society, and government may legitimately act to promote it. Similarly, though more controversially, common cultural traditions provide the matrix without which the exercise by individuals of their autonomy becomes impoverished and attenuated, and government may act to promote the common culture by the support of the arts and by other measures. Here we may mention an important maxim, the first among several we shall invoke for the restraint of government:

> *Government may act to provide a public good so long as the coercive aspect of such action is confined to its financing from taxation and the provision of the good by government does not tend to monopolize or dominate any market which may exist in that good.*

[. . .] By this criterion, state support for the arts may be legitimate, but the present near-monopoly in schooling is not. The maxim we have enumerated has a corollary which is also worth mentioning. This is that policy should be guided by the aim that, aside no doubt from the core services of national defence and law enforcement, *government should, so far as is possible, always be constrained in its activities by market competition*. As we shall see, this is a maxim with far-reaching and sometimes radical implications.

The Ethics of Market Freedom

But what is the moral justification of relying so heavily on market competition? What, in other words, is the ethical argument for market freedom?

In classical liberal writings, market freedom and its precondition, private property, are often defended negatively, as shields against coercion by other men or by a tyrannous state. This is, at best, only half of the story. The most fundamental argument for market freedom is in its contribution to individual wellbeing by positively enabling people to act in pursuit of their goals and to express their values and ideals. Unlike any collective decision-procedure, however democratic, the market enables individuals to act to achieve their ends without the necessity of consulting their fellows, a procedure which often occasions social conflict, where it does not result in majoritarian tyranny. The market provides the positive freedom of autonomy and self-determination, accordingly, and not only the negative freedom of non-interference. Where, as with us, human values and goals are indefinitely various, and society harbours a diversity of cultural traditions and conceptions of the good life, market provision of most goods is a condition of peace, since each may act with his own resources to achieve the good without thereby depleting any collective resource. [. . .]

The ethical argument for the market is, then, not only that it allows practitioners of different traditions and values to live in peaceful co-existence, but also that it allows for innovation and novelty in thought and practice in a way that collective decisions cannot. This is to say that market freedom protects the very basic freedom to think new thoughts and try out new practices. At its most fundamental, the moral argument for the free market is one that appeals to its indispensable role in *enabling* people to implement their ideas and realize their goals. The language of 'enablement' is particularly apt, since it has lately been co-opted by critics of the market. Such critics do not (or will not) see that it is only the institutions of the market that accord full respect to human agency, while efforts to 'empower' people through government intervention typically turn them into passive consumers of impersonal bureaucracies.

The Market Is Indispensable to Liberty

The justification of the market is, in the end, then, as an indispensable condition of autonomy and self-determination. The claim that free markets best achieve prosperity, like the claim that markets allocate scarce resources most efficiently, though true, is not fundamental. Again, Adam Smith's famous observation that we rely on the self-interest, and not the benevolence, of the butcher for our provisions, does not go to the bottom of things, despite its being indisputably correct. The case for the market is not that it allows for the motive of self-interest – for who supposes that motive to be absent when resources are subject to collective, political allocation? – but that it allows for the whole variety of human motives, in all their complexity and mixtures. The defence of the market goes astray, accordingly, when it represents it as a means to aggregate social welfare. Instead, we should see the ethical standing of the market in its respect for human agency and its contribution to human autonomy.

In order to participate fully in the free market, people sometimes need resources the market has not conferred on them. It is for that reason that a limited government, committed to the market economy, may and often ought to act to provide those with small resources with the wherewithal to make good use of market freedoms. When government so acts, it does so in accordance with the maxim that *a necessary background condition of a stable market order is a wide diffusion of wealth and a reasonable measure of equality of opportunity*. [. . .] However a limited government acts to confer resources and opportunities on those who have hitherto had few assets or options, it best prepares people for responsible life in a market economy by using the institutions of the market itself. It is for this reason that, when government acts to provide an underproduced public good, or to correct distributional anomalies, it should do so, in most contexts, by providing purchasing power and not by the direct provision of goods or services. It thereby conforms to the maxim that *markets are best reformed by the further development of markets*.

4

The Criterion of Efficiency

H. Simon

The Nature of Efficiency

The criterion of efficiency is most easily understood in its application to commercial organizations that are largely guided by the profit objective. In such organizations the criterion of efficiency dictates the selection of that alternative, of all those available to the individual, which will yield the greatest net (money) return to the organization. This 'balance sheet' efficiency involves, on the one hand, the maximization of income, if costs are considered as fixed; and on the other hand, the minimization of cost, if income is considered as fixed. In practice, of course, the maximization of income and the minimization of cost must be considered simultaneously – that is, what is really to be maximized is the difference between these two.

It will be seen that the criterion of efficiency is closely related to both organization and conservation objectives. [. . .] It is related to the organiz-ation objective in so far as it is concerned with the maximization of 'output'. It is related to conservation objectives in so far as it is concerned with the maintenance of a positive balance of output over input.

The simplicity of the efficiency criterion in commercial organizations is due in large part to the fact that money provides a common denominator for the measurement of both output and income, and permits them to be directly compared. The concept must be broadened, therefore, if it is to be applicable to the process of decision where factors are involved that are not directly measurable in monetary terms. Such factors will certainly be present in noncommercial organizations where monetary measurement of output is usually meaningless or impossible. They will also be present in commercial organizations to the extent that those controlling the organization are not solely directed toward the profit motive – i.e. where they are concerned with questions of the public interest or employee welfare even when those factors are not directly related to the profit and loss statement. Moreover, non-monetary factors will also be involved in the internal operation even of purely commercial organizations where specific activities are concerned whose relation to the profit-and-loss statement cannot be assessed directly.

From H. Simon, *Administrative Behavior*, New York: Macmillan, 1957, pp. 172–97 (abridged).

For example, decisions in a personnel department cannot always be evaluated in monetary terms, because the monetary effect of a particular personnel policy cannot be directly determined.

The Cost Element in Decision

In both commercial and noncommercial organizations (except for volunteer organizations) the 'input' factor can be largely measured in money terms. This is true even when the organization objectives are broader than either profit or conservation of the organization. That is, even if the organization is concerned with the cost *for the community*, this cost can be fairly valued in terms of the goods and services that the organization buys.

This point may not be entirely evident in the case of the evaluation of the services of employees. The tasks to which employees are assigned are not all equal with respect to agreeableness, hazard, and the like; and, to the extent that they are not, the money wage (unless this accurately reflects these elements – which it usually does not) is not an accurate measure of input in an organization where employee welfare takes its place among the organization objectives. In such cases, organization decisions must balance not only money input against output, but money input against output *and* employee welfare.

There are other cases, too, where input is not accurately measured by money cost to the organization. An industrial concern, for example, which is not penalized for the smoke and soot it distributes over the community has a cost factor, provided the organization objectives include concern for community welfare, that does not appear in the accounts.

When the decision is being made for a public agency that embraces among its objectives the general stability and prosperity of the economy – the federal government, for example – still other considerations must enter in. In the case of a private business, interest on invested capital, at the market rate, must be included in calculations as a cost. In the case of government, if the effect of spending is to employ investment capital that would otherwise be idle, the interest on this capital is not really a cost from the standpoint of the economy as a whole. Moreover, the 'output' of government investment may include effects of this investment on the level of income and employment in the economy, and these effects must be included in the measurement of product.

Likewise, when a private business employs an unemployed person his wage is an ordinary cost; while when the government employs such a person it makes use of a resource that would otherwise not be utilized, and hence the wages of those employed do not involve any real cost from the standpoint of the community.

These comments are not intended to defend any particular concept of the role of government spending in a modern economy – a subject that evokes sufficient controversy among the various competing schools of modern economists – but merely to point out that the criterion of efficiency cannot be applied to decisions in governmental agencies without consideration of the economic effects that the activities of these agencies may have. In the language of the economist, the problem of efficiency in the public agency must be approached from the standpoint of the general, rather than the partial, equilibrium.

Positive Values in Decision

While the negative values involved in decision can usually be summarized in terms of time or money costs, the positive values present a somewhat more complex picture. [. . .] In a commercial enterprise, money value of output plays somewhat the same role as cost of production (input) in summarizing the value element involved. From a positive standpoint the kind of product manufactured is a valuationally neutral element. Not so in the case of public services. Hence, some substitute must be found in public administration for money value of output as a measure of value.

This substitute is provided by a statement of the objectives of the activity, and by the construction of indices that measure the degree of attainment of these objectives. Any measurement that indicates the effect of an administrative activity in accomplishing its final objective is termed a measurement of the *result* of that activity.

Definition of Objectives.   The definition of objectives for public services is far from a simple task. In the first place, it is desirable to state the objectives so far as possible in terms of values. That is, only if they are expressions of relatively final ends are they suitable value-indices. When objectives are stated in terms of intermediate goals, there is a serious danger that decisions governed by the intermediate end will continue to persist even when that end is no longer appropriate to the realization of value. The proliferation of forms and records in an administrative agency, for instance, frequently evidences a failure to reconsider activities which are aimed at some concrete end in terms of the broader values which that end is supposed to further.

On the other hand, however, the values which public services seek to realize are seldom expressible in concrete terms. Aims, such as those of a recreation department – to 'improve health', 'provide recreation', 'develop good citizens' – must be stated in tangible and objective terms before results can be observed and measured. A serious dilemma is posed here. The values toward which these services should be directed do not provide sufficiently concrete criteria to be applied to specific decisional problems. However, if value-indices are employed as criteria in lieu of the values themselves, the 'ends' are likely to be sacrificed for the more tangible means – the substance for the form.

Further difficulty arises in the lack of a common denominator of value. An activity may realize two or more values, as in the case of the recreation department mentioned above. What is the relative importance of the various values in guiding the department's activities? The health department provides an illustration of the same problem. Shall the department next year redistribute its funds to decrease infant mortality or to increase the facilities of the venereal disease clinic? Observations of results, measured in terms of value-indices, can merely tell the extent to which the several objectives are realized if one or other course of action is taken. Unless both activities are directed toward exactly the same value, measurement of results cannot tell which course of action is preferable. Rationality can be applied in administrative decisions only after the relative weights of conflicting values have been fixed. [. . .]

Accomplishment a Matter of Degree.   Defining objectives does not exhaust the value element in an administrative decision. It is necessary to determine, in addition, the degree to which the objective is to be attained. A city charter or ordinance may define the function of the fire department as 'protecting the city from damage due to fire'; but this does not imply that the city will wish to expand the fire-fighting facilities to the point where fire damage is entirely eliminated – an obviously impossible task. Moreover, it begs the question to say that the fire department should reduce losses 'as far as possible', for how far it is possible to reduce losses depends on the amount of money available for fire protection and fire prevention services.

Value questions are not eliminated from the fire protection problem of that city until it has been determined that (1) the fire department should aim to limit fire losses to x dollars per capita; and (2) the city council will appropriate y dollars which, it is anticipated on the basis of available information, will permit (1) to be carried out. Values are involved, then, not only in the definition of objectives, but in the determination as well of the level of adequacy of services which is to be aimed at. Attainment of objectives is *always* a matter of degree.

The processes of 'policy determination', as they take place in our governmental institutions, seldom cope with these questions of degree in determining the objectives of governmental services. It will be urged in later sections of this chapter that extension of policy determination to such questions is of fundamental importance for the maintenance of democratic control over the value elements in decision. It will be shown that a large measure of this procedural reform can be attained by a modification and extension of budgetary techniques.

Distributive Values.   Thus far, the discussion has centered on values which are 'aggregates'. That is, the community measures its fire loss in terms of total dollars of destruction during the year. It does not distinguish the loss of $1,000 in Smith's store from a loss of $1,000 in Jones's store. The police department, in attempting to reduce the number of robberies, does not give a robbery on Third Street a different weight from a similar robbery on Fourth Street.

Nevertheless, questions of 'distributive' value enter into almost every administrative decision – if in no other way than in an assumption of 'equal weight' like those cited above. A playground built on the West Side will not serve children on the East Side. If chess classes are offered at the social center, there may be no facilities available for persons interested in social dancing.

Many distributive questions are geographical, but they may involve social, economic, or innumerable other 'class' distinctions. The importance of such considerations in administration can be appreciated when it is recognized that agencies for assessment administration, administrative tribunals, and even welfare agencies are concerned primarily with questions of distributive rather than aggregate value.

As will be shown later, distributive questions are also of great importance when the work of an organization is specialized by 'area' or by 'clientele'. In these cases, the objective of the organizational unit is immediately restricted to a particular set of persons, and interjurisdictional problems of the greatest consequence may arise.

A Common Denominator for Value – the Criterion of Efficiency

A fundamental problem involved in reaching a decision is the discovery of a common denominator between the two values which have been mentioned: low cost and large results. How is the choice made when the two conflict? Four relations are conceivable between choices A and B. If I_A is the input for A, and I_B for B, and O_A and O_B are the respective outputs, then these four possible relations may be expressed as follows:

1 I_A is less than I_B, and O_A is greater than O_B.
2 I_B is less than I_A, and O_B is greater than O_A.
3 I_A is less than I_B, and O_A is less than O_B.
4 I_B is less than I_A, and O_B is less than O_A.

In cases (1) and (2) the choice is unequivocal; but not so in cases (3) and (4). That is, when possibility A involves a larger cost than possibility B, but produces a smaller result, B obviously is preferable. But when possibility A involves a lower cost as well as a smaller result than B, cost must be weighed against result before a choice can be made.

The path to the solution of this difficulty has already been indicated. Underlying all administrative decisions is a limitation – a 'scarcity' – of available resources. This is the fundamental reason why time and money are costs. Because they are limited in quantity, their application to one administrative purpose prevents the realization of alternative possibilities. Hence, the administrative choice among possibilities can always be framed as a choice among alternatives involving the same cost, but different positive values.

An administrative choice is incorrectly posed, then, when it is posed as a choice between possibility A, with low costs and small results, and possibility B, with high costs and large results. For A should be substituted a third possibility C, which would include A *plus* the alternative activities made possible by the cost difference between A and B. If this is done, the choice resolves itself into a comparison of the results obtainable by the application of fixed resources to the alternative activities B and C. The efficiency of a behavior is the ratio of the results obtainable from that behavior to the maximum of results obtainable from the behaviors which are alternative to the given behavior.

The criterion of efficiency dictates that choice of alternatives which produces the largest result for the given application of resources.

It should be noted that this criterion, while it supplies a common denominator for the comparison of administrative alternatives, does not supply a common numerator. Even though all decisions be made in terms of alternative applications of the same resources, the problem still remains of comparing the values which are attained by the different courses of action. The efficiency criterion neither solves nor avoids this problem of comparability.

Note on the Term 'Efficiency'

The term 'efficiency' has acquired during the past generation a number of unfortunate connotations which associate it with a mechanistic, profit-directed, stop-watch theory of administration. This is the result of the somewhat careless use of the term by over-enthusiastic proponents of the 'scientific management' movement. Nevertheless, no other term in the language comes so close as 'efficiency' to representing the concept described in this chapter. The term has therefore been employed, with the hope that the reader will understand the criterion in the sense in which it has just been defined, and will be able to dissociate from it any unfortunate connotations it may have had in his mind.

Until practically the end of the nineteenth century, the terms 'efficiency' and 'effectiveness' were considered almost as synonymous. The *Oxford Dictionary* defines 'efficiency' as ' 'Fitness or power to accomplish, or success in accomplishing, the purpose intended; adequate power, effectiveness, efficacy.'

In recent years, however, 'efficiency' has acquired a second meaning: the ratio between input and output. In the words of the *Encyclopaedia of the Social Sciences*:

> Efficiency in the sense of a ratio between input and output, effort and results, expenditure and income, cost and the resulting pleasure, is a relatively recent term. In this specific sense it became current in engineering only during the latter half of the nineteenth century and in business and in economics only since the beginning of the twentieth. [. . .]

It must be noted that there is a difference in computing an output–input ratio in the physical and in the social sciences. For the engineer, both output and input are measured in terms of energy. The law of conservation of energy tells him that the output of useful energy cannot exceed the energy input. Hence arises the concept of 'perfect' efficiency – that is, a situation in which output equals input. In the social sciences, output and input are seldom measured in comparable units; and even when they are, as in a comparison of cost of fire protection with dollar losses from fire, there is no 'law of conservation of energy' which prevents the output from exceeding the input. Hence, the concept of perfect efficiency, if it is used at all, must be redefined. As a matter of fact, the concept of perfect efficiency will not be required in the present study. Actual problems, as they present themselves to the administrator, are always concerned with *relative* efficiencies, and no measure of *absolute* efficiency is ever needed. Moreover, the theory does not require a numerical measure of efficiency, but merely a comparison of *greater* or *less* between the efficiencies of two alternative possibilities. Under these circumstances, the definitions of efficiency as ratio of output to input and as ratio of the actual to the maximum possible amount to the same thing. [. . .]

Criticisms of the Efficiency Criterion

Criticisms of 'efficiency' as a guide to administration have been frequent and vociferous. One group of criticisms need not concern us here, for they refer to definitions of the term different from the one proposed here. In this category must be placed attacks on efficiency which equate the term with 'economy' or 'expenditure reduction'. As we have used 'efficiency', there is no implication whatsoever that a small expenditure – or, for that matter, a large expenditure – is *per se* desirable. It has been asserted only that if two results can be obtained with the same expenditure the greater result is to be preferred. Two expenditures of different magnitude can, in general, be compared only if they are translated into opportunity costs, that is, if they are expressed in terms of alternative results.

'Mechanical' Efficiency

Others have objected to 'efficiency' on the ground that it leads to a 'mechanical' conception of admiration [sic, administration]. This objection, too, must result from the use of the term in quite a different sense from that proposed here. For a mere criterion of preference among possibilities does not in any manner limit the administrative techniques which may be employed in attaining the possibilities, nor, as we shall see in the next section, does it in any way reduce the role of the administrator's judgment in reaching decisions. Furthermore, the efficiency criterion is in the most complete accord with a viewpoint that places the social consequences of administration in the forefront of its determining influences.

'The Ends Justify the Means'

Two other lines of criticism assert that the criterion of efficiency leads to an incorrect relationship between 'means' and 'ends'. On the one hand it is alleged that, in the interests of efficiency, ends are taken to justify any appropriate means. As we have noted [. . .], the terms 'means' and 'ends' must be employed carefully in order to avoid contradictions; and for this reason we have preferred to talk of the value and factual aspects of alternatives. Suffice it to say that if the evaluation of the results of administrative activity takes into account *all* the significant value elements of the administrative alternatives, no undue subordination of 'means' to 'ends' can result.

'Ruthless' Efficiency

On the other hand, it is charged that efficiency directs all attention to the means, and neglects the ends. This charge has already been answered in pointing out the integral role which valuation plays in the employment of a criterion of efficiency. It may be freely admitted that efficiency, as a scientific problem, is concerned chiefly with 'means', and that 'efficient' service may be efficient with respect to any of a wide variety of ends. But merely to recognize that the process of valuation lies outside the scope of science, and that the adaptation of means to ends is the only element of the decisional problem that has a factual solution, is not to admit any indifference to the ends which efficiency serves. Efficiency, whether it be in the democratic state or in the totalitarian, is the proper criterion to be applied to the factual element in the decisional problem. Other, ethical, criteria must be applied to the problem of valuation.

Common to all these criticisms is an implication that an 'efficiency' approach involves a complete separation of 'means' and 'ends'. We have already seen that, strictly speaking, this is not the case – that the only valid distinction is one between ethical and factual elements in decision. Yet, in the actual application of the efficiency criterion to administrative situations, there is often a tendency to substitute the former distinction for the latter, and such a substitution inevitably results in the narrower, 'mechanical' efficiency which has been the subject of criticism.

How this substitution comes about may be briefly explained. The ethical element in decision consists in a recognition and appraisal of all the value elements inhering in the alternative possibilities. The principal values involved are usually expressed as 'results' of the administrative activity, and, as we have seen, the activity itself is usually considered as valuationally neutral. This leads to the isolation of two values: (1) the positive values expressed as 'results'; and (2) the negative values, or opportunity costs, expressed in terms of time or money cost.

In fact, to consider the administrative activity itself as valuationally neutral is an abstraction from reality which is permissible within broad limits but which, if carried to extremes, ignores very important human values. These values may comprehend the remuneration and working conditions (using these terms broadly) of the members of the group which carries out the activity.

We may enumerate some of these value elements more explicitly:

1   If cost is measured in money terms, then the wages of employees cannot be considered as a valuationally neutral element, but must be included among the values to be appraised in the decision.
2   The work pace of workers cannot be considered as a valuationally neutral element – else we would be led to the conclusion that a 'speed-up' would always be eminently desirable.
3   The social aspects of the work situation cannot be considered as a valuationally neutral element. The decision must weigh the social and psychological consequences of substituting one type of work-situation for another.
4   Wage policies, promotional policies, and the like need to be considered not only from the viewpoint of incentives and result-efficiency, but also from that of distributive justice to the members of the group.

It must be emphasized, then, that when a choice between alternatives involves any valuationally significant difference in the work activity this difference must be included among the values to be weighed in reaching a decision.

Valuational Bias

A closely related fallacy in the application of the efficiency criterion is to include in the evaluation of alternatives only those values which have been previously selected as the *objective* of the particular administrative activity under consideration. The effects of some administrative activities are confined to a rather limited area, and indirect results do not then cause much difficulty. The activities of the fire department usually have an effect on fire losses, but very little relation to the recreation problem in the community (unless ardent fire fans form a large part of the community). Hence the fire chief does not have to take recreation values into consideration in reaching his decisions. It is very fortunate that the consequences of human activities are so strictly segregated; if they were not, the problem of reaching rational decisions would be impossible. But the mere fact that activities do not *usually* have valuationally significant indirect effects does not justify us in ignoring such effects if they are, *in fact*, present. That is, the fire chief cannot, merely because he is a fire chief, ignore the possibility of accidents in determining the speed at which his equipment should respond to alarms.

This all seems commonplace, yet [. . .] in actuality, administrators in reaching decisions commonly disclaim responsibility for the indirect results of administrative activities. To this point of view we oppose the contrary opinion that the administrator, serving a public agency in a democratic state, must give a proper weight to *all* community values that are relevant to his activity, and that are reasonably ascertainable in relation thereto, and cannot restrict himself to values that happen to be his particular responsibility. Only under these conditions can a criterion of efficiency be validly postulated as a determinant of action. [. . .]

Factual Elements in Decision

We have seen that the criterion which the administrator applies to factual problems is one of efficiency. The resources, the input, at the disposal of the administrator are strictly limited. It is not his function to establish a utopia. It is his function to maximize the attainment of the governmental objectives (assuming they have been agreed upon), by the efficient employment of the limited resources that are available to him. A 'good' public library, from the administrative standpoint, is not one that owns all the books that have ever been published, but one that has used the limited funds which are allowed it to build up as good a collection as possible under the circumstances.

When a decision is made in terms of the criterion of efficiency, it is necessary to have empirical knowledge of the results that will be associated with each alternative possibility. Let us consider a specific municipal function, the fire department. Its objective is the reduction of the total fire loss, and results will be measured in terms of this loss.

The extent of the fire loss will be determined by a large number of factors. Among these are natural factors (frequency of high winds, heavy snowfall, severe cold weather, hot dry weather, tornadoes, hurricanes and cyclones, earthquakes, and floods), structural and occupancy factors (exposure hazards, physical barriers, density of structures, type of building construction, roof construction, contents, and risk of occupancy), the moral hazard (carelessness and incendiarism), and finally the effectiveness of the fire department itself. The loss, then, will be a function of all these variables, including the performance of the fire department itself. The fire chief must know how the activities of his department affect the loss if he is to make intelligent decisions.

How does the fire department perform its task? It inspects buildings to eliminate fire hazards, it carries on campaigns of education against carelessness, it fights fires, it trains firemen, it investigates and prosecutes arsonists.

But we can carry the analysis a step farther. Of what does fire-fighting consist? A piece of apparatus must be brought to the scene of action, hose laid, water pumped and directed upon the flames, ladders raised, and covers spread over goods to reduce water damage. Again, each of these activities can be analyzed into its component parts. What does laying a hose involve? The hose must be acquired and maintained. Equipment for carrying it must be acquired and maintained. Firemen must be recruited and trained. The firemen must spend a certain amount of time and energy in laying the hose.

A final level of analysis is reached by determining the cost of each of these elements of the task. Thus, the whole process of fire-fighting can be translated into a set of entries in the city's books of accounts.

The problem of efficiency is to determine, at any one of these levels of analysis, the cost of any particular element of performance, and the contribution which that element of performance makes to the accomplishment of the department's objectives. When these costs and contributions are known, the elements of performance can be combined in such a way as to achieve a maximum reduction in fire loss.

There are at least four rather distinct levels at which the analysis of the administrative situation may be carried out. At the highest level is the measurement of results, of the accomplishment of agency objectives. Contributing to these results are the elements of administrative performance. Subordinate to these, in turn, is input measured in terms of effort. Effort, finally, may be analyzed in terms of money cost.

The mathematically minded will see in this structure a set of equations – strictly identical with the economist's 'production functions'. The first equation expresses the results of government as a function of the performance of certain activities. Further equations express these performance units as functions of less immediate performance units, the latter in terms of units of effort; and finally effort is expressed as a function of expenditures. The problem of efficiency is to find the maximum of a production function, with the constraint that total expenditure is fixed.

The Determination of Social Production Functions

It follows from the considerations which have been advanced that that portion of the decision-making process which is factual, which is amenable to scientific treatment, resolves itself into the determination of the production functions of administrative activities. This is a research task of the first magnitude, and one which as yet has hardly been touched.

Progress toward an understanding of these functions involves a series of well defined steps:

1   The values, or objectives, affected by each activity must be defined in terms that permit their observation and measurement.
2   The variables, extra-administrative as well as administrative, that

determine the degree of attainment of these functions must be enumerated.

3   Concrete, empirical investigations must be made of the way in which
results change when the extra-administrative and administrative variables are altered.

The necessary scope and difficulty of a research program which would
make a substantial contribution to our knowledge of these functions can
hardly be exaggerated. The principal progress to date has been in the first
step, and, as yet, empirical studies involving steps (2) and (3) are almost
nonexistent. [. . .]

The fact of the matter is that momentous decisions are made every day as
to the allocation of resources to one or another competing purpose, and
that, particularly in noncommercial organizations, the decisions are made in
an almost complete absence of the evidence which would be necessary to
validate them. The principal reason for this, of course, is the difficulty,
except in enterprises that have a relatively tangible product, of determining
the actual production functions.

To recognize how far actual decisions fall short of rationality is no
criticism of the administrator, who must act whether or not he possesses the
information that would be necessary for the complete rationality of his
decisions. It is, however, a criticism of apologies that would make his
ignorance a virtue, and would question the need for extensive programs of
research in this direction.

Functionalization in Relation to Efficiency

A few words need to be said now about the bearing of this efficiency criterion
upon organizational problems. [. . .] It was noted that specialization in
organization often follows functional lines. This functionalization involves
the analysis of the organization objective into subsidiary objectives. One or
more of the subsidiary objectives may be assigned to each of the organizational units.

Thus, a fire department may be divided into a fire prevention bureau, and
a number of fire-fighting divisions. The function, or objective, of the former
will be defined in terms of prevention, that of the latter in terms of
extinguishment. A health department may include a communicable diseases
division, a division for prenatal care, a vital statistics division, and so forth.
Similar illustrations can be found in every field of governmental service.

Under these circumstances, there will be a hierarchy of functions and
objectives corresponding to the hierarchy of divisions and bureaus in the
agency. In general, the hierarchical arrangement of functions will correspond to a means–end relationship. Fire losses, for instance, can be
conceived as a product of number of fires by average loss per fire. Hence, a

fire department might take reduction in number of fires and reduction in average loss per fire as subsidiary objectives, and assign these objectives to subsidiary units in the organization.

There are several prerequisites to effective functionalization. First, as indicated above, the general objective must be analyzed into subsidiary objectives, standing in a means–end relation with it. But further, the technology of the activity must be such that the work of the agency can be broken into distinct portions, each contributing primarily toward one, and only one, of the subsidiary objectives. Thus, it would be useless to divide a recreation department into 'good citizenship', 'health', 'enjoyment', and 'education' divisions. Although these might be defended as subsidiary objectives of recreation work, it would be impossible to devise a scheme of organization which would break activities into component parts, each contributing to only one of these objectives. [. . .]

Specialization by 'Area' and 'Clientele'

It has not generally been recognized in the literature of administration that specialization by 'area' and 'clientele' are, in fact, merely a particular kind of functionalization. This follows from the fact, already noted, that the complete definition of an objective involves the specification of the group of persons to whom the value in question refers.

The fire department of Podunk, for instance, has as its objective not 'minimization of fire losses', but 'minimization of fire losses *in Podunk*'.

If specialization by area and specialization by clientele are merely forms of functionalization, then, to be successful they must satisfy the conditions of effective functionalization: (1) it must be technologically feasible to split the work activity, as well as the objective, along functional lines; (2) these segregated work activities must not affect, to a substantial degree, values extraneous to the specified functions. [. . .]

Efficiency and the Budget

As a practical application of the approach set forth in this chapter, we may consider the public budget-making process, and the form which this process will have to take if it is to conform to the requirements of rationality.

It has been asserted that the concept of efficiency involves an analysis of the administrative situation into a positive value element (the results to be attained) and a negative value element (the cost). For the practical execution of this analysis, a technique is needed that will enable the administrator to compare various expenditure alternatives in terms of results and costs. The budget document will provide the basis for such a comparison.

The essence of the public budget process is that it requires a comprehensive plan to be adopted for *all* the expenditures that are to be made in a limited period. But if the budget is to be used as an instrument for the control of efficiency, substantial improvements must be made in present techniques.

Inadequacy of Customary Budget Methods

What does the typical governmental budget include? It tells how much each department will be allowed to spend during the subsequent year, and how it may spend it. How are the particular figures to be found in budgets arrived at? How is it determined that 14 per cent of the budget shall be devoted to fire protection and 11.6 per cent to highways?

A different answer to this question would be given in every community in which it was asked. Some budgets are made by copying off the figures of the previous year's expenditures. Some are constructed by increasing or decreasing appropriations by a fixed percentage. Some are determined by allotting to each department a certain percentage of its request – he who shouts loudest gets most. Some have even less systematic plans.

If this seems exaggerated, the following justifications for increased appropriations in the supporting schedules of one city budget should serve to convince even the most skeptical:

'Salaries should be commensurate with duties and responsibilities of office.'

'Naturally with increased work more supplies will be necessary and the cost will be greater. My postage bills alone amount to $2,500 a year.'

'Time and skill required for this work before and after election.'

'A larger increase was asked last year and refused.'

There are, of course, a few exceptional cities and other agencies which attempt to substitute a more rational budget review for this hit-or-miss process. A number of federal departments, including the Department of Agriculture, may be cited in this connection.

The Long-Term Budget

If budgeting is to serve as a basis for the rational allocation of expenditures, two comprehensive budgets must be substituted for the present inadequate documents: an annual budget and a long-term budget. However, since the annual budget is merely a segment of the long-term budget, only the latter need be discussed.

The long-term budget will be made up of several parts: (1) long-term estimates of trends in problem-magnitude for the various departments – distribution and concentration of burnable values which must be protected against fire, mileage of streets which must be kept clean, population which must be served by libraries, etc.; (2) long-term estimates of service adequacy

– that is, the level of services which the city intends to provide its citizens, so many acres of park per 1,000 population, a specified fire loss, etc.; (3) a long-term work program, showing in work units the services which will have to be provided and facilities to be constructed to achieve the program outlined in items (1) and (2); and (4) a financial program which will relate the work program to the fiscal resources of the community.

Item (1) involves primarily factual considerations. The determination of item (2) is primarily a matter of value judgments. Items (3) and (4), after the first two items have been determined, become largely factual questions. Hence, it would seem to be a legislative task to weigh (2) against (4), and to determine the budget program. On the other hand, the legislature would need assistance in developing the factual information for (1), (2), and (3).

Under present budgetary procedure, items (1) and (2) are seldom even a part of the budget document, and the entire discussion is carried on in terms of items (3) and (4). Furthermore, usually a single budget plan is presented to the legislature, for its approval or amendment. It would seem much preferable, if the necessary information were available, to present directly to the legislature the policy issues involved in (2), and to present the legislature with alternative budget plans, indicating the implications for policy of increases and curtailments of expenditure. Modifications along these lines would seem to be absolutely essential if the legislature is to be returned to a place of influence in the determination of public policy.

Too often, under current practice, the basic decisions of policy are reached by technicians in the agency entrusted with budget review, without any opportunity for review of that policy by the legislature. That this condition is tolerated results partly from general failure to recognize the relative element in governmental objectives. Since most legislative declarations of policy state objectives of governmental activity without stating the level of adequacy which the service is to reach, it is impossible for an 'expert' to reach on factual grounds a conclusion as to the adequacy of a departmental appropriation. Hence, present procedures would not seem to safeguard sufficiently democratic control over the determination of policy.

Progress Toward a Long-Term Budget

Public agencies have made considerable progress within the past few years toward long-term plans that include a work program and a financial plan. Little progress has as yet been made toward a program that will tell the legislator and the citizen what this program means to him in terms of specific governmental services. Furthermore, little progress has as yet been made toward estimating the cost of maintaining governmental services at a particular level of adequacy, or determining when expenditures should, in the interests of efficiency, be turned from present channels into other, more useful directions.

Illustration of a Rational Budget

As an illustration of the line of development which needs to be pursued, the budget procedure of the California State Relief Administration will be described briefly. The agency for several years employed a well designed procedure of budget estimating. One reason for its successful performance of this difficult task was the nature of its objectives.

The major task of an unemployment relief agency is to provide a minimum level of economic security to needy families. The family budget which the agency employs to effect its policies provides an immediate translation of 'cost' into 'result'. That is, it is immediately possible to visualize what a specific expenditure means in terms of the level of economic assistance which the agency provides. The policy-forming body can decide how large a family budget it is willing to authorize, and this decision can be immediately translated into cost terms. In this way 'service adequacy' is determined.

Similarly, the State Relief Administration had worked out a detailed procedure for estimating over a period of time how many cases would be eligible for assistance; that is, what the problem-magnitude would be. With these two steps completed – the level of service determined and the problem magnitude estimated – it was a simple matter to develop the work budget and estimate financial needs.

This illustration has been oversimplified to emphasize its salient features. An unemployment relief agency must provide certain types of service as well as cash relief. The operating expenses of the agency have been left out of consideration also. But, except for this oversimplification and these omissions, the budget procedure which has been described closely approximates the ideal of a rational budget process.

Summary

In this chapter we have seen that, in the factual aspects of decision-making, the administrator must be guided by the criterion of efficiency. This criterion requires that results be maximized with limited resources.

On the other hand, criteria of 'correctness' have no meaning in relation to the purely valuational elements in decision. A democratic state is committed to popular control over these value elements, and the distinction of value from fact is of basic importance in securing a proper relation between policy-making and administration.

Improvement in the quality of decision awaits empirical research into the production functions that relate activities to results. Our knowledge of these functions is fragmentary at present, yet they are indispensable as a tool of reason, without which it operates in a factual vacuum.

The value of organization along functional lines lies in its facilitation of decisional processes. Functionalization is possible, however, only when the technology permits activities to be segregated along parallel lines.

A potent device for the improvement in governmental decision-making processes, both legislative and administrative, is the budget document. The improvement of budgetary methods will (1) permit a more effective division of labor between the policy-forming and administrative agencies; and (2) focus attention upon the social production functions and their critical role in decision-making.

5

Management in the Public Domain

John Stewart and Stewart Ranson

The public domain has its own purposes. It expresses collective purpose in society. That sets the conditions and the tasks for management. This chapter develops ideas appropriate for management in the public domain by

- exploring the inadequacy of private sector models of management for the study of management in the public domain and arguing the need for a distinctive approach;
- starting the process of building distinctive approaches to management by setting out the purposes, conditions and tasks of the public domain;
- setting out dilemmas that have to be faced in building those approaches to management in the public domain;
- developing an approach to management in the public domain that recognizes both its distinctive purposes, conditions and tasks as well as its dilemmas.

Inadequacy of the Private Sector Model

There are dangers if, consciously or unconsciously, management in the public domain adopts models drawn from outside organizations. That is not to say that management in the public domain cannot learn from management in the private sector, or vice versa. Specific management ideas can be transferable. What is not transferable is the model of management – its purposes, conditions and tasks.

Yet, the private sector model dominates thinking. This leads to the task of management in the public domain being defined negatively rather than positively. It is common to use such phrases as 'management in not-for-profit organizations' or 'management in non-market organizations' to describe not merely management in the public domain, but also management in voluntary organizations. One is told that the public sector organization does not aim for profit, but not what it does aim at. This is no basis on which to develop a purposive approach to management in the public domain.

From *Public Money and Management*, Spring/Summer 1988: 13–18 (abridged).

The private sector model defines the nature of management in relation to the purposes and conditions of the private sector. Although a management approach developed for the private sector can have relevance to the public domain, that approach may have to be transformed in its application. There are also many aspects of management in the public domain that find no ready parallel in the private sector.

Strategic management

This is concerned with the competitive stance of the organization. It concentrates on organizational strengths and weaknesses in relation to a changing environment in order to determine the product/market mix that will achieve optimum organizational performance.

There is much in the ideas of strategic management that has meaning for the public domain – for example, the review of the organization's activities in relation to a changing environment and the analysis of organizational strengths and weaknesses. Yet, approaches to strategic management based on the private sector cannot be applied directly to the public.

It is not meaningful to think of the competitive stance of the public sector except in certain fields. Government cannot opt out of a product or a market merely because the environment seems unfavourable. It may well have to opt in because of market failure. None of this is to argue that strategic management is not required in the public domain, but that strategic management cannot be based on the competitive stance of different organizations and cannot choose product/market mixes on the basis of profit margins. Strategic management in the public domain expresses values determined through the political process in response to a changing environment. It requires its own model.

Marketing and the Customer

The marketing role is critical to the private sector model and can lead to an emphasis on the relation of the firm to its customers. Undoubtedly there is scope for marketing approaches in the public domain and not merely where there are direct trading relationships. Equally, it can be argued that it can be helpful for a public organization to think of those who use its services as customers.

Thought about marketing and customers can be a stimulus to management in the public domain, but if used uncritically it can distort. A public sector organization can and should have many relationships with its public. However, there are customers, clients, consumers and there are citizens. The public sector organization can and should be concerned with a particular customer, but has also other concerns. Consumerism is by itself no guarantee of the public interest.

If marketing's scope covers the relationship between an organization and public behaviour, it has a wide role in the public domain. It is not, however, necessarily the same role as in the private sector. The private sector is concerned with demand for products at a price in the market. The public domain extends beyond the limits of market demand. It can be concerned with need, both in establishing its meaning in the public arena and in discovering it in practice. Marketing in the public domain is about matching provision to a publicly established concept of need, which is different in quantity and quality from demand. Marketing can be learning from citizens about their understanding of need. It can be about searching out need hidden by apparent demand. It can also be about influencing behaviour to discourage demand but to provide access for need. Marketing for collective purpose cannot be modelled on the private sector alone.

The Budgetary Process

The budget has a different significance in many public sector organizations from that in the private sector – and certainly for non-trading organizations. In the private sector, the budget is based on a forecast of likely sales. It is a means of relating expenditure to likely revenue. If sales can expand above the forecast, the private sector organization will, as far as possible, adjust production and expenditure accordingly.

By comparison, the budget in the public domain is an act of political choice. Government taxes rather than sells. The budget sets out the choice as to the desirable level of taxation and expenditure and the choices made on the allocation of that expenditure. That budget will not be changed merely because demand for a service is greater than is provided for.

Management approaches developed for budgeting in the private sector have little value in the public domain. Management in the public domain has to see budgeting as political choice. Scarce resources have to be fitted to unmet need. That involves collective choice both in the definition of need and in the allocation of resources to need. The effective budgetary process in the public domain recognises the necessities of choice.

Public Accountability

Organizations in the public domain exercise substantial power for which they are accountable. The private sector model also assumes accountability, but that accountability is found in the market.

Public accountability is both wider and deeper. The public organization is accountable to all – to the public at large and to individuals. Accountability cannot therefore be defined in a single dimension. Public accountability is required to explain and to justify actions taken. It has to find many languages to give many accounts. It has to encompass quality and quantity. Public accountability is through a political process which responds to many voices.

Management in the public domain is therefore a process, subject to challenge and debate. The pressure is for greater rather than less accountability. There are demands for open government and in local authorities much wider access to information has been conceded. The model of management in the public domain has to accept and meet the requirements of public accountability.

Public Demands, Pressure and Protest

These are a condition of the public domain. They belong to the public arena of debate in which collective purpose is sought and the basis of collective action determined. They have, however, no necessary part in the private sector model. The private sector model deals with the public in the market. In so far as the private sector has to deal with views and protests, these are defined as problems to be overcome, not as the means by which decisions are made. 'Exit' from the market is the signal to which the private sector responds.

Management in the public domain has to be based on acceptance not merely of the reality but of the legitimacy of public demand pressure and protest. In the public domain it is through their voices that the public assert their views. In the public domain all voices have a right to be heard, and it is to 'voice' that government responds (Hirschmann, 1980).

Political Process

This can be seen as an inherent feature of management in the public domain, or, it can be treated as a constraint as when the phrase 'the costs of democracy' is used, as though it is a special difficulty to be overcome, rather than a basic condition expressing the purposes of the public domain. One does not speak of 'the costs of profit-making' when describing management in the private sector.

The political process is a basic condition of management in the public domain. It is the means by which collective needs are defined in the arena of debate. It is the process by which choices are made for collective action. Out of the variety of different interests and values, the political process is the means by which meaning is given to common interests. [. . .]

Purposes, Conditions, Tasks

Our discussion so far suggests the need to find a different basis for public sector management. It is only if the distinctiveness of management in the

Public Domain Model

The public domain has its own conditions, which are ignored at their peril. These conditions are themselves an expression of the fundamental reason why management in the public domain requires its own model. The public domain is the arena in which values can be realized, which cannot adequately be realized outside it. Economists may see the public domain as required to correct market imperfections, to provide services which cannot be provided by the market or to redistribute resources.

Such statements are, however, inadequate because they still define the public domain negatively. It is also possible to see the domain as a public arena, not merely where the defects of the market can be corrected but where distinctive values can be realized.

Thus, in the public arena many will assert the value of equity in meeting needs that cannot even be expressed in the market. If equity is sought in the public arena then it must influence the nature of management. In the search for value for money, emphasis is placed on economy, efficiency and effectiveness. For at least the first two of those values the private sector model may suffice. Yet, if the value of equity is sought, distinctive management processes are required. Need has to become a management concept.

Again, in the public domain justice can be sought. Justice is a product of the public domain. It represents an appeal from individuals to the wider public arena. Justice cannot be determined by the individual but for the individual. If justice is sought in the public domain, then management must support justice. It is not sufficient to ask whether management is efficient, it must be asked whether it is just.

The public are not merely clients or customers of the public sector organization. They are themselves a part of that organization as citizens. Citizenship can be a basic value in the public domain. In building citizenship management has to encompass a set of relationships for which the private sector model allows no place.

The values given expression in the public domain set the purposes for management, determine its conditions and specify its distinctive tasks. They constitute the basis for a model of management in the public domain that has its own rationale distinguished from management in the private domain.

Private sector model	Public sector model
Individual choice in the market	Collective choice in the polity
Demand and price	Need for resources
Closure for private action	Openness for public action
The equity of the market	The equity of need
The search for market satisfaction	The search for justice
Customer sovereignty	Citizenship
Competition as the instrument of the market	Collective action as the instrument of the polity
Exit as the stimulus	Voice as the condition

The dilemma for the private sector is that the public domain sets its conditions and on those conditions the private sector depends. The dilemma for the public domain is that while it has its own rationale, it must encompass the private sector. The definition of public and private depend on each other. They have, however, to be distinguished for it is only then that they can be understood by and for management.

public domain is grasped that it is possible to identify where and how approaches developed within the private sector model can be applied.

The public domain is constituted not to replicate behaviour in the private sector but to support behaviour which is different. If the public domain were constituted to operate as the private sector there would be no rationale for the public domain. To make the assertion that the public domain is constituted to operate in different ways, subject to different modes, guided by different criteria from the private sector is not to argue about the appropriate scale of the public domain. It is to argue that whatever its scale, the public domain has its own purposes, conditions and tasks.

We have already suggested some of the elements that have to be taken into account in building a model of management in the public domain (see Public Domain Model). We now broaden the discussion to consider:

- the purposes of the public domain;
- the distinctive conditions that constitute the public domain;
- the distinctive tasks of government that are carried out in the public domain.

Purposes of the Public Domain

The public domain can be described as the organization of collective purpose, the area in which collective values are pursued. That is its rationale and its purpose.

Politics is the process of determining collective values out of the diversity of social and economic interests. Without that foundation little else in society can proceed.

Democracy is therefore a basic value for management in the public domain. Lawrence Rutter (1980), writing of local government, said

> Yet democracy is the very foundation of professional local government management. Indeed in many respects the job of the administration reduced to its basics is to make democracy work.

Making democracy work can involve a commitment to representative government, but also to an active citizenship. The value of citizenship can underlie the relationship between government and its many publics. [. . .]

In management in the public domain, community values can be sought and concepts of the public interest can be searched for. Equity can be sought and justice can be established; co-operation can be sought as well as competition. Community can be given meaning. The ordering of society can be undertaken.

A public organization provides services determined by collective choice through the political process rather than by market conditions. The services can be, and often are, provided free of charge or at a price below the cost of production. The services provided by a public service organization can, of course, be sold at market prices but it is a matter of collective decision so to do.

Conditions Which Constitute the Public Domain

In any society the public domain is constituted by certain conditions. Those determine authoritative behaviour within the public domain. They express the purposes of the public domain. They have to be met by management. They should not be seen as constraints but as the means by which collective action is undertaken in society. Without those conditions there is no legitimate basis for collective action. In our society decisions in the public domain are taken through political processes. Debate, discussion, pressure and protest are all part of that political process. Voice and the right to voice is a condition of the public domain.

Action within the public domain is subject to public accountability. That places upon those with power the duty to give an account and to citizens the right to hold them to account. Elections provide the legitimate basis for collective action and the means of enforcing public accountability.

The political process is not a bounded process. Its boundaries are those of society. All voices are entitled to be heard. No issue can be assumed to be of no concern. [. . .]

It is because the public domain is unbounded, that collective action faces necessities as well as choice. Collective action cannot be opted out of. Collective action expressing collective purpose is a necessary condition for society, and indeed for the operation of the market-place. The market is a social institution and all institutions can only proceed if underwritten by collective agreement grounded, ultimately, in law.

Tasks of Government

The public domain has its own distinctive tasks. These we characterize as the tasks of government. They give expression to the purposes of the public domain.

Only in the public domain can collective values be established. Collective values are arrived at through debate and discussion in the public arena. Interests have to be balanced. Particular values are expressed. The balancing of interests and the search for collective values beyond the particular is a task distinctive to the public domain. Other organizations balance particular interests, but in the public domain no interest can be excluded.

The tasks of government encompass the establishment of law and the maintenance of order. Particular organizations impose their own order and enforce their own practice, but their very existence assumes the public domain. The task of government is to give meaning to justice within the framework of law and the necessities of order.

In the public domain need has to be assessed. It is a task for government with its own purposes. In the private sector need is established, in order to establish demand. In the public domain need is assessed as a condition of government. Choices have to be made.

Beyond the distinctive tasks of government a range of activities has to be carried out. Many of those activities are also carried out in the private sector. Letters are typed, vehicles are maintained and invoices are checked in both sectors. Children are educated; residential homes are provided for the elderly and medical operations are undertaken in both. Activities in the public domain are also contracted out to the private sector.

The distinctive tasks of government have their own quality. Other activities do not necessarily vary because they are carried out in the private sector or the public domain. The purpose of the activity, those for whom it is provided and the role of the activity can vary, because those are determined through the political processes of collective decision-making rather than the market. These can affect the nature of the activity, but need not necessarily do so. The immediate management of such activities may need to be little different in the public domain from the private sector.

The management of activities is, however, set within wider management processes. Those processes can and should be different for they reflect the purposes and conditions of management in the public domain. Within those processes the questions can be raised not merely whether, but should, the management of schools be different in the public domain? Or, should the management of a direct labour organization be different from that of a private contractor?

Dilemmas To Be Faced

Management approaches have to be developed that support the purposes, meet the conditions and achieve the distinctive tasks of the public domain. This is no easy task. Purpose can conflict with purpose or tasks fit uneasily with the conditions under which they have to be carried out. We look to the public domain to reconcile interests that may be unreconcilable and to meet aspirations that may not be capable of attainment. We look to the public domain to provide the rigidity of direction and the responsiveness of service.

The dilemmas which characterize management in the public domain are inherent in its nature. Thus it is because the public domain is in principle unbounded, in that any interest or individual can make claims upon it, that dilemmas are inherent in its management. A private sector organization is limited and can limit its concern. A private sector organization can resolve the dilemma by defining it as out of its area of organizational concern. The public domain provides an arena in which all claims have to be heard.

Collective and Individual

The public domain is the domain of collective action. The public domain is, however, also the domain of individual citizens, each of whom may have views, demands or complaints. The collective has the power to impose on the individual, but action requires justification.

Representative and Participative

Collective action can be determined by elected representatives acting on behalf of the community or by active participation by that community. In our society power is normally exercised by the elected representative. Yet, the reality of representative government is challenged by the ideal of the participating community.

Bureaucracy and Responsiveness

In the rules of bureaucracy, political will is expressed, yet in those same rules responsiveness to individual need can be denied. Bureaucratic order can ensure impartiality of service, but cannot easily encompass a responsive service. Large-scale delivery of a uniform service is grounded in bureaucracy, but a service may be over-defined in its uniformity. It is difficult for bureaucracy to break its own rules.

Order and Service

In the public domain order is maintained and regulation imposed. But in the public domain, services are also provided, often by the same organization. An activity undertaken can be both a means of securing order and the provision of a service, yet each has its own management requirements.

Controlling and Enabling

Complex urban society depends upon a network of control. Society is grounded in a framework of regulation, upon which its functioning depends. Control derives from the public domain. Yet the public domain facilitates the achievement of collective aspirations. The public domain has to control but also has to facilitate and enable.

Political Conflict and Institutional Continuity

In the public domain, decisions are made through a political process. Debate, argument, pressure and protest all have their place in that process. Political conflict tests decisions. Yet political conflict presupposes and is grounded in institutional continuity. While the public domain provides the arena for the political process, it also provides the organizations that both support and act on that process.

Stability and Flexibility

Any organization faces a tension between the stability necessary for performance of its tasks and the flexibility required to adapt to change in its external environment. For the public domain the tension is deeper. For in its stability, society finds its order and yet that order depends upon a capacity to change.

Customer and Citizen

In the public domain many services are provided for the public. The public can be regarded as customers entitled to good service but they are also citizens. The public as customer and the public as citizen can share needs and wants, but can also differ in their purposes.

A Choice of Values

Values are sought in the public domain, but there can be a conflict of values between need and growth, equity and reward, competition and co-operation, liberty and equality, etc. In the end there has to be choice made and balance struck.

A Balance of Interests

Management in the public domain is set in a world in which many interests seek to achieve their aims. Balance is sought and resought in a continuing process.

The distinctive nature of management in the public domain lies in the dilemmas faced. The mistake is to act as if the dilemmas did not exist. One reason why models drawn from other sectors distort the nature of management is that they assume the dilemmas do not exist or do not have the depth implied, because they do not do so in other sectors.

The dilemmas are never finally resolved. In the public domain balances are achieved between the factors which constitute the dilemma. It is in the search for balance that management in the public domain has to be developed.

New Approaches to Management

Management has to develop approaches that recognize the distinctive purposes, conditions and tasks of the public domain and the dilemmas which they raise for management.

The Learning Process

The public domain is the setting for societal learning. The process of governing can be seen as a process of learning. There is a rhythm of problem and aspiration, response and action, failure and success. The rhythm is set by the changes in society, themselves intertwined with government.

The process of management can itself assist the process of learning or can limit it. Organizations lay down procedures and those procedures become channels through which learning flows. Those channels are, however, often determined by the existing pattern of activities and restrict learning to a perspective set by that pattern. Government learns from its own procedures about the number of cases dealt with more easily than those cases not dealt with (whether that is claimants to social security, applicants for library books, or the operation of environmental controls). The organization and the procedures can themselves limit learning from the political process, moulding it to predetermined patterns.

The need for learning can be too easily overlooked in the public domain because of the boundaries set by past practice. There is a perceived organizational necessity in existing activities. There is no market that enforces review. Instead of the market there is the politics of protest and demand, pressure and problem. That is part of the politics of learning, but it can be restricted by existing organizational patterns.

Yet, the public domain is in principle unbounded. It is open to all citizens, alert to need, subject to argument. It is no part of management to close off the learning process, but rather to sustain many channels of learning, not all of which are controlled by past practice.

In learning, management faces the tensions between past action and future potential and between the continuities of existing service provision and the demands of government.

Response and Direction in Strategy

The process of government is one of being governed and governing, of response and direction. The political process can guide both response and direction.

It is possible to envisage the process of response and direction as strategic planning, if it is not constructed from the private sector model. The strategy should express political purpose, not competitive strategy. Strategy expresses public aspiration realized in public debate.

The nature of strategy in the public domain is formed by the impossibility of drawing boundaries to public concern, the political process as the guiding principle, the many values sought and the many interests to be balanced. The task for management is to develop processes of strategic planning grounded in that reality.

It may well be that processes of strategic planning will be marked by selectivity in identifying key areas for directed change, while allowing space for responsiveness; by recognizing that in the public domain many values can be balanced in the single activity and that strategy centres more on the balances than on a single objective; by assessing a strategy in a political context and finding the language that enables that to be achieved; by recognizing the necessities of bargaining in a political process but by appraising the organizational framework within which bargaining takes place; by seeing the organizational framework as determined by and determining strategic purpose.

The Budgetary Process

In the public domain the budget expresses the choice between public purpose and private action, expressed in the decision on levels of tax. To price goods or services in the private domain is less a choice than an instrumental decision, determined by market position.

The allocation of expenditures within a budget expresses a choice too – between the values embedded in different activities and services. It will be achieved through bargaining and a balancing of interests. It will reflect assessments of needs, themselves derived from the values that emerge from collective debate in the political process. In the public domain the allocation of values, the balancing of interests and the assessment of need is made through the political process. Choice can be dependent on the vote.

The distinction is between the budget as a choice decision, to which in principle there is no right answer beyond the choices actually made in the political process, and the budget as an instrumental decision, to which in principle, if not in reality, there is a right answer to be found in the market. Management in the public domain has to focus on the budget as choice determined through a structure of bargaining in the political process.

The Management of Rationing

In the public domain many services are rationed. Services are not normally provided on demand – in one sense there is no limit to the demand for a free service and even a subsidized service generates demand beyond that of the market. Indeed, it can be to generate such demand that public provision is established. But the allocation of services can be by need rather than demand.

The management of rationing requires an understanding and an assessment of need, and an identification of choice, but also an understanding of how rationing is carried out. For wherever limited service meets unmet demand rationing takes place, consciously or unconsciously, by political will or by bureaucratic inertia, by budgetary choice or under work pressure, by frustration or by idealism. In the management of rationing the challenge is to match practice to purpose.

Decision-making

Decisions made in the public domain are value laden. That does not entirely separate them from decisions made outside the public domain. The distinction is that the achievement of collective values is the purpose of the public domain and not of other domains. Management in the public domain has to be sensitive to the values inherent in its actions, for if it is not it denies the purposes of the public domain. The building of a road or of a hospital, the drafting of supplementary benefits regulations, selection of books for libraries – all deny and assert values.

Decision-making is subject to public pressure and governed by politics. In these processes collective values are established. It is therefore a process, which in principle is open. Interests cannot be excluded. Pressures cannot be denied. Management in the public domain cannot operate in an enclosed world. It cannot make the assumption that public concern is limited or that political views are fixed.

The criteria for decision-making are subject to debate. Management in the public domain has to recognize that there are gainers and losers from any decision, and that both have voices.

Not all decisions will be subject to the same pressures; not all decisions have a high political salience; not all decisions will be recognized as embodying values. Decisions can be routinized.

Management in the public domain has to develop approaches to decision-making that recognize criteria cannot be fixed; that values have to be looked for; that results emerge from political processes and that costs and benefits from decisions can rarely be simply arrayed. Techniques that appear to predetermine decisions may well be inappropriate. The public interest is rarely clear. It is at the heart of debate and challenge.

Management Control and the Management of Action

Action in the public domain expresses collective purposes settled through political processes. It can express the values of impartial or equitable treatment. In rules and procedures the implementation of collective purpose is sought and impartiality and equity are established.

Yet, action in the public domain cannot deny the individual, whether as citizen or customer. To respond to a claimant for supplementary benefit or to an appeal by an income tax payer can be to break a rule. In the management of action or in management control, responsiveness has to be reconciled with the existence of rules and procedures.

Bureaucratic principles are designed to ensure impartial and equitable expression of collective decisions. Management in the public domain both requires bureaucracy and must seek to overcome it. Representative government, collective purpose, due process and public accountability all require rules and procedures to secure their observance. If collective action is limited to bureaucratic principle, collective action is limited in potential.

Collective action need not be limited to uniformity. Public provision does not necessarily eliminate individual choice. The problem for management control must be to distinguish that which must be controlled and that which should not be or need not be.

The Management of Interaction

The many organizations in the public domain are the shared expression of collective purpose. In principle, therefore, they are in a co-operative relationship. The reality can be different. Organizations have their own dynamic and those who work in them have their own purposes. Health and local authorities seeking their separate purposes can easily deny collective purposes. Different parts of the same organization may be in competition for public funds.

Management involves the management of interaction between different agencies and organizations. Management has to examine how, while recognizing the reality of competition, the practice of co-operation can be enhanced. Joint action can and does happen.

Performance Monitoring

Performance can rarely be defined in single outputs, because single outputs have many outcomes, none of which are beyond the concern of the public domain. Outputs can be defined and have value in work control, but those outputs are never an adequate basis for assessing performance. The number of child-care cases dealt with in a social services department gives no guide to performance.

The phrase 'value for money' sums up the dilemma. To seek value for money is a proper objective. The dilemma is that cost (money) is more easily established than value. The tendency is to resolve the value issue in simple measures of output. But to do so denies value for money, because value is not expressed.

There are many levels of performance monitoring. There is the simple measure of efficiency often expressed in a single dimension of cost of output. There are the more difficult assessments of the multi-dimensioned concept of effectiveness and beyond effectiveness there is the assessment of impact and of values achieved. Performance monitoring in the public domain is not merely concerned with effectiveness in achieving stated values, but with the unexpected impact, and of values denied.

Management has to assist assessment as well as measurement, encompass a multi-dimensioned performance, use indicators of quality and recognize the values hidden in analysis.

Staffing Policies

There is a tension that has to be faced in the public domain between concern for staff and concern for the public as customer, while recognizing that the public are also citizens – as are the staff. Neither representative democracy nor participatory democracy sits easily with industrial democracy.

In the past, emphasis has been placed on the public service ethic, as motivation and purpose. Yet the public service ethic alone is inadequate. Staff have trade union rights and have proper demands to make. The public service ethic is misused if it leads to low wages and salaries and poor conditions of service.

Staff have views, ideas and suggestions. Senior staff are powerful in the determination of policy. They hold resources of information, skill and access, which can weaken political control.

Management has to assist the development of staffing policies that recognize the tension between political control and the position of the staff, between citizen rights and staff rights, or between public accountability and staff initiative. The dilemma is to reconcile political control and staff potential.

Relations with Customer and Citizen

The public is both customer and citizen. That does not lessen the rights of the public in the public domain. It should enhance them. It means however that the relationships with the public are more complex than in the private sector. In many a decision on location of new public buildings, the interests of different customers and citizens have to be balanced.

The customer of a public service does not and should not behave like a customer of a private firm. At one level, management in the public domain can learn much from thinking of the public as customer. But the private sector model, although a stimulus, is not adequate by itself to the demands of the public domain.

Management has to develop theories of consumer behaviour, to reconceptualize marketing as the influence of public behaviour, to develop approaches based on the recognition of the role of both customer and citizen and to recognize that the interests of customers have to be balanced as well as met.

Public Accountability

This depends upon public organizations which are subject to political processes and in particular, directly or indirectly, to an electoral process. But public accountability requires more than the electoral process. An electoral process is the means by which those who make political decisions are held to account. Public accountability involves more than holding to account – it involves the need to give an account.

This is often interpreted in formal terms. Public accountability involves preparing proper financial accounts, scrutiny by audit and by ombudsman, and open decision-making. The emphasis is upon the carrying out of proper procedures and upon being able to show that decision-making has been carried out in the proper way. The established traditions of public accountability can encourage caution and the maintenance of past practice.

These traditions reflect a limited concept of public accountability. They reflect an accounting for probity and propriety rather than for policy and performance, yet it may be more important to consider public accountability in these latter senses than in traditional terms. Initiative, innovation and experiment should not be limited by public accountability, but should be encouraged in responsiveness to the public.

Public accountability will not be achieved by the reporting of simple performance measures. The services provided have many aspects and many publics. They need many forms of accounting in contact and involvement. The main requirement is that those who work in public service organizations should feel responsible and accountable to the public for whom they work.

References

Hirschmann, A. O. (1980) *Exit, Voice and Loyalty: Responses to Decline in Firms, Organizations and States*. Cambridge: Harvard University Press.

Rutter, L. (1980) *The Essential Community: Local Government in the Year 2000*. Washington: International City Management Association.

6

Professional Ethics, Government Agenda and Differential Information

Leonard Wrigley and David McKevitt

This chapter is about the interrelationship overall between professional ethics, the *agenda* of government, and differential information. Clearly, the subject is important, particularly for those concerned with public sector policy and management, but seems hitherto not to have been seriously explored.

The issue is not new. It was, indeed, formulated 200 years ago by Edmund Burke in his idea of the finest problem in legislation: 'namely, to determine what the state ought to direct by the Public Wisdom, and what it ought to leave, with as little interference as possible, to individual exertion' (Bullock and Shock, 1967: 254; the authors were questioning an argument made by Keynes in *The End of Laissez-Faire*).

That is also the fundamental question explored in this chapter. Our proposition is that in developed countries in socially important areas like health, education, welfare, and security (HEWS), where there exists differential information in favour of the producer, responsibility for progress is necessarily on the agenda of government, in the public domain, and the service delivery activities of the professional specialists in these areas is properly structured not by the market system, but by institutions of social responsibility, like legal regulations, civil law, and a rigorously grounded, well understood and properly enforced code of professional ethics. This proposition has its practical roots in our research on the workings of regional hospitals in Ireland, and its theoretical roots in the writings of Edmund Burke, Carr Saunders, Herbert Simon, Michael Oakeshott and Kenneth Arrow. Like all propositions of its kind, it might be wrong.

Concept of Progress

Our first step is to develop a concept of progress. The concept we seek must have the characteristic of being generally workable and acceptable as a first criterion of what should be done by social action.

Let us suppose that progress (or reform) means movement in a desirable direction. Here is the problem. In important areas of social action, citizens are not agreed on what it is they want for themselves or for their society. Irreconcilable differences about means and ends are endemic in the human condition. Innovation or change which is beneficial for some does not imply benefits for all. This distinction between innovation and progress is crucial in shaping our concept, but is not new. Indeed, the distinction was often articulated down the ages, particularly during the eighteenth century by conservatives, like Burke and Montesquieu, against the optimists of their day, like Condillac and Helvetius, who believed that, because of new social discoveries, all good things entailed each other, and innovations and progress were therefore identical. Burke did not agree with that at all.

Nowhere did Burke push the distinction between innovation and progress with greater force than in his famous polemic against the French Revolution. Writing in 1795, six years after the storming of the Bastille, he argued:

> To innovate is not to reform. The French Revolutionists complained of everything; they refused to reform anything; and they left nothing, no, nothing at all unchanged. The consequences are before us – not in remote history, not in future prognostication: they are about us; they are upon us. They shake the public security; they menace private enjoyment. They dwarf the growth of the young; they stop our way. They infest us in towns; they pursue us to the country. Our business is interrupted, our repose is troubled, our pleasures are saddened, our very studies are poisoned and perverted, and knowledge is rendered worse than ignorance, by the enormous evil of this dreadful innovation. (O'Brien, 1992: 537)

According to this light, movement which brings great benefit to some at the cost of great harm to others does not provide a workable definition of progress. We would agree. As a first criterion, progress has to be a movement towards benefits for all, or, to adapt the homely but magnificent language of Sean Lemass, Prime Minister of Ireland in 1958, 'Like as a rising tide to lift all boats.'

For the purpose of developing a workable concept of progress, we make three assumptions. First, we assume that society is the historic personality known as the nation state, working through innumerable arrangements where all the participants are endowed from their mother's milk with a sense of community. Secondly, we also assume that society over the long term will always organize itself to seek an optimal state, and correspondingly, to escape from a suboptimal state. And thirdly, we assume that society will have reached an optimal state when it is exactly and precisely in the following condition: 'There is no other movement of activities or resources which will make all the participants of society better off' (adapted from Arrow, 1975). Correspondingly, we assume society is in a suboptimal state if there exists a feasible movement of activities and resources which would make all participating members better off.

In the literature, these states are known respectively as Pareto optimality and Pareto suboptimality (named after the Italian economist, Pareto, who developed them). In that light, it seems reasonable to present a workable concept or definition of progress as that change of activities and resources which moves society from a Pareto suboptimal state to a Pareto optimal state. Obviously, definitions are just definitions, and imply no particular stance in regard to social and personal values and ethics, either positive or negative. Nonetheless, our definitions can be contentious.

While, according to our concept, it is clearly desirable for society to seek Pareto optimality, we need to accept that optimality in this sense is not the only possible criterion for individual or social action. A Pareto optimal society may yet contain great inequality of wealth or talent or happiness. For example, only a few individuals in such a society may be extremely happy or talented or wealthy, and yet the society may be Pareto optimal according to our definition if there is no way of moving activities and resources to increase the happiness or talent or wealth of the many without hurting the few. We accept that this brings to our definition some qualifications. Obviously considerations of equity do have a valid role in shaping the social policy of a modern society.

Moreover, the concept of Pareto optimality implicitly contains the assumption that all economic agents, whether as sellers or buyers, as producers or clients, do know what they want, today and for all the tomorrows. This implies that customers are clear about the consequences for themselves of making a purchase, that they are certain of the satisfaction to be derived from the products they buy, and that they can forecast accurately the utility they will get in the future from their purchasing arrangements today. But this assumption is most shaky. From time immemorial, society has had to cope with the problem that not all citizens (including children and the elderly) are necessarily always in possession of the information needed to render valid such an assumption. To satisfy better the expressed wishes and desires of all citizens, everywhere, at all times is not necessarily the sole or ultimate criterion of social progress. Pareto optimality may be an ideal state only for the happy uplands, where free choice is always exercised to favour the general good.

Yet, however important such qualifications are in practical affairs, we still hold firm to our concept of progress as movement of activities and resources to change society from a Pareto suboptimal to a Pareto optimal state. We accept that this may not be – and even should not be – the only workable definition of progress, but, we argue, it is one that is always central, always important, and always capable of serving as a valid first criterion of what should be done by social action. Moreover, with this criterion in our kitbag, we can return to the level of ordinary language and robustly look at the problem of differential information.

Differential Information

It is on their assumptions that social scientists can either make great contributions to their society or perfect fools of themselves. In discussions on promoting the efficiency of the market, politicians and economists tend to assume equality of information as between sellers and buyers. Of course, no one would seriously defend the assumption regarding inputs or methods of production. Here the seller will clearly have superior knowledge. This is not the issue. The issue concerns outputs. If there is differential information in favour of the producer, then the market is defective as an institution for progress: the greater the differential information, the more defective the market.

Our proposition requires us to treat differential information as an independent variable of massive proportion. It is quite clear that the great inequality of the late twentieth century is not wealth or talent or happiness. These are the outcomes. This is clear to those with experience on the one hand of Dublin or Boston or London or Stockholm or Paris, and, on the other hand, of Addis Ababa or Baghdad or Jakarta or Manila or even Cairo.

It is also perfectly obvious in respect of individual transactions and personal relationships that those with the education, training and scholarship going into professional specialisms in health, education, welfare and security have a far higher level of knowledge in these matters than the mass of ordinary citizens. Indeed, the significant attribute of professional workers compared with ordinary citizens is differential information.

However, before looking at differential information we need to consider the role of the market in resources allocation. In recent years, economists like Arrow, Debrue and Godley, who have done so much to clarify the workings of the market, have been at pains to identify and highlight the necessary conditions for market efficiency and these conditions are not trivial.

It is generally accepted that when certain conditions are satisfied, the competitive market will promote a socially (Pareto) optimal state. We accept that argument. However, amongst the conditions to be satisfied is the marketability of all goods and services relevant to costs and utilities in the society. Here is where we see the problems. Not all goods and services are marketable.

Nonmarketability can be traced to the intrinsic characteristics of a product which prevent price from being agreed and enforced (for example health care for an individual with a contagious disease). It can also be traced to social values which prohibit the sale of a product because of social repugnance at the consequences (for example the sale of one's own children). But the important factor making a service nonmarketable that is of direct relevance to this chapter is differential information in favour of the producer as to the consequences for a customer or client of the acquisition of a product or service.

Differential information in favour of the producer is a characteristic of those services which are so complicated in their nature, and about which there is such uncertainty as to their effects for the recipient, that the producer has to be especially and carefully trained over a lengthy period on the varying characteristics of the services. In the end, the information possessed by such producers concerning the most likely consequences for a particular client of acquiring the service is very much greater than that of the client. In such circumstances, a price relationship is not a valid basis for an optimal level of transactions, particularly in relation to those services the proper distribution of which is deemed important for a sense of community to be maintained.

In this argument, it is accepted that information can be difficult to transfer. The problem is in the receiver. Learning takes time. The effort required for success can be very great in respect of certain services that are of community importance. Indeed, it is the difficulty of information transfer that renders so significant the phenomenon of differential information.

The most obvious areas where such conditions of differential information are significant are health care, education, welfare and the law. Let us focus here on health care. Because of the complexity of the human body and of modern techniques to cure the sick, and also because of the supreme importance of the outcome for the client, the doctor has to undergo lengthy, rigorous and highly specialized training before he or she is deemed qualified to practise. Because of this training, the doctor possesses far more information than the client on the consequences for the client of, and the possibilities open for, particular forms of treatment. So once the client has chosen their doctor, then he or she has to rely on the doctor to determine the type, quality and quantity of health care that the client needs in order to be cured of sickness.

Thus the doctor is not merely a provider of medicine, but also, necessarily, an agent of the client in providing information. The issue is crucial. In the decision to acquire health care, the sick cannot stand alone. They need the doctor to advise them, to be on their side, to wish them well. They cannot themselves predict the likely consequence of acquiring a particular treatment. They rely upon the doctor to advise them not just on what medicine to have, but also how much and what and where. Thus, the doctor has two roles: provider and agent. This duality of roles has important consequences. The doctor, historically, is bound by society not to seek to maximize profit, but to seek to maximize the welfare of the client.

There is another aspect. If an error is made in diagnosis, the consequences for the doctor may be loss of income; for the client, it may be death. So the two sides of the coin are quite different. It is very much in the client's own interest that the doctor is not at arm's length, but on their side, as their agent.

Duality of role of the producer also characterizes, in greater measure or less, the areas of education, welfare and security, including the law, because here too there is differential information, and here too the producer needs to be the agent of the client. The very basis of the market as an optimal-seeking institution does not exist, cannot exist, where the producer is also the client's agent. The essential characteristic of the market system – arm's-length negotiation – is lacking.

Kenneth Arrow, in his paper on resource allocation in US medical care, noted the problems facing the market (or price system) in health care: 'the agent in the simplest model is assumed to predict correctly the satisfaction he will get from consumption in the future. Now an essential characteristic of medical care as a commodity is that such certainty is absent' (Arrow, 1972: 397). Arrow's main concern, however, was uncertainty regarding the incidence of sickness, where insurance is the solution. The concern is with the uncertainty regarding the outcome of medical care for a client who is sick, and when the solution is 'best practice', as identified through proper training, by the doctor, as agent of the client.

It is necessary to emphasize that the inequality of information on the consequences of acquiring a service has to be significant to render the product nonmarketable. In those areas where the client can have, or can reasonably acquire, as good or nearly as good an understanding as the producer of the utility of the product, then the product is marketable.

In summary, defenders of the market assume that the client is well informed of the consequences for him or her of a purchase, or that they can become so informed by their own experience – in repeat purchases – or by relying on the experience of others. In the areas of health care, education, welfare and security this defence is not valid. The risks, including death or a wasted youth, can be so great that even one bad experience is fatal. In these areas the market cannot make for progress. Movement towards social optimality calls for them to be placed on the agenda of government, in the public domain.

Agenda of Government

This chapter opened with Burke's question, 'What should the state direct by the public wisdom?' The traditional answer relates (in one variant or another) to 'market failure', namely, the areas where the market would necessarily fail to operate as an institution for progress. Such an answer always casts the government as an 'add-on' to the social structure. However, many people, given equal efficiency of government and market, would prefer the use of the government, or public sector, if only because it allows greater accommodation for altruistic motives. But more mundane forces drive our argument here.

Historically, for the provision of important social services, government has explicitly or implicitly been held out as the institution which is an alternative to the market in the allocation of resources. This position has long been implicit in discussions of the functions of government. That society will seek to achieve optimality by government (or other social) action if it cannot achieve it by the market is amongst the oldest traditions of Western civilization. The public sector has a particular role in areas where private interests may not lead to progress. This is the aspect of interest to us.

Because of differential information, there is no reason why private interest in the supply of health care, education, welfare and security will ever coincide with social optimality. In areas where there is differential information, it is not true that 'the invisible hand of self-interest' will guide suppliers towards the collective needs of society. In such instances there will be enormous social pressure on the government to take responsibility for progress as part of its agenda. Democracy cannot resist such pressure. Moreover, areas where differential information exists are likely to be part of the stable agenda of government. Because of this stability and the defining nature of the areas, we give the term 'Core Public Sector' to these areas. The core has certain characteristics to which we must give attention.

Once in the public domain, as part of a stable core public sector, public services tend to become legal entitlements for all the relevant citizens and, in consequence, tend to lead in time to deeply valued arrangements in which citizens live out their lives. Amongst other effects, this evolution limits the scope for public sector managers. In areas where citizens are entitled by law to a given service, and have developed corresponding arrangements, the scope for decentralized initiative is very small. The need for stability and continuity is then very large.

There is more than that. If attempts are made to make great change in these areas there is a risk that society will become disorientated. The innovations in health, education, welfare and security now being pushed through with unprecedented energy in the United Kingdom, United States and New Zealand are not necessarily progressive. Indeed the changes may greatly harm many people. At a technical level, an important reason for caution in effecting change in the areas of health, education, welfare and security is the sheer magnitude of these areas collectively.

For ease of exposition we defined as HEWS the general area embracing health, education, welfare and security, which we term the core public sector. HEWS is a huge area in all modern societies, now tending to stabilize in size after growing very rapidly in the 1950s and 1960s. The proportion of Gross National Product that has been expended on HEWS since the Second World War has varied over time but less so between countries, at least between the countries of Western Europe. In broadest measure the proportion of GNP for HEWS in the Western world (not including the USA, but including Canada) was about 20 per cent in 1950, about 30 per cent in 1960, and has reached and remained at about 40 per cent since. No other general area in society is of such magnitude. This too brings problems.

In recent decades there has been a continued increase in demand, which leads to the problem of rationing in health, education, welfare and security. Broadly, the services here are free to the client, but paid for out of taxation. The trend in recent decades is for public demand to increase disproportionately to the resources that society as a whole has been willing to make available through taxation. The result is a shortfall of supply relative to demand. Consequently, each core public service enterprise has to develop a rationing system to allocate supply to individual clients. The term 'rationing' here means allocation by a system other than price. Hospitals, schools, welfare offices and the law, all develop a system of rationing to ensure 'fairness' – or optimality – in distribution. The need to ration the service at an operational level is a major factor that makes the activities of professionals in core public services quite different to those of the professionals in business firms in the market system. It is professional judgement not customer affluence which largely determines the allocation of resources within the areas of health, education and welfare. But, of course, professionals' judgement can be affected by many factors, including fear of malpractice suits, difficulty in coping with political pressures, as well, of course, as assessment of what the client really needs.

Public sector managers and professionals have to cope with the problems resulting from rationing, particularly the problem articulated through the political system as pressure to do something for some special person or class of person. Stewart has argued that a central concern of public service managers (and professionals) has to be the political dimension inherent in their work. In his words, 'The Manager needs to be aware of political aims and priorities, possible areas of conflict, and sources of political difficulty' (Stewart, 1989: 171). It is scarcely necessary to mention that nowhere is the political dimension more significant than in areas and conditions where rationing of a core public service has to be severe because of demand or supply conditions (see McKevitt, 1990: 158). All this puts pressure on professional specialists to develop and embellish strong institutions of social responsibility.

Allocation of scarce resources, rationing, in the market system is done by price. In the public domain, it is done by the decisions of professional specialists. But these specialists decide within a framework of social obligations, and the efficacy of government in service delivery activities is very largely affected by the strength and appropriateness of social obligations.

Exhortation and expectations of good behaviour have their place in public affairs. However, to be effective in bad times as well as good, and over the long term, such exhortations and expectations have to be embodied in the specific form of social institutions, of which three are particularly relevant to HEWS services:

Legal regulations;
Civil law; and
Codes of professional ethics.

The legal regulations specify the rights and duties under law relating to the specific services. Civil law enables the law courts to be brought into public service to legislate on damages suffered by clients from defective delivery, as characterized by malpractice suits. Institutionalized codes of ethics prompt good behaviour not by an appeal to individual conscience, but by well enforced and a well understood and rigorously grounded definition of good and bad behaviour and practice.

For better preparation to meet future challenges, there is much to be said for the public sector's allowing some private initiative in relation to the HEWS areas. In fact society has been vigorous in enabling that allowance. Surprisingly, there has been much less vigour in enabling developments in codes of professional ethics, notwithstanding the organic relationship between differential information and ethical codes, and the changing environment of health, education, welfare and security. It does not seem too much to say that development in professional codes of ethics should now become a priority on the agenda of government in the various countries of the developed world.

Code of Professional Ethics

An historical association is not necessarily a logical one, but it can be evidence. Over the centuries since professional specialists emerged, there have also emerged related codes of professional ethics. This has led to the notion that there is a logical relationship between professional activities and the codes. For us, that notion is much too loose.

Ethical codes appropriate to professional activities are organically related to differential information in favour of the producer in respect of services which carry a high risk for the client. We present this judgement without reservations or equivocation. The organic nature of this relationship has consequences of importance for the possibilities of progress. In areas where there is a large difference in information in favour of the producer, strong ethical codes can make a difference, immediately in terms of greater economic efficiency, more fundamentally in strengthening the power of altruistic motives and sense of community, through greater trust between government and people and between professionals and clients.

All professions, by the very definitions appropriate to each one, involve a large measure of differential information in favour of the producer. In the first place, ethical codes evolved to protect the client. But such codes, if strongly institutionalized in the form of widespread understanding and proper enforcement, provide, as it were, a 'level playing field' in which each professional can compete with his or her fellows without short-changing the client. Moreover, such codes provide information and guidance to new entrants to the profession as to good and bad practice. Client protection, a level playing field for competition, and information and guidance to new entrants are major benefits. But there is more than that.

Rationing is inevitable in public service delivery. Legal regulations may stipulate priorities for service, but it is the strength of the ethical code which determines whether effect is given in practice to the legal regulations, and whether the regulation is complied with in spirit as well as letter. In the absence of a strong ethical code, corruption is inevitable and endemic, and the whole purpose of the core public sector is reduced to mere words about other words. Ethical codes are useful, therefore, when widely understood, generally accepted, and seen as giving benefits to all if all comply with the codes. Given that codes do strengthen society, the question arises of how the codes become accepted.

Historically, the acceptance of ethical codes is an integral part of the lengthy training of professional specialists. Indoctrination in the codes has been a central part of professional education in a crucial sense. The efficacy and progress of the core public sector is largely influenced in the professional schools. And this influence takes the form not of lectures or specific training, but of indoctrination in a way of life, as at Sandhurst or West Point. It highlights the enormous social importance of the faculty of such schools. All this was recognized well in the past, but is now under threat by thoughtless efforts at shortening professional education.

The role of the professional schools is also important in the evolution of codes. The impetus for such evolution may be problems in the field, which have been seriously explored by researchers and written about and discussed in learned journals and professional conferences. But the impetus may also come from the impact on the public of a breakdown in the enforcement of such codes and with public pressure on the political parties to develop a response.

What is important is that the codes seem unable to develop beyond a certain point without institutional support from relevant organizations, including government, trade unions, concerned groups and members of the profession itself. Such support is needed to render explicit a change in the code, and to enforce widespread acceptance of changes.

Since it is always a benefit for a minority to cheat on the code, the strength of the ethical code largely depends on the mechanisms used by the institutions to enforce compliance. In this regard it is strange that society spends so much effort in providing resources for the public sector, and even for professional education, and yet almost none in enforcing compliance with the ethical codes. Of course the codes are not a substitute for the other two institutional social obligations: legal regulations, and civil law. But without a vibrant set of ethical codes, legal regulations and civil law are like wax images that shock by their resemblance: they may hope to have everything – but not life itself.

Management of Professionals in the Public Sector

We have to examine how developed countries evolved quite different institutional arrangements and organizational routines for the management of professionals and the recruitment and development of public service managers. Societies evolve complex arrangements for social control: organizations do likewise as they seek to accommodate competing and conflicting demands from their citizens/clients. In this context, we need to remember that the Anglo-Saxon tradition of public service is only some one hundred years old. Hitherto, doctors, lawyers, teachers and engineers were self-employed or dependent on political patronage for their income. Organizational and institutional arrangements for the provision of core public services are quite recent. Their impetus lay in the sweeping away of poor law paternalistic arrangements and their zenith was in the recent past, from 1946 to 1970. The new orthodoxy of privatization and market arrangements for public service provision is some fifteen years old. If society is not to be buffeted by changes which presage disruption of social cohesion rather than maintenance of social solidarity, then it is the responsibility of professionals and managers to understand (and respond to) the character of the core public service; to attend to its purpose rather than to tinker with its structures and organizations.

The development and maintenance of a code of professional ethics and rules of behaviour is inseparable from the general development of a society's norms and traditions. Thus, for example, the German tradition of a salaried and university-educated professional civil servant paralleled the more general developments of the Bismarckian welfare state in the late nineteenth century. In large measure, the north European tradition of professional development and institutional cohesion was a reciprocal relationship between the emerging professional class and the modern nation state. Hence, the professionals were instrumental in legitimizing the governance of the modern welfare state as they embodied the act of service to the citizenry. Such developments were reflected in the wider development of the socio-legal arrangement whereby citizens' rights and entitlements were embodied in the law. The idea (or ideal) of a code of professional ethics, incorporating notions of internal social control, was seen by writers as diverse as Durkheim and Talcott Parsons as an important part of a wider modernizing process.

The Anglo-Saxon tradition of professional development (and, indeed the academic and critical commentary on this development) was one whereby, in general, professionals were granted great autonomy in their arrangements for self-regulation and control. Doctors, lawyers and teachers, overwhelmingly state employees, were (and still are) allowed to codify their own standards and guidelines, entry requirements and promotion criteria. It is only in the last decade that sustained state attention has been given to the curtailment or abridgement of these professionals' 'freedoms'. This process has largely been an adversarial one, reflected in the idea that a managerialist ethic is now in the ascendant, with the professionals on the defensive, ethically, socially and economically. Such a perspective is, of course, overblown; yet it does reveal an important point. The professional cadre of public service employees *is* on the defensive, their traditions and sapiential authority *is* being questioned, their legitimacy *is* under close and sustained scrutiny. Academic commentary on professionals is largely couched in terms of power analysis: its framework is underpinned by the notion that professionalism is, by and large, a cloak for self-interest, that its ethical base is a measure of social closure not a means for standards in service delivery.

It would be unwise to view recent curtailment of some professional claims to autonomy and self-regulation as intrinsically a 'bad thing': one has to acknowledge that professionals' claims to act on an ethical basis in their relationships with citizen/clients has to be balanced against widespread public disenchantment with a perceived poor standard of service delivery. Similarly, as their system of internal regulation has yielded little in the way of consistent debarment of its personnel, one can legitimately question whether self-regulation is working to the advantage of the client. Yet to refashion important relationships with the professionals through a series of laws and systems of crude performance measurement frameworks is not necessarily the best way of ensuring progress. Recent research in this area has found that professionals may indeed be seeking to 'hold the line' between pressures for cost containment and emerging evidence of a decline in service quality (McKevitt and Lawton, 1993). That is, professionals are a possible bulwark between the state's need to curtail expenditure and the necessity to maintain minimum standards of services that promote and sustain social cohesion and interdependence. Countries as diverse in their historic and cultural traditions as Sweden, Canada and Germany have succeeded in mediating between professional self-interest and the maintenance of social cohesion and high standards of service delivery. The relationship between professionals and clients, and between professionals and managers, is one of mutual respect and trust.

In the United Kingdom, Ireland and the United States the situation is different; here, professional claims to autonomy are uneasily balanced against the legitimate claims of government to ensure efficiency and efficacy in service delivery and to curtail general public expenditure. The reforms of public regulation and control have, in large measure, been crude attempts to impose mechanistic controls in an environment where organic relationships are dominant. It is not surprising that there is little evidence of public satisfaction with these reforms. They are misdirected and inappropriate in their mission: the provision of core public services is not inconsistent with a need to seek 'value for money', nor is it incompatible with a desire to ensure responsible behaviour by professionals. To ensure responsible behaviour by professionals, however, requires working with the grain of professional interest in quality, granting professionals a voice in the formulation of performance standards and attending to their historic role in civilizing state–citizen relationships. Replacing power with patronage is not how modern democratic nations evolved, nor is it the way to resolve complex and important social problems. Each country should undertake more research on the best practices of other countries to discover clues as to how to improve the management of professionals in their own public sector.

Implications

We have, we believe, documented the validity of our proposition. There is a relationship between professional code of ethics, the *agenda* of government, and differential information. This has not, we believe, been recognized before, so we have made an original contribution to the corpus of knowledge of public policy and public sector management. We have also formulated certain concepts, like core public sector, which seems likely to enter the language of public policy.

So what? Are there here any significant implications for politicians or managers, or for our fellow academics? If so, what things should be done differently? We will now seek to answer these very real questions.

For politicians, the implication of this chapter is that 'market failure' is a workable concept to identify what should be directed by the public wisdom, and what should be left to private enterprise. Clearly, health care, education, welfare and security should largely be on the agenda of government, part of the public domain, as these are the major elements of the core public sector. But the public sector does have problems, including the system for rationing usage. Hence, areas and activities outside the core public sector seem best left to private action and enterprise.

For public sector managers, the major implication is that the public sector really is different from the private sector, and all those ideas about reinventing government to bring in the management practices of private enterprise are just cocktail party chatter. Important similarities do exist between public and private management – we know that from such writers as Hebert Simon. But the differences are no less profound. These relate to differential information, the legal imperatives of public service, and inflexibility arising from the institutions of social obligation. The differences should be accepted, and pride taken in the fact of public service, in the scope and the room for altruistic motives, particularly amongst professionals and managers and the public employee working 'at the coal face'. However, similarities with private enterprise should not be ignored: there is a case for far more information, in the form of easily understandable advertisements about the various public sector enterprises.

Our fellow academics will, of course, see our concern that there should be more research on professional ethical codes as an institution, and on the relationship both with differential information and with the other two institutions of social obligations, legal regulation and civil law. At this moment we would argue that the interrelationship of all three institutions of social obligation and responsibility would enable a major step forward on the road to progress and the delivery of public service. But in making this suggestion, we do not underestimate the difficulties: they will be huge. The rewards could be greater.

References

Arrow, Kenneth (1972) 'Problems of resource allocation in United States medical cases', in R. M. Kenz and H. Fehr (eds), *The Challenge of Life*. Basle and Stuttgart: Berk Bauer.

Arrow, Kenneth (1975) 'Economic development: present state of the art', *Papers of the East–West Communications Institute*, 14.

Bullock, Allen and Shock, Maurice (eds) (1967) *The Liberal Tradition from Fox to Keynes*. Oxford: Clarendon Press.

McKevitt, David (1990) *Health Care Policy in Ireland*. Hibernian University Press.

McKevitt, David and Lawton, Alan (1993) 'The manager, the citizen, the politician and performance measures'. Paper prepared for Public Administration, 23rd annual conference, York.

O'Brien, Conor Cruise (1992) *The Great Melody: A Thematic Biography of Edmund Burke*. London: Sinclair-Stevenson.

Stewart, John (1989) 'In search of curriculum for management for the public sector', *Management Education and Development*, 20(3): 168–75.

PART 2
CONTROL AND
IMPLEMENTATION

Introduction

Part 1 examined the political, economic, social and moral assumptions that underpin arguments justifying the scope, role and size of the public sector. Another set of assumptions is concerned with the values deemed appropriate for the processes and outcomes of public services organizations. Managers are encouraged to be more economic, efficient and effective in what they do. Organizations are encouraged to be more responsive to the customer, and managers are expected to be more accountable. It is assumed that such terms can be clearly specified and that their definition is unproblematic. Greater choice for the customer is advocated and increased competition is seen as a means to improve efficiency and effectiveness. Means proffered to achieve such effects include moving organizations from the public sector to the private sector, deregulation, the creation of internal markets, a concern with tighter financial controls and attacking the perceived power of the professionals.

In Chapter 7 Rose examines the use of the price mechanism as a means of allocating resources in the 'public provision of private benefits'. Whether such measures have improved the effectiveness of public services organizations is open to debate. In the next chapter Dunsire *et al.* examine how a change in status, as organizations move from the public to the private sector, has affected the performance of those organizations. This chapter looks at organizational change, linking changes in market status to changes in internal management structures. The evidence it presents suggests that a change in ownership does not necessarily lead to a change in the performance of the organization. Clearly there is more research to be done on how a change in status affects organizational performance.

One of the issues highlighted by Dunsire *et al.* is the location of control within public services organizations. Control issues in such organizations are not confined to simple issues of ownership. One of the defining characteristics of these organizations is said to be the requirement to respond to a multiplicity of different stakeholders, internal and external to the organization. Issues of control will need to include the role and status of professionals and managers within the organizations, the role of politicians and the relationship with the citizen, consumer and client.

Jacob, in Chapter 9, argues that the changes within the NHS, responding to legislation, have raised issues concerning the role of professionals within public services organizations. Jacob puts forward the proposition that the legal status of some of these changes is unclear and that this may lead to an increased role for lawyers. Furthermore, within the NHS, Jacob argues, the demands for quantification have come to replace professional judgement. 'Effort and striving are turned into cost; practice into performance; trust into negotiated consent; cure into discharge; anguished choice into efficiency.' Control is inextricably linked to performance and to accountability.

The concern with measuring performance and ensuring accountability through quantification represents a triumph of technique over judgement. In Part 1 Oakeshott counselled against this, and from a different perspective Hopwood in Chapter 10 argues that the increasing importance of accounting in public services may be unhealthy: 'A world of the seemingly precise, specific and quantitative can, in this way, emerge out of that of the contentious and the uncertain.' Technical expertise can come to dominate political debate. Accounting may be seen as a symbol of the organization's commitment to efficiency and economy. As a technique of control, accounting may give the appearance of certainty in an uncertain world.

Organizations are messy; policy-makers seem to assume that the process of implementation is unproblematic and that what goes into the 'black box' of public services organizations will smoothly lead to intended outputs. In Chapter 11 Baier *et al.* argue that 'Policy-makers often ignore, or underestimate considerably, the administrative requirements of a policy, and thus make policies that assure administrative incapacity.' Top-down implementation ignores the concerns of middle managers and the training requirements involved in implementing internal markets, contract cultures or Citizens Charters. Top-down implementation takes a simplistic view of organizations. Baier *et al.* argue that multiple stakeholders and values are features of public services organizations and that 'Conflict of interest is not just a property of the relations between policymakers on the one hand and administrators on the other; it is a general feature of policy negotiation and bureaucratic life.'

In a companion piece Challis *et al.* indicate the implementation problems of managing across organizations and the difficulty of policy co-ordination. Challis *et al.* point to the interaction of organizations, groups and individuals and urges us to look at patterns of dependence in terms of bargaining and power. As public services organizations are encouraged to provide services through a multitude of other organizations and to change from providers to purchasers, has enough consideration been given to the problems that managers may face in securing compliance, co-ordination or collaboration through a number of formal and informal agreements? Community Care, for example, requires implementation through a range of organizations, each with different values, goals, structures and cultures.

7

Charges as Contested Signals

Richard Rose

Allocating resources is a common problem of both states and markets: governments need means of deciding how much education, transportation and military defence should be provided, just as a clothing manufacturer needs to allocate resources between producing white and striped shirts. In principle, the supply of particular public policies should meet the demand for these policies; in practice, whether they do is contested.

Although politics and markets are both about supply and demand relationships, they differ fundamentally in the way in which demands are signalled: votes are the currency of political demands, whereas money is the currency of the market. The theory of democracy is that public policies are produced by popularly elected representatives in response to signals from individuals *qua* voters. Economic theory views individuals as consumers signalling demands by their willingness to pay a price for goods and services produced for sale in the market-place.

Votes determine who governs but not what governors do. Just as the market model of neo-classical economic theories is so stylized as to be inconsistent with much empirical reality, so a model of government being steered by the signals of the electorate is a simplification offering little guidance to officials facing decisions about the actual allocation of resources for public policies. As Day and Klein (1987) have shown, when a public agency is faced with decisions about how much money to spend on a service or whether to increase or cut a particular programme, elected officials usually lack knowledge of the technicalities of supply and demand of programmes, and thus rely upon experts for guidance (see also Rose, 1989: chapter 4).

In the belief that the price mechanism offers an effective method of allocating such publicly provided goods and services as education, health care and housing, free market economists often advocate charging. [. . .] Such proposals may be less radical than privatization, accepting that the government may still own and operate agencies providing services at a charge, or they may be a prelude to subsequent privatization by generating revenue that could then be used to finance a privatized agency. Charging is

From *Journal of Public Policy*, 1989, 9(3): 261–86 (abridged).

also less radical than libertarian claims that the state should be confined to the provision of pure collective goods, such as defence and diplomacy. It also accepts that the state may provide individuals with such private discrete benefits as education and health care that could be (and sometimes are) sold in the market. Ingenious proposals for awarding vouchers that can be spent at public or private agencies even accept public finance of social benefits; the idea of a voucher is that it will act as a signal identifying and rewarding those who provide services that best satisfy their users.

Whether political or market signals should be primary signals guiding public programmes is contested. Economists disagree among themselves about whether or not markets always make efficient provision; the logic of market failure is used to justify public provision of services without charge. Political parties often differ along left–right lines about the principle of charging. There are also organizational differences within government between Ministry of Finance officials, cautious about open-end commitments to finance 'free' (that is, uncharged) services that claim funds from the fisc, and spending ministers who can take credit for providing benefits without charge.

Charges can be rejected as morally unsatisfactory, politically unwise, economically inefficient, or administratively cumbersome – and on all these grounds. The moral opposition to charges emphasizes the primacy of non-pecuniary values. The prudent politician reckons that people will be more likely to vote for a party that offers them something for nothing (that is, social benefits without charge) than for a party that only makes services available at a price. A variety of economic arguments can be marshalled against charges, such as the positive externalities of such things as a well educated citizenry. When the administration of charges involves the exemption of those without the means of payment, the difficulties and inequities of means-testing can be grounds for opposition.

Nor does government need charges as a signal of demand. The major programmes of the mixed-economy welfare state can be financed from general tax revenue. In the extreme case of free, compulsory education, individuals may even be compelled to consume a public service free of charge. After a decade in which free-market ideas as well as market-oriented politicians have achieved political prominence, in both Britain and America providing public services without charge remains the norm for public practice.

Although charging for public services is just as much a theoretical anomaly as government subsidy of the market, in fact the government of every OECD nation imposes charges upon users of a wide variety of its goods and services. This is true not only of the outputs of public utility enterprises, such as electricity and transport, but also for a host of classic services (e.g. bridge tolls); programmes for which there are private sector counterparts (public housing); and to some extent for welfare state benefits (e.g. a more or less nominal charge to use parts of a health service). If a government provides military equipment to another country, it may decide to charge for the tanks or planes it supplies rather than gift them.

Even if money talks, it is not clear what charges say about the demand for public programmes. Therefore, this chapter examines empirically the use and non-use of charges by government. The potential scope for charges is considered first; three-quarters of public expenditure is allocated to programmes that could, in principle, be subject to charge. The substantial dispute on political and economic grounds about whether charges ought to be imposed is reviewed in the second section. The range and volume of charges are examined in the third section. Although some charges are imposed on a wide variety of public policies, for the most part governments reject marketing what is marketable. Charges tend to be imposed only for fringe services, such as school trips abroad. Theoretical inconsistencies in government imposition of charges reflect political inertia; each government tends to accept commitments inherited from its predecessors and avoids the political and fiscal costs of introducing major changes. The conclusion offers an analytic paradigm for interpreting charges, since an accurate interpretation of the signals sent depends upon attributes specific to a given public programme.

Scope for Charges in the Mixed Polity

The scope for charges depends in part upon how broadly the term is defined. It also depends upon what government does, for it is much easier to impose charges on some types of programmes than others, e.g. it is easier to charge a rent for a house than to rent the services of a nation's diplomats. [. . .]

Definition

Charges involve payment of money as a condition of use of a specific public good or service. The forms of charges are variable in the extreme, between the strictly voluntary payment that an individual may make to attend a performance in a state-owned theatre through rent paid for use of a municipally owned house to the fee paid for a passport; at the margin the term 'charges' can overlap with payments conventionally classified as taxes (OECD, 1986: 37f.). The payments that government collects may be labelled a charge, a fee, a fine, levy, licence, rent, toll, or even a price. Since custom rather than reason tends to determine the use of different labels, it would be unwise to interpret verbal differences as signals of differences in meaning. Therefore, the word charge is here used as an inclusive term.

A critical distinction between a tax and a charge is that a tax is compulsory and it is also unrequited; a person *must* pay a tax on income, and does not *ipso facto* receive particular services or goods by doing so. By contrast, charges are not compulsory: an individual does not have to attend the opera, live in a council house, or travel abroad. Charges are also requited; in return for paying a charge a person is entitled to use a public service. [. . .]

The High Volume of Collectively Provided Private Goods

Analytically, public policies can be divided between those concerned with collective (often called public) goods and those providing private goods. *Collective* goods and services are consumed on a non-excludable basis; everyone can enjoy their benefits. Equally important, they are non-rival, that is, one person consuming a collective good does not diminish the quantity available to others. Defence, diplomacy and clean air are classic examples of collective goods. Diplomats represent the whole of a country's population, the armed forces defend all of its territory, and public programmes to prevent air pollution benefit everyone breathing the air.

Collective goods cannot be sold in the market, since it is not possible to exclude individuals who wish to be 'free riders' from receiving the benefits of collective goods though they do not pay for them. Collective goods must be provided by the state or a similar institution with all-encompassing interests, since it is impossible to charge each person for their use. The state finances collective goods by levying compulsory taxes that produce income for the fisc that can be allocated by public laws rather than market signals.

By contrast, *private goods* are excludable and rival in consumption. Health care, education and housing were bought and sold in the market before they became responsibilities of the contemporary welfare state. Those who do not pay could be excluded from medical treatment, access to a particular school or the tenancy of a house. Consumption of private goods is rival: if one family occupies a house another cannot live there. Whereas demand for collective goods does not affect their supply, demand for private goods requires investment in resources to increase their supply e.g. building more houses or schools or hospitals.

The distinction between collective and private goods is not necessarily absolute, and considerable technical ingenuity can be devoted to devising means of capturing the cost of use of public services. For example, even though charging for the use of city streets may present practical difficulties, the negative externalities of urban traffic may be captured through high parking charges, or a municipal petrol tax. By not expanding an urban road system a notional congestion 'tax' may be imposed on motorists – albeit it is one that does not benefit the fisc. [. . .]

Charging was impossible as long as the state concentrated upon collective goods. While mid-nineteenth-century data is only approximate, government spent little, and that was mostly for collective goods. For example, in Britain in 1840 more than four-fifths of public spending was for collective goods, and in France then more than nine-tenths of spending was for

Table 7.1 *Government spending concentrates on private benefits*

	Average for OECD nations	
	Gross Domestic Product %	Public expenditure %
Private benefits		
Social security, social services	14.1	32
Health	5.6	13
Education	5.5	13
Other	8.0	18
Subtotal	33.2	76
Public goods		
Debt interest	5.1	12
Defence	3.0	7
Other	2.5	6
Subtotal	10.6	24

Sources: Calculated from OECD data as reported in Rose (1989) Table 1.2.

collective goods; the same was broadly true in the United States (Flora, 1983, as reported in Rose, 1989: Table 1.1). Moreover, some private goods now provided by government, for example roads and schools, were financed by private capital and charges made for their use.

Today, the bulk of public programmes are, in economic terms, private goods delivered to individuals, households or corporate users. Education, health care and other familiar public services are private goods because charges could be levied as a condition of use and those who did not pay could be excluded from their receipt. Moreover, consumption is rival. As the number of people claiming such benefits increases, the cost of provision tends to rise.

Three-quarters of public spending in the average advanced industrial nation today is allocated to programmes that are *marketable but not marketed*, that is, private benefits. The activities of government are no longer confined to a few traditional collective concerns; public revenues now finance such programmes central to the lives of ordinary people as education and health care. Since every nation's economy has grown greatly in the past century, historically high tax rates give government large sums to spend; in OECD nations on average public spending on private benefits is equal to one-third of a country's Gross Domestic Product (Table 7.1).

The biggest programme, social security, provides a material and personal benefit – cash in hand – to each household receiving a payment. In theory, many social security benefits could be covered by private insurance, and private sector pensions demonstrate that many people rely for income in old age upon paying insurance premiums as well as paying taxes. Health care ranks second in public expenditure; it too is a private benefit that can be sold. Education is the third biggest claimant on public funds; it too is sold by profit-making or not-for-profit agencies as well as being provided free of charge by public schools. An additional sixth of public spending is accounted for by programmes providing such individual benefits as housing, and subsidies to farmers and businesses. Paradoxically, the most costly collective good – payment of debt interest – also involves charging, although in this case the fisc must pay lenders for the use of their money.

Moreover, in almost every welfare state the market remains of first importance. Three-fifths of the national product of a European nation is channelled through the private sector, where charges allocate goods and services. If welfare is defined as those material goods and services significantly affecting everyone on a continuing basis (such as food or clothing or housing) or at a major stage in the life cycle (such as education), then charges play an important part in the way in which people meet most welfare needs. Of seven basic welfare needs, most people normally pay charges for food, housing and transportation, and a significant portion of income and health care is bought and sold in the market (Rose, 1986). Primary and secondary education is free but higher education is usually not. Personal social services – parents caring for children or elderly couples caring for themselves and each other – are distinctive as a 'priceless' service supplied without regard to money. Even here, the readiness of families to pay charges (sometimes subsidized by public funds) for day care centres and residential homes for the elderly shows how the market can signal fresh demands for social services. [. . .]

Conflicting Theories about Charges

Even though there is potentially wide scope to charge for publicly provided goods, the imposition of charges is problematic. Logically, the private benefits provided by public agencies might be: free of charge (e.g. primary education); subject to a submarket price that signals individual demand (e.g. bus fares); or subject to a charge that recovers the cost of provision (patents). There are conflicting political and economic arguments about which programmes ought to be subject to or exempt from charges and thus, the interpretation of charges as signals for government (see e.g. Heald, 1983: 299 ff.).

Subjecting Programmes to the Market

The new right asks: why should private goods and services be provided by government? After all, people devote much more time to their role as a consumer spending money than to their role as a voter. Moreover, ordinary people expect that many basics of welfare, such as food and housing, will be allocated through the price system. Radical free-market economists argue that government need only finance collective goods, and privatizers argue that public agencies could buy more of their services at market prices fixed by competitive tender (OMB, 1988) and impose charges to finance these services.

The first assumption in the new right case for charging is that money is a good measure of the value of public policies. Public expenditure is frequently used as an indicator of political priorities. Proponents of social programmes and national defence analysts are alike in evaluating programmes not so much in terms of their outputs (for good health or national security are not easily reduced to money terms) but by government inputs: how much money is government spending on this service, and is its claim on the budget increasing or not? Given that we already judge the supply of programmes by budget spending, introducing charges could provide a money signal on the demand side.

The cash nexus is necessarily present in public policy. To speak of publicly provided private benefits as 'free' is a half-truth. While public agencies may provide their benefits free of charge, they are not free at the point of production. Producers of public services expect to be paid for their work. In the case of health and education, the wages of producers are the principal cost of the services. [. . .]

Secondly, charging is said to introduce the efficiency of the market to the allocation of public programmes. Prices are meant to signal what consumers will give up to receive a product, and give producers information about how much to produce of a given good or service. If people are not prepared to pay for a particular benefit, then it should not be produced; public money can then be re-allocated to goods that people are willing to pay for. 'Government failure' is assumed to result when budget decisions must be made between competing claims – should more be spent on meals-on-wheels for the elderly, or on meals served in communal centres? – without measures of market demand. The absence of signals from charges leads to outcomes determined by factors extrinsic to the benefits of programmes, e.g. the political status or personality of competing spending departments, or bureaucratic empire-building

In the absence of charges signalling demand, experts can be producers in the role of Platonic guardians rather than producers responding to consumer demand.

> Teachers and social workers as well as doctors now claim that only qualified professionals have the knowledge and expertise to define the needs of clients in their particular field, and that neither the clients themselves nor other groups in society such as politicians or ratepayers have sufficient expertise to participate in the definition of welfare needs. (Foster, 1983: 25; see also Day and Klein, 1987: chapter 2)

The distinction between priority needs (what people must or ought to have) and wants (what people might like) is a matter of political debate.

Thirdly, charging is said to be equitable in so far as each individual enjoying a particular benefit pays for its cost. A US General Accounting Office (GAO, 1980: 29) statement declares: 'User charges are advantageous because they can equitably place the cost burden of goods and services produced by the government on recipients.' For the state to provide private benefits without charging their consumers is deemed inequitable because most of the cost will be paid by those who do not benefit directly and may not perceive any indirect benefit. [. . .]

Charges are fourthly recommended to reduce taxation: 'The only way to bring home to voters how much public service costs is to charge them when they use it' (Letwin, 1986). Imposing charges will increase revenue as long as there is some demand for a service, and in so far as some recipients are unwilling (or unable) to pay a charge for a service, public expenditure will tend to fall as output is reduced. For a market-oriented political economist, a reduction in taxation has pervasive benefits for society as a whole. [. . .]

Finally, charges can be a device for regulating the market, including the production of such public 'bads' as environmental pollution. The starting point is the assumption that government regulation is inefficient, because of difficulties in deciding how much is too much of an undesirable activity, e.g. producing chemical pollutants. In place of legal standards, the behaviour of firms could be regulated by imposing charges for the emission of pollutants. The payments are better considered charges than fines, for the emission of pollutants is costly but not illegal. Such charges give firms a cash incentive to invest in equipment to reduce pollution, in order to reduce their payment of pollution charges. Marginal monetary incentives are meant to replace the absolutes of statutory regulation.

Proponents of charges normally admit one inherent difficulty: some people lack the income to pay for benefits now received free of charge from the mixed-economy welfare state. This problem is often met by exempting individuals from payment on the basis of a financial means-test or by waiving charges for categoric groups such as children or pensioners. A radical response would be a Negative Income Tax, extending the logic of tax assessments to making cash payments to those whose assessed income is insufficient to maintain a given minimum living standard. A Negative Income Tax could leave individuals 'free to choose' how to spend their money for a mixture of public and private goods and services appropriate to their tastes.

Valuing Solidarity More Than Money

Opponents of charges believe first of all in the solidarity of society. Individuals are viewed as having solidary ties and mutual responsibilities superior to the cash nexus. The state sees to it that everyone can have access to many benefits, just as a household would look after its members without charge. [. . .] Davies (1980: 133) suggests that providing social benefits free of charge has the significant externality of 'increasing the degree of social cohesion'. In so far as goods provided free of charge are financed by progressive taxation, then the resulting more egalitarian distribution of income is considered as enhancing solidarity too.

The public provision of private benefits extends the concept of citizenship beyond the ballot box. In T. H. Marshall's (1950) famous formulation, the provision of such social benefits as education, health care and income security was a natural evolution from the granting of civil and political rights. The public provision of education is justified as necessary to create an informed citizenry. Votes are the signal giving direction to public policy; the governing party is accountable to the electorate at the ballot box rather than to shareholders through a balance sheet. If elected officials endorse laws that provide private benefits without charge to recipients, this is deemed to reflect popular preferences. The process of election legitimizes the decision of governors about what citizens ought to be given free of charge.

Thirdly, it is argued that money cannot be used to value all political concerns. In *What Price Incentives?*, a comparison of political and economic approaches to the prevention of environmental pollution, Kelman (1981) argues against charges, because they imply that at the margin everything is interchangeable. He states that government should signal that some things (e.g. human life) are more valuable than others (e.g. corporate profit): 'The very act of keeping something outside the realm of the market, then, is a way of proclaiming its special value; most things are bought and sold, but special things are not.' The idea that government can signal its dislike of pollution by imposing charges upon firms dumping noxious wastes is rejected because it reduces matters of morality to matters of degree. A government ought to decide how much or what types or quantities of pollution are acceptable and which are not: it should then prohibit everything that falls outside its normative definition of the tolerable. Similarly, the allocation of public resources for health care on pecuniary or 'shadow price' cost-benefit criteria is regarded as morally wrong, or offensive. In 1989 the British Medical Association argued against Conservative government attempts to promote greater efficiency in spending £18 billion a year on the National Health Service budget; its press advertisements proclaimed: 'In Mr Clarke's sharp new Health Service, making medicine pay could become more important than making people well.' [. .]

Fourthly, externalities can be cited as an economic argument against full cost charges for private benefits. There is market failure if the market will not supply the amount of a given service that would maximize welfare in society. For example, education can be described as an investment in training a labour force to a higher level than any individual employer would finance, in so far as this creates a higher standard of living for society as a whole. The existence of an externality can be coincidental with the existence of private benefits: and education benefits an individual as well as the society of which a well-educated individual is a part. In such 'mixed' cases it is technically possible to impose user charges related to the benefits that individual users internalize, and to provide public funds that subsidize the external benefits. For example, a public subsidy for urban mass transit may be justified as a signal from government encouraging people not to drive to work, and fares may be charged as a signal that people should pay something for their benefit.

Administrative impracticality, arising from problems of exempting (or refusing to exempt) people from charges, are a fifth objection against charges. Categoric exemptions are rejected as illogical, since many people for whom charges may be waived could pay for services. Exempting individuals from charges through a means test is attacked as a stigmatizing intrusion into private life, and likely to discourage some people from taking up a benefit to which they are entitled because they do not want to submit to a test of means. It also creates a disincentive to work by creating a poverty trap, since the benefits of exemption are quickly withdrawn and high marginal rates of income and social security tax become effective as a person rises above the subsistence-level income that entitles individuals to a means-tested waiver of charges.

Critics of charges tend to be ambivalent about the place of money in public policy. Proponents of the public provision of private benefits invariably invoke public expenditure as a test of policy, assuming that the more money that government spends, the higher the level of social benefits. They argue that charges are wrong because the solidaristic claims and needs of citizens should be independent of purchasing power, and more important than pecuniary values. But such general principles give no signals to policy-makers responsible for allocating resources between priceless programmes.

The extent of disagreement about charges at the theoretical level should not be surprising, for questions about whether charges should be imposed affect central political and economic values, and this in turn affects how signals are interpreted. A proponent of charges can thus interpret a reduction in the number of health service prescriptions issued after a rise in prescription charges as a sign of previous waste, whereas a critic of charges will interpret the same phenomena as signs of an increase in unmet need. Since politics is about the articulation of conflicting views about what government ought to do, controversy is inherent. Because they rest on conflicting political values, such disputes cannot be resolved by logic. Yet it is possible to use empirical analysis to test which side of the debate is favoured by the practice of government.

Wide Range but Shallow Depth

We can conceive of charges in two dimensions. The first is their *range*: how many programmes are subject to charges? Proponents and opponents of charges tend to favour one or another extreme in a range of possibilities. Either charges should be systematically applied to all publicly funded private benefits, or they should be systematically avoided. Given that at least three-quarters of public expenditure is devoted to programmes for which charges could be imposed, the potential range for charging is great.

The *depth* of a charge can refer to the amount of money paid by an individual or the total sum collected for a programme, or the ratio of the individual payment to the cost of a unit of a service, or the ratio of total receipts from charges to total programme expenditure. Individuals are likely to judge charges in terms of the unit cost of using a service, and how this compares with private sector charges for a comparable service. A tripwire charge, such as a fine for the late return of a library book, is small in absolute terms but has a symbolic value in reminding individuals to return their books on time. It is also low in relation to the cost of running a library. By contrast, a charge for rent of a public property could be substantial and could not only cover the cost of a building but also provide a return on capital. A charge that covers only a small part of the cost of using a public service nonetheless remains a consumer-driven signal of demand, but does little to reduce the gross cost of public expenditure.

Aggregate Revenue from Charges

Since revenue from charges is a part of the cash flow of government, the International Monetary Fund compiles such data as part of its routine monitoring of the financial circumstances of governments around the world. While problems of comparability arise from differences in national account-ing practices and government structures, the figures should give a reason-able guide to the magnitude of charges in aggregate. The IMF (1986: 138: category V) distinguishes seven different categories of non-tax current revenue, including operating surpluses from trading activities of govern-ment departments and public enterprises, other property income, fines, employee contributions to government welfare funds, and miscellaneous other contributions and gifts. Category V.9, administrative fees and charges, nonindustrial and incidental sales, comes closest to the concept of charges used here. It includes payments for the use of government hospitals, schools, admission fees, passport fees, sales of products of service agencies and rents of buildings.

In absolute terms charges in aggregate raise substantial sums of money (Table 7.2). Charges raise tens of billions of dollars in the United States, tens of billions of Deutschmarks in Germany, and billions of pounds in Britain. On a per capita basis, charges in Germany are equivalent to approximately DM 850 a year, in Britain to about £150, and in the United States to about $250 per capita. If these figures are multiplied by three or four, to reflect the number in an average household, the significance of charges is increased, even after discounting payment of some charges by corporations (including public sector institutions) rather than individuals. Nonetheless, charges of hundreds of dollars or pounds do not appear large

Table 7.2   *Receipts from government charges as % tax revenue*

Country, year	Charges	Tax revenue	Receipts as % rev.
Germany, 1983 DMmn	51,990	625,690	8.3
United Kingdom, 1982 £mn	7,996	108,368	7.4
USA, 1982 $bn	59.5	923,123	6.4
Spain, 1983 Psbn	280	6,200	4.5
France, 1984 FFr milliard	51	1,948	2.6
Sweden, 1984 SKr mn	5,610	397,194	1.4

Sources: OECD, *Revenue Statistics of OECD Member Countries, 1965–1985* (Paris: 1986), principally part VII, reporting IMF statistics for fees, sales, etc. lines 10, 11 for central, state and local government together.

when compared with a contemporary household budget, or the total taxes that a household pays.

Charges nonetheless have a relatively low profile in the public budget and national income accounts. The revenue produced by charges is very small in relation to tax revenue; it is less than 2 per cent of tax revenue in Sweden, and even where it is least low, in Germany, charges are less than one-twelfth of tax revenue. All countries raise at least ten times as much in tax revenue as they report from charges. Nor do the differences between countries appear to conform to any meaningful theoretical pattern. Charges are relatively highest in Germany, very much a mixed-economy welfare state rather than aggressively free-market, and they are low in France, where historic difficulties in collecting income tax might be expected to encourage their use. Since public expenditure claims less than half the Gross Domestic Product of nearly every OECD nation, charges appear even more shallow when they are measured as a proportion of the national product. [. . .]

Charging for Specific Programmes

Examining aggregate government revenue shows that charges are of relatively low priority in the budget overall. But aggregate receipts from charges are not a macroeconomic policy target, as is total public expenditure or the public sector deficit. Charges are part of the world of micro-politics; a charge is always imposed in return for a specific good or service. The evidence of Table 7.2 is consistent with two very different possibilities: that charges bear down deeply upon a small number of programmes or that they are widespread but shallow across many areas of public policy. [. . .]

The evidence shows that charges for public programmes are very widespread throughout British government. Every department – whether notionally concerned with collective goods as is defence, or private enterprise benefits as is trade and industry – is responsible for some charges

Table 7.3   *Income from charges by British government departments*

	Charges	As % dept. £mn	Number expenditure
Defence	1,619	7.9	40
N. Ireland	159	3.1	28
Trade & Industry	198	15.7	26
Home Office & Legal	533	7.4	26
Employment	505	11.3	21
Scotland	434	5.0	21
Wales	187	5.3	19
Health & Social Services	969	4.7	16
Housing, environment	893*	11.5	15
Treasury depts	135	5.5	13
Transport	280	5.6	11
Arts & Libraries	87	9.0	10
Energy	115	29.9	8
FCO	39	1.9	5
Agriculture	47	2.2	4
Education & Science	1,322	7.1	4
Social security	701	1.5	2
Misc.	920	38.5	18
Total	9,143	5.7	287

* Excludes rents received by local authorities.

Source: Heald (1989) Tables 3, 5, and 8.

(Table 7.3). The most money is raised by the Ministry of Defence, which also imposes the largest number of different charges; it provides weapons, training and equipment services for foreign defence forces and also manages large complexes of land, supplies, equipment and personnel in ways that generate revenue. When charges are related to total departmental spending, their significance is diminished, for in aggregate charges are equal to less than 6 per cent of total expenditure. In 14 of the 18 headings by which charges are reported, charges are less than 10 per cent of expenditure – and their proportion is well below average in the biggest spending departments, Social Security and Health. The Department of Energy, responsible for North Sea oil, ranks highest in charges as a percentage of its expenditure, but its total expenditure figure is the lowest of any government department.

Total income from charges represents the aggregate of receipts from a total of 287 different programmes; the total is actually greater than that shown in Table 7.3 since government often aggregates many charges into a single line, for example, £691 million raised in social security is opaquely labelled as 'other running cost receipts'. The average British government spending department is responsible for 15 different programmes involving one form or another of charges. Although the vagaries of accounting practices urge caution in pursuing detailed analysis of official data, the overall position is clear: departments responsible for classic collective concerns of the state, such as Defence and the Foreign Office, are as ready to impose charges for programmes as are departments responsible for social benefits to individuals or benefits to enterprises.

The variety of charges can be illustrated by examining the official record of the English Home Office and the associated legal departments having the responsibilities of a continental Ministry of the Interior and of Justice. As the agencies responsible for maintaining law and order, we would expect their services to be priceless. In fact prices are put on many aspects of the administration of order, law and justice: charges are collected for 26 different programmes (Heald, 1989: Appendix Table A.11). The largest sum is generated by a programme that is a classic public service, the police. It raised £195 million by selling its services. It did not 'sell' protection to criminals; the police can charge for maintaining order at commercial events, such as rock concerts or football matches. The courts rank second in the amount of money raised. When the courts are used for private purposes which are not integral to the pursuit of justice, e.g. a civil dispute, charges can be levied. Notwithstanding the centrality of citizenship, the state charges for the issuance of passports, visas and for registering citizenship. The annual register of electors also generates incidental revenue, being bought by market research firms drawing random survey samples. By comparison with expenditure of more than £7 billion a year, the charges levied by the Home Office and the legal departments are relatively small, 7 per cent of total spending by the ministry, but they are substantial in aggregate and their range and variety are important in principle.

Policy-makers are interested in particular policies for their own sake: a Minister for Health is concerned with the provision of health care, and a Minister of Defence with maintaining the nation's security. No cabinet minister sees himself as a businessman responsible for producing programmes that cover their costs by revenue from charges. Spending ministers expect to finance their programmes by claiming money from the Treasury in the annual round of public expenditure negotiations. They look upon recipients of their services as beneficiaries and political supporters, not as customers. Nor would the Treasury readily allow a government department to retain any 'profit' that might accrue to it from charges; it seeks to claw back sums raised by charges for general revenue funds, or to reduce a department's Treasury funds if it raises more from charges. [. . .]

When charges are levied they often depart substantially from formal stipulations that charges should cover costs. For example, the British Treasury declares that charges should in principle meet costs, and its rule of thumb for pricing is between 75 to 125 per cent of the identifiable current costs. Any charge lower than this is regarded as a subsidy. In practice, the subsidy element is often very large, for example, the flat-rate charge for prescriptions in the health service is one-third the cost of filling an average prescription (Birch, 1986: Tables 2, 3). In Washington a Congressional

Budget Office (1983: 5) survey of seven services for which charges were made found that in six of seven instances – cargo shipping, barge freight, coastguard services, general aviation, irrigation of Western farms, and the strategic petroleum reserve – less than 15 per cent of federal costs were recovered.

Three major findings from the British evidence are consistent with the aggregate IMF figures in Table 7.2. Charges tend to be spread widely across a range of policy areas and programmes; charges are more likely to be levied on fringe or peripheral elements of a policy area rather than upon central activities; and charges usually do not recover the full cost of the service provided. [. . .]

The broad albeit shallow use of charges for some public programmes rejects any simple notion that the use of charges depends upon whether a right-wing or left-wing party is in office. Charges are used where nominally pro-market parties dominate, as in the United States and Britain, and in social democratic Sweden and the German *Sozialstaat*. Kjell-Olof Feldt, Sweden's social democratic minister of finance, endorses the efficiency of the market economy 'as long as it is influenced by the democratic forces' (Taylor and Webb, 1989). Changes in Eastern Europe emphasize that socialist states committed to centralized planning as the primary means of allocating resources are now seeking to give greater priority to the role of prices and charges in allocating resources produced by public agencies.

Detailed studies in Britain have found that local authorities under Labour control are less likely than those under Conservative control to levy charges, but these are marginal differences of degree rather than the differences in kind implicit in the contest of political values reviewed above (Judge and Matthews, 1980: chapter 5; Straw, 1987). Labour councils see nothing un-socialist in charging for a wide variety of services, nor are they deemed in breach of party rules or ideology. Nor have Conservative councils been pressing the Thatcher government for the power to raise charges for many of the services that they deliver.

In public policy, unlike business, you normally do *not* get what you pay for. The characteristic policy output of government is not a classic collective good; it is a service that is marketable but not marketed.

Interpreting Contested Signals: A Paradigm for Analysis

The signals provided by the crazy-quilt pattern of imposing or avoiding charges are contradictory as well as contested; any generalization can thus be refuted. A major GAO (1980: ii) study of federal United States practice concludes: 'Pricing practices are inconsistent both within and across agencies.' The author of a British ESRC report on pricing policy in the public service (Stewart, 1980: 7) has described the contemporary variety of charging practices as operating on 'unclear' principles with the result that the overall pattern of charges is 'bewildering'.

The apparent confusion is simple to resolve if attention is turned from charging in principle to charging in practice, abandoning the normative as well as scientific *a priori* assumption that the same principle must govern all publicly provided private benefits. If one expects uniformity and does not find it, then either government stands condemned as illogical or theories of free-market economists or proponents of social solidarity are misleading. The latter is the case: any attempt to predict or prescribe charging or not charging from first principles is ahistorical. To understand what happens we need a paradigm for analysis that will capture the observable variety in the use of charges and provide a historically meaningful explanation.

Interpreting Specific Charges: A Multi-dimensional Paradigm

Given that charges do exist in many areas of public policy, to understand their use we must consider the specifics of the programme for which a particular charge is levied. Unlike taxes, which normally go into the general revenue fund of government, charges are paid in return for specific benefits. Differences of opinion about whether taxes or charges are a superior form of finance derive from this distinction between fungible taxes paid into a common fund, and specific charges paid as a condition of using specific services. We cannot deduce what government does from a simple theory of 'doing good' or 'making people pay'.

In order to understand what a particular charge may signal, we must pose a number of analytic questions. Each point in the following analytic paradigm allows for more than one empirical answer. In place of a one-dimensional concern with the morality of the market or of non-pecuniary social solidarity, we must have a multi-dimensional perspective, since charges are only one aspect of a programme. Accounting data is thus meaningful only in so far as it can be integrated with information about laws, administration, partisan values, the distribution of public benefits, and the income of those who pay. [. . .]

Who Pays?   While economics textbooks often illustrate market processes by reference to individuals paying for services, many public goods and services are bought by organizations, including some in the public sector. A Ministry of Defence can supply military equipment or training facilities to a foreign nation, a Department of Trade and Industry supplies services to profit-making organizations, and a National Opera House provides benefits to a relatively prosperous segment of the population. Public agencies responsible for housekeeping, such as the management of government buildings or telecommunications networks, deliver services to other government agencies. In short, charges are not necessarily regressive levies falling on the poor harder than the well-to-do – and this may sometimes be true in Third World countries too. They are paid by people at many different income levels and many charges are paid by large organizations.

Subject to What Exemptions? Exempting from charges those deemed unable to pay but meriting a benefit is a corollary of imposing charges on those able to pay. Means-testing is the most familiar form of exemption; charges for public services may be waived for those whose earnings or assets are deemed inadequate to meet a charge. Means-testing is contentious because it can discourage some people from claiming benefits to which they are entitled because of the way in which it can be administered. [. . .]

How Much? When a charge is small, debates about amounts are more likely to express political values or emotions than financial considerations, for example, parking-meter charges do not impose large financial hardships on individual motorists. Rents to tenants of public housing usually involve significant sums to public authorities running multi-million housing programmes, and to tenants for whom rent is a significant portion of their weekly income. [. . .] The political 'heat' generated by a charge may vary inversely with the amount of money involved; for example charges for school meals may stir up more debate than charges for the rent of large public buildings.

To Whom? Although the agency collecting a charge is usually that providing a service, often the money obtained is not added to its budget to spend as the collecting agency would like. In central government all receipts may become part of the pool of funds controlled by the Treasury. Even if it does not pocket the money it can offset income against departmental expenditure, thus discouraging public agencies from charging since the income received does not augment its funds. [. . .] When collection of a charge involves friction with clients, an agency has a strong incentive to oppose charges that require more work but give it no more revenue.

For What Goods or Services? By definition, charges can only be imposed for the provision of private benefits, and there is a greater likelihood of a charge being made if a public service operates in parallel with a similar market service. For example, elderly people are asked to contribute to the cost of meals on wheels or accommodation in a centre providing residential care, since in the absence of such services they would have to buy food and pay rent. When goods and services are inputs to profit-making companies, the likelihood of charging also increases. When a service is central to public policy it is more valued in non-pecuniary terms, and thus a charge is less likely. Hence, a health service may charge for dentistry or chiropody but not for heart surgery or perinatal care.

Produced at What Cost?   Wages are an important element in the current cost of such labour-intensive public services as education and the police. The determination of public sector wages, and thus of a large element of costs, is perennially subject to dispute as public sector wage bargaining is not constrained by the market, since settlements can be underwritten from tax revenue. A variety of public services such as roads and housing are capital- rather than labour-intensive, and the calculation of capital costs is contingent too. [. . .]

When?   Even though most charges are levied at the time of delivery, for example admission to a public monument, others are billed after delivery, for example a weekly rent, or a public dockyard refitting a foreign ship. [. . .] However, if ex-post payments are slow in coming, a public agency is forced to choose between accumulating bad debts or making politically difficult demands. A local housing agency has a choice between evicting a family for non-payment of rent and then having to rehouse it because it is homeless, or letting debts accumulate. A farm-credit agency either carries some bad debts in its accounts receivable or forecloses on farm properties and sustains capital losses. Debts of Third World countries to government agencies in advanced industrial nations create large financial as well as political difficulties.

Subject to What Statutory Conditions?   The simplest statutory command to administer is a declaration that a service shall be provided free of charge. If an Act specifies the value of a charge in money terms, inflation will soon erode its value. If a statute allows the charge to be set by ministerial directive, this is a 'poisoned chalice' that the minister of the day may pass to his successor, for no politician wants to be known as the person who increased charges on a popular public service.

The paradigm for analysing who pays what to whom, when and why demonstrates that charges cannot be analysed solely in terms of a money balance at the bottom line of a set of accounts. Public agencies are not businesses concentrating upon money and profits; their starting points are values articulated in political debates about policy-making. Nor do policy-makers start with a free hand; they inherit programmes and practices accumulated through the generations. In the practice of charging, there is no bottom line; there are only many sides.

Who or What Determines Charges: People or Inertia?   Since abstract principles do not determine the observed pattern of charges, then charges may be reckoned to reflect calculations of decision-makers. A behavioural explanation is also appropriate with conventional public choice models, which see calculating politicians as central in what government does. If we assume that politics is about maximizing benefits and minimizing costs, the politicians have good reason to avoid taking decisions about charges. Introducing a charge for the first time is bound to stir up very considerable controversy and cause a politician to be attacked by recipients of a service and public sector providers. Increasing a charge that is already in effect will attract a lesser degree of unpopularity. Efforts to reduce or repeal a charge involve risks too, for budget officials may make compensating cuts in the department's spending a condition of eliminating or reducing a charge. Once a programme is deemed a merit good it is politically difficult to reclassify it as 'unmeritorious', that is suitable for charging. Equally, if charges have been levied for a service as long as people can remember, it is politically easy to continue it. The simplest thing for a risk-averse politician to do is to leave charges as they are (Rose, 1985; Weaver, 1986).

An impersonal force – political inertia – provides a better explanation of the structure of charges in force at any given moment of time. *Political inertia* is the tendency of a policy to remain in force once adopted; the momentum to sustain it comes from laws that remain on the statute book from one decade to the next, authorizing organizations and public employees to charge for some public services and not for others, and leading recipients of public programmes to expect to pay for some services but not for others. Since inertia also sustains a high and buoyant tax revenue, entitlement programmes can be funded without elected politicians having to raise taxes or charges (Rose and Karran, 1987).

Each incoming government inherits hundreds of programmes from its predecessors, some involving charges and others not; officials are legally bound to continue to deliver all these programmes as long as the government of the day chooses to repeal particular statutes. [. . .]

The manifold of government programmes at any given point in time is the accumulation of generations of legislation; each measure was adopted for reasons specific to a time and place; it is therefore hardly surprising that the pattern formed by the accumulation of programmes is not consistent with any single theory of charging. [. . .]

Programme-specific practices have persisted through the force of political inertia. Charges are levied for one municipal service regarded as socially desirable as well as individually beneficial (the use of swimming baths) but not for another that also has both collective and individual benefits (the use of public library services). [. . .] The practice of charging in the mixed polity reflects an inheritance of past choices more than it does the logic of economic or political principles.

References

Birch, S. (1986) 'Instructing patient charges in the National Health Service', *Journal of Social Policy*, 15(2): 163–84.

Congressional Budget Office (1983) *Charging for Federal Services*. Washington DC: Government Printing Office.

Davies, Bleddyn (1980) 'Policy options for charges and means tests', in K. Judge (ed.), *Pricing the Social Services*. London: Macmillan, pp. 132–52.

Day, Patricia and Klein, Rudolf (1987) *Accountabilities*. London: Tavistock.

Flora, Peter (1983) *State, Economy and Society in Western Europe 1815–1975*. London: Macmillan, Vol. I.

Foster, Peggy (1983) *Access to Welfare: an Introduction to Welfare Rationing*. London: Macmillan.

GAO (General Accounting Office) (1980) *The Congress Should Consider Exploring Opportunities to Expand and Improve the Application of User Charges by Federal Agencies*. Washington, DC: Comptroller General of the United States. PAD-80-25.

Heald, David (1983) *Public Expenditure*. Oxford: Martin Robertson.

Heald, David (1989) *Charging by British Government: Evidence from the Public Expenditure Survey*. Glasgow: University of Strathclyde Studies in Public Policy No. 173.

International Monetary Fund (1986) *A Manual on Government Finance Statistics*. Washington, DC: IMF.

Judge, Ken and Matthews, James (1980). *Charging for Social Care*. London: George Allen & Unwin.

Kelman, Steven (1981) *What Price Incentives? Economists and the Environment*. Boston: Auburn House.

Letwin, William (1986) 'Charge more and standards too will rise', *The Times*, 21 July.

Marshall, T. H. (1950) *Citizenship and Social Class*. Cambridge: Cambridge University Press.

OECD (1986) *Revenue Statistics, 1965–1985*. Paris: OECD.

OMB (Office of Management and Budget) (1988) *Enhancing Governmental Production through Competition*. Washington, DC: OMB Office of Federal Procurement Policy.

Rose, Richard (1985) 'Maximizing tax revenues while minimizing political costs', *Journal of Public Policy*, 5(3): 289–320.

Rose, Richard (1986) 'The dynamics of the welfare mix in Britain', in Rose and R. Shiratori (eds), *The Welfare State East and West*. New York: Oxford University Press, pp. 80–106.

Rose, Richard (1989) *Ordinary People in Public Policy*. London: Sage Publications.

Rose, Richard and Karran, Terence (1987) *Taxation by Inertia: Financing the Growth of Government in Britain*. London: George Allen & Unwin.

Stewart, Murray (1980) 'Issues in pricing policy', in K. Judge, *Pricing the Social Services*. London: Macmillan, pp. 7–23.

Straw, Jack MP (1987) 'Parental contributions to the cost of school activities'. London: House of Commons, duplicated.

Taylor, Robert and Webb, Sara (1989) 'A champion of market socialism: Kjell-Olof Feldt', *Financial Times*, 17 April.

Weaver, R. Kent (1986) 'The politics of blame avoidance', *Journal of Public Policy*, 6(4): 371–88.

8

Organizational Status and Performance: summary of the findings

Andrew Dunsire, Keith Hartley and David Parker

I

An earlier article in *Public Administration* (Dunsire *et al.*, 1988) surveyed the popular beliefs and academic theories which support the contention that a change in the legal status of an enterprise (for example, from ministerial department to executive agency, or from the public to the private sector) improves its performance. Much current public policy in this country and elsewhere has been based on the belief that resources are more efficiently used in the private sector, or under public sector emulations such as the trading fund.

Perhaps few would hold that a measure like privatization by itself affects performance. The operative mechanisms usually posited are (a) the policing role of the capital market (Kay and Thompson, 1986); and/or (b) an increase in competition (Millward and Parker, 1983); and/or (c) a change in managerial incentives (Alchian and Demsetz, 1972; De Alessi, 1980). It is commonly appreciated, too, that the latter two mechanisms may be installed *without* a change in ownership, and that change in ownership does not necessarily entail them. 'Selling a government firm makes no difference to the competitive environment in which it operates; ownership and competitive structure are separate issues' (Forsyth, 1984: 61); and 'privatization involves more than the simple transfer of ownership. It involves the transfer and redefinition of a complex bundle of property rights which creates a whole new penalty–reward system which will alter the incentives in the firm and ultimately its performance' (Veljanovsky, 1987. 77–8).

Incentives are altered because the 'penalty–reward system' is linked not (as in the archetypal bureau) with input or process measures but with measures of output: payment is by results. But managers held accountable for results must have control over the factors contributing to those results; and this may require better management information, and even a reorganization of the enterprise on an output rather than an input or functional basis.

From *Public Administration*, 69 (Spring 1991): 21–40.

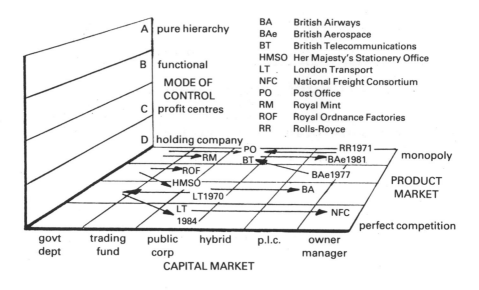

Figure 8.1   *The basic model*

Equally, change in the quality of information and in management structure in an enterprise may produce a change in performance irrespective of change in ownership or of degree of competition in the environment.

These considerations suggested a model of organizational change in three distinct dimensions, as portrayed in Figure 8.1:

1   a change in the *capital market*, associated with status change, where an enterprise can take up a position along a 'west–east' spectrum, from pure government department through trading fund and other hybrids to public limited company and, at the extreme 'private' end, the owner-manager;

2   a change in the *product market*, where an enterprise can be placed somewhere on the axis between monopoly and perfect competition; and

3   a change in the *internal management structure*, where an enterprise falls somewhere on a 'top–bottom' axis between command-orientation and results-orientation, intermediate points corresponding to, for example, Williamson's (1970) 'U-form' and 'M-form' types.

This is the model which underlay our research programme into the relationship between organizational status change and performance in the UK in recent years, outlined in the earlier article and reported here.

A number of hypotheses for testing were deduced from the public choice and other literatures. The three main hypotheses concerned propositions that improvement in enterprise performance is associated with:

Table 8.1   *The organizations*

Type of change	Organization	Date
I *Movements within the public sector*		
(a) Government department to trading fund	Royal Ordnance Factories	Jul. 1974
	Royal Mint	Apr. 1975
	HMSO	Apr. 1980
(b) Government department to public corporation	Post Office (incl. posts and telecomms)	Apr. 1969
(c) Public corporation to separate public corporation	British Telecommunications	Jul. 1981*
(d) Public corporation to local government	London Transport	Jan. 1970
(e) Local government to public corporation	London Transport	Jun. 1984
(f) Trading fund to Executive Agency	HMSO	Dec. 1988*
II *Ownership change*		
(a) Private to public (nationalization)	Rolls-Royce	Feb. 1971
	British Aerospace	Apr. 1977
(b) Public to private (privatization)	Rolls-Royce	May 1987*
	British Aerospace	Feb. 1981
	National Freight	Feb. 1982**
	British Telecom	Aug. 1984*
	Royal Ordnance Factories	Jan. 1985*
(c) Anticipating privatization	British Airways	1980–87**

  * Event not included in performance tests (section II)
** Event not included in section III analysis

1   a change in *capital market*, marked by a shift in status in a west to east direction (the 'central hypothesis');
2   a change in the *product market* or degree of competition encountered;
3   a change in *internal management structure* marked by movement away from command-orientation towards results-orientation.

Two subsidiary hypotheses explored relationships between the dimensions of the model, concerning propositions that:

4   a management change from command-orientation towards results-orientation is associated with an increase in competition; and
5   change in internal management structure is associated with change in capital market or in status.

Figure 8.1 summarizes the status changes for each of the organizations. Only in three cases – British Aerospace (BAe) on nationalization, London Transport (LT) in the mid-1980s, and Her Majesty's Stationery Office (HMSO) from 1982 – was there evidence of a status change associated with a significant change in the degree of competition in the product market. Our main investigations therefore concerned associations between status change and performance, between management change and performance, and between status change and management change, although changes in competition are noted where relevant.

The empirical material was drawn from studies of ten organizations which were subject to one or more changes in legal status within the last twenty years or so, embracing changes within the public sector as well as changes from the public to the private sectors and vice versa. The ten organizations, with the types and dates of the status changes, are listed in Table 8.1. For each organization there was at least one major status change with a substantial amount of publicly available data both before and after the change, so permitting adequate testing of the hypotheses. The exception was British Airways (BA) which was included as an example of a publicly owned organization which might have improved performance *in anticipation of* privatization.

A number of the organizations, as shown in Table 8.1, were involved in more than one change of status, but the later changes in most cases were excluded from the studies of performance owing to the lack of sufficient post-change data at the time of the research. Analyses of two of the organizations (BA and the National Freight Corporation/Consortium (NFC)) were incomplete and not included in the survey of management change.

II

Capital Market/Status Change: Measuring Performance

Testing the central hypothesis required the selection of appropriate indicators for measuring the performance of an organization. The study focused on identifying changes in production efficiency, on how well an organization uses its resources. Three sets of indicators were used to measure organizational performance before and after the status change:

1 *Productivity* measured by both labour and total factor productivity, with the latter relating output changes to changes in *all* factor inputs (capital and labour). It was predicted that a west-to-east status change would result in higher productivity.
2 *Changes in employment levels*, particularly the possibility of a 'shake-out' of labour following a status move from west to east. A standard employment model was used to estimate any employment effects of a status change. This model allowed for other determinants of employment, namely, output, technology, the capital stock and a lagged adjustment mechanism, as well as the influence of status change. In this way, it provided a more accurate and reliable estimate of the effects of a status change.

3 *Financial ratios.* This study used profitability, and the ratios of stocks to sales, debtors to sales, and sales to fixed assets, together with the proportion of labour costs in total expenditure and value-added per employee. Improvements in enterprise performance were expected to be reflected in higher profitability, lower ratios of stocks and debtors to sales, a higher sales to fixed assets ratio, a reduction in labour's share in costs (i.e. a shake-out), and higher value-added per employee.

Empirical work in this field is not without its problems. Often, output data are available only in value rather than volume terms and an appropriate price deflator is required. Also, a transfer of ownership is likely to result in the pursuit of different objectives so that focusing on a limited set of efficiency indicators might fail to provide a comprehensive appraisal of an organization's performance (e.g. are we comparing like with like?). Further problems arise where an organization's peformance improves either well before, or considerably after, the official date of the status change, raising doubts about relying on the promulgated date alone for all the indicators (see section III).

Allowance also has to be made for what might have happened without the status change. For example, in the 1980s labour productivity in the UK rose substantially, so that the 'successes of privatization' need to be assessed against general improvements in the economy's performance. Our solution was to present the results in relation to general trends in productivity for public corporations and for the UK economy as a whole (the counter-factual).

Status Change: The Empirical Results

A considerable amount of empirical work was undertaken and this section can only provide a summary and overview with examples for each of the three sets of performance indicators and an evaluation of the consistency of the results.

Productivity Data on average annual growth rates of labour and total factor productivity were estimated for four years before and four years after each organization's status change. To allow for national trends, the productivity figures for each organization were compared with the corresponding estimates for the UK economy, for public corporations and, where appropriate, for UK manufacturing. The results are summarized in Table 8.2. There were organizations where *some* but not all of the productivity and national comparisons when subjected to an analysis-of-covariance test supported the hypothesis: hence these are shown as mixed results.

Table 8.2 shows that the productivity results provide unanimous support for the central hypothesis (No. 1) for the Royal Mint (RM), LT (1984 change) and British Airways (BA). Looking for confirmation from three out

Table 8.2 *Summary of productivity results*

Organization	Prediction of central hypothesis	Labour productivity	Total factor productivity	Labour productivity compared with national trends	Total factor productivity compared with national trends
Royal Mint	Improved performance	Confirmed	Confirmed	Confirmed	Confirmed
London Transport (1984 change)	Improved performance	Confirmed	Confirmed	Confirmed	Confirmed
British Airways	Improved performance	Confirmed	Confirmed	Confirmed	Confirmed
British Aerospace (nationalization)	Deterioration in performance	Confirmed	Confirmed	Confirmed	Mixed result
British Aerospace (privatization)	Improved performance	Confirmed	Confirmed	Confirmed	Mixed result
National Freight	Improved performance	Confirmed	Mixed result	Confirmed	Confirmed
London Transport (1970 change)	Deterioration in performance	Confirmed	Confirmed	Not confirmed	Confirmed
Post Office Postal	Improved performance	Confirmed	Not confirmed	Confirmed	Mixed result
Post Office Telecommunications	Improved performance	Confirmed	Not confirmed	Confirmed	Mixed result
Her Majesty's Stationery Office	Improved performance	Confirmed	Mixed result	Mixed result	Not confirmed
Royal Ordnance Factories	Improved performance	Not confirmed	Confirmed	Not confirmed	Mixed result
Rolls-Royce	Deterioration in performance	Not confirmed	Not confirmed	Not confirmed	Not confirmed

of four productivity measures identifies another group of organizations, namely National Freight (NFC), LT (1970 change), and both changes of ownership for BAe. In contrast, the productivity results did not support the hypothesis for Rolls-Royce (RR) and possibly for Royal Ordnance Factories (ROF). The results for the remaining organizations were less conclusive, with only two of the productivity measures confirming the central hypothesis, the Post Office Postal and Telecommunications businesses (for details, see Hartley, Parker and Martin, 1991).

Employment changes   The possibility of a labour shake-out was tested by including a dummy variable for organizational status into a standard employment function (see Dunsire *et al.*, 1988: 384).

Various employment equations were estimated using both intercept and slope shift dummies to capture the effects of status change. For the intercept dummy, a shake-out of labour would be reflected in a negative relationship. Also, to allow for possible anticipation effects (and delays) in adjusting an organization's performance, the date of the status change was varied by two years. A summary of the results is presented in Table 8.3 (for further details see Hartley and Parker 1991). There were examples where the employment model showed that moves to trading fund status and actual or anticipated privatization gave results which were consistent with our central hypothesis (HMSO, RM, BAe, NFC, BA). However for both the ROF and RR, the sign of the status change dummy was contrary to expectations, so supporting the productivity results (Table 8.3). The ROF's apparent failure to produce the expected gains in employment efficiency might have reflected the lack of any change in their position as a defence contractor operating in a protected and regulated market (see also section III below).

Table 8.3   *Employment changes*
Q. Did the employment model provide support for the central hypothesis?

A.	Yes	Limited support	No
	HMSO	BAe (1977 change)	Post Office (Postal)
	Royal Mint	London Transport (1984)	London Transport (1970)
	BA	Post Office (Telecom)	ROF
	BAe (1981)		Rolls-Royce
	NFC		

Financial ratios   Using various financial ratios two sets of tests were undertaken. First, averages were estimated for four years before and four years after the status change. Second, to allow for long-run trends in performance and to assess the statistical significance of any change in performance, an analysis-of-covariance model was used where performance measured by different financial ratios was determined by a dummy variable for status change and a time-trend.

Table 8.4   *Summary of financial results*

Organizations where
1   *most financial ratios supported the central hypothesis*
     Royal Ordnance Factories
     British Airways
2   *only 40–50 per cent of the results supported the central hypothesis*
     Her Majesty's Stationery Office
     Post Office (Postal)
     Post Office (Telecommunications)
     London Transport (1984 change)
     British Aerospace (1981 privatization)
     National Freight Corporation
3   *Most of the financial ratios did not support the predicted deterioration in performance*
     Rolls-Royce
     British Aerospace (1977 nationalization)
     London Transport (1970 change)

Notes: Classification based on aggregating averages and covariance results.
       The Royal Mint is not included in this table.

Inevitably, using a variety of financial ratios meant that not all of them necessarily pointed in the same direction and, in some cases, differences also occurred between the averages and covariance results. Aggregating both sets of results the predicted improvement in across-the-board financial performance was confirmed for the ROF and BA (i.e. 66 per cent or more of the results supported the hypothesis). Elsewhere, support for the hypothesis was more limited, much depending on the choice of financial ratio. For example, using profitability as the *key* ratio, the predicted improvement was confirmed for the ROF, HMSO, NFC and BA. Results completely contrary to our predictions were obtained for RR, LT (1970 change) and BAe (1977 nationalization). For these three organizations, across-the-board financial performance either improved or did not deteriorate as predicted. A summary of the financial results is shown in Table 8.4 (a fuller account can be found in Parker, Hartley, Martin, 1990).

From our three sets of empirical results (productivity, employment, and financial), we can be reasonably confident that the central hypothesis (No. 1) was supported for three organizations, namely, National Freight, British Airways and the privatization of British Aerospace. The central hypothesis was also supported for the Royal Mint, although the data only allowed two sets of tests for this organization (productivity and employment). Similarly, the results for Rolls-Royce consistently contradicted the central hypothesis. What all this means is that over the available tests, although a substantial number of organizations provided partial support, fewer than half of those studied provided completely convincing support for the hypothesis that improvement in enterprise performance is associated with status change away from public towards private ownership.

III

Management Change: Model

If enterprise performance does (or does not) change in these ways when status changes, is it because status has (or has not) changed, or is it because there has (or has not) also been simultaneous change in the competition and/or internal management change dimensions? What is the relationship between performance and competition (hypothesis 2), performance and management change (hypothesis 3), competition and management change (hypothesis 4), status change and management change (hypothesis 5)?

These are the questions we pursued, using non-quantitative methodology and mainly public sources to make in-depth studies of the management history of the organizations studied, in the manner of Chandler (1962) and Channon (1973) for the private sector, both to demonstrate the potential of the method for the public and hybrid sectors and to explore the possible mechanisms of the performance changes reported in section II.

From annual reports to parliament or shareholders, supplemented sometimes by internal documents of a non-confidential nature made available to us, changes in the divisional structure of the organizations studied were logged for each year over a period of about twenty years, along with changes in management accounting systems and changes affecting the competitive environment. Certain regularities emerged, and a model of internal control modes was developed to help in demonstrating them.

This model was described in Dunsire *et al.* 1988, and its current (much simplified) version is portrayed in Figure 8.2. It builds on the work of Thompson (1967), Williamson (1970, 1975), Mintzberg (1979, 1983), and later students of strategic management (see accounts in Bowman and Asch, 1987; Johnson and Scholes, 1988) but was specially adapted to the 'status change' thesis explored here. It starts from the well-established antonyms 'markets' and 'hierarchies', but postulates that all real organizations of this kind will fall somewhere between 'pure hierarchy' (or 100 per cent 'command-orientation') and 'pure market' (or 100 per cent 'results-orientation').

No example of 'pure hierarchy' (point A in Figure 8.2) was found among the organizations studied (though several were perhaps nearer A than B to begin with), and only one clear illustration (BAe after complete privatization) of a 'holding company' mode of control (point D). Most organizations could be placed either around point B (emphasizing managerial 'functions', broadly corresponding to the 'staff and line' pattern of classic scientific management, to Chandler's (1962) 'centralized' and Williamson's 'unified' form (1970)); or around point C (stressing their distinct 'businesses', the idea of cost- and profit-centres, which broadly corresponds to Chandler's multidivisional or 'decentralized' structure and Williamson's 'M-form'). The 'functional' form is characterized by a large HQ with organization-wide planning, finance, personnel, purchasing, marketing and research departments, monitoring inputs and outputs for the organization as a whole; the

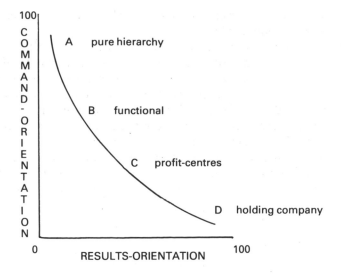

Figure 8.2   *Modes of control*

Salient Characteristics in Brief

A 'Orders of the Day', 'Daily Duties List', 'Daily Postings' etc. for whole organization.
   Large manuals of procedure.
   Itemized release of funds – few internal budgets.
   Upward referral of all problems expected.
   High visibility of rank and status; salary scales by rank and seniority.
B Large proportion of total managerial staff located in HQ departments for planning, financial control, personnel, procurement, marketing, R&D, etc.
   'Policy' replaces instructions; operational decisions delegated to divisional management.
   Centrally approved budgets for money, staff and other resources.
   Several HQ inspectorates, on quality, O&M, maintenance, etc.
   Many formal reports to HQ, on production, working days lost, sickness, stoppages, vehicle miles travelled, etc.
   Outcomes monitored for organization as a whole.
   Salary scales by specialism and comparability.
C Small HQ as facilitator, common and support services.
   Production, finance, personnel, etc. choices for division delegated to division management.
   Separate cost centres or 'businesses' identified in accounts; costs and outcomes monitored output by output; performance targets set.
   Large capital projects, promotion across divisions and to centre, and internal restructuring, remain an HQ prerogative.
   Personal salaries by individual management contract, performance-related.
D Very small corporate HQ, with some arm's-length financial monitoring but no staff or production performance monitoring.
   Congeries of distinct subsidiary companies, each with own board of directors, accounts, markets, etc.
   No corporate salary except for HQ personnel.

'profit-centres' form by a smaller 'facilitating' HQ, monitoring inputs and outputs of divisions individually.

Mapping any shift from one point to another is what the model is for. But we do not attempt to document here the reasons for an observed shift, or to reconcile the popular doctrines behind our hypotheses with the results of research in organizational management (see for example, Johnson and Scholes, 1988: ch. 10). Decentralization, for example, may not necessarily and always be a 'good thing' in itself for a particular organization at a particular time. The organizational design literature agrees that there are contingencies for which any particular structure will be the most appropriate. It is the adoption of a mode of control apparently incongruent with an enterprise's situation internal or external that may lead to reduced performance.

Management Change: Empirical Findings

In this section we report as fully as space will allow the findings from an analysis of eight of the ten organizations listed in Table 8.1 (omitting NFC and BA). Additional status change events excluded from the analysis reported in section II have, however, been included here (see Table 8.1 for details) to further test hypotheses 4 and 5, unrelated to performance.

Her Majesty's Stationery Office Trading Fund (TF) status for HMSO in 1980 meant the end of the 'allied service' principle, by which government departments ordered their stationery and printing requirements from HMSO free of charge (HMSO accounting for the expenditure on its own vote), and of the 'tied procurement' principle, by which departments could order *only* from HMSO; and thus the introduction of a requisite change in 'culture', from reactive administration to proactive competition with private suppliers. Preparation for the change had actually begun in 1972, with the design of a new management accounting system to provide detailed costings and statistics like turnover per employee, neither available nor necessary for vote accounting.

Top management structure in 1971 was virtually unchanged from what it had been in 1921, and corresponded to the 'functional' control pattern normal to government departments, with directorates for Accounts, Establishments, Contracts, Printing Works, Printing and Binding, and so on. What happened between 1972 and 1977 was the structural recognition of four main 'businesses': Print Procurement (not even mentioned in the 1971 chart), Production, Publications (the bookshops, etc.), and Supply (the stationery business), each accountable for its costs and results – a shift towards the 'profit-centres' form.

But all this had actually begun well before the status change. The mixed performance for HMSO noted in section II might be explained by the relatively short period covered, considering the amount of capital re-equipping undergone. The shift from a captive market to a competitive one was, however, successfully made, without importing managerial expertise, and on civil service salaries. However, one of HMSO's first actions on becoming an Executive Agency in December 1988 (the second status change) was to use this additional freedom to restructure its entire remuneration system, including a performance reward element.

Royal Mint The Mint became a trading fund in 1975, which is a west-to-east shift in capital market, and it subsequently achieved high growth in many of the performance indicators. But although TF status does entail a different 'capital market' relationship with the Treasury, it would seem to expose the agency to no greater risk of takeover and the like; and it is hard to identify any major corresponding change either in competitiveness or in management structure and management accounting systems, much less in reward systems, to account for the improvement.

The Royal Mint is a relatively small organization, relatively undiversified, with a simple functional-type structure. It began to export worldwide (competitively) in the 1920s, and achieved its first Queen's Award to Industry for exports in 1966, without any marketing function appearing in the staff listings, even as late as 1971. There was a remarkable stability of top management structure between the late nineteenth century and 1965 (even to nomenclature – deputy master, chief clerk, superintendent, chief assayer, etc.); and the structure was not basically changed with the announcement in 1972 of impending TF status, except for some modernization of titles. Nor was there any marked change in accounting: the Mint had published annual reports including output figures since 1871, and full trading accounts since 1948. Staff remained on (relatively low) civil service grades and salaries.

How, then, are we to account for the performance improvement on gaining TF status? One possible explanation is 'technological change', concerning the coincidental shift from several old London buildings to new purpose-built plant in Wales, occasioned by the need for massive investment in new machinery following the decision to decimalize the coinage in 1966, with a deadline for its introduction in 1971. The move to Wales took eight years (1968 to 1976) to complete; but effects on costs and productivity were apparent as soon as production started.

Royal Ordnance Factories   Here the change to TF status in 1974 appeared to have made performance worse. In 1966 the 44 wartime Ordnance factories had been reduced to eleven, grouped under three directorates for Ammunition, Explosives, and Weapons and Fighting Vehicles, from which in 1969 was carved out a Small Arms group. With HQ directorates for Administration and Finance, Accounts, and 'Civil Work', this was the top management structure in May 1972 when the TF decision was announced. Although the four manufacturing divisions were not full 'profit-centres', the Mallabar Committee in 1969 had found a largely decentralized structure and praised the cost-conscious system of management accounting (Cmnd. 4713, 1971, p. 25), enhanced by a system of fixed-price quotations. In the ROF no 'allied service' principle applied, and supply was on repayment (though usually a non-competitive UK defence market); they had been producing trading accounts for over a century.

This structure was altered in 1973, just before the status change, to a more 'functional' one. Under the newly titled managing director there were Directors-General for Production, Procurement and Administration, and Finance. The D-G Procurement and Administration supervised directors for Plans and Secretariat, Personnel, Procurement, and Quality. In 1974 a marketing coordinator was appointed from outside. But when in 1984 ROF was being groomed for privatization, consultants advised the formation of four 'operating companies': Ammunition, Explosives, Small Arms, and Fighting Vehicles.

It is tempting, therefore, to postulate that one of the reasons for relatively poor post-TF performance was the adoption in 1973 of a centralized-function top management structure in place of what had seemed a perfectly well-adapted four-business structure.

Post Office Postal services and telecommunications had been run as separate operations since the 1930s, but neither had its own accounts or engineering service or field organization. The significant development was less the status change (to a public corporation) in 1969, than the 1967 decision to create two *businesses* (the word used), each with its own personnel, accounts, engineering, and research functions, within the one corporation, until the split into two corporations in 1981. Thus the Post Office as a whole moved to a 'profit-centres' form in 1967. But it was much later before either Posts or Telecommunications did so individually.

Posts remained 'functional' in form and was heavily criticized by the Carter Committee in 1976 for its highly centralized decision-making and marked rises in administrative costs per unit of output since status change. But the period was also one of intense government intervention, first by Conservatives insisting on price restraint, and then by Labour insisting on economic pricing. The combination may explain the poor performance reported in section II. In the 1980s the Post Office identified its four real 'businesses' (Royal Mail, Post Office Counters, Parcel Force, and Girobank – later privatized) and made profit-centres of them. By 1988 the chairman reported that his Post Office was the only one in the European Community to have made a profit for twelve successive years with no form of subsidy.

British Telecommunications The telecommunications side also remained highly centralized under the Post Office Corporation, in spite of much 'commercial' rhetoric and 'market talk'. In 1979, ten years after the status change, the centre did not trust its field staffs (Beesley and Laidlaw, 1989: 21). Several minor activities were brought into a profit-centre subsidiary British Telecom Enterprises, but it proved extremely difficult to define 'businesses' (sets of activities that can be ring-fenced in costs, marketing, and results) in either the international or the inland telephones fields. In 1990 BT, although privatized in 1984, is still trying to get its structure right, as between massive 'divisions' and multiple decentralized subsidiaries.

Rolls-Royce   As reported in section II, the performance of Rolls-Royce improved on its nationalization in 1971. There is no space to tell here the saga of the RB 211 engine, with which the company hoped to break into the US market, and the ruinous contract that had been negotiated with Lockheed in 1968. But according to the DTI inspectors' report (MacCrindle and Godfrey, 1973) the company was being weakly run well before this, particularly in the divisional and corporate accounting function. It effectively had a multidivisional 'profit-centres' structure; but the main board, heavily overweighted with engineers and long-serving non-executive members, did not receive the information that would have shown it that one division, Aero Engines, was running the whole company into dire trouble; and what it did receive, it discounted.

When Rolls-Royce went bankrupt (creating a profound shock effect throughout the company), the government let it, and then bought the aero-engines businesses from the receiver, so that they would not inherit the Lockheed contract. A completely new board was appointed, and a new Lockheed contract negotiated. It is not therefore surprising that the recorded performance improved. Performance deteriorated badly in the mid-1970s, and it was many years until the company was brought fully round. It may be significant that just before overall profitability was attained, a restructuring took it back up the control curve towards a more functional form: the management of straight production, and that of design for production (the more standardizable activities) were centralized into functional divisions, leaving the essentially risky activities of developing new products and landing contracts with the three 'businesses' (Aero Engine, Small Engines, and Industrial and Marine Engines). The company was reprivatized in 1987.

British Aerospace   When after a series of amalgamations aircraft manufacture was nationalized in 1977, the Act required that the corporation would 'promote the largest degree of decentralization of management consistent with the proper discharge of its functions'. In fact, the corporation structure simply retained the old companies, each division having its own board and chairman, with small corporate departments – a typical multidivisional form. It cannot be said that nationalization produced bureaucratic fetters on management – in any case, it only lasted four years. The drop in performance reported in section II probably was owing to the disruptive effects of change – or possibly to 'lack of managerial incentives'.

BAe was partially privatized in 1981, without major internal change. That came in 1983, when a new managing director was appointed on a wave of centralizing tendencies – marketing unified, then research, cost controls tightened, and a whole tier of management abolished 'in order to improve strategic decision-making and cohesive management'. By 1986 there were no 'business-based' directors at all on the main board: all were either functional or non-executive. BAe (freed from the statutory injunction to decentralize) had moved decisively back up the curve towards the functional mode in the name of 'unification'.

Remaining government shares were sold in 1985, a new chairman in 1987 immediately reversed the tide of centralization, floating all the 'major businesses' off as separate limited companies, as well as expanding BAe massively by new acquisitions outside its traditional aerospace activities. By 1988 the board was composed mainly of directors with responsibility for one or more of these subsidiaries – a complete turnaround from 'functional' directly to 'holding company' form in two years.

London Transport   The London Passenger Transport Board (LPTB) was formed in 1933 out of a welter of private and municipal transport undertakers, as one of Britain's first 'public corporations'. In 1947 LT (as we shall refer to it) became an arm of the British Transport Commission, until 1963 when it was once more an independent public corporation, though (in the face of large social changes in demography and travel habits) it was kept going only on Exchequer subsidies. When the Greater London Council was formed in 1965, agreement was reached for it to become responsible for all aspects of traffic and transport in its area, and LT, although remaining a statutory corporation, answered to the GLC on policy matters, including fare levels and finance generally. The Transport Tribunal lost its control over fares, and the GLC supported by grants and cross-subsidization a policy of concessionary fares for special groups. For a few years after 1970 LT ran a small surplus, but from about 1974 the performance, both financial and in quality of service, began to decline again markedly.

In the 1960s LT had still the highly centralized functional board structure created by the LPTB to weld together many disparate elements, with some 15 or 20 specialist departments coordinated only by reporting to a particular board member. Even in 1962, not all the six 'railway' departments reported to the same member, nor did the three 'bus' departments, and engineering was quite separate from operations. In so far as structural change took place, the watchword was still 'rationalization' – bringing together similar activities whether serving rail or bus services – even as late as 1971. Although bus and rail operations respectively were gathered and given to separate board members in 1971, neither had planning, engineering, supply/stores, person-nel, industrial relations, or financial responsibilities for their operations, these being the province of other members.

It was in 1978 that large-scale reorganization began, in a conscious drive to improve LT's perilous financial position. A new chairman, and a deputy chairman appointed from outside, took three actions: they created two 'businesses' absorbing most of the engineering and supplies functions;

decentralized management within them into smaller units, each with budgeting and personnel powers; and instituted performance measures for management at all levels.

Politically this was a calamitous time. The sacking of that chairman by the GLC after a hard-hitting consultants' report was followed by the 'Fares Fair' controversy, when the courts declared illegal the GLC's policy of cheap fares which had decisively reversed the decline in LT's passenger traffic, and forced a doubling of fares which started it off again. 'Political' interference by GLC-appointed board members (although quite within their rights) led to low managerial morale, until the London Regional Transport Act of 1984 put LT once more directly under the minister.

The Act required the board to set up subsidiary companies for its bus and underground services, and in the next few years the strategy was applied by LT to most of its activities, so that by 1988 a small central HQ confining itself to corporate planning and financial oversight was surrounded by half a dozen subsidiary companies and as many 'business boards' (including LT Advertising, LT Catering, LT Museum, LT Property, etc.). The Act had also enjoined competitive tendering not only for central services but for bus routes; and building services, computing, architects, and medical services departments were made 'profit centres', charging for their services in order to establish their real costs. Thus it can be said that the structural groundwork of the performance improvements after the 1984 status change was laid by the reorganization of 1978 onwards, and built on by the statutory provisions of the 1984 Act reflecting 'New Public Management' doctrines.

Management Change: Analysis

The results of the analysis are summarized in Table 8.5. Hypothesis No. 3 was that improved performance is associated with management change from A towards D on the curve. HMSO supported this, if weakly; but the Mint did not, since performance improved without movement along the curve. In the cases of ROF, Post Office and Telecommunications, Rolls-Royce, London Transport and the later BAe status change, the hypothesis was confirmed either positively or negatively (if there was the requisite movement, performance improved; if performance did not improve, no movement was observed). The earlier BAe case went against the hypothesis, however: performance worsened although no movement was observed.

Thus the result on this hypothesis was somewhat mixed. But from one perspective, as suggested in section II, perhaps one should not have expected this hypothesis to be confirmed, except by accident. Performance figures gathered on the basis of the date of legal status change will not test a hypothesis about the effect of change of control mode unless the dates of the two changes coincide (see below, on hypothesis 5).

Table 8.5   *Summary of findings on management change*

Name	Movement along curve		Hypoth. 3 Performance	Hypoth. 4 Competition	Hypoth.5 Status
	Expected	Found			
HMSO	B–C 1980 +	B–C 1977 +	Yes (+)	Yes (+)	No
R Mint	B–C 1975 +	C 1948 +	No	Yes (−)	No
ROF	B–C 1974 +	C–B 1973 +	Yes (−)	No	No
PO ('69)	B–C 1969 +	B–C 1967 +	No	No	No
PO Posts	B–C 1969 +	B–C 1983 +	Yes (−)	Yes (−)	No
PO Telec	B–C 1981 +	B?C 1983 +		Yes (−)	No
BT ('84)	C–D 1984 +	B?C 1983 +		No	No
R-R	C–B 1971 +	C–B 1983 +	Yes (−)	No	No
BAe ('77)	C–B 1977 +	C 1977 +	No	No	No
BAe ('81)	B–C 1981 +	C–B 1983 +	Yes (+)	No	No
LT ('70)	C–B 1970 +	B 1933 +	Yes (−)	Yes (−)	No
LT ('84)	B–C 1984 +	B–C 1978 +	Yes (+)	Yes (+)	No

'Movement Expected': On assumption that mode of control will follow status change: west–east on Figure 8.1 = A–D on Figure 8.2.

'Movement Found': direction and date of movement observed.

'Hypoth. 3 Performance': association between change in performance as reported in section II and movement found is confirmed positively (+) or negatively (−). (Column covers only those status change events for which section II performance data are available.)

'Hypoth. 4 Competition': association between movement found and change in degree of competition is confirmed positively (+) or negatively (−).

'Hypoth. 5 Status': association between dates of movement found and of status change is confirmed positively (+) or negatively (−).

HMSO status change 1988 to Executive Agency, and ROF privatization in 1985, omitted for lack of data.

Hypothesis No. 4 was that movement from A towards D is associated with increase in competition. This too was only partly supported by the evidence of change in these eight organizations. The HMSO case was good positive confirmation; the Royal Mint provided a negative confirmation – there was no marked change in control mode, but there had been no marked change in competition. The two Post Office businesses and the two London Transport status changes gave both positive and negative confirmation: while there was little or no increase in competition, there was little or no decentralization; if competition (or its threat) became more evident, the predicted movement took place. The ROF move just prior to status change, however, went quite the wrong way, given that degree of competition remained the same. In the Rolls-Royce and BAe cases, movement away from D towards A occurred when competition had not changed, also contradicting the hypothesis. Thus of the ten status-change events for which we have section II data, six confirmed the hypothesis, four did not – sometimes, apparently, a tightening of control is indicated by internal contingencies even in a competitive environment.

Hypothesis 5 was that movement along the curve is associated with status change. This was amply refuted. In all cases studied, the timing of the legal status change was different from that of the managerial control change: or else, negatively, there was no perceptible managerial control change although there was change in legal status. But if one takes the date of *announcement* of an impending status change as the significant event (typically two years or so in advance), the coincidence of event and control mode change was more marked. The threat of status change may be sufficient to trigger adaptive managerial behaviour.

Answering the question posed at the beginning of this section (were the performance results found related not only to status change but also to simultaneous change in the competition and/or internal management change dimensions?) is not a simple matter. Of the ten status-change events studied, only one (the BAe privatization), as reported at the end of section II, was clearly associated with performance improvement on all three sets of measures, with RM doing well on the two tested. The BAe improvement was not associated with increased competition, though it might have been associated with a slightly earlier change in control mode; but that change was in the direction opposite to the prediction – away from results-orientation, not towards it. The RM results cannot be put down to associated change in either competitiveness or internal management, for there was none.

Only three cases for which we have section II data were associated with change of competition: the BAe nationalization (less competition), HMSO, and the 'delocalizing' of LT in 1984 (both increased competition). For both of the latter, a clear shift in mode of control, in the predicted direction (towards a 'profit-centres' form), was also observed. So for these two all three postulated mechanisms for improved performance through status change were in place. Yet their performance results were rather mixed – some predictions confirmed, some given only limited support. No clear lesson, therefore, on competition: performance was as likely to improve in the absence of increased competition as in its presence.

Out of the ten cases for which performance figures were available (a further four status events were mentioned in this section but were not the subject of performance testing), we found only four cases of control-mode shift: the three mentioned in the previous paragraphs, and ROF. Of these, two (HMSO and LT) were towards a 'profit-centres' operation, two (BAe and ROF) were in the opposite direction, towards centralized functional control. Only one (BAe) showed clear improvement in performance. No structural change involving shift of control mode preceded or accompanied the status change event in RM, PO (Posts), BT, RR, the LT 'localization', or the BAe nationalization. RM showed improved performance, as did RR but against prediction; the BAe nationalization confirmed the predicted worsened performance; and the others showed mixed results. No clear lessons there either: performance was as likely to improve in the absence of change of control mode as it was following it.

In short, there was no clear relationship between enterprise performance and status change, change in competition, or change in control mode, singly or in combination.

IV

Conclusions

On the whole, then, the results of the investigations reported in section III are as cloudy and perplexing as are those reported in section II. As so many social scientists find, life is rather more complicated than the prescriptive theories assume. Certainly, neither investigation supports the simple assertion that change in ownership necessarily changes enterprise performance, even in its sophisticated form, where capital market change is assumed to be accompanied by increased competition and improved managerial incentives. Sometimes it does, sometimes it doesn't.

In this study we have been very conscious of the benefits of multidisciplinary collaboration. Much of the established public choice literature is by economists, who tend to assume 'efficiency' is good, and have traditionally got by with very simple models of 'the firm' and 'the bureau', regarding internal organization as a black box into which it is not necessary to enquire; and when political scientists join the fray, they tend to discuss 'objectives' and social accountability rather than costs and financial accounting – but agree with the economists about the black box. The management analyst, on the other hand, is often happy to spend his life inside the black box. It has done all of us good to be forced to look beyond our disciplinary blinkers.

This kind of exercise needs replication with other cases and perhaps improved data and methods. We should like to see the question of managerial incentives, for example, probed empirically. Does managerial remuneration go up before improved enterprise performance, or after, or anyway? Again, much research concerns itself with the difficulties of performance measurement; but surprisingly little on how to recognize and ring-fence a 'business', whether in the private or the public sector. It is not a matter for accountants only. Not only are party politics involved (seen, for instance, in the arguments about London Transport's fares cross-subsidization policies), but also organizational politics and personalities, which this account of our research has hardly touched upon.

Another avenue of research would explore the possibility that, by a variety of the 'Hawthorne Effect' (Roethlisberger and Dickson, 1939), *any* sort of major change will lead to improved performance, for a while, since it opens up opportunities for the ambitious and staff generally get more attention than usual. On the other hand, all major change carries disruption costs which could in the short term depress performance or mask improvements. Testing empirically for these two effects in our organizations would have needed another research programme.

To a strategic management theorist our results (though admittedly on a very small sample) may be interesting in that, out of eight major structural changes noted over the period studied, only five (HMSO, ROF pre-privatization, PO Posts 1985, LT 1978, and BAe 1987) were in the direction one would expect from US and UK business history, that is, from functional to multidivisional or holding company form – the direction also being pushed hard under the British government's 'Next Steps' programme even for non-commercial and regulatory agencies. The other three (ROF pre-TF status, RR and BAe before privatization) were functional centralizations. Chandler in 1962 for USA and Channon in 1973 for UK both reported massive movements in business firms of any size towards M-form structures; but, significantly, studies in other countries have failed to find this, leading Bowman and Asch (1987: 251) to suggest that structure will change only where increased competition obliges it; otherwise the existing (inefficient) structure will prevail.

This produces a hypothesis for testing among the new executive agencies in the UK. Will their *internal* structure change on their change of status, and will it too move in the cost- and profit-centres direction even in the absence of competition?

References

Alchian, A. A. and Demsetz, H. (1972) 'Production, information costs and economic organizations', *American Economic Review*, 62; reproduced in A. A. Alchian (1975) *Economic Forces at Work*. Indianapolis: Liberty Press.

Beesley, M. E. and Laidlaw, B. (1989) *The Future of Telecommunications* (IEA Research Monographs No. 42). London: Institute of Economic Affairs.

Bowman, C. and Asch, D. (1987) *Strategic Management*. London: Macmillan Education.

Carter Committee (1976) *Report of the Post Office Review Committee*, Cmnd. 6850. London: HMSO.

Chandler, A. D. Jr. (1962) *Strategy and Structure: Chapters in the History of the Industrial Enterprise*. Cambridge, MA: MIT Press.

Channon, D. (1973) *The Strategy and Structure of British Enterprise*. London: Macmillan.

De Alessi, L. (1980) 'The economics of property rights: a review of the evidence', *Research in Law and Economics*, 2: 1–47.

Dunsire, A., Hartley, K., Parker, D. and Dimitriou, B. (1988) 'Organizational status and performance: a conceptual framework for testing public choice theories', *Public Administration*, 66(4): 363–88.

Forsyth, P. (1984) 'Airlines and airports: privatisation, competition, and regulation', *Fiscal Studies*, 5(1): 61–75.

Hartley, K. and Parker, D. (1991) 'Organisational status and performance: the effect on employment'. *Applied Economics* [forthcoming].

Hartley, K., Parker, D. and Martin, S. (1991) 'Organisational status, ownership and productivity', [Mimeo: publication forthcoming].

Johnson, G. and Scholes, K. (1988) *Exploring Corporate Strategy*, 2nd edn. Englewood Cliffs, NJ: Prentice-Hall.

Kay, J.A. and Thompson, D. J. (1986) 'Privatisation: a policy in search of a rationale', *Economic Journal*, 96 (March): 18–32.

MacCrindle, R. A. and Godfrey, P. (1973) *Rolls-Royce Limited: Investigation under Section 165(a)(i) of the Companies Act 1948*. Report by the inspectors appointed by the Department of Trade and Industry. London: HMSO.

Mallabar Committee (1971) *Report of the Committee on Government Industrial Establishments*. Cmnd. 4713. London: HMSO.

Millward, R. and Parker, D. (1983) 'Public and private enterprise: comparative behaviour and relative efficiency', in R. Millward, D. Parker, L. Rosenthal, M. T. Sumner and N. Topham, *Public Sector Economics*, London: Longman.

Mintzberg, H. (1979) *The Structuring of Organizations*. Englewood Cliffs, NI: Prentice-Hall.

Mintzberg, H. (1983) *Power in and around Organizations*. Englewood Cliffs, NJ: Prentice-Hall.

Parker, D., Hartley, K. and Martin, S. (1990) 'Do changes in organisational status affect financial performance?' [Mimeo].

Roethlisberger, F. J. and Dickson, W. J. (1939) *Management and the Worker*. Cambridge, MA: Harvard University Press.

Thompson, J. D. (1967) *Organizations in Action*. New York: McGraw-Hill.

Veljanovsky, C. (1987) *Selling the State: Privatisation in Britain*. London: Weidenfeld & Nicolson.

Williamson, O. E. (1970) *Corporate Control and Business Behavior*. Englewood Cliffs, NJ: Prentice-Hall.

Williamson, O. E. (1975) *Markets and Hierarchies: Analysis and Antitrust Implications: a Study in the Economics of Internal Organization*. London and New York: Free Press.

9

Lawyers Go to Hospital

Joseph M. Jacob

Discussion of the changes to the British system of health care made by the new Terms of Service of general practitioners, the National Health Service and Community Care Act 1990 and by associated reforms has tended to focus on such questions as efficiency, management, participation, and the adequacy of the funding. This chapter is not concerned with these doubtless important issues. Instead it makes a forecast. Whether desirable or undesirable, intended or unintended, many of these major changes are likely to prove a fertile ground for lawyers: they and their allies, particularly in accountancy, are likely to become significant players in the administration of medical practice. Now lawyers are not concerned only with conflict, but clearly as the prospect of that increases, including but also beyond the malpractice action, they are gaining in prominence. This chapter suggests that this new role is a by-product of a more important concern, and returns also to a thesis I have offered before: medicine and health are so central to our experience of living that their interaction with rules tells us a great deal about the place of regulation in life, and frequently, even without the distraction of the debates about medical ethics, causes us to revise more general philosophies. In one field it describes the adaptation of the machinery of government to what perhaps can be called its modern or post-modern purpose. [. . .]

The changes to be discussed here are: (1) the preventative and screening provisions of general practitioners' new Terms of Service; (2) new requirements for audit and associated measures; (3) reforms to the general practice complaints scheme; (4) new arrangements for defending malpractice actions; (5) increased reliance on ministerial and other circulars consequent on the new constitutions of health authorities; (6) the creation of *NHS trusts*; and (7) the introduction of the 'internal market' and of *NHS contracts* between NHS bodies.[1] As will be argued, these seven alterations together represent a change to the system of health care at least as fundamental as those accomplished by the Labour government of 1945–51. The structures previously established in the NHS are not abolished, but are subordinated to a market which at least in the rhetoric is 'internal'. These changes add the

---

From *Public Law*, Summer 1991: 255–81 (abridged).

control mechanisms necessary for a market to those already existing for the professional and state-run bureaucratic regulation of health care. Although government has consistently denied the intention, they also make it more possible for the increasingly important market mechanisms, in effect, to be deregulated so as to achieve the legal privatization of health care including, if that is desired, an increasing emphasis on private funding. It is crucial to their image, but not to the changes themselves, that these market mechanisms are internal, for if they are justiciable the major step to privatization has already been taken. This chapter argues that their combined effect is in fact to make that step.

Now is not the occasion to seek a definition of all the circumstances necessary for litigation to be predicted, but these changes in the health service enable some of the conditions to be 'separated out', to use a metaphor from chemistry. Thus we may say that litigation is more likely where: (a) the content of the legal obligation is uncertain; (b) victory is seen as worth the effort to each party; (c) the possibility of each side needing the other for future transactions is less than the importance to them of the current dispute; and, (d) in considering each of these factors, the officer who will make the decision whether to litigate, that is, the manager, is working to criteria and goals separated or different from those of the institution for which he works. Litigation is also more likely where (e) a threshold of disappointment is crossed. This threshold is dependent on a variety of factors: where it is increased by the commitment of personal choice, for example by the purchase of a service, the first reaction is of increased satisfaction which, if realization of its frustration dawns, may result in a sharp shift to disappointment and litigation.

In relation particularly to the fourth of these (the separation of the manager from his institution), it is of some importance that modern health service administrators are given individualized and distinct incentives, notably by way of performance-related earnings. The consequence is that the ideological and other gaps between these managers (who will negotiate *contracts*) and the medical staff (who will execute them) isolate the manager from the organization's other staff so that their best interests may not be his. Doctors still use the language of medicine and caring, managers that of commerce: patients are customers; the art of medicine becomes a business and the act of medicine a product. Effort and striving are turned into cost; practice into performance; trust into negotiated consent; cure into discharge; anguished choice into efficiency. The performance of professional duty becomes doing a job, and job satisfaction ceases to be a smile on a grateful patient's face or the earning of respect and becomes, at best, the creation of goodwill for further business and, more normally, monetary reward.

The Preventative and Screening Provisions of the New Terms of Service in General Practice

The new provisions seek to create a novel relationship between patients and their general practitioners whereby patients are compelled to be explicitly responsible for their own health and doctors are to police the new obligation. The terms of service for NHS doctors in general practice are contained in Schedule 1 to the General Medical and Pharmaceutical Services Regulations 1974. These terms were radically altered by amending regulations issued in 1989. Of note here are the provisions in paragraph 13B (new patients) and paragraph 13D (patients aged 75 years and over) and, of the widest application, paragraph 13C (patients not seen within three years). Typical is this last: that the doctor shall invite his patient for a consultation and that this meeting shall include details of the patient's and the patient's consanguineous family's 'lifestyle (including diet, exercise, use of tobacco, consumption of alcohol, and misuse of drugs or solvents)'. Paragraph 13D(5)(e) adds, in respect of the aged, that the doctor shall make an assessment of the 'social environment'. It is not sufficient to say that the concern is only with, to use the words of the paragraph, 'lifestyle affecting the patient's medical history'. Health and ill-health are in everything we do and, on some views, think: 'our bodies are the informers'. As one of the health ministers said: 'Eating for health is a choice everyone can make. Those who choose not to are *failing to take responsibility for their own health.*[2] Any records generated will not belong to the doctor. He is likely to be their custodian, but there is no 'Chinese wall' between the doctors and their governing Family Health Service Authority (FHSA). Whatever else, these provisions represent new levels of surveillance, albeit on their face medical, which can raise a profound threat to freedom. For example, how far it is compatible with rights to privacy, for example under article 8 of the European Convention on Human Rights, for a state-run service to acquire this type of information? It is no answer to rely merely on the legalistic point that patients are not under a duty to have the consultation or to reply to questions, for that is to mistake the normative character of medicine encapsulated in the expression 'doctor's orders'. [. . .]

What is interesting about these new demands is the expression they give to individual choice. It seems clear that this provision taken with the rest of the paragraph requires a negotiated relationship with explanation and choice, not merely, as in the past, as to proposed medical intervention, but also now as to lifestyle. Each of us will have to justify our way of life to our doctor. Choice [. . .] implies a regard for self; regard for self gives prominence to individual rights; and, such rights deny trust. On this basis, it is quite reasonable to say that the decay in trust has been a principal cause of the increase in litigation by patients against their doctors and to predict that it will cause more.

The New Requirements for Audit and Associated Measures

The new terms of service require that doctors police the patient's obligation to be healthy. But these new policemen are themselves to be policed. Under previous legislation, general practitioners had almost unlimited rights to prescribe within their clinical judgement. Now that right is curtailed by the imposition of cash limits. GPs will practise under the supervision of a FHSA. Each year most will have access to an 'indicative prescribing amount': it will be open to negotiation and be based on past levels deemed reasonable or adequate by the authority. Doctors will refer patients to hospitals which may be within or without the district under arrangements (see below) which the relevant District Health Authority (DHA) has made. Whilst it remains true that overspends will result in renegotiation rather than penalty, and the 'indicative prescribing amount' was described as 'a management tool and a way of monitoring precisely what is happening', these are signs that some doctors are becoming both more aware of the cost of prescriptions and more reluctant to write expensive ones. Other GPs will elect to become part of a 'fund-holding practice'. Here, they will receive an amount deemed sufficient to cover the costs of both their prescribing and any contract or *NHS contract* they make for the provision of further services (particularly hospital treatment) for their patients. The important point of both these arrangements is the change from practice without regard to cost, to cost-controlled practice.

General practitioners are now required under paragraph 43A of the terms of service to make an annual report to their FHSA. This report is to set out matters specified in the regulations. Ostensibly this requirement is merely a management tool, enabling the Authority to acquire precise details about referrals and some other topics. [. . .]

More general implications underlie the change. The change is about the nature of the control to which GPs are subjected. [. . .] There should be little surprise that cash-limited practice and the annual reports were introduced at the same time. What was once to be left to professional judgement and common sense is now to be defined and, having been defined, is to be watched by managers The reason is quite simple. It is that the new world of the NHS holds to a philosophy based in commerce and contract; and in that philosophy obligations are meaningless if they are defined by those who have assumed them. On the other hand, as practice becomes monitored, its goals and the basis of self-esteem are changed, for, unless practice is objectified, success and failure cannot be measured. [. . .]

This shift from judgement to criteria is accented by the application of *audit* to the NHS. The jurisdiction of the Local Government Audit Commission, with some modifications, has been extended to it (and the Commission is renamed accordingly). The Commission was established in 1983: its purpose is not merely to provide 'probity' auditing, that is, some assurance of the reliability of the accounts and the legality of its transactions; rather, it provides machinery for ensuring there is 'value for money'. McSweeney provided an assessment of its work in local government. He argued: 'The pre-Commission discourse [had an] inherent belief in the reforming and revelatory power of auditing. . . . Calls for greater accountability . . . pervaded the debate. Not surprisingly, the concept of accountability advanced has had a constrained meaning.'[3] He added: 'there are extensive gaps in the required data and knowledge about appropriate processes and accomplishments. . . . This has led to a continuing search, for surrogate or proxy data, known as performance indicators.'[4]

To McSweeney, the difficulties of these devices include: the necessity in their construction drastically to simplify; a preoccupation with quantification and consequent disregard for the qualitative; and their use in isolation, unrelated (or inadequately related) to other indicators implying knowledge of the accomplishments and processes far in excess of what actually exists. [. . .]

Perceptively, McSweeney argued that the new audits with their universal model of rational decision-making, their partial performance indicators and the rest, are not just descriptions or even judgements. The values and priorities underlying these audits do not just influence behaviour in the sense of altering responses to evaluation criteria. More profoundly, they can influence the awareness of both alternatives and priorities.

The second method of objectifying medicine is the use of the so-called medical audit. As with financial audit, there is hope in its 'reforming and revelatory power'. At times it is linked with resource management. So too, there is some idea of 'accountability'. The differences between financial and medical audit are that the latter is to be conducted by peer review. With financial audit, organizational goals are set within limits established by outsiders. In medical audit, they are set by the brotherhood of the profession: medical audit represents an extension of epidemiological techniques from disease, through particular treatments, to the effectiveness of particular practitioners. The similarity between the two types of audit is that both assume that to some degree the results of the activity are measurable. In the case of medicine, the assumption is that one doctor practises or ought to practise in the same way as another.

One can perhaps see why the medical profession has embraced medical audit. It reinforces its claim to practise a science. But this reason is not the government's, whose concern has been accountability. To an extent, government has been misled by the profession's rhetoric. But so also has the profession itself. The rhetoric of audit and the rhetoric of science pretend to an objectivity which practice, particularly primary care rather than surgery, denies. It may be inevitable and even accurate for modern medicine to claim a scientific base. But the claim to objectivity is also a strategy which contradicts important elements of the art of medicine and which has, if only as a by-product, the effect of reducing its dependence on trust and thus increasing the prospect of complaints, including litigation, consequent on the creation of self-interested suspicion, if not distrust.

The Amendments to the Complaints Scheme for General Practice

New rules have been made to make it easier for patients both to choose their practitioner and to complain about him or her. Pursuant to the first of these, despite the General Medical Council's long-standing opposition to advertising, all GPs are now required to publish a 'practice leaflet' and update it each year: patients can both change their GP and know something about what they are changing. Related to these, and of as much significance, are the reforms relating to complaints in general practice. In strict law, a complaint within the health service about general practice amounts to an allegation of breach of the contract between the GP and the service. [. . .] If, however, a complaint is upheld by a service committee, it has power only to withhold remuneration: a compensatory order in favour of a patient cannot be made. The time limit within which complaints may be accepted has been extended from eight to 13 weeks. FHSAs are now required to provide an informal procedure for patients who do not wish to pursue more formal procedures. The new mechanisms provide that FHSAs shall accept oral complaints from people unable to make complaints in writing. One of the previous areas of criticism was that doctors dominated the service committees. Under a further set of new measures there is now a majority of lay members. The reforms are reinforced by a novelty within the health service: service committees and the Secretary of State are given power to refer a case to a practitioner's professional registration body.

These reforms are in part due no doubt to the feeling that patients should be involved but also in part to the desire to make the policing of the terms of service more effective. That the reforms can be presented as an advance in the rights of patients is an advantage to government but, if that were a main purpose, it is hard to see why a complainant should not be able to get compensation. Underlying these changes is the desire to make individuals who enter contracts (in this case, to become a NHS GP) honour them.

The Arrangements for Defending Malpractice Actions

As before the 1990 Act, where a medical service is improperly performed, those who perform it (i.e. the practitioners) may be personally liable and the provider of that service, commonly the employer, may be directly and vicariously liable for the acts of its staff. This meant that there could be two heads of liability for the organization which was legally responsible for a hospital, commonly the DHA. These reasons do not apply to the discharge of an authority's own direct statutory duties to provide general medical services to residents of its area: it may have difficulties in showing that this duty has been discharged if it has turned a 'blind eye' to a series of defaults by a particular practitioner.

Now, with the new separation of acquiring and supplying authorities under the provisions for *NHS contracts* described below, the acquiring authority (DHA or fund-holding practice) which placed the *NHS contract* with that provider will have corresponding duties to ensure that the *contract* specifies adequate standards and that the provider is reasonably believed to be able to carry it out. Of course, a patient will not be able to sue on the *contract* itself, mainly because of the terms of section 4(3) of the 1990 Act but partly also because of the doctrine of privity. However, as will be argued, this head of liability (for failure to maintain adequate standards) lies outside contract, although the terms of the arrangement will be relevant in determining the extent of the duty. [. . .]

Of greater novelty, in 1989 the Department of Health issued circular HC(89)34. Under it, health authorities were required to undertake the full cost of the defence of malpractice actions and they were empowered to employ private solicitors. [. . .]

Thirdly, in April 1990 changes were made to the legal aid rules so that children are no longer assessed jointly with their parents. The result is that many more children have become eligible for legal aid and so able to pursue malpractice actions, particularly in respect of injury at birth. [. . .]

The New Reliance on Ministerial and Other Circulars

The increased reliance on circulars is consequent on the new constitutions of health authorities and is symbolized by the removal of their Crown status. Lord Bridge said in *Gillick* v. *West Norfolk AHA*:

> The issue by a department of government with administrative responsibility in a particular field of non-statutory guidance to subordinate authorities operating in the same field is a familiar feature of modern administration . . . . The question whether the advice tendered in such non-statutory guidance is good or bad, reasonable or unreasonable cannot, as a general rule, be subject to any form of judicial review.

The remarks almost seem as if they have been taken from a different age. The health service has long recognized that in respect of many important matters ministers have a choice whether to use a binding statutory instrument (which would be published) or a binding circular (which may not be). Today, non-statutory guidance is not only familiar, it may well be the precursor of directions and resort to the courts. In the course of the debates on the 1990 Act, the government's attitude was explained: 'guidance is stronger than guidelines . . . if an authority did not take note of guidance, the Secretary of State has the power to make directions . . . guidance is expected to be followed. In the absence of it being followed and there being breaches, the Secretary of State can use powers so to direct. [. . .]

The NHS provides yet another layer of difficulty. The central administration of the service is no longer conducted by a minister. It is carried out by the National Health Service Executive. Many circulars are issued by this 'body'. However, unless it exists under an unpublished use of the prerogative, the Executive itself has no statutory or other legal existence. It can have no authority to issue binding guidance. The status of its directives is uncertain. Possibly, its officers have the same authority as civil servants so that they act on behalf of the minister. If not, in the event of a health service body defying its guidance, the Executive would have to ask the Secretary of State to issue directions requiring compliance with its instructions.

NHS Trusts

The legal position of these new institutions is *sui generis*. The *trusts'* financial and other obligations are defined by statute (including the statutory instruments which establish them and, of course, ministerial directions). But these obligations disguise a series of discretions which ministers sometimes call freedoms. On the establishment of a *trust*, it is required to produce a prospectus dealing with its overall aims, its progress in arranging *contracts*, the way in which it will develop its services, the quality that will be assured, its leadership and management arrangements, personnel issues, information systems, finance and estates.

New instruments make it clear that some of these *NHS trusts* will be hospitals; others will supply other services and facilities (a term broad enough to include the supply activities of a district health authority or an ambulance service). [. . .] As with other corporations in the NHS, *NHS trusts* themselves can become trustees. Their capacity to raise extra money for the NHS by way either of the sale of services or of charitable appeals is perhaps their *raison d'être*. Despite the ministerial control, and despite the fact that in some cases they will lack the depth of tradition which attached to the old boards of governors, it would seem that these sources of non-NHS money will provide the motor for them to assert their independence of government, if need be by testing the *vires* of some of the guidance and directions which ministers may seek to impose. If recent experience with local government is anything to go by, we can expect *NHS trusts* to seek to preserve their autonomy against government and also to have their own implied duties tested by relevant local authorities on behalf of their resident populations.

The management of these *trusts* is to be conducted by a 'board of executive and non-executive directors'. The non-executive directors are to be appointed by the minister and the Regional Health Authority (RHA). The executive directors are to be officers of the *trust*. The legal status and responsibilities of *trust* directors are obscure. Almost certainly, *NHS trusts* are not 'trusts' or 'charitable trusts' in the usual legal sense of the words and their directors are not trustees. For this reason, and to avoid the rhetoric implied by the use of the benign word 'trust', they have been called 'NHS Corporations'. But this hardly simplifies things because there are many other corporations lurking in the NHS: the Secretary of State is himself a 'corporation sole', RHAs, DHAs, FHSAs are statutory corporations, and so also are the 14 or so 'special health authorities'. It is, however, reasonable to surmise that the 'directors' will be subjected to similar fiduciary obligations as attach to the members of local authorities so that they will have obligations relating to the need to provide proper management of public funds, and to analogous obligations to those of directors of companies incorporated under the Companies Acts to avoid a conflict of interest.

NHS Contracts and the Internal Market

[. . .] The funding of the health service is altered so that instead of money being given to a district authority in respect of the services it provides, money is now given on the basis of 'residency': DHAs, FHSAs, and 'fund-holding practices' make 'arrangements' with suppliers to provide services to those for whom they have responsibility. This process of public money following the patient is said to establish the internal market. The suppliers of services may be 'directly managed' in the same district, or elsewhere in the NHS or in what is sometimes called 'the private sector', although the wider term 'outside the NHS' is to be preferred (because a considerable part of non-NHS care is offered by charities). Where a district makes such arrangements with a unit which it itself runs, despite the changes in the managerial mechanisms, there can be no change in the legal relationships because no legal entity (except through a legally distinct subsidiary) can contract with itself. Where 'arrangements' are made with suppliers outside the NHS, it is inevitable that they have to be by contract. The *NHS contract* operates in the intermediate zone where one NHS body makes arrangements with another.

It is to be noted that so far individual patients (consumers) are not players in this internal market: it is their district of residency, not they, who are the purchasers. It is a paternalistic sort of market. The stage is set, however, for a further possible change. In the private health insurance and life assurance markets, lifestyle is already relevant. It would not be out of place for the logic of the individual's personal responsibility for his or her own health to be given legal meaning so that the choice of the distribution of public money will be made by the patient not the district authority. The public and private purchasers of health care would become the same. At this point, it would become possible to reduce or phase out the use of public money in individual health care. To an extent this process has already begun with undoubted pressure (via charges for dental and optical tests and hospital waiting lists) for individuals to seek private care.

One of the circulars describing the new system said of arrangements within an authority that they would be 'structured as contracts but enforced through management processes'. It is a source of confusion that members of the NHS Executive include these internal arrangements within their use of the phrase *NHS contract*. However, such *contracts* are defined by section 4(1) of the 1990 Act as 'an arrangement under which one health service body . . . arranges for the provision to it by another health service body . . . of goods or services'. [. . .]

There are also difficulties to be noted concerning the *NHS contract*. First, the usual public law principles developed in relation to local government will apply so that acquiring authorities will have a general fiduciary duty to place *contracts* with the most advantageous provider (who may not necessarily be the cheapest) and they must not have regard to irrelevant considerations. Secondly, section 4(1) of the 1990 Act says that it is an arrangement under which an acquiring health service body arranges for the provision to it 'of goods or services which it reasonably requires for the purposes of its functions'. That is, an arrangement is not an *NHS contract* if the acquirer did not *reasonably* require the goods or services. If the goods or services were not reasonably required, the arrangement cannot be an *NHS contract* and the rest of the section making provision for such *contracts* does not apply. It is not difficult to imagine situations where goods or services may not be reasonably required but nevertheless their acquisition may not be *ultra vires* the corporation. Suppose an NHS body decided to acquire more goods than it reasonably needed for a particular year in order to dispose of a cash surplus (for example, to prevent it committing itself to recurrent expenditure or to guard against projected price rises or to be able to sell them out of a dominant market position). It is perhaps important that these last may be caught by European Community competition rules, and their application may itself depend on whether the arrangement was enforceable as a contract, that is, was not *reasonably required* so as to prevent it becoming an *NHS contract*. [. . .]

The white paper, the government's notes on clauses, and expressions of ministerial intent indicated that section 4(3) was intended to prevent *NHS contracts* being the subject of litigation. The problem that was not faced is whether the words are technically sufficient to achieve that purpose. But, initially, a more important point needs to be made. The autonomous *NHS contract* is not fundamental to the scheme of the 1990 Act. Rather, the Act's purpose here is to subject the NHS to a market discipline. The purported autonomy of the *contract* merely serves to aid the political acceptance of the idea. The terms of section 4 need to be read not so much as timeless law, but as a device to facilitate the shift of public and administrative attitudes from reliance on bureaucratic machinery to that of the market. If later litigation

opens the section to review by the courts, that will not matter – partly because litigation is the hallmark of a market and partly because if the courts
do intervene it will be seen as the action of an independent agency. The
loss of powers the government does not want will not be seen to be its fault.

[. . .] There are six reasons why it is doubtful if the intention that *NHS
contracts* will not be litigated has been adequately expressed. It is necessary
to take some time to consider them.

First, as already noted, the acquiring authority has a duty to the residents for whom it is responsible to ensure that it makes adequate arrangements with a supplier and it is these residents who may therefore be able to
sue, not on the arrangement, but because the arrangement is not adequate.
There need be no enforceable duty on the authority of residence to make
the arrangements for this head of liability to arise: it is sufficient that in
doing so it has failed to make prospectively reasonable arrangements. On
this basis, there is no need to postulate [. . .] that the doctrine of 'legitimate expectation' may be applied to *NHS contracts* in order to give consumers access to the courts concerning the definition of the quality of
services. Consumers (patients is a better word) would only need the extra
scope of that doctrine in order to complain that no arrangement had been
made.

Secondly, assuming that the statutory scheme works as intended, it
seems likely that determinations of the Secretary of State will be subject to
judicial review under RSC, Ord. 53 so that all the matters which could have
been argued had the action lain in contract can be brought to the court.
This view is based on the supposition that these arrangements between
NHS bodies are impressed with a public character concerning the discharge
of statutory duties. If, *per contra*, the court regards these arrangements between independent autonomous corporations (and, in the case of fund-
holding practices, partnerships) as private, an action for a declaration
under RSC, Ord. 15(16) will lie.

Thirdly, subsections (6) and (7) of section 4 provide that 'it shall be the
duty of the parties' to comply with any directions given as a result of arbitration proceedings under the section. It would seem odd that a *duty*
should arise only after such proceedings, because normally arbitration *determines* what rights and liabilities the parties had: it only *creates* them in
the sense of building on that foundation. Here, if rights are not created by
the arrangement, the arbitration has nothing to build on: it has to be regarded as yet another *sui generis* creation of the Act.

Fourthly, the departmental guidance as to the content of these *NHS contracts* in effect insists that the only difference between them and an arrangement enforceable as a contract is that both parties are health service
bodies: an identical arrangement with a non-health-service body, e.g. a
private hospital, is an ordinary contract. The language of the Act and the
language of the guidance is of commerce, albeit between parties who
expect long-term relationships and thus the emphasis is on arbitration
rather than litigation. But quality and standards are to be defined in the

arrangement, cross-subsidies between one *contract* and another are to be discouraged, and the accounts within each year must be balanced.

Fifthly, the provision that 'an arrangement' shall not be regarded for any purpose as giving rise to contractual rights and liabilities does nothing to prevent those rights and liabilities which arise outside contract (if any) from being sued upon. It is at this point that one begins to think there may be a major error of law. Put simply, one cannot say that, in the absence of a legally enforceable contract, there is no need to pay for goods or services which were both requested and have been supplied or performed. [. . .]

Related to this action [. . .] it appears likely that the section mistakes the legal nature of the obligation assumed by authorities (and practitioners) within orthodox medicine. That obligation rests, without more, on the fact of their occupation and the extent of their undertaking, regardless of whether there is a contract. [. . .] There seems no reason why, merely because the *content* of the obligation of health authorities is defined by an arrangement (under whatever name) or regulations made under statute, the *basis* of the obligation should be altered.

The difficulty that the draftsman has got into lies in supposing that common law obligations lie either in contract or in tort with nothing in between. Speaking generally, the failure by doctors and hospitals to perform their undertakings creates a liability which cannot be in contract with its insistence on express agreement between parties. Nor can it be in the legal idea of *negligence* with its dependence on foreseeability. Neither concept permits the legal consequences ascribed by the courts to malpractice actions.

As to contract, in the pre-health service days, a general practitioner no doubt owed contractual duties to the paying member of a family. The doctor's failure to give proper treatment was, however, also actionable at the suit of the injured patient – with consequences attached in terms of the proper party to the suit and the measure of damages. In such cases the courts were not interested in the doctrines of privity of contract or consideration. This is contrary to the general rule that a third party cannot sue in tort for breach of a contract between two parties. [. . .]

In medicine, there is scarcely an act or an abstention from action that does not carry risks foreseeable by the profession; that is, most of the time cure and injury are both foreseen. But in the malpractice action, foresight is rarely the issue. In such actions, the questions are 'was the act justifiable in relation to its purpose, to other values, and to the alternatives?' and 'was the exercise of discretion (the judgement) reasonable in all the circumstances?' Crucially, in negligence theory there is no room for 'error of discretion'. The insistence on neglect prevents any meaning being given to the expression 'gross negligence' (a mistake of the sort that is not encompassed within the bounds of acceptable error of discretion) because as a specific tort negligence requires no epithet: there cannot be degrees of inadvertence. On the other hand, to refuse to use the epithet in issues of vocational liability invites a disregard for the idea of the forgivable mistake. It is somewhat difficult to speak of 'errors being made with all proper care'.

If then, we cannot use either contract or negligence theory to describe the malpractice action, what of the middle course? [. . .] The source of this action against an individual practitioner may be called 'situation liability'. It arises out of the public interest in the occupation and the assumption of the occupation by the practitioner or the institution. [. . .]

On this basis, the liability for failure to perform an *NHS contract* is not a contractual liability (which s.4(3) of the 1990 Act would have excluded) but a liability arising out of the situation determined by the undertaking (which the subsection does not exclude). This basis in all material respects renders the practice of medicine a 'common calling'. It may seem somewhat strange today that an occupation which is so dependent on high technology should be subjected to a legal regime which, if it is noticed at all, is regarded as archaic. The strangeness [. . .] is itself not new: it puzzled the authors of the major text for practitioners in the middle of the last century, and is caused by seeking to impress on the common law a classification system which has no relevance to it and which was created after the nature of common law liability had been established. The peculiar legal regime of the common calling implies a series of obligations which themselves cannot be excluded by agreement. It is not applicable to any occupation: it applies only to those services with some special public interest where a purchaser somehow has to trust a supplier. It applies at common law a policy now largely reflected in the Consumer Protection Act 1987.

The voluntary undertaking is necessary to this situation liability. The duty which arises out of the defendant doctor's situation is not infused with generalized considerations of foreseeability. It arises because the defendant has undertaken to care for patients who present themselves. The content of the duty is defined by this undertaking. Accordingly, where a person is possessed of skills and has undertaken to use them, his or her intention, as defined by the expectations that other practitioners would have as well as the terms of any arrangement (so long as they are not regarded as unacceptable by these others), is crucial to the determination of the standard of care. This view by way of modern legal principle underlines the idea that the distinction between contract and tort was never very successful or very important. In the medical malpractice action, the acceptance of the situation by the defendant is the necessary precondition of liability and the standards of care to be applied are those determined by the general expectation of his or her peers.

It is precisely the separate base of malpractice liability that section 4(3) ignores: there is no reason to suppose that the obligations of a supplying health authority are any different from the obligations of any other supplier of medical care. *NHS contracts* are to become the cornerstone of the market in medical care. The attempt by the subsection to make them unenforceable was an attempt to make this market internal. It can be conceded that it is not clear whether the action on the *arrangement* will lie in public or private law; but this lack of clarity reflects the difficulties of that distinction. The doubt does not affect the justiciability of the *arrangement*. The internal market may be the dream of the politician and the administrator: the law cannot recognize it. In the eyes of the law, this 'internal market' becomes a contradiction in terms because it is a market based on a cash nexus in which choices are made whether to spend within or outside the NHS and which implies access to the courts.

Conclusion

Each of the changes considered in this chapter is a manifestation of a consistent (that is, not self-contradictory) political approach – one which is used in other fields, such as education and, increasingly, social services. They constitute a reliance on autonomous management units (in health care, *NHS trusts* and fund-holding practices) largely market driven (via contract and the *NHS contract* but elsewhere by competitive tendering) with control exercised in three ways: by ministerial guidance enforceable by direction through the courts; by concepts of audit; and by preference of individual claims against professional power (manifested in health care by the greater chance of succeeding in a malpractice action and the new procedural ease accorded to hearing allegations of abuse in general practice, but elsewhere by other changes directed against professional domination). Together, they provide an illustrative essay on the adaptation of the machinery of government. Given the intended use of the ministerial discretion, the whole represents an attempt to use the invisible hand of the market instead of what in places was the bureaucrat's benign anonymity and in others the professional's paternalism. The invisible hand is to replace mechanisms which permitted and even required the expression of humane values. Previously medicine had no purpose except to combat suffering: now it is a product to be valued to the extent of its profitability. But then, so are the results of other vocations. The invisible hand is itself dependent on the imposition of choice. We can no longer accept our lot; we are to choose it, and in that we have no choice; we are not allowed to abstain, for even abstention is choice. These forced decisions compel us to consider our position and our wants and to think of ourselves instead of our place in our world. Our social being is fragmented by this raising of consciousness of self. Choice and the insistence on a private domain, it may be said, sever bonding.

Reflecting the needs of our times, academic lawyers commonly make a distinction between public and private law. It is artificial (that is, does not reflect a distinction drawn by the courts) and hardly ever helpful. Despite the obvious fact that all law in the courts is literally public, it is a necessary strategy to maintain a 'private domain'. It is not to be a matter of looking at the same thing in different ways or at different times. There has to be belief that the public and the private are separate. Only with a 'private' can there be autonomous individuals, and only these can have choice. To conceive of individuals, who are varyingly dependent on their society's collectivity and their own and each other's individuality, *choosing* is to accept great complexity. It is also the world of our reality. The simplicity of the choiceful private individual satisfies what some call our reason but not our experience: 'There is more to us than us.'

In 1979 Daintith drew attention to what he called 'The New Prerogative', but the mechanisms described in this chapter are at once more simple and more subtle. Daintith argued:

> government has discovered means of using its increasing economic strength vis-a-vis private industry so as to promote certain policies [mainly incomes policy] in a style, and with results, which for a long time we have assumed must be the hallmark of Parliamentary legislation: that is to say, officially promulgated rules backed by effective general compulsion. This means the power to rule without parliamentary consent, which is the hallmark of prerogative.[5]

The modern mechanisms now exemplified in health care are more simple because, once they have been created, tension in the public domain is diffused: all becomes subjected to the 'private' and government is absolved from responsibility. The fundamental issues are [. . .] of the change of the system. Responsibility is passed to institutions, not just doing government's bidding, but also in competition with each other. As regards individuals, when they do not like what they get, they have it in their own hand to complain, not as previously about government, but about the defaulting supplier. Unresolved discontents and complaints are to be seen by suppliers and consumers, in the case of institutions, as a result of their own management weaknesses and, in the case of individuals, as a result of their failure to defend their interests. The government's concern is merely to provide the 'level playing field' by way of either using its rule-making powers to control these transactions or establishing new agencies. The most important example of the creation of this 'level playing field' is the imposition of the so-called capital charges scheme under which in order to balance the accounts in each year, each health service unit is to be required to allow at least 6 per cent of the current (not historic) value of all its assets as part of its notional expenditure. By such devices, government claims to be removed from accountability for what happens during the 'game'. It is in this sense that the health service is to be privatized, to the exclusion of the traditional concerns of 'public lawyers': there is no accountability to public institutions because the world is deemed private. [. . .]

But, *per contra*, unthinkable as it may be to those with different values, there is nothing that government has done that precludes the consequences of commercial risk, that is, the liquidation and asset-stripping of hospitals and other health service units. In a competitive environment, it is economic, psychological and semantic illiteracy to suggest that everyone can be successful. Where there are winners, there must be losers.

The new mechanisms of government illustrated in the health service are more subtle than those identified by Daintith because 'the only way to influence lasting change . . . is by influencing the conditions that determine the interpretation of situations and regulation of ideas'.[6] The new machinery is intended to change the conditions for debate (for deciding, for living) in a way that Daintith's 'New Prerogative' was not. This chapter has argued that the legal effectiveness of some of them is not what it seems. Important as this is, it is beside the central point: there is no reason to think that government will be unduly dismayed if the prediction in this chapter (that there will be an increase in the activities of lawyers and their allies) is fulfilled. It may even be taken as a sign of the success in altering the conditions of debate. The fact that the language of business seems so natural is a reflection, not of its truth, but of its effectiveness in reformulating ideas. If we want to know how to change the basis of debate so as to permit other values (including not least personal self-fulfilment) to be recognized we need, in a word, to 'unscramble' these new mechanisms: to re-establish trust in place of claims to objectified fact as the fundamental organizing thought. In the new world of these verities, major institutional and personal resources are committed to planning inputs, recording results and justifying outcomes. Hopwood once remarked: 'The facts, accounts and economic statistics to which policy appeals are made seem to be increasingly seen as moveable and manageable phenomena . . . . Apparently the facts are not the facts.[7] Aided by the new governmental mechanisms, there is a conspiracy of the calculating professions to maintain a faith in the fixity of facts they know to be fluid: accountants in the valuations and forecasts of their balance sheets; doctors in attributing significance to selected symptoms and in giving numerical probabilities to prognosis; lawyers in marshalling persuasive evidence and calling it the 'facts' and in formulating a rule and describing it as the 'relevant' rule; managers in setting goals and judging outcomes dependent on all these uncertainties.

The problem of quantification in place of judgement of quality is not confined to the NHS. It is one of the central questions of our era. Instead of relying on the frailty of the decisions of an elite, it substitutes apparently detached facts or criteria. It is a problem because, in this substitution, decision-makers are compelled to disregard any factor not susceptible to measurement. The question for those whose intuition reacts against the rhetoric and the deception of the objectified fact, against the substitution of judgement by criteria, against the reduction of individuals into cyphers, is how to delimit measurement so that it does not interfere with the achievement of non-quantifiable ambitions. After all, it was never true that there is no alternative, but it requires not an article nor a book but a programme to get to it.

Notes

1 This chapter refers to the changes made in England and Wales. There are corresponding reforms in Scotland. References to the new *NHS trusts* and *NHS contracts* have been kept

throughout in italics to distinguish them from the words 'trust'and 'contract' in their ordinary meanings.

2 Baroness Hooper, 21 March 1991. DoH Press Release H91/128, emphasis added. EC Health Ministers have designated 1994 as 'European Year of Nutrition'.

3 B. McSweeney (1988) 'Accounting for the Audit Commission', *Political Quarterly*, 59: 28, 30 . He cited A. G. Hopwood, 'Accounting and the pursuit of efficiency', in A. G. Hopwood and C. Tomkins (eds), *Issues in Public Sector Accounting* (1984), p. 173.

4 Ibid., 36–7. And see N. Flynn, 'Performance measurement in public sector services' (1986) *Policy and Politics*, 14: 389.

5 T. Daintith (1979) 'Regulation by contract: the new prerogative', 32 C.L.P. 41. And see also V. Korah (1976) 'Counter-inflation legislation: whither parliamentary sovereignty?' *LQR*, 92: 42.

6 R. Norman (1977) *Management for Growth*, cited in McSweeney ['Accounting for the Audit Commission' (1988) 59 *Political Quarterly*], at p. 42.

7 A. G. Hopwood (1985) 'Accounting and the domain of the public: some observations on current developments, in *Price Waterhouse Public Lecture on Accounting*. Leeds: University of Leeds.

10

Accounting and the Pursuit of Efficiency

Anthony Hopwood

> Every society keeps the records most relevant for its major values.
> (Lazarsfeld, 1959: 108)

Accounting for the public sector has become a major issue for both discussion and action. In the last few years both the language and the practices of accounting have entered much more frequently and forcefully into debates about the efficiency, accountability and even scope of public sector activities. Appeals are now being made to the apparent inefficiency, lack of cost-effectiveness, unprofitability and waste associated with the public sector. Referring to the existing economic calculus, it is being said that we are now 'living beyond our means', supporting that which is not 'economically viable', and either unable or unwilling to face 'the facts of economic reality'. Although there is a long history of investing in accounting mechanisms for recording, planning, controlling and making visible public sector activities, within a very short period of time indeed recent pressures for change have succeeded in challenging the adequacy of existing public accounts and management accounting practices. New demands are now being made for the practices of accounting to become even more implicated in public sector management.

Where have these pressures for change come from? What form do they take? And what are their implications? How, in other words, can we not only better understand the forces at work but also attempt to gain a more adequate appreciation of their consequences for both the technical practice of accounting and the conduct of business within the public sector?

Before focusing on these questions, however, it is useful to consider some of the ways in which existing accounting practices have become intertwined with quite substantive issues of public policy. For, like today, much of the power of the public accountings of the past derived from their ability to move beyond merely facilitating the operation of pre-given and relatively unproblematic forms of economic and financial management. Accounting has already been implicated in a more positive shaping and influencing of that which is regarded as problematic, the forms which public debates take and the options seemingly available for management and public action.

From A. G. Hopwood and C. Tomkins (eds), *Issues in Public Sector Accounting*, Philip Allen, 1984, pp. 167–87 (abridged).

Accounting and Public Policy

Accounting records provide a way of freezing the decisions of the past
(Bahmueller, 1981: 193). What was problematic and debated can become
lost within the accounting archive. 'Facts' can thereby be created out of
dissent and disagreement. An aura of the obvious and the unchallengeable
can and does emerge out of the residues of past actions which accounting
presents.

The significance of the ability of accounting to forge a domain of the
factual in this way can be seen in the patterns of both relative and absolute
performance of many public sector bodies. Past subsidies, allowances and
provisions, decisions on transfer prices and payments, and the specific
means used for their financing, play a significant role now in determining
where current costs are incurred, continuing subsidies required and profits
and losses both generated and shown. The relationships between past
policies in the areas of defence, industrial development and regional
support, all have current impacts of this type. Examples abound in the
interplay of taxation, economic and social policies. For the National Coal
Board, British Rail, London Transport and the Central Electricity Generating Board the patterns of present financial performance emerge out of a
complex array of decisions of a social and political, as well as purely
economic, nature. But those decisions give rise to accounting residues which
can be and are used independently of the contexts out of which they
emerged. Being 'profitable' or 'unprofitable', 'subsidized' or 'a drain on the
Exchequer', can have a powerful contemporary significance. In this way
accounting seems to provide a means of judiciously selecting the time-scale
for comment and debate. The compelling obviousness of the present can
overwhelm the contingencies of the past.

The fact that accounting, as we know it, provides a partial record of
organizational choices and actions has also been of enormous importance.
Organizational accounts both reflect and, in turn, influence the emphases
that are given in public debates. Consequently, the economic has undoubtedly been made more visible than the social and the political, in many
spheres of public life. Now, however, the imperatives of those economic
'facts' can be contrasted with the more questionable dictates of political
ideology and•social preference, illustrating, in the process, the powerful
influence that the recording tools of the public domain can have. [. . .]

Accounting has also become implicated in the development of the
institutional structures and linkages which today characterize the public
sector. Particular forms of accounts have been used to buffer certain
organizations from the dictates of government policy and intervention.
'Losses', for instance, have served as a pretext for price increases which have
provided subsequent investment autonomy, sometimes on a very large
scale; profits, similarly, have been used as evidence of both the granting of
greater autonomy and its positive achievements. More frequently, accountings have served to tighten the relationships between different parts of the

public sector. They have been used as a means of restraint; to constrain expenditures, actions and policies. The selective visibility created by organizational accountings has served to further the salience of imposed patterns of standardization and uniformity. The information which they produce is used to monitor and evaluate the actions of others, and more frequent plans, budgets and reports can facilitate centralized control at the expense of local discretion.

All told, accounting is already centrally implicated in the institutional frameworks, language and patterns of power and influence that characterize the public sector. As a means of collecting and reporting selective patterns of information it has played a not insignificant role in the construction of public organizations and policies as we now know them. There are, however, yet further pressures for public sector accounting not only to change but also to expand its sphere of influence.

Pressures for Public Sector Accounting to Change

The pressures for the expansion and reform of public sector accounting are numerous, diverse and even conflicting in nature. Moreover, the emphasis given to particular factors can change remarkably over time, as recent decades have illustrated. In what follows, an attempt is made to outline only some of the main forces at work in recent debates in the area.

Changing Conceptions of the State

One of the major factors behind the current interest in public sector accounting is the changing view of the state that has entered political discourse in recent times. The legitimacy and value of at least some state actions and prerogatives are now being questioned from the perspective of a very different ideological stance. Indeed, a new way of examining and managing the state is emerging, and accounting is being implicated in that process.

Agencies of the state are now being asked to account for their aims, actions and achievements. Many more of their activities are coming to be seen in quite explicit economic terms. Cost and efficiency rather than effectiveness are being highlighted and debated. Information on economic consequences is being demanded. 'Value for money' has now entered the vocabulary of government.

[. . .] Economic calculations are now being seen as a way not only of reforming the management of the state but also of influencing the priorities which are given in policy determination and decision-making. Accounting is quite explicitly becoming implicated in the construction of different views of the problematic, the desirable and the possible.

Accounting and Economic Restraint

Organizations tend to increase their investment in economic calculation and visibility during periods of restraint. In what has become known as 'newly poor behaviour' (Olofsson and Svalander, 1975), the constrained organiz- ation places a renewed emphasis on costs, financial information and the calculus of economic decision-making. Mechanisms for enhancing economic visibility extend further into the organization. Financial standards, budgets and plans become both more detailed and more subject to change. The organization overall becomes more economically orientated, more influ- enced by economic calculation and, somewhat paradoxically (given that very frequently the economic difficulties emanate from without rather than from within), more orientated towards the seeming dictates of its own internal economic circumstances rather than the pressures of the world at large. [. . .]

During periods of economic difficulty, accounting and accountants have consistently expanded their sphere of influence in the UK. However, the relatively large British investment in the profession remains quite localized in its influence, having, until recently, much less of a presence in the service, financial and governmental sectors than in the area of manufacturing industry. Now, it seems, the current recession is providing a pretext for that to change, at least for the public sector. As the economic receives more emphasis in government, and as economic decision-making itself becomes more constrained, more and more demands are being made for the type of economic calculations that accounting provides.

The Search for Greater Efficiency

Continued economic restraint has given a new urgency to demands to improve the efficiency of management in the public sector. More and more accusations of waste, maladministration and inefficiency have been made. High staffing levels have been pointed out. The traditionalism and sluggishness of decision processes in the public sector is noted repeatedly. Although it is sometimes realized that the demands of public accountability and decision-making in a political context can serve to limit the extent to which concepts of efficiency derived from the private sector can be applied uncritically in the public domain, there nevertheless remains a feeling that much could be done to improve resource utilization. Efficiency remains a very real and persuasive dream.

To this end, there is a renewed interest in importing into the public sector management practices developed in the private sector. Reference is made to the valuable roles that might be served by more adequate instruments for management planning and control. Appeals are made to the potential offered by improved costing procedures, more specific criteria for resource allocation, improved management information systems, investigations of administrative efficiency and better audits (which compare actual accomplishments with both original intentions and experience elsewhere). Such improved management practices, including those related to accounting itself, are seen as being able to assist in locating the inefficiencies of the past and ensuring that better performance is achieved in the future, not least by making public sector management and employees accountable for their actions and decisions.

Accounting and the Demand for Accountability

Appeals to the concept of accountability pervade many discussions concerned with the advance of accounting practice in the public sector. Accounting is seen as a way of both making visible and disciplining performance so that accountability can be demanded, policed and enforced.

A major impetus to the development of financial accounting in the private sector occurred when a separate cadre of managers came to be recognized as being accountable for their actions and performance to shareholders, the legally recognized owners of business. Since then, periodic crises of confidence have resulted: first, in more and more elaborate and detailed accountings of both organizational aims and achievements being demanded; and second, in the supply of such accountings by managers who have tried to maintain respect for their ability to manage the assets of others. Equally, in the public sector, accounting has been implicated with the development of notions of stewardship and accountability. Accounting information has flowed from agencies of the state to parliament and the public at large in recognition of the emerging constitutional requirement for the former to provide an account to the latter.

In the 1960s and early 1970s there were, in many Western countries, quite major pressures to expand the concept of accountability. In the name of social performance, environmental impact and the quality of working life, attempts were made to redefine the basis of organizational accountability to include aspects of performance broader than the purely economic. Related efforts were orientated towards expanding the information provided by the organization in order to enable assessments to be made of its performance in new areas of concern. Notions of social, environmental and energy accounting and auditing were discussed and experimented upon. In the public sphere not unrelated developments were under way. Wider audiences started to demand the right to question the actions of the state. Not only was the state increasingly being asked to account for its actions and achievements, but greater demands were also being made for the right to assess public information, attend public meetings and more generally observe and interrogate the machinery of the state so that others might construct their own accounts of its performance. Concepts such as 'freedom of information' and 'the right to information' started to enter the language of political negotiation and debate.

However, in retrospect, it is interesting to note that most of these developments were much less significant in the UK than elsewhere. [In the UK] they did not result in any appreciable questioning of, let alone change in, concepts of either accountability or accounting. Ideas of wider accountings of the social remained peripheral to UK concerns. Nor was the traditional secrecy of the state effectively challenged in the name of wider rights to public information. Accounting maintained its emphasis on the economic, and disclosure, rather than access, remained the vehicle by which information flowed. The reasons for this relative lack of debate and change in the UK are little understood. However, it is possible to point to the continual dominance of the economic over the social in the UK, the emphasis that all sides of the political spectrum have put on the primacy of the ownership of assets (be they in private or public hands), rather than on other strategies for regulating their deployment and use, and the long history of constraints on the dissemination of information which still pervade our legal, administrative and constitutional systems.

From such a perspective perhaps we should not be surprised that recent discussions of the advance of public sector accounting in the UK continue to emphasize the narrowly economic. Efficiency and value for money, rather than effectiveness, are the focuses of attention. Equally, we can note how little attention continues to be given to strategies for the wider dissemination and use of information, accounting or otherwise. Although demands for more accounting are still permeated with the rhetoric of accountability, the latter continues to have quite a constrained meaning. Indeed, many recent discussions appear to emphasize the role that accounting can serve in advancing accountability within the machinery of the state, rather than between it and the public at large. Administrative rather than public accountability appears to be the problem at issue.

[. . .] Accounting is explicitly implicated in the development of quite strategic interests and concerns. Rather than emanating from the specifics of particular accountings, deficient or otherwise, current pressures for change have stemmed from views of the role which the particular might play in mobilizing more general strategic arguments.

However, such strategic interests in accounting are now attempting to grapple with questions of the particular and the specific. A rhetoric of economy, efficiency and value for money is now being used to call for a detailed concern with the specific accounting innovations that can service these wider ends.

The direction of change, from the general to the specific, has important implications for those interested in understanding and directing the practical process of accounting reform in the public sector. The generality, and indeed ambiguity, of notions such as efficiency and value for money must be recognized. For, although the ideas appeal to the comparison of inputs and outputs, and financial resources with their consequences, the delineation of those inputs, outputs, resources and consequences remains both a practically and conceptually difficult endeavour, not least in organizations which are complex, have little tradition of financial administration and economic record-keeping, and where outputs and consequences repeatedly arise in organizations different from those initiating the developments. In fact, very little is known about not only the practice of the new public accountings but also the wider impacts which might stem from such an intensification of economic visibility in the public domain. To date, accountings for efficiency and value for money have been advanced in the name of their presumed potential rather than their practical possibility or actual consequences.

On Examining the Practices of Accounting

In order to facilitate an examination of the practical consequences of public sector accounting developments, we now consider some of the ways of examining and questioning proposals for such accounting changes. Attention is directed towards the technical practices of accounting themselves, the ways in which they are embedded in organizations, and the wider issues to which extensions of accounting give prominence and significance.

Accounting as Technique

Given the ambiguity which pervades such notions as 'efficiency' and 'value for money' when used in public debate, it is always important to analyse proposals for the practical assessment of these concerns carefully and precisely. Only rarely can it be presumed that there will be a direct and unproblematic relationship between the issues of concern and their measurement in practice. More frequently, there will be a gap between the policies which mobilized interest and the specific accounting practices that result from them. Accounting, in practice, invariably requires a specification of detail and a reliance on other organizational practices and procedures that make the final assessments arrived at only partially dependent on the initial interest in them. When subsequently taken up and used in decision-making and policy formulation, practical accountings can, and do, have the potential to result in consequences very different from those originally envisaged for them.

Discretion often exists as to what inputs are deemed to be relevant, the costs that are assigned to the resources used, the outputs that are seen to flow from them, and their assessment in both financial and other terms. Issues of organizational interdependency will invariably arise, questions of presumed patterns of causal relationships will need to be debated, and proposals for specific valuations, weightings and assignments of priority will rarely be straightforward and unproblematic. Indeed, the difficulties of accounting in practice are such that it is often easy to arrive at a whole array of costs, efficiencies and value-for-money assessments. Many of these never see the light of day, however. Some are buried as a result of seemingly technical accounting choices; others fail to be recognized because of the dominance of particular organizational emphases and favoured theories of the determination of outcomes and consequences; and still others never emerge from internal discussions of 'the message to be presented'. [. . .]

Accounting and the Process of Organizing

Accounting has the potential to have organizational consequences beyond merely facilitating, in a technical manner, the processes of decision-making and policy formulation. By making visible what was previously unknown, it can open up different areas of the organization for examination and debate. That visibility can also transcend different levels of the organizational hierarchy. What is accounted for can thereby shape the patterns of power and influence both within the organization and without. Those with the power to determine what enters into the organizational accounts have the means to articulate and diffuse their values and concerns, and subsequently to monitor, observe and regulate the actions of those that are now accounted for. An expanded flow of information on organizational resources, capabilities and achievements can enable the monitoring, control and planning of organizational actions to be more readily abstracted from their execution. Management, in other words, can become more centralized. New linkages can be drawn both within and between organizations. Different and more abstract criteria can be used for resource allocation. And opportunities can be created for new specialists to enter into the processes of decision-making and policy formulation. [. . .]

Accounting and the Creation of the Significant

The selective visibility which accounting gives to organizational actions and outcomes can play an important role in influencing what comes to be seen as problematic, possible, desirable and significant. Neither organizational participants, nor interested parties outside, can ever know the whole extent of organizational life. Direct observation can play a vital role in determining what is seen and valued. However, in organizational hierarchies and in those circumstances where geographical distance and organizational boundaries restrict what is directly visible, observation is soon supplemented and often superseded by that which is recorded. 'Information', both accounting and otherwise, then comes to play a significant role in determining what is known of the organization and what is expected of it.

In such circumstances, those who influence what enters into the organizational accounts have a powerful and influential role. Some organizational disturbances are more likely to be seen as problematic than others. Some organizational options for change will be able to appeal more readily to supportive information and facts than others. Some criteria for the evaluation of change will likewise find it easier to relate to the partial mappings of the organization that are incorporated into the accounting system. In these and other ways, not only can the emphasis given to different aspects of the organization be changed, but also different values can more readily enter into decision processes, and appeals can be made to different legitimacies for action. The economic, for instance, can be given more attention than the social. The internal workings of the organization can be emphasized rather than its external context. The immediate can be given priority rather than the longer term. Accounting, by shaping the realm of the visible, can have a major impact on the significance that is attached to both organizational life as it is and the directions of change which are considered desirable. Both the organizational landscapes of the present and the future are in part, at least, a creation of the accountings that are given of them.

A very conscious attempt has been made to emphasize the need to interrogate and understand proposals for accounting change in terms different and wider than those in which they are usually presented. The ambiguity and generality of the accounting desirable needs to be confronted by an insight into the specificity of actual accounting practice. This needs to be done in terms of its precise operationalization, the impacts that it has on organizational functioning and the emphasis that it creates in discussions and debates. Just as accounting is called upon to serve more than the merely technical, so it needs to be evaluated in commensurate terms.

Accounting for Accounting

It is possible to examine developments in public sector accounting on numerous grounds and from a variety of different perspectives. In the discussion which follows, emphasis will be placed on just a few axes for questioning which, nevertheless, raise issues of quite widespread significance. Stemming from an appreciation of how the technical practice of accounting intermingles with the fabric of political and organizational life, the aim is to identify some issues which are worthy of consideration by a much wider audience than they attract at present.

Accounting, Technical Practice and the Realm of Politics

Accounting has the potential to create 'facts' out of the uncertain world of the past and even, in a planning context, the future. What was, and still is, debated and challenged can give rise to a residue of accounting calculations of what is costly, beneficial and of value. A world of the seemingly precise, specific and quantitative can, in this way, emerge out of that of the contentious and the uncertain.

A calculative priority can be given to the economic rather than the social. Costs, consequences and benefits can come to be divided into the defined and known, and the imprecise and intangible. In such ways accounting can create very different maps of organizational and social functioning. Particular emphases are given. Only certain chains of reaction are made visible. Only some consequences of actions enter into the world of the precise, the known and even the knowable. In part, at least, what comes to be known of organizational reality starts to be created by the accountings of it. A different view of what is central, and what is residual and peripheral, can start to be reinforced by the ways in which the calculations of accounting intertwine with the complex functionings of organizations as we know them.

Such changes in the visible are accompanied by other changes in organizational life. Expertise in the creation of particular organizational realities starts to emerge and be rewarded. Different legitimacies can come to be attached to arguments and viewpoints, depending on the extent to which they appeal to the domain of the newly factual. Quite specific calculative procedures for decision-making and resource allocation can come to be used in contexts where underlying disagreements remain.

Accounting, in other words, can become implicated in the creation of a domain where technical expertise can come to dominate political debate. By appealing to the centrality of the newly visible, be it the economic or whatever, an imperative for technical action can more readily be justified. What were previously seen to be problems of political priority can now start to be seen as requiring management guidance and expertise. We must now face the facts of the newly emerged reality. Rather than debating and arguing, we must appeal to those with expertise in the technical. Politics must stay at the door of public organizations. Within them, so it is said, planning, decision-making, resource allocation and the evaluation of performance must come to be seen in management terms. The emerging domain of the technically factual and necessary must be given priority over the domain of the political.

Such attempts to restructure the sphere of legitimate political debate and action have profound consequences for the nature of the society in which we live. Is it necessary, one wonders, for politics to be thus confronted by the domain of the technical? From what political strategies does this itself emerge? And what are the wider consequences for political and social life? Just what might be at stake in such a juxtaposition of the rhetoric of efficiency with that of democracy? Is it really necessary, one wonders, for the enhancement of the legitimacy of the technical to be gained at the expense of the legitimacy of politics?

Of course, not all changes in public sector accounting raise such fundamental questions. Indeed, accounting itself can be used to mobilize political arguments and debates. The ambiguity of technical accounting practice is such that it often has an uncertain relationship to political practice. Nevertheless, both some specific proposals for accounting change and the general emphasis which together they place on the managerial and the economic, suggest that, at times, accounting developments do need to be seen in such wider terms. Although often masked by the language of the technical and the procedural, accountings can have quite profound consequences in the political sphere.

Accounting, Organizational Visibility and the Centralization of Authority

Accounting can also become implicated in the creation of very different patterns of organizational influence and control. The selective patterns of visibility which it creates can enable the local to become known to the centre. Institutional boundaries can be made less opaque. Different patterns of local behaviour can come to be seen, compared and more readily labelled as conforming to, or deviating from, the dictates of the centre. Equally, the preferences of the centre can more easily become known to the local. Procedures for planning, budgeting and performance assessment can serve to both disseminate and make real the demands of the centre. Constraints on local behaviour can be imposed on the basis of the calculative visibility created by accounting systems. Specific behaviours can be monitored and more readily restrained. The local can, in this way, come to be managed as a part of the centre. Organizational interrelationships can become tighter. Discretion can more readily be specified and monitored. Indeed, the local can start to enter into the plans, policies and strategies of the centre so that the meaning of the distinction between the local and the centre can be radically changed.

Yet again, accounting can become implicated in the attainment of a set of consequences which extend far beyond the merely technical. Questions, therefore, can be, and perhaps should be, asked of the organizational and wider consequences of accounting developments.

Just who is made visible to whom? Are the patterns of visibility symmetrical or otherwise? Can only the centre observe the local? Or can the local also observe the centre? Equally, what emphasis is placed on the forging of a visibility within the system of public administration, as compared with the creation of an external account? In other words, just what concepts of accountability (as distinct from accounting) are implicated in the process of accounting change?

Accounting and the Enhancement of Organizational Legitimacy

Accounting can also provide quite a direct basis for enhancing organizational legitimacy. Investments in rational organizational accounts and
technical management procedures can be used to demonstrate to others that
the organization accepts the legitimacy of economic and technical bases for
action and is seeking to further these ends. Accounts, plans, budgets and the
practices of efficient management then become symbols of the organization's commitment to efficiency both as an aim and a particular strategy of
rational governance and management.

The manifestation of such accounting symbols need not result in their
coupling to organizational action, however (Meyer, 1979; Meyer and
Rowan, 1977). The display of the rational accounts may be orientated to
those who ask questions of the organization and seek to probe into its affairs
from without, rather than to those who determine from within the
organization's course of events. So, somewhat paradoxically, if the investment in accounting provides sufficient evidence of the organization's
commitment to the course of rational economic and technical action, the
discretion so gained might be used to uncouple organizational actions from
the accounts which are made of them. Accounting might, in such circumstances, provide the freedom for the organization to be unaccountable. By
successfully appealing to the symbols of legitimate action, accounting might
enable the internal affairs of the organization to have a looser relationship to
the external accounts of them.

Accounting and the Routinization of Concern

Thus, the practices of accounting can come to be valued independently of
the precise ways in which they intermingle with other organizational
practices to influence the course of practical events. In any event,
accounting, often stemming from more wide-ranging and ambiguous
concerns, can have difficulty reflecting the specificity of both particular
mobilizing concerns and particular organizational phenomena, not least in
the public sector. In addition, accounting can also come to function as a
specialist area of activity in its own right. Technical questions of accounting
can arise independently of the contexts in which it functions; accounting can
be changed in the name of its own organizational bases and management
rather than the wider concerns of the organizations in which it operates.

Such tendencies serve to detach accounting from the organizations in
which it functions and the concerns in the name of which it was mobilized.
Efficiency, for instance, can lose its force as the basis for accounting
changes, to be replaced by a more procedural concern for accounting for
efficiency. Similarly, plans can become more important than planning;

budgets than the process of budgeting; and costing than the ascertainment of costs. A routine emphasis on accounting as procedure and technique can, at times, supersede accounting's initial concern for the issues in the name of which it was introduced and reformed. [. . .]

However, the tendency for accounting over time to emphasize the procedural and the routine, to the detriment of the managerial and the strategic, has recently been recognized as a problem in the industrial sector (Kaplan, 1983). There accounting's routine emphasis on the short-term economic has been seen to constrain the organization's strategic vision and posture (Simmonds, 1983). Concerns have been expressed about the rigidity of the information and control practices which accounting has traditionally advanced. Accounting has been seen to emphasize the proliferation of routine techniques in the absence of a concern with the specific managerial consequences which they have. And quite active attempts are now being made in some parts of the private sector to reform accounting in the name of what it should be doing rather than what some now see as what it has done.

Accounting and Its Use

Accounting developments do not always lose contact with either the organizations or the missions which they seek to serve. Similarly, accounting does not have any automatic relationship to shifts in organizational legitimacy, the location of social power and influence, and what are seen to be legitimate or illegitimate bases for political action. Moreover, even when accountings of organizational actions and achievements do become intertwined with such substantive concerns, they do not necessarily have any automatic effects. Accountings can counter accountings: those provided by one organization can confront those made by others. The routinization of accounting can even limit the changes in organizational power that might stem from accounting developments. The legitimacy that a particular accounting helps to establish at the organizational boundary can protect rather than necessarily disrupt the internal political processes of decision-making.

[. . .] The effects of accounting are determined by the uses that are made of it, the organizational and social roles which it is made to serve, the ways in which it intersects with other organizational and social processes and practices, and the resistances which its use engenders. Rather than being either a unitary or automatic phenomenon, accounting comes to function in a variety of very different ways in very different settings. And it is those ways and settings which influence the effects that it comes to have.

However, such a contingent view of accounting and its consequences does not deny that accounting can raise quite legitimate and significant questions at levels far beyond the purely technical. If for no other reason than this, accounting developments should be examined in a wider forum. Attempts should be made in this way to account even for accounting itself.

Accounting and That Which Happens in Its Name

Throughout this discussion an attempt has been made to demonstrate that the consequences of accounting do not necessarily have a close and automatic relationship with the aims in the name of which it is introduced and changed. For one thing, the aims that are expressed on behalf of accounting are general and often ambiguous. Stemming from political and managerial rhetoric, they are rarely expressed in terms of the specific operational and pragmatic questions which accounting must address before it can give rise to its technical procedures and practices. However, that gap between the general and the specific can be a very large one. As a result, the precise operationalization of accounting's aims can introduce quite significant elements of technical autonomy into the accounting process. These elements serve to distance the specific from the general to which it seeks to appeal. Equally significantly, accounting practices come to be enmeshed in wider organizational processes and concerns. The domain of the factual, which they create, gives rise to a visibility, emphasis and basis for governability that can enable the consequences of accounting to become both more pervasive and more independent of the original aims which might have been advanced on its behalf.

It is, therefore, always legitimate to seek to confront accounting with an analysis of the specific consequences which it has had. What has been changed in the name of accounting both within the organization and without? What effects have attempts to increase efficiency actually had? What precisely has happened to costs, resources and outcomes? What organizational actions have been curtailed or expanded? What changes, if any, have been introduced into the power structure of the organization and its processes of management and governance? And how do any such precise consequences of specific accountings relate to the missions and rationales which mobilized them in the first place?

Although such an examination should not be alien to the accounting perspective, accounting itself has only rarely been accounted for. The furtherance of accounting in the public sector could, however, provide an ideal context in which to ask questions of accounting; for its use in this sector can raise questions of a wider organizational, social and even political nature. Given this, perhaps we should use the current pressures for change as a basis for starting to account for accounting and to ask questions about what is actually achieved in the pursuit of efficiency.

References

Bahmueller, C. E. (1981) *The National Charity Company: Jeremy Bentham's Silent Revolution*. Berkeley: University of California Press.

Kaplan, R. S. (1983) 'Measuring manufacturing performance: a new challenge for management accounting research', *Accounting Review*, October.

Lazarsfeld, P. F. (1959) 'Sociological reflections on business: consumers and managers', in R. A. Dahl, M. Haire and P. F. Lazarsfeld (eds), *Social Science Research on Business: Product and Potential*, New York: Columbia University Press.

Meyer, J. (1979) 'Environmental and internal origins of symbolic structure in organisations', Paper presented at the Seminar on Organizations as Ideological Systems, Stockholm.

Meyer, J. and Rowan, B. (1977) 'Institutionalised organisations: formal structure as myth and ceremony', *American Journal of Sociology*, September: 340–63.

Olofsson, C. and Svalander, P. A. (1975) 'The medical services change over to a poor environment'. Unpublished working paper, University of Linköping.

Simmonds, K. (1983) 'Strategic management acccounting', in D. Fanning (ed.), *Handbook of Management Accounting*. Aldershot: Gower.

11

Implementation and Ambiguity

Vicki Eaton Baier, James G. March and Harald Sætren

The 'Implementation Problem'

One of the oldest topics in the study of organizations is the relation between policy and practice, the way general directives and programs adopted by legislatures, boards of directors, or top managements are executed, modified, and elaborated by administrative organizations. Contemporary forms of this interest are found in studies of program evaluation and policy implementation. Although there is no question that central policies affect organizational behavior students of implementation frequently report complications in moving from adoption of a policy to its execution (Marshall, 1974). They often describe a scenario in which the wishes of central offices and policy-making bodies are frustrated by the realities of a decentralized administrative organization (Levine, 1972; Pressman and Wildavsky, 1973; Edwards and Sharkansky, 1978; Hanf and Scharpf, 1978).

Two interpretations of implementation problems are common. The first interpretation attributes difficulties in implementation to bureaucratic incompetence. Sometimes bureaucracies are unable to accomplish the tasks they are assigned. The technical difficulties of organizing for major programs are often substantial; the technical skills needed for a specific job may be unavailable (Allison and Halperin, 1971; Pressman and Wildavsky, 1973; Bardach, 1977). The second interpretation attributes difficulties in implementation to conflict of interest between policy-makers and bureaucratic agents, and thus to deficiencies in organizational control. [. . .]

The two interpretations are not mutually exclusive, and they are sensible. In the present chapter, however, we wish to suggest some limitations to such analyses and the importance of including an appreciation of the policy-making process in a discussion of implementation. [. . .] Analyses of the United States Congress, for example, suggest that the act of voting for legislation with appropriate symbolic meaning can be more important to legislators than either its enactment or its implementation (Mayhew, 1974). This is not because legislators are unusually hypocritical. It comes from

From *Scandinavian Journal of Management*, May 1986: 179–212 (abridged).

practical concerns with maintaining electoral support and the substantial symbolic significance of political actions. Voters seek symbolic affirmations as well as mundane personal or group advantage. An interest in the support of constituents, whether voters or stockholders or clients, leads policy-makers to be vigorous in enacting policies and lax in enforcing them.

A desire to maintain the values, ideals, and commitments of an organization or society can easily lead to a similar course (March and Olsen, 1976). Political actors, citizens as well as legislators, workers as well as managers, symbolize their virtues and proclaim their values by seeking and securing policy changes. Policies are not simply guidelines for action. Often they are more significantly expressions of faith, acknowledgements of virtue, and instruments of education. Individuals and groups support (often with extraordinary vigor and at considerable cost) the adoption of policies that symbolize important affirmations, even where they are relatively unconcerned with the ultimate implementation of the policies. As Arnold (1935: 34) observed: 'It is part of the function of Law to give recognition to ideals representing the exact opposite of established conduct. Most of the complications arise from the necessity of pretending to do one thing, while actually doing another.'

Cases of such clear intentionality are, however, only a minor part of the story. They dramatize the limitations of talking about 'implementation problems', but they do not define those limitations. We will argue the more general point that an understanding of implementation cannot be divorced from an understanding of the processes that generate policies, and that some conspicuous features of policy-making contribute directly to the phenomena we have come to label as problems of implementation.

Bureaucracies as Instruments of Policy

Despite the pervasiveness and effectiveness of bureaucratic organization, there are ample grounds for doubting that a modern administrative agency will fulfill any policy directive that it might be assigned. For example, bureaucratic inability to cope with the size or scope of new responsibilities has been used to explain the difficulties of some business organizations implementing policies that lead them into foreign markets and of military organizations implementing policies that ask them to fight limited wars. One typical situation in the public sector involves the implementation of new national programs through local departments or bureaus seemingly ill-equipped to administer them.

Consider, for example, Sutherland's (1975: 74–6) portrayal of problems in implementing the Elementary and Secondary Education Act of 1965 in the United States:

> Although some state agencies in 1965 were considered to be well managed, most were thought to lack sufficient personnel to supervise existing state programs or

the capability to assume new responsibilities needed to meet future educational needs. Although all state departments of education had professionals capable of providing consultative and technical service to local educational agencies, the number of staff members available on a full-time basis was limited. Only one-fifth of the states had two or more supervisors of teacher education and 15 did not have a part-time employee for this activity. One-third of the states provided no services or supervision of school libraries. Twenty-nine did not provide for the supervision of industrial arts programs and the remaining states had only a supervisor of vocational education. Four state agencies had no full-time staff members to consult with local school systems for special education and only 13 had one or more full-time consultants for the development of programs for the gifted. . . . Persons in possession of skills and the training to conduct research, evaluate findings and test and implement new instructional programs were also needed by state educational agencies. Although more than two-thirds of the state agencies had departments that included the word 'research' as a part of the title, only 108 persons were employed for research purposes, and nine state departments of education listed no research personnel.

[. . .] The idea that implementation is made difficult by the possibly unavoidable, and certainly ubiquitous, problems of bureaucratic and individual incompetence is found in many analyses of modern administrative agencies. Logistic complications are not solved in time. Coordination among agencies is not accomplished, even when there is no significant conflict among them. Materials, plans, and people are not available when needed; personnel are not trained properly or are given inadequate instructions or supervision (Allison and Halperin, 1971).

Agencies are sometimes sloppy, disorganized, inadequately trained, poorly staffed and badly managed; but gross incompetence is not required to produce significant bureaucratic inadequacy. Some tasks are not feasible; some policies are ill-suited to administrative agencies. Moreover, it is possible to recognize the considerable individual and organizational skills represented in a bureaucracy and still observe a mismatch between a particular organization and a particular task. For example, the United States Forest Service has had difficulty playing the role of a narcotics police force in national forests.

These difficulties are frequently further complicated by a need to coordinate several different organizations in order to implement a single general policy (Elmore, 1975; Hanf and Scharpf, 1978). Central policy may require coordination among organizations with sharply contrasting objectives, styles, or normal activities. Managing several relatively autonomous groups often demands capacities beyond those of elaborate bureaucratic structures, not to mention the largely ad hoc structures that are sometimes used. Policy-makers often ignore, or underestimate considerably, the administrative requirements of a policy, and thus make policies that assure administrative incapacity.

The problems of incompetence are paired with problems of control. Administrative organizations are neither reliably neutral nor easily controlled. They seem persistently to modify policies in the course of implementing them. Descriptions of such local adaptations tend to overestimate the extent to which official policy, as interpreted by interested observers, can be equated either with the public interest or with the intentions of legislatures (Lynn, 1977). They are likely to picture national officials, top management, or major policy-makers as defending general interests against the predations of local officials, subordinates, and special interest. The core idea, however, does not depend on that particular representation of a morality play. Whenever an agent is used to execute the policy of a principal, control problems arise. The problems are endemic to organization and have been extensively discussed in the literature on organizations (March and Simon, 1958; Crozier, 1964), as well as in treatises on optimal contracts, incentive schemes, and theories of agency (Hirschleifer and Riley, 1979).

Bureaucracies appear often to be thoroughly political, responding to claims made in the name of subunits, clients, and individual organizational actors. Political processes continue as policies filter through a bureaucracy to first-level administrative officials. Agencies adopt projects and implement programs in response to political pressure or financial incentives; they exercise discretion in order to improve their local position or address specific problems of interest to them; they interpret policy directives in ways that transform their prior desires into the wishes of policy-makers. For example, the Fort Lincoln project, seen by political leaders as a way to help poor people escape city slums, was converted into a program to build model communities and to try out the newest ideas in community planning (Derthick, 1972).

In dealing with organizational actors, policy-makers find it hard to ensure that incentives for following official policy are adequate to overcome incentives to deviate from it (Christie, 1964). Organizations, their clients, and their subunits pursue political tactics seeking renegotiation of policies and practices. Since from the point of view of most other groups and institutions, any new policy announced by policy-makers is primarily an opportunity to pursue their own agenda, those responsible for implementing policy have constituents who seek deviations from policy. Some parts of any administrative organization will have incentives for pursuing objectives that deviate from any policy that might be adopted (Downs, 1967).

The difficulties in coordinating the agendas of multiple actors are compounded by the way political and organizational actors move in and out of the arena in response to various claims on their attention (March and Olsen, 1976). An organization is pressed to meet the inconsistent demands of a continually changing group of actors. Pressman and Wildavsky (1973) suggest some reasons for the inconstancy of attention: actors may find their commitments to a policy incompatible with other important commitments; they may have preferences for other programs; they may be dependent on others who lack the same sense of urgency; they may have differences of opinion on leadership or proper organizational roles; they may be constrained by legal or procedural questions or demands. In general, a shifting pattern of demands for attention made on the individuals involved in and around an organization tends to make the climate of implementation unstable in many small ways that cumulatively affect the course of events (Kaufman, 1981).

Programs for Reform of the Policy Process

Because it is part of classical administrative dogma, and because bureaucratic organizations do, in fact, have a rather impressive record for successfully coordinating large numbers of people in service of policies imposed from outside, it is persistently tempting to picture administrative agents as natural implements of prior policy. They are made innocent by an act of will or good management. In this spirit, problems of implementation lead to proposals to increase competence and control by hiring new personnel, developing new training or procedures, improving accountability, and providing new incentives. For example, foreign service organizations may respond to diagnoses of incompetence by increasing the length of service at a particular station for individual officers; they may respond to diagnoses of lack of control by requiring more frequent rotation of officers through stations. Implementation failures may lead to new organizational forms, for example divisional management; to new investments, for example in management information systems; to new routines, for example evaluation studies; or to new personnel, for example new top executives.

Such changes are intended to make an organization into a competent, reliable agent, executing a wide range of possible policies. They picture the problems of implementation as problems of securing neutral administrative compliance with prior, exogenous policies. This view of administration has, however, long been in disrepute among students of organizations. It suggests more clarity in the distinction between policy-making and administration than can usually be sustained; and it leads to a mechanistic perspective on the management of organizations that seems likely to be misleading. Trying to keep administrators innocent may, of course, simply reflect an instinct to use unachievable aspirations as a means of achieving less heroic, but admirable outcomes (March, 1978, 1979); but it tends to delusion. Consequently, many sophisticated observers of organizations take a more strategic posture with respect to designing administrative organizations.

Suppose we accept the proposition that bureaucracies are limited instrumentalities, that there are constraints on our abilities to make them more competent or to avoid the demands of self-interest. Then implementation problems are attributed not to characteristics of organizations – which are taken as essentially intractable – but to the naivety of policy-makers. In this view, policy-makers do not specify objectives clearly enough (Løchen and Martinsen, 1962; Jacobsen, 1966; Lowi, 1969; Sabatier and Mazmanian, 1980), provide inadequate resources, fail to build a proper administrative organization, fail to consult with affected groups, or have too high expectations. Such a strategic vision leads to recommendations to improve the policies, make them clearer and more consistent with the attitudes of the groups involved, and strengthen the incentives and capabilities for bureaucratic conformity to policy directives.

[. . .] Many problems in implementation might be avoided if policy-makers made less ambiguous policies and designed simple procedures that protected their intentions from the inadequacies and self-interest of administrative agencies. Rather than expecting to change the character of administrative organizations, we might design strategic policies, quasi-price systems, and incentive contracts that are likely to lead to desired ends even when executed by administrative organizations that are neither perfect nor neutral.

These efforts to increase the sophistication of policy-makers in dealing with administrative agencies, like earlier attempts to improve the competence and reliability of the agencies, are vital to good administration. Without a struggle to link policy and action, any social system suffers. However, we want to argue that the problems of implementation are obscured by the terminology of implementation, even in its more sophisticated forms, that discussions of implementations assume a coherence in policy objectives that rarely exists. Understanding administrative implementation cannot be separated from understanding the ways in which policies are made and the implications of the policy-making process for administrative action.

Policy-Making and Policy Ambiguity

Proposals for implementations reform treat policy – or policy objectives – as given. They assume that policy goals and directives are (or can be) clear, that policy-makers know what they want, and that what they want is consistent, stable, and unambiguous. The assumptions are similar to assumptions about preferences made in standard decision theory, and they have some of the same advantages (Raiffa, 1968). They made administration, like decision-making, a difficult technical job of optimization, subject to prior exogenous policies established by legitimate authority. They also have many of the same disadvantages (March, 1978; Elster, 1979; Cronbach *et al.*, 1980).

In particular, the assumptions are often not true. They are frequently false in a way that makes the concept of implementation not only inaccurate as a portrayal of organizational reality, but often an inappropriate base for organizational reform. For example, the frequent advice that policies should be clear seems to assume that policy-makers can arbitrarily choose the level of clarity of a policy, that policies are ambiguous because of some form of inadequacy in policy-making. Such a view ignores what we know about the making of policies. In fact, policies are negotiated in a way that makes the level of clarity no more accessible to arbitrary choice than other vital parts of the policy.

Forming a coalition in order to support a policy, whether in a legislature or a boardroom, involves standard techniques of horse-trading, persuasion, bribes, threats, and management of information. These are the conventional procedures of discussion, politics, and policy formation. They are well conceived to help participants form coalitions, explore support for alternative policies, and develop a viable policy. Much of the genius of modern organizational leadership lies in skills for producing policy from the conflicting and inchoate ideas, demands, preconceptions, and prejudices of the groups to which organizational leadership must attend. At the heart of several of these techniques for achieving policies, however, are features that make implementation problematic.

Adopted policies will, on average, be oversold. Even unbiased expectations about possible policies will lead to bias in the expectations with respect to those that are adopted. Since proposed programs for which expectations are erroneously pessimistic are rarely adopted, the sample of adopted programs is more likely to exhibit errors of over-optimism than of over-pessimism (Harrison and March, 1984). Inflated expectations about programs that are successful in gaining support from policy-makers make subsequent disappointment likely. Thus, great hopes lead to action, but great hopes are invitations to disappointment. This, in turn, leads both to an erosion of support and to an awareness of 'failures of implementation.'

Such a structural consequence of intelligent decision-making under conditions of uncertainty is accentuated in situations of collective choice. Competition for policy support pushes advocates to imagine favorable outcomes and to inflate estimates of the desirability of those outcomes. Developing and communicating such expectations are a major part of policy discussions. Expectations become part of the official record, part of collective history, and part of individual beliefs. Others will, of course, try to deflate the estimates of advocates; but the advocates usually write the stories for their preferred policies and often come either to believe them or to be committed publicly to them. Tactical supporters of policies (i.e., those who support policies for reasons extraneous to their content) do not resist being misled. Extravagant claims justify their support and provide a basis, if one is ever needed, for claims that they are duped.

In addition, the centripetal processes of policy-making exaggerate the real level of support for policies that are adopted. Although commitment to a policy or program in its own right may be important for some coalition members, few major policies could be adopted without some supporters for whom the policy is relatively unimportant except as a political bargain. They may be persuaded to join a coalition by a belief the policy is sensible, by claims of loyalty or friendship, or by a logroll in which their support is offered in trade for needed support on other things in which they have a direct concern. There is no assurance that such groups and individuals will be equally supportive of its implementation. Except in so far as their continued active support is a part of the coalition agreement, and such extended coalition agreements are difficult to arrange and enforce, supporters will turn to other matters. Consequently, a winning coalition can easily be an illusion (Sætren, 1983).

Finally, one common method for securing policy support is to increase the ambiguity of a proposed policy (Page, 1976). It is a commonplace observation of the legislative process that difficult issues are often 'settled' by leaving them unresolved or specifying them in a form requiring subsequent interpretation. A similar observation can be made about policies in armies, hospitals, universities, and business firms. Particularly where an issue is closely contested, success in securing support for a program or policy is likely to be associated with increasing, rather than decreasing ambiguity. Policy ambiguity allows different groups and individuals to support the same policy for different reasons and with different expectations, including different expectations about the administrative consequences of the policy.

Thus, official policy is likely to be vague, contradictory, or adopted without generally shared expectations about its meaning or implementation. Aubert, in his study of the enactment of a Housemaid Law in Norway (Aubert 1969: 125), discusses the apparent anomaly of legislation that paired a policy proclaiming the protection of household workers with a set of procedures for redress that were effectively inaccessible to victims:

> What is pretended in the penal clause of the Housemaid Law is that effective enforcement of the law is envisaged. And what the legislature is actually doing is to see to it that the privacy of the home and the interest of housewives are not ignored. . . . The ambivalence and the conflicting views of the legislators, as they can be gleaned from the penal clause, appear more clearly in the legislative debate. A curious dualism runs through the debates. It was claimed, on the one hand, that the law is essentially a codification of custom and established practice, rendering effective enforcement inessential. On the other hand, there was a tendency to claim that the Housemaid Law is an important new piece of labour legislation with a clearly reformatory purpose, attempting to change an unacceptable status quo. . . . The crucial point here is the remarkable ease with which such apparently contradictory claims were suffused in one and the same legislative action, which in the end received unanimous support from all political groups.

In this way, the ambiguity of a policy increases the chance of its adoption, but at the cost of creating administrative complications. For example, Øyen (1964) observed that the ambiguous text of a Norwegian welfare statute was simultaneously a necessary condition for the unanimity of its political support and a basis for considerable administrative discretion. As a policy unfolds into action, the different understandings of an ambiguous political agreement combine with the usual transformation of preferences over time to become bases for abandoning support, deploring administrative sabotage of the program, or embracing a special fantasy of what the policy means. As a result, many coalition members can easily feel betrayed; and observers can easily become confused.

In the long run, of course, political institutions learn from their experience. Administrative agencies seem likely to adapt to a history of ambiguous, contradictory, and grandiose policies by an administrative posture that tends to emphasize creative autonomy. They learn to establish independent political constituencies, to treat normal policies as problematic (or at least subject to interpretation), and to expect policy-makers to be uncertain, or in conflict, about the expected consequences of a policy, or its importance. They come to realize that they cannot escape criticism by arguing that they were following policy but must develop an independent political basis for their actions.

Similarly, policy-makers learn from their experiences with administrative agencies. As administrative practices become flexible, it becomes easier to use policy ambiguity as a basis for forming coalitions. It becomes plausible to attribute failures in programs to failures in implementation and thus to avoid possible criticism for mistakes. Policy ambiguity encourages administrative autonomy, which in turn encourages more policy ambiguity. Thus, it is not hard to see why we might observe organizations functioning with only a loose coupling between policies and actions, between plans and behavior, and between policy-makers and administrators (March and Olsen, 1976; Weick, 1976).

The Concept of Implementation

The terminology of implementation conjures up a picture of clear, consistent, and stable policy directives waiting to be executed. It encourages us to think that a reasonable and responsible person can easily measure the discrepancy between policy and bureaucratic action, that the discrepancy can be attributed to some properties of the organization (e.g. its competence and reliability) or to some properties of the policy (e.g. its clarity and consistency), and that the properties of the organization and the properties of the policy can be chosen arbitrarily and independently in order to reduce the discrepancy.

As we have noted, studies of policy-making cast doubt on such a characterization. The implementation of policies is frequently problematic; but the difficulties cannot be treated as independent of the confusions in the policy. Those confusions, in turn, cannot be treated as independent of the ways in which winning policy coalitions are built. Policies are frequently ambiguous; but their ambiguities are less a result of deficiencies in policy-makers than a natural consequence of gaining necessary support for the policies, and of changing preferences over time. Conflict of interest is not just a property of the relations between policy-makers on the one hand and administrators on the other; it is a general feature of policy negotiation and bureaucratic life. As a result, policies reflect contradictory intentions and expectations and considerable uncertainty.

It may be tempting to deplore a policy process that sometimes seems to restrict us to a choice between inaction and ambiguity, and to wish for some alternative system in which policy agreements would be clear and their execution unproblematic. But that concern should be paired with an awareness of the complications. The problems involved in establishing and maintaining an effective policy-making and an administrative system that provides responsiveness, coherence, and symbolic affirmation of social values have occupied philosphers and managers for long enough to suggest that they are not trivial. Certainly, contemporary theories of policy-making and administration have not solved them. Nor have we. As a preface to such an effort, however, we have argued that the terms of discourse for discussing policy-making and implementation are misleading. Any simple concept of implementation, with its implicit assumption of clear and stable policy intent, is likely to lead to a fundamental misunderstanding of the policy process and to disappointment with efforts to reform it.

References

Allison, Graham T., and Halperin, Morton H. (1971) 'Bureaucratic politics: a paradigm and some policy implications', *World Politics*, 24: 40–79.

Arnold, Thurman (1935) *The Symbols of Government*. New Haven, CT: Yale University Press.

Aubert, Wilhelm (1969) 'Some social functions of legislation', in Vilhelm Aubert (ed.), *Sociology of Law*. London: Penguin.

Bardach, Eugene (1977) *The Implementation Game*. Cambridge, MA: MIT Press.

Christie, Nils (1964) 'Edruelighetsnemnder: Analyse av en velferdslov. (Temperence committees: Analysis of a welfare state)', *Nordisk Tidshrift for Kriminaluitenskap*, 52: 89: 118.

Cronbach, Lee J., *et al.* (1980) *Toward Reform of Program Evaluation*. San Francisco: Jossey-Bass.

Crozier, Michel (1964) *The Bureaucratic Phenomenon*. Chicago: University of Chicago Press.

Derthick, Martha (1972) *New Towns – In Town*. Washington, DC: Urban Institute.

Downs, Anthony (1967) *Inside Bureaucracy*, Boston: Little, Brown.

Edwards, George C., and Sharkansky, Ira (1978) *The Policy Predicament*. San Francisco: W. H. Freeman.

Elmore, Richard F. (1975) 'Lessons from follow through', *Policy Analysis*, 1: 459–67.

Elster, Jon (1979) *Ulysses and the Sirens*. Cambridge: Cambridge University Press.

Hanf, Kenneth, and Scharpf, Fritz W. (1978) *Interorganizational Policy Making: Limits to Coordination and Central Control*. London: Sage.

Harrison, J. Richard, and March, James G. (1984) 'Decision-making and post-decision surprises', *Administrative Science Quarterly*, 29: 26–42.

Hirschleifer, J., and Riley, John C. (1979) 'The analytics of uncertainty and information – an expository survey', *Journal of Economic Literature*, 17: 1375–421.

Jacobsen, Knut D. (1966) 'Public administration under pressure: the role of the expert in the modernization of traditional agriculture', *Scandinavian Political Studies*, 1: 69–93.

Kaufman, Herbert (1981) *The Administrative Behavior of Federal Bureau Chiefs*. Washington, DC: Brookings Institution.

Levine, Robert A. (1972) *Public Planning: Failure and Redirection*. New York: Basic Books.

Løchen, Yngvar, and Martinsen, Arne (1962) 'Samarbeidsproblemer ved gjennomføringen av lovene om attføringshjelp og unføretrygd' (Cooperation problems in the implementation of laws dealing with aid to the handicapped and disability insurance), *Tidsskrift for Samfunnsforskning*, 3: 133–68.

Lowi, Theodore J. (1969) *The End of Liberalism*. New York: W. W. Norton.

Lynn, Laurence E. (1977) 'Implementation: will the hedgehogs be outfoxed?' *Policy Analysis*, 3: 277–80.

March, James G. (1978) 'Bounded rationality, ambiguity, and the engineering of choice', *Bell Journal of Economics*, 9: 587–608.

March, James G. (1979) *Science, Politics, and Mrs. Gruenberg*. Washington, DC: National Academy of Sciences.

March, James G., and Olsen, Johan P. (1976) *Ambiguity and Choice in Organizations*. Bergen: Universitetsforlaget.

March, James G., and Simon, Herbert A. (1958) *Organizations*. New York: Wiley.

Marshall, Dale Rogers (1974) 'Implementation of federal poverty and welfare policy: a review essay', *Policy Studies Journal*, 2: 152–7.

Mayhew, David R. (1974) *Congress: The Electoral Connection*. New Haven, CT: Yale University Press.

Øyen, Else (1964) *Sosialomsorgen og dens Forvaltere* (Social care and its managers). Bergen: Universitetsforlaget.

Page, Benjamin I. (1976) 'The theory of political ambiguity', *American Political Science Review*, 70: 742–52.

Pressman, Jeffrey L., and Wildavsky, Aaron B. (1973) *Implementation*. Berkeley, CA: University of California Press.

Raiffa, Howard (1968) *Decision Analysis*. Reading, MA: Addison-Wesley.

Sabatier, Paul, and Mazmanian, Daniel (1980) 'The implementation of public policy: a framework of analysis', *Policy Studies Journal*, 8: 538–60.

Sætren, Harald (1983) *Iverksetting av offentlig politikk*. (Implementation of public policy). Bergen: Universitetsforlaget.

Sutherland, B. H. (1975) *Federal Grants to State Departments of Education for the Administration of the Elementary and Secondary Education Act of 1965*. Ann Arbor, MI: University of Michigan Press.

Weick, Karl (1976) 'Educational organizations as loosely coupled systems', *Administrative Science Quarterly*, 21: 1–19.

12

Investigating Policy Coordination: issues and hypotheses

L. Challis, S. Fuller, M. Henwood, R. Klein, W. Plowden, A. Webb, P. Whittingham and G. Wistow

Attempts to improve coordination are only one manifestation of the long historical search for greater rationality in public affairs, but they have been central to the history of social policy. From the Charity Organization Society and the Royal Commission on the Poor Laws to the Central Policy Review Staff and JASP, the leitmotif of coordination has traced a path through a century of concern about social problems. Motivations and objectives have varied greatly, but underlying them has been a constant reality: social issues, needs and problems – and the responses which they invoke – are usually complex and interrelated. As a consequence, a call for greater coordination flows almost ineluctably from any discovery of duplication, inefficiency, ineffectiveness, or of 'holes in the safety net'.

Perhaps surprisingly, given the historical background, coordination in social policy tends to be regarded as neutral and innocuous at worst and as self-evidently good for consumers and clients at best. We do not make this assumption. Coordination can be pressed to the service of many causes and interests; who gains and who loses from coordinative successes and failures must be investigated, not taken for granted. As Pressman and Wildavsky note, in the absence of consensus and common purpose 'coordination becomes another term for coercion'.[1] More specifically, Glennerster has argued that in recent times centrally coordinated social planning has been at least as much about the control and rationing of public expenditure as about the effective meeting of social need.[2] Similarly, social service professionals who ostensibly seek to improve coordination in order to benefit their clients can easily be seduced by that which is personally rewarding or professionally appealing; they can lose sight of how the consumers actually experience services and of what for them amounts to accessible and useful forms of help. These are matters of evaluation which we did not broach systematically in

From L. Challis et al., *Joint Approaches to Social Policy*, Cambridge: Cambridge University Press, 1988, pp. 24–51 (abridged).

our empirical research. Our sights were firmly set on policy and administrative processes, not on outcomes as such. Nonetheless, there can be no doubt that the search for rationality which characterized the 1970s was strongly motivated, at least in part, by a desire to produce policies and outcomes which would be better for the immediate client or consumer. We therefore set off in search of coordination in the belief that it – and the wider demand for rationality in social policy which it represents – could certainly, in principle, be in the interests of the public in contact with the social services.

Coordination: Its Meaning and Political Relevance

Precision about the meaning of coordination is rare. We have broadly characterized it as a pursuit of coherence, consistency, comprehensiveness and of harmonious or compatible outcomes. In the 1960s and 1970s, however, it took on a more specific, dominant form. Within the belief in rational, synoptic planning was to be found a search for *policy* coordination – coordination at the strategic level. Coordination was central, not peripheral to the style of governance. Indeed, the preoccupation with administrative technique and organizational machinery was at times so strong that it became the major form of substantive policy. The reorganization of the personal social services, the health service, and local government could all be seen in this light; so, too, could the partnership policies and 'total approach' towards the inner cities.

Coordination is above all the rationalist's technique for embracing the complexity and interrelatedness of social issues and problems, and there can be no doubt that at times rational planning has come to resemble the triumph of administrative technique over the craft of politics. Planning in the 1960s and 1970s was primarily conceived, by default as much as by design, as a centralized and essentially technical process. As such it threatened to bypass the political masters it was supposedly serving, but it also seemed poised to supplant the more obscure and mundane craft of bureaucratic politics – the bargaining, trade-offs and fancy footwork by which professionals and administrators in the public services defend or promote sectional goals and interests.

It is important to note and hold on to both these notions of politics: what might be called 'high politics' and 'low politics'. The search for rationality in public affairs usually expresses an impatience, even distaste, for the former and always for the latter. It represents an attempt to marshal and discipline the chaos which can arise from a multiplicity of competing, often conflicting, interests. The political craft, on the other hand, is embedded in the recognition of divergent interests – or at least some of them. Our own contrast between the politics of rationality and the rationality of politics must be seen in this light. It is not merely party politicians who threaten to upset the rationalist's carefully arranged apple-cart, it is all actors – high or low – who exhibit a leaning towards *ad hoc* negotiations, deals and opportunistic actions.

To characterize the rational planning of the 1970s as essentially a centralist dead hand on party and bureaucratic politics would be misleading. The tendency was discernible, but the practice was never sufficiently developed to have that outcome. Moreover, the trend towards centralization was matched by a desire to achieve decentralized forms of coordination. The inner cities provided one notable, not to say notorious, example; the health and personal social services provided another. Both examples added a further piece to the coordination jigsaw: while centrally devised plans could aid coordination by providing a coherent framework, the need at the local level was for collaboration. It was seen to be necessary for local actors and organizations to rise above any minor differences of opinion and interest in order to pursue the common good of the local community in concert. Indeed, it is an abiding feature of the rationality game that people who can see many reasonable – and rational – reasons for differences of opinion and divergences of interest at their own level of operation tend to emphasize the rationality of collaboration at other levels (and fail to see why there should be barriers or obstacles in the path of such a self-evident good).

Centralization is an inherently relative concept. What was perceived by central government as a valuable or even essential attempt to develop decentralized collaboration was often perceived by local actors and observers as further evidence of centralization. Corporate planning in local government was a prime example. The attempt, in itself laudable and long overdue, to achieve greater coordination across local government departments became inseparably entwined with the reorganization of local government into much larger, more remote and more bureaucratically complex units. The same was true of collaboration between the health and personal social services. Moreover, the collaboration in question was between whole departments and organizations and was designed to promote another layer of rational planning. The term 'collaboration' has warmer and more personal overtones than the term 'coordination', but in practice it did not imply too many cosy chats about mutual interests – it merely entailed some attempt to harmonize the actions of large organizations characterized by divergent interests. As we shall illustrate from our own empirical work, it was generally as resolutely technical and technocratic (few local politicians played a decisive role) as the attempt at rational planning initiated within central government.

Nonetheless, these different developments highlighted a single and crucial issue: the large-scale state social services which had been developed in the post-war years could fail to meet – or could even exacerbate – people's needs, as well as resolve them. One central reason for this was that policies, the structure of service systems, and the actual delivery of services all exhibited gaps in coverage, conflicts of aim and failures of communication. Better coordination was the solution and it could take several forms (that there could possibly be other sources of failure and other potential solutions is a point to which we shall return).

The two forms of coordination which we have mentioned – rational planning and collaboration – require a further word of explanation. In one sense they represent the difference between technique and process. *Rational planning* is one technique by which a framework to guide and coordinate action can be achieved. Collaboration is a process of interaction in which two or more parties identify mutual interests and freely agree to work together towards a common goal. *Collaboration* is therefore one way of *developing* a rational plan, and it was seen to be a necessary way at the local level (because many autonomous agencies needed to work together and there was no acceptable means of coercing them to do so). By way of comparison, a second way of engaging in rational planning is for an acknowledged authority to require different groups and interests to submit to a single coherent strategy. *Imperative* (or coercive) and *collaborative* processes may both be involved in the process of rational planning, therefore. Government departments engaged in planning might do so through a combination of these processes. Ministers, cabinet and trans-departmental bodies [. . .] might exercise authority or persuasion, but much might also hinge upon unforced collaboration across sections, divisions and departments. [. . .]

However, we later use the term *collaboration arena* in a quite specific sense which should be distinguished now. It is used to refer to the field of local interaction between the health authorities, local authorities and voluntary agencies. Its use reflects the fact that central government policies have characterized coordination and joint planning at this level as *essentially* collaborative precisely because the organizations involved are autonomous of one another and, to varying degrees, of central government. Any plan of action agreed by such agencies would immediately take on a different role within those separate agencies – it would be authoritative – but it would itself be the product of purely collaborative interaction. In reality, joint planning has never been innocent of authoritative action by central departments. [. . .] Joint planning has been heavily mandated from above. Nonetheless, central government writ runs but imperfectly at such local levels and collaboration has remained the essential ingredient. Hence we use the term *collaborative arena* to specify joint planning between health and local authorities and voluntary bodies.

Even before 1979, no actuary would have taken a risk on the life expectancy of rational planning; the more grandiose hopes and ambitions had already begun to crumble and decay. Once the first Thatcher administration had come to power, it was only a matter of time before the life support machine was switched off altogether. What had finally disappeared, after a long period of false alarms, was the entire post-war tradition of consensus politics. Most fundamentally, the competence and role of the state had been re-evaluated and re-defined. State paternalism – and 'dirigiste' central planning – were anathema. Yet, as we have argued

[. . .] the need for policy coordination has survived this dramatic change in political ideology. It has everywhere undergone a change of style or of name, it has on occasions gone underground, but in only a few cases has it gone out of the window. A considerable degree of continuity of practice has accompanied sharp changes in principle. What, then, is to be learned about coordination and the politics of rationality from the experiences of the early 1980s?

The first lesson is that a market-oriented philosophy throws a different light on the whole issue of rationality and coordination in the social policy field. It redefines the problems and highlights different potential solutions. Ideally, rational decision-making and coordination is left primarily to the individual consumer at the point of consumption. The emphasis, in principle, is on consumer choice between outputs rather than on political or bureaucratic decision-making and the coordination of inputs and policy processes. Consumers are expected to be able to put together their own package of social provisions. Coordination is still necessary if government is to create the right framework within which a mixed economy of statutory, voluntary or private producers can operate. It is also still necessary within and between statutory producers. But the weight of coordinative responsibility is decentralized somewhat and the parties covered by the coordinative imperative are different – coordination between public and private producers grows in importance.

The second lesson is that the 'rationality of politics' has been reasserted in a major way at the strategic level. The tendency to depoliticize policy issues has been swept aside. What was always clear to many has become perfectly clear to all: rationality resides in the choice of means to ends, but the choice between ends is inherently political. Faith in consensus has been at a minimum; divergent and conflicting interests have come out of the closet. Yet this reassertion of the rationality of politics has been highly selective. It has been confined to the national tier of government and to 'high politics'. Neither differences of interest and viewpoint between centre and locality, nor bureaucratic politics, has been countenanced as a legitimate barrier to the implementation of key policies. Coordinated action has remained very much in demand once political decisions have been made: *instrumental* rationality has lost none of its appeal. It is any lingering belief in *substantive* rationality – a uniquely appropriate understanding of the public good which can be discerned through sophisticated policy analysis – which has disappeared from view.

A third, obvious but often overlooked, lesson has also been forcibly restated. The more grandiose formulations of the rational synoptic planning approach contained a deep-rooted paradox. They were an attempt to contain and discipline the *ad hoc* and short-term nature of purely political decision-making and yet they were fundamentally dependent on the support and commitment of politicians. [. . .] The British civil service is deeply conservative in its ways and resistant to implanted foreign bodies such as policy units and think-tanks; only civil service loyalty to committed ministers could offset the deleterious consequences of departmental and sectional loyalties for the vital organs of the rational approach. Ministerial support for synoptic planning was patchy and uncertain at best before 1979, but it ceased altogether thereafter.

Coordination: Components and Dimensions

Coordination remained a key aspect of the style of governance which characterized the early 1980s, but it was shorn of most of the trappings of rational planning. The issues to which it was seen to be most pertinent also changed. Public expenditure control moved sharply up the agenda, as did law and order and, more gradually, the link between education/training and 'manpower planning'. But what does coordination entail? What kind of phenomenon or process are we discussing? Now that the rhetoric and organizational machinery of the rational planning era have been jettisoned, it is somewhat easier to perceive the essential elements. Coordination in social planning may refer to one or more of the following:

(a) ensuring consistency and coherence between the *various objectives and elements of a single policy or project*;
(b) ensuring consistency and coherence within a *set of interacting policies or projects* 'owned' by one or more departments or organizations;
(c) ensuring that policy is translated into a consistent and coherent set of *appropriate actions* within one or more departments or organizations;
(d) ensuring that *service delivery practices* at the field level are such that a consistent, coherent and comprehensive package of help is available to people with specified needs;
(e) ensuring that the *services actually consumed* by the public in contact comprise a consistent, coherent and comprehensive package appropriate to expressed wants.

To begin with the last, we have noted that the market philosophy places considerable emphasis on coordination at this stage as a function of consumer choice. In a more traditional public service frame of analysis, this view of implementation implies the evaluation of outputs and outcomes from the consumer's perspective. The first four forms of coordination fit readily within the public service perspective: the first two emphasize coordination in policy-making, and the second two underline the importance of policy implementation. Both these 'levels' of coordination were covered in our empirical research. [. . .]

Coordination can also be specified in terms of the kinds of activities involved. Three distinctions are especially pertinent:

(a) coordination as a *cerebral or analytical activity* (e.g. establishing an appropriate mix of objectives and methods in a policy or project at the planning stage);

(b) coordination as the *interaction of formal organizations* (agencies or departments of a large organization) *or groupings* (e.g. professions) and the possibly competing or conflicting interests which they contain or represent;

(c) coordination as the *interaction of individuals* – usually as representatives or members of organizations or groupings (e.g. politicians, chief officers, middle managers, professionals and other field workers).

Each of these facets of coordination presents different issues. The first was the jewel in the rational planning crown, though some account had necessarily to be taken of the second. However, the rational planning era did tend to obscure the importance of the second and third; they were less glamorous and also less amenable to centralized control through paper planning exercises. But for our own purposes they are central: the interactive elements of the coordination process were the key object of our empirical research.

Coordination can finally be characterized in terms of a series of dichotomies. Two of the most significant – *centralized/decentralized* and *authoritative/collaborative* – have already been mentioned. They are broadly indicative of important variables rather than precise specifications. The third – *formal/informal* – is similar in this respect. By formal we mean coordination attempted through official channels or special machinery (e.g. joint consultative committees); by informal we mean the interaction of individuals or small groups as representatives and as people. The latter introduces the human element: the importance of personalities and interpersonal interaction. As such it is pervasive. Interpersonal interaction may tip the balance in favour of a particular outcome within a highly formal committee meeting just as much as over a drink at the bar afterwards. We do not intend these dichotomies to be seen as mutually exclusive polarities, therefore. They are important dimensions of our analysis which are best summarized briefly in this manner for the time being.

The analytical component of coordination was explored at considerable length in a large body of academic writing before and during the rational planning era. Changes in the process of governance were strongly underpinned by theory. But they were also strongly criticized by alternative bodies of theory. Moreover, once the emphasis shifts from coordination as policy analysis to coordination as organizational interaction it is quite apparent that the body of academic writing which could be drawn upon as a guide to understanding is immense. Consequently, in developing guiding hypotheses for our research we had to be severely selective. We drew upon a wide range of literature, but concentrated on key ideas relating to the interactions which we most wanted to study and understand. It is to this academic framework that we must now turn.

Theories and Hypotheses

To begin to understand the approach taken towards rationality in the 1970s one has only to look at the one comparatively coherent and manageable body of literature advocating rational synoptic planning, or – in later revisionist versions – mixed scanning. But there is also a need to understand the likely limits of and impediments to these routes to coordination, and the literatures in this case are altogether more diverse and intimidating. It is true that the rational planning literature was counterbalanced by the 'incrementalist school'[3] which trenchantly criticized both the feasibility and desirability of the rational synoptic approach, but simply to draw on this would not be wholly appropriate. The image of a sharp antithesis between the 'rational planning' and 'incrementalist' schools was always overdrawn and resulted in fundamentally distinct issues being conflated. For example, the idea of incremental policy processes seemed to convey a single, coherent phenomenon, but incrementalism could, in fact, convey any or all of the following:

the avoidance of grand strategies in favour of single-issue decision-taking;
the avoidance of elaborate policy analysis in favour of political judgement
  and the 'intelligence of democracy';
the avoidance of centralized policy-making in favour of more decentralized
  decision-taking;
the avoidance of dramatic change in policy objectives in favour of more
  conservative patterns of change; and
the acceptance of undramatic or conservative shifts in policy outputs at the
  expense of radical change.

Neither sophisticated analysis nor radical policies necessarily means radical changes in outputs (or vice versa), but these small matters of causality were often lost sight of in the partisan heat of a great academic debate. However, given the qualifications and intellectual disentangling which are now possible, the incrementalist literature obviously proved to be a valuable source of ideas and guiding hypotheses when first we began our research. Nonetheless, we faced a further problem. Both the rational synoptic planning literature and – to a lesser extent – the incrementalist rejoinder concentrated on 'high politics': on the nature of policy-making rather than on the whole politico-administrative process. We therefore needed to draw additional perspectives, especially on organizational interaction, into our theoretical net. We had also to identify a simple framework within which ideas from these various literatures could be marshalled.

Notwithstanding the dangers of over-generalizing and of drawing unduly hard distinctions between literatures characterized by diversity and subtlety, two broad traditions of thought can certainly be discerned. We will label them, for convenience, the 'optimistic' and 'pessimistic' traditions. However, it is important to emphasize that we only present them as optimistic and pessimistic in relation to our chosen issue: the possibility and likelihood of achieving coordination as an expression and outcome of a wider commitment to rationality in public affairs.

The 'Optimistic' Tradition

The 'optimistic' tradition is characterized by persistence in the face of recurring disappointments; it follows a cyclical pattern of enthusiasm, disillusionment and resurrection. Its rhetoric is enduring because it evokes commitment to a particular way of viewing the world:

> The first of the shared commitments is to rationality. Coordination strategies carry an authoritative ring of technical competence and planning . . . The most obvious point is that integration of human services makes sense . . . A reform strategy that claims to bring order out of chaos becomes very appealing. There is a deep and pervasive vein of current conventional wisdom, namely that all things should be unified, quantified, ordered, consolidated and computerised . . . Unification is good, duplication is bad . . . official order is safe, pluralistic order is less than safe. Coordination appeals to this proposition.[4]

In short, the 'optimistic' tradition survives because it reflects and embodies the ideology of public bureaucracies concerned to bring about predictability and regularity in a turbulent world. Without coordination there will be conflict or wasteful competition.

The primary focus of this tradition in recent times, apart from the process of rational synoptic planning itself, has been the organizational framework necessary for the survival of that process. Organizational dysfunction, as we have noted, was widely diagnosed as the major barrier to effective coordination throughout the 1960s and 1970s: organizational structures, formal machinery and planning processes were highlighted as the crucial prerequisites of progress. [. . .]

The prerequisites and assumptions entailed in the 'optimistic' tradition underline the organizational and behavioural demands and expectations which it involves. At minimum, the idea of rational planning implies:

(a) a broad, system-wide perspective rather than a narrow or sectional view of problems, needs and issues;
(b) the existence, or achievement, of broad areas of consensus on goals, the nature of the problems to be tackled, the most acceptable and efficacious methods of intervention, and on priorities;
(c) a significant capacity for rational analysis, combined with authoritative backing;
(d) organizational arrangements appropriate to the analysis of problems and the implementation of solutions.

The assumption is that rational planning springing from such a conducive environment will provide the authoritative framework within which coordination will occur at all levels. As we have noted, the exception – a very major exception – arises from the frequent absence of imperative coordination: collaboration is necessary if policy and action are to be coordinated across the boundaries of autonomous organizations and groupings. However, collaboration, as Webb and Wistow have indicated,[5] implies further and no less demanding requirements:

(a) that a system-wide perspective will pervade all organizations and groups which do, or which ought to, interact;
(b) that 'system-gain' (e.g. the greater good of the client or community) will be readily identified by all and will act as a sufficient reward for the achievement of consensus;
(c) that where pursuing system-gain conflicts with short-term and sectional interests, the latter will triumph – 'organizational altruism' will be the order of the day.

The matter of organizational altruism is crucial precisely because the rational tradition underplays the power of divergent interests. It assumes that consensus is readily achievable and it has no solution to offer – other than authoritative action by a higher body – if it is not forthcoming. Given the reality of divergent sectional interests, collaborative rational action must therefore depend to some extent, possibly a major extent, on the altruistic willingness of organizations or groupings to forgo some of these sectional interests. It is one of the issues we clearly had to build into the hypotheses and propositions which guided our empirical research.

The 'Pessimistic' Tradition

While the rational tradition optimistically posits an underlying social harmony, the many alternative viewpoints are united precisely in their pessimism – or realism – on this point. The assumption is that 'harmony of needs is not only undiscoverable but non-existent'.[6] In the tradition of Hayek and Popper, true rationality resides in process – the interplay of individual preferences and decisions – not in the imposition of a collective strategy. 'Pluralistic disorder' is positively embraced, or at the very least acknowledged. The notion of an overarching rationality is seen as a snare and delusion leading to the 'preceptorial society'.[7]

Beyond the prescriptive and tendentious elements of this perspective there is a central observation with which observers from all points of the ideological compass have been able to concur: individual and group interests are multiple and divergent, and the net result is competition, bargaining and conflict. As with the tradition of optimism about rationality, routes back to some form of relatively harmonious social order are typically sought and prescribed – whether in the classical liberal advocacy of the market or the classical Marxist advocacy of a wholly novel socioeconomic order. Nonetheless, theorists in the 'pessimistic' tradition begin by recognizing divergent and conflicting interests and it is this preliminary observation which throws much light on the deficiencies, and indeed the potential dangers, of the search for a rational consensus in public affairs. Without a class or conflict perspective, for example, it would be much more difficult to highlight the enormous potential of 'coordination' as an instrument of neglect (benign or otherwise), of official evasion, or of repressive social control. But for the purposes of guiding our empirical research, a potentially vast literature which was explicitly or implicitly critical of the rational optimistic tradition had to be translated into a manageable number of insightful propositions and guiding hypotheses on three topics central to the coordination issue:

information;
the nature of policy; and
the nature of interaction between organizations.

Information: Coping with Overload

Failures of communication and pleas for better information exchange are perennial. They are the smokescreen for incompetence and bad faith, but also the time-honoured figleaf with which to disguise the unpalatable fact of divergent interests where harmony and rational collaboration are presumed to reign. However, even assuming that communication is the problem and not the scapegoat, the 'optimistic' tradition tends towards naivety. Information is treated as costless, as self-evidently good and as a force for unity rather than division. The alternative is to stress the costs of both generating and processing information, and the problems of coping with it.

The most familiar result of viewing information as problematic is to conclude, with Simon, that individuals and organizations will tend to 'satisfice' rather than 'optimize'.[8] The rational model assumes that maximizing information and analysis will maximize the quality of decision-making. That, in practice, the costs of pursuing perfect information are great is indisputable, but the argument can be taken further. For the individual actor learning to cope with a particular kind of information is an 'irreversible investment'; the 'code' has to be learned. For the organization this process represents a significant accumulation of 'capital': once created, therefore, organizations have distinct identities which are comparatively inflexible due to the costs involved in changing codes.[9] The process of coping with information consequently erects barriers to coordination, especially to collaboration.

The more efficient an organization (or profession) is in developing its own code – i.e. its way of handling and interpreting information – the more difficult it may be to communicate with other organizations. A similar conclusion is suggested by cognitive theory. Organizational actors develop analytical paradigms which allow them to cope with uncertainty and ambiguity in dealing with information. In Steinbruner's words, 'Pertinent information may enter the decision process or it may be screened out, depending on how it relates to the existing pattern of belief';[10] information 'which is threatening to established belief patterns' may be rejected. This, in turn, may lead to 'grooved thinking': the organizational actor's decisions 'are programmed so that once he determines which category obtains, the decision follows without further question'. This is first cousin to the notion of Standard Operating Procedures (SOPs), described as follows by Allison:

> Rules of thumb permit concerted action by large numbers of individuals, each responding to basic cues. The rules are usually simple enough to facilitate easy learning and unambiguous application. Since procedures are 'standard' they do not change quickly or easily. Without such standard procedures, it would not be possible to perform certain concerted tasks . . . Some SOPs are simply conventions that make possible regular or coordinated activity. But most SOPs are grounded in the incentive structure of the organisation or even in the norms of the organisation or the basic attitudes and operating style of its members. The stronger the grounding, the more resistant SOPs are to change.[11]

Once again, the more efficient organizations are in developing their own analytic paradigms and SOPs – i.e. in coordinating their internal activities – the more difficult they may find it to enter into a dialogue with other organizations, since they will be using different organizational languages.

The problems of organizational information-handling raise some further questions about the assumptions made – if only implicitly – in the 'optimistic' rational model. If coordination is about information exchange (among other things), what actually is being exchanged, and by whom? One way of organizing the collection of information within the organization is through hierarchy: the information flows up the official lines of authority. But this, as Downs argues,[12] introduces bias since 'all types of officials tend to exaggerate data that reflect favourably on themselves and to minimize those that reveal their own shortcomings'. Such bias introduces information distortion. Thus Tullock calculated that if, in an organization with seven levels, the average official screens out only half the data given him by his subordinates, the winnowing process would eliminate 94.8 per cent of the data originally gathered by the time the information reached the top of the office.[13] Yet a central feature of coordination, as we discovered, is precisely that it depends both upon detailed understanding of the key issues at the level at which coordination is to occur and upon decision-making authority. The choice of personnel to discuss and negotiate new arrangements is therefore a perennial problem and a crucial determinant of outcomes.

Policy: A Misleading Concept

The very idea of policy implies a degree of orderliness, even consensus; a way forward has been agreed and delineated. In the social policy field, moreover, the term 'policy' is typically taken to refer to the specification of the needs which are to be met and the means by which this is to be achieved. The implication – widely reflected in official policy on the inner cities and on the care of the elderly and other 'priority client groups' – is that what is required is coordination between different policies, each of which is designed to meet one of an interlocking set of needs. The real problem of coordination is seen to lie at the interface between the major strands of social policy and the major service departments and agencies which enact them.

This is a wholly misleading picture and it is one which arises from the conceptualization of policy as a coherent, relatively self-contained, complete and authoritative guide to future action. However, this misleading picture also arises from the tendency in the post-war decades to split social policy off from the rest of the body politic and to treat it as a hermetically sealed arena of state intervention coterminous with the departments and agencies of social policy. In reality, policy processes are altogether more complex and messy. The conflicts and power struggles which determine the *outcomes* of social policy (as opposed to the content of statements of objectives which are merely *inputs*) are to be located throughout the government system and not only in the 'social policy departments'.[14]

One way of expressing some of this complex reality is by thinking, as Webb and Wistow suggest,[15] in terms of *streams of policies* which interact, compete and conflict, rather than in terms of policies as discrete and authoritative blueprints. They argue that social policy outcomes are best seen as the end-product of at least three streams of interacting policies:

1 *service, or output, policies* – which specify the social needs to be met and the choice of appropriate means and methods of intervention;
2 *resource policies* – which specify broad patterns of expenditure, detailed allocations between competing uses, and the dominant approaches taken to resource management (e.g. to maximize long-term cost-effectiveness or to minimize total expenditure in the short term);
3 *governance policies* – which specify the general view taken of the role of the state as well as the philosophy of management and control to be adopted within public authorities (e.g. centralization or decentralization, detailed intervention or *laissez-faire*).

To these can be added a fourth:

4 *fiscal policies* – which specify the general view taken on the level and structure of taxation to be aimed at as well as the specific tax 'subsidies', benefits or breaks which are to be permitted.

What this formulation immediately reveals is the importance of seeing policies as a means of *expressing* conflicting interests rather than as the product of conflict resolution. A policy to ease the lot of institutionalized mentally ill people which founders for lack of resources can only be seen in the rational 'optimistic' tradition as a failure of communication and coordination. But it may more accurately be understood as the triumph of one interest (expressed through resource allocation policies) over the interests of mentally ill people (expressed through a service policy). It is therefore essential to look for competition and conflict between policies and also to recognize the divergent value systems, goals, dominant interests, and informational codes which may underpin differences between various policy streams.

To turn this perception of conflicting interests on its head is to reveal another dimension of coordination: to achieve a particular outcome for a vulnerable and weak interest group such as the mentally ill will not only depend on coordinating different social service organizations and objectives. It will depend on the degree of coordination achieved across the service, resource and fiscal policy streams, which in turn will depend upon the adoption of a governance strategy designed to effect congruence between service goals and resource commitments. In short, coordination is not merely a neutral technique. It can be a crucial element of any strategy to overcome – or to enhance – the bias in favour of dominant interests and ideologies which is inherent in our – and every – system of government. Coordination is itself about power and the purposeful use of power.

Power-Dependence and Organizational Interaction

The rational tradition tends to assume that the guiding ideology of public service organizations is the pursuit of the common good. One of the popular alternative viewpoints is that organizational actors are self-interested 'utility maximizers':

> Bureaucratic officials in general have a complex set of goals including power, income, prestige, security, convenience, loyalty (to an idea, an institution, or the nation), pride in excellent work, and desire to serve the public interest . . . But regardless of the particular goals involved, every official is significantly motivated by his own self-interest.[16]

This view of organizational actors as economic men who will weigh up the costs and benefits to themselves of any given course of action, sensitizes us to incentives and disincentives to coordination (or any other desired objective). [. . .]

Viewing public service organizations as bodies dedicated to protecting their resource base (as distinct from necessarily seeking to maximize their budgets) has some further implications. It suggests that such organizations will seek to mobilize political support for their activities – and budgets – just as private sector business firms will seek to attract customers for their products. After all, in a period of resource stress even support for baseline activities cannot be taken for granted. Such support mobilization strategies may take a variety of forms, but one self-evident strategy consists of proclaiming the organization's special and unique role in protecting the interests or well-being of a popular or politically strong client group. To establish a monopoly of care or provision for such a group is to assert the claim that any attack on the organization – such as budget retrenchment – is also an attack on those clients. In a sense, popular clients are valuable property, to be defended against other, competing organizations. Conversely, of course, one might expect public sector organizations to be less interested in the care of less popular client groups. Willingness to collaborate would, therefore, be most unlikely where one organization sees itself as having established a desirable monopoly and most likely where a client group is seen as marginal to the agency's main role or as imposing burdens which do not bring in any compensatory inputs of support. In this respect, the rational strategy for public sector organizations would be similar to that for professions, in so far as the process of professionalization can be seen as the assertion of monopoly control over certain social functions or skills (a conclusion which would, in turn, suggest that a public sector organization containing a strong professional element would have a double incentive to warn possible competitors off its policy patch). [. . .]

The rational perspective draws heavily on Weber and a host of modern interpreters united by the basic tenets of the classic theory of bureaucracy, but alternative viewpoints spring from a variety of disciplinary perspectives and often lack even a common vocabulary. Nonetheless, a central theme is the insistence on viewing organizations as 'bargaining and influence systems'. If individual actors seek to maximize utilities, groups and even whole organizations can be understood in the same terms. Organizations compete for resources with the result that the normal mode of co-existence is not harmonious collaboration but bargaining, power play and conflict.

Lindblom's early contribution to the debate rested on the assumption that organizations would coordinate their activities only if it was in their own self-interest; attempts at exhortation or at establishing formal coordinative machinery would not be likely to have much effect.[17] Lindblom's approach was consistent with a heterogeneity of literature sailing under the flag of exchange theory. One of its great merits is that it identifies many of the barriers and opportunities which shape bargaining processes.[18] The starting point is that bargaining, or exchange, is a function of interdependence: interdependent organizations 'must take each other into account if they are to accomplish their goals'. Interdependence consists of interlocking patterns of demand and supply for resources: material resources such as capital, income flows, labour and clients, but also less tangible resources such as information, expertise, authority and the capacity to authorize. Bargaining depends upon complementary patterns of demand and supply for such resources and also upon the likelihood of substituting readily available alternatives for needed resources possessed exclusively by a rival organization. [. . .]

Aiken and Hague have argued that for bargaining and exchange to take place 'there must be some slack in the resource base'.[19] Subsequent empirical findings suggested that scarcity may provide the motive but that 'those agencies most willing to act upon this motive are those relatively rich in clients and non-human resources'.[20] The obvious proposition – which informed our own choice of empirical research sites – is that a finely balanced experience of pressure and comparative security (or room for manoeuvre) provides the strongest spur to exchange through bargaining.

However, the picture is further complicated by the transaction costs involved in inter-organizational exchange. Negotiation ties down staff and involves uncertainty and risks. These costs may in turn depend upon the networks, if any, which link organizations. As Thrasher has argued, 'networks which persist over time are likely to exhibit different exchange patterns than those which are newly created.[21] The need to create networks and engender trust can be a major transaction cost. What this suggests is that formal machinery may have no relevance where the preconditions for bargaining are absent, but it may play a real role in giving permanence to networks and lowering transaction costs.

The importance of networks underlines the fact that the rewards sought on behalf of organizations and those sought by their representatives as individuals differ. Individual actors may aspire to many non-material rewards: status, social approval and friendship. Nonetheless, the individual actor, just as much as the organization, is viewed essentially as self-interested rather than altruistic.

To recognize networks and diverse non-material rewards is to accept that exchange and bargaining constitute a complex social game which is likely to be played according to rules – rules which define socially acceptable behaviour and transactions. Relationships between organizations, groupings and policy streams may be based on competition and conflict rather than on consensus, but competition and conflict are constrained by 'basic rules of conduct'. Moreover, interlocking transactions may take place in more than one arena: 'some resources gained in one arena may be used to win prizes in another arena'.

The complexity of the bargaining relationships through which policies and actions may become more (or less) coordinated points to two crucial issues for empirical research: the structuring of arenas by government and the role of 'middlemen'. The first of these is summarized in Webb and Wistow's phrase, 'the structuring of local policy environments'.[22] Health and local authorities, for example, do not relate one to another in a vacuum. Central government systematically, though not necessarily intentionally, influences the resources needed by and available to these organizations. It structures the formal organizational arrangements which impinge on the development of networks of relationshps, and it determines many of the costs and benefits of interaction. It may also affect the availability of 'middlemen'. [. . .]

The superficial attractions of the rational 'optimistic' tradition are even clearer when it is remembered that stable patterns of exchange and bargaining rest upon a broad symmetry between organizations and a recognition that opportunities exist for rewarding exchange. The first is crucial, not least because it raises the ghost at this feast: power. Bargaining and exchange arise from dependence: a wholly independent organization with no pressing unmet resource needs can afford to go its own way without reference to others. But dependence bestows power on the resource-rich party; undue dependence implies dominance by another. Reasonably symmetrical patterns of dependence are therefore the stimulus to exchange. Moreover, a symmetrical pattern of dependence has to be *perceived*. Opportunities for exchange which go unnoticed, and exchange possibilities which are seen to include unduly high costs, or risks of dominance, will simply result in non-interaction – even the active avoidance of interaction. [. . .]

The obvious caveat which must be appended to this power-dependence/bargaining-exchange model of organizational interaction is that power may be too narrowly conceived. Wrong suggested the narrowness of the approach taken by arguing: 'I do not see how we can avoid restricting the term "power" to intentional and effective control by particular agents'. Emerson, even more specifically, asserted: 'The power of A over B is equal to, and based upon the dependence of B upon A.[23] These views of power could be stretched to include all that we would wish to include, but it is better by far to follow Lukes and adopt a more catholic formulation. The kind of power most readily incorporated within the approach suggested by Wrong and Emerson and many others, is essentially overt – it is a behavioural approach to power. It comprises what Bachrach and Baratz called the first face of power.[24] In their terms, the second face of power added another ingredient: non-decisions. This concept has been greatly ill-used, but Bachrach and Baratz applied it in situations in which possible lines of action or behaviour were intentionally excluded from discussion, or were kept off the agenda, by power-holders. To take an example, a highly self-sufficient organization may perennially disregard calls to coordinate its actions with those of a less powerful organization; an arrogant insularity may keep the coordination issue off the agenda altogether. [. . .]

From the point of view of central government departments seeking to encourage coordination in social policy, the 'pessimistic' tradition of academic analysis makes dismal reading. The central government tendency has always been to rely on the rational model. Organizations and professions are exhorted to look beyond their sectional interests and to work together for the greater good of clients and the community. Such altruism is expected to be its own reward. The 'pessimistic' academic tradition underlines all the barriers not only of self-interest *per se*, but of exceedingly complicated patterns of self-interest. Interaction may occur through bargaining and exchange and it may possibly lead to desired patterns of coordination. But it may, even more plausibly, lead to no such thing. Organizational relationships, where they occur, may fall far short of such well-developed exchanges. Partisan mutual adjustment, to use Lindblom's old expression, may merely involve organizations in changes of practice which are designed to avoid or minimize conflict. It may facilitate unilateral development, which Glennerster identifies as the dominant contemporary mode of action in the social policy field,[25] rather than presaging close collaboration.

Unilateral change by one organization to accommodate the policies of another may produce desired coordination, or it may merely represent two ships of state passing in the night.

While non-interaction and failures of coordination may be the most readily explained phenomena, the 'pessimistic' tradition does hold out hope of more concerted action. It points to the possibility of systematically structuring arenas so that they facilitate and promote collaborative exchange. The conditions may be demanding and government action may need to be finely tuned if it is to succeed, but the message – in essence – is simply that 'policy implementation' ought to be as central and as well informed a feature of government as 'policy-making'. That opportunities for concerted influence do exist is the optimistic part of the 'pessimistic' tradition from a governmental point of view.

What is also apparent is that these academic perspectives are substantially complementary, rather than in conflict. The great rational synoptic planning versus incrementalism debate obscured this complementarity. An emphasis on power-dependence and bargaining needs to be balanced by reference to the possibility – however slight – that social service organizations and professions may at times take a broad, altruistic view and elevate system (or client) gain above sectional interests. However, to speak of altruism in this context could be misleading, for it is the value base and service ethos of the social services which may produce such a 'rational' outcome. If government neglects to build and mobilize such a value base, it is indeed relying upon pure altruism to generate collaboration.

Similarly, the 'pessimistic' emphasis on processes of interaction, bargaining and conflict is needed to balance frequent references to structures. The elegant mansion of rational synoptic planning was constructed without sufficient regard to the need for adequate foundations or to the problems of managing a large and disputatious household. Nonetheless, it did at least recognize that walls and roof are more likely to join, and skilled workers are more likely to be brought together, when everyone has a blueprint in their hands. Neither the emphasis on structure nor that on planning is irrelevant; together they may, as we have argued, provide the context in which networks develop and flourish – networks which are vital to processes of interaction. [. . .]

Notes

1 J. L. Pressman and A. Wildavsky (1979) *Implementation*. Berkeley: University of California Press.

2 H. Glennerster, *et al.* (1983) *Planning for Priority Groups*. Oxford: Martin Robertson.

3 C. E. Lindblom (1959) 'The science of muddling through', *Public Administration Review*, 19(2): 79–88; Lindblom (1965) *The Intelligence of Democracy*. New York: Free Press.

4 J. A. Weiss (1981) 'Substance and symbol in administrative reform: the case of human service coordination', *Policy Analysis*, 7(1): 21–47.

5 A. L. Webb and G. Wistow, 'Collaboration: a case study in social planning', *Journal of Social Policy*, forthcoming.

6 C. E. Lindblom (1977) *Politics and Markets*. New York: Basic Books, p. 251.

7 Ibid.

8 H. Simon (1965) *Administrative Behavior*. New York: Free Press.

9 K. J. Arrow (1974) *The Limits of Organisation*. New York: W. W. Norton.

10 J. D. Steinbruner (1974) *The Cybernetic Theory of Decision*. Princeton, NJ: Princeton University Press.

11 G. T. Allison (1971) *Essence of Decision*. Boston: Little Brown.

12 A. Downs (1967) *Inside Bureaucracy*. Boston: Little Brown.

13 G. Tullock (1975) *The Politics of Bureaucracy*. Washington, DC: Public Affairs Press.

14 R. M. Titmuss (1968) *Commitment to Welfare*. London: Allen & Unwin; H. Heclo and A. Wildavsky (1981) *The Private Government of Public Money*, 2nd edn. London: Macmillan.

15 A. L. Webb and G. Wistow (1982) *Whither State Welfare?* London: Royal Institute of Public Administration; Webb and Wistow (1986) *Planning, Need and Scarcity: Essays on the Personal Social Services*. London: Allen & Unwin.

16 Downs (1967), *op. cit.*, pp. 212–13.

17 Lindblom (1965), *op. cit.*

18 Peter Abell (ed.) (1975) *Organisations as Bargaining and Influence Systems*. London: Heinemann; S. B. Bacharach and E. J. Lawler (1981) *Bargaining*. New York: Jossey-Bass. For a comprehensive summary of power-dependence/bargaining-exchange literatures as they apply in this field, see R. Rhodes (1981) *Control as Power in Central–Local Relationships*. London: Gower; see also Glennerster *et al.* (1983), *op. cit.*

19 M. Aiken and J. Hage (1968) 'Organisational interdependence and Intra-organisational structure', *American Sociological Review*, 33: 912–30.

20 E. Litwak and L. P. Hylton (1961) 'Intcrorganisational analysis: a hypothesis on coordinating agencies', *Administrative Science Quarterly*: 395–420.

21 Michael Thrasher (1983) 'Exchange, networks and implementation', *Policy and Politics*, II(4) October: 375–93.

22 A. L. Webb and G. Wistow (1985) 'Structuring local policy environments', in S. Ranson, *Studies in Central–Local Relations*. London: Allen & Unwin.

23 D. H. Wrong (1967) 'Some problems in defining social power', *American Journal of Sociology*, 73: 673–81, R. M. Emerson (1962) 'Power dependence relations', *American Sociological Review*, 27: 31–41.

24 P. Bachrach and M. S. Baratz (1970) *Power and Poverty: Theory and Practice*. London: Oxford University Press.

25 Glennerster *et al.* (1983), *op. cit.*

PART 3
RESPONSIVENESS AND PERFORMANCE

Introduction

Managers in the public services are required to be accountable in a number of different ways – financially, legally and politically. Accountability is central to the debate concerning control and performance measurement. Who is accountable for what and to whom are key questions for public services organizations.

Day and Klein, in Chapter 13, examine different perceptions of accountability and different forms of it. They conclude that 'accountability is problematic precisely because of the assertion by many service providers that only they can define and evaluate competence'.

Day and Klein argue that different perceptions of accountability are held by different stakeholders, and they suggest that managerial accountability and political accountability often do not appear to mesh. In Chapter 14 Carter considers how organizations move from hands-on to hands-off control and whether performance indicators can aid this. Carter argues that as constitutional accountability becomes more problematic because of the creation of arm's-length agencies such as those involved in Next Steps then performance indicators can 'help fill this accountability gap'.

From a different perspective Kanters and Summers argue that there will inevitably be different constituencies with an interest in public services organizations and these multiple stakeholders have to be catered for when assessing the performance of organizations. Organizations have a number of different functions reflecting their different aspects. Each function services a different constituency – outside stakeholders who confer legitimacy upon it such as elected representatives; managers concerned with internal processes and resource allocation; customers or clients in receipt of the service or product. In order to respond to the latter groups of stakeholders, some control has to be given up by managers. How do organizations become more responsive and in what areas do managers have to respond if consumer interests are to be given greater prominence? In Chapter 17 Potter looks at five key factors which need to be addressed: access, choice, information, redress and representation. Potter indicates the challenge for managers: 'It requires an imaginative leap to consider consumers as equals in a three-cornered exchange with politicians (who possess the power) and professionals (who possess the skills and the expertise, and any delegated or assumed power as well).'

In Chapter 16 Bertillson cautions us against the strength of professional power, arguing that 'it is indeed possible to claim that the welfare state is as much a professional as it is a political achievement', and argues that we need professionalism but not 'blind faith in its decisions'.

In order for organizations to become more responsive, management gurus urge changes in culture. Meek, in 'Organizational Culture', cautions against simple panaceas, since 'culture is the product of negotiated and shared symbols and meanings'. It cannot be mechanically manipulated: 'culture should be regarded as something that an organization "is", not something that an organization "has": it is not an independent variable, nor can it be created, discovered or destroyed by the whims of management'.

Notwithstanding the arguments of Meek, greater attention has been paid in recent years to the development of human resource strategies. In the final chapter Weggemans examines the different values involved in managing human resources in public services organizations and contrasts the concern by central government to control expenditure on public employees with the need for local autonomy to respond to local political choices and labour markets. Weggemans argues that public services organizations need to develop human resource strategies to take account of the link between the organization and its environment.

The readings in Parts 2 and 3 are concerned with the core issues of control, accountability performance, the role of professionals, implementation and responsiveness and reflect the tension between control and responsiveness.

13

Interpretations and Implications

Patricia Day and Rudolf Klein

[. . .] Our starting point, anchored in the logic of the academic literature on the theory of accountability and the assumptions of public policy pronouncements, was that to be fully accountable implies the ability to exercise control. If service providers are not accountable to authority members, that is if the links in the chain are broken, then how can authority members be accountable, be it to voters or to a secretary of state? In our study, however, we found that members of some authorities saw no incompatibility between perceiving themselves as accountable, while yet lamenting their own lack of control. The difference between the authorities made up of directly elected members and those made up, to varying degrees, of nominated members, did not stem from different perceptions of their own role. It reflected, rather, differences in the way in which they responded to and interpreted the tensions inherent in that role.

Consider first the non-elected members of the health and police authorities. In both cases members were worried about their ability to control the services for which they were responsible. And, in line with our expectations, they were also worried about their own ability to be accountable for those services. In short, their attitudes were consistent in that they were aware of the tension between the requirements of formal accountability and the reality of lack of effective control. Consider next, however, the directly elected members of the education and social services committees. In the former case [. . .], the members expressed considerable doubts about their ability to control the service; in the latter case [. . .], they had far fewer doubts. But both sets of authority members, to a remarkable degree, saw the exercise of their accountability as unproblematic. This would, in turn, suggest that directly elected members differ from nominated members not so much in their perceptions of accountability as in their ability to convince themselves that accountability is unproblematical and to ignore the relationship between accountability and control. From their perspective, the fact of election, the constitutional myth that election *ipso facto* makes members accountable, washes away the contradictions involved in the role. Accountability is taken for granted.

From P. Day and R. Klein (1987) *Accountabilities: Five Public Services.* London: Tavistock, 1987, pp. 228–50 (abridged).

The contrary does not follow, however. Here, the case of the non-elected members of the water authority is instructive. These were unique among the members of the non-elected authorities in our study in that they saw neither the exercise of accountability nor that of control as problematic. They were as confident about their role as the local authority members, despite lacking the imprimatur of elections. Their confidence stemmed from their perceptions of congruity between practice and theory in their exercise of their own role, inasmuch as accountability and control marched hand in hand.

The evidence therefore suggests that the distinction in much of public discussion between elected members as being accountable by definition and non-elected members being non-accountable by definition, is oversimple. And it is oversimple because it ignores the link between control and accountability. Our findings would suggest that the real distinction is in the perceptions of members. It is between those elected members who perceive themselves to be accountable, even when the requirement of effective control is lacking, and those non-elected members who feel themselves to be accountable only when the necessary condition of effective control is met. The paradox would seem to be that the rhetoric of election as synonymous with accountability may, in fact, divert attention from the conditions that have to be met if accountability in the full sense is to be achieved; in contrast, members who lack the legitimacy of election appear to be more conscious of their need for control.

All this is, however, to assume that accountability itself is an unproblematic concept. Again, our findings would suggest the need for a more finely shaded interpretation, as well as providing a warning against assuming that members of authorities necessarily read the textbooks which tell them what their accountability role is. The different ways in which the authority members thought aloud about their role, in response to our questions, in themselves illustrate the ambiguities of the concept. They often tended to use a clutch of words – accountability, answerability, and responsibility – as though they were interchangeable. Few appeared to use accountability in the strict sense, that is the revocability of a mandate. There was little sense, either among the members of nominated authorities (whose mandate could, in theory, be revoked by the Secretary of State or his agents) or among the members of elected bodies (whose mandate could, in theory, be revoked by the voters) of sanctions if their justification failed to satisfy. More frequently their implicit definition of accountability seemed to shade into answerability: the duty to provide explanations or to give visibility to their actions. Lastly, many members tended to define accountability in terms of their responsibility, either to the community being served or to use their own sense of what was sensible or proper: they internalized accountability, as it were, as a general duty to pursue the public good according to their own criteria of what was right. As they saw it, their mandate also imposed a duty on them: the real sanction was not revocability of the mandate, but their own civic super-ego. They saw themselves as trustees or tribunes rather than delegates.

It is this perhaps which helps to explain a pattern running right across our services: the emphasis among members on seeing accountability, answerability or responsibility as being directed *to* the 'community' at large, rather than following the lines of constitutional accountability. Whether nominated members of health, police or water authorities or elected members of education or social service committees, it was this emphasis which provided a common thread through the responses. The nominated members did not, for the most part, see themselves directly accountable to a secretary of state, as they are in theory (the main exception being the chairmen of the authorities concerned). The elected members did not, for their part, see themselves directly accountable to the voters, as they are in theory. Some Labour councillors saw themselves accountable to the party; but interestingly the Conservatives did not. This indeed was one of the very few issues where there was even a hint of consistent differences between political parties: going through the notes of the interviews, it was often impossible to tell the political allegiance of the respondents.

In adopting a 'community' view of accountability, members may in fact have been reflecting the actual pattern of their day-to-day linkages, which have little to do with such remote abstractions as the Secretary of State or voters. [. . .] They rarely discussed their services with individual citizens or voters: [. . .] even in the case of councillors, most of the issues raised by members of the public were, in fact, to do with public housing. They were, however, involved as active citizens themselves in a variety of contacts, responding to pressures and demands and thus forced to justify the actions of the authorities of which they were members. This would suggest that the way in which members of authorities define their accountability – as a general, diffuse duty to justify or explain to that nebulous notion, the 'community' – reflects their position as public persons, rather than the route (nomination or election) by which they arrived at that position. It is because they are publicly exposed to scrutiny that they feel themselves accountable, in one or other meanings of that concept. It is their own, personal visibility – whether as magistrates on a police authority or councillors on a local authority committee – which makes them sensitive to the need to explain and justify themselves in face-to-face encounters. In other words, the subjective sense of accountability of authority members has its roots – our evidence would imply – as much in the social context in which they operate, as in constitutional doctrine.

Performance, Policies and Actions

But for what do authority members see themselves accountable? What is their language of evaluation? Again, our discussion must start with a puzzle, this time stemming from the discrepancy between the conventional doctrine of accountability and our own findings. The drift of public policy [. . .] has been towards conceiving accountability as being responsible for the overall performance of a service and using what might be termed managerial tools of analysis as the language of evaluation. However, our interviews provide little evidence that the members of the five authorities in our study – with one significant exception – saw their own role in the way assumed in public policy and much academic discussion. Moreover, they also suggest that many of the assumptions made are unrealistic – given the characteristics of the services themselves.

First, our use of the notion of performance in public services needs some explanation. This encompasses two concepts which stalk the literature: policy-making and policy implementation. To talk about the performance of a service is to combine these into one concept: to convey the idea that a service is to be evaluated by what it does, which will inevitably be a combination of what policy decisions have been taken, often over a very long period of time, and the processes whereby those policies are translated into action. To be accountable for the performance of a service, in our definition, is thus to be answerable for the achievement of multiple objectives (which may or may not be expressed in terms of explicit policy decisions of either policy-makers or service providers). It is from these objectives that the language of evaluation is derived, since there can be no criteria of assessment without a sense of what is desirable. The objectives may be about ends or about means. [. . .] They may involve either political accountability or managerial accountability: argument about what should be done and argument about whether what is being done is being done efficiently and effectively. The notion of performance thus embraces the various dimensions of accountability in that it assumes that members of authorities will be answerable not just for the different strands of service delivery but for the way in which these combine to form a total tapestry of service provision. Using this wide sense of the term there is little evidence that members of the various authorities in our study – with the single exception of the water authority – had any sense of being accountable for the performance of their services. They may have perceived themselves as 'owning' particular policy strands: that is for being accountable for pursuing specific policies (perhaps because these were in the party manifesto; for example, in the case of the education committee members, abolishing corporal punishment, and introducing peace studies in schools). [. . .] Where members of the various authorities tended to differ was chiefly in whether or not they found their inability to set some overarching set of goals bothersome. Again, the members of the elected authorities tended to find this issue unproblematic, while others (notably the members of health authorities) were worried about their inability to define performance in terms of the efficient and effective pursuit of specific objectives. Even in the case of the elected members, there were signs of a dawning interest in the notion of performance among the young councillors: in this respect, as in some others, there were signs of a generational split.

There are a number of reasons for the apparent lack of interest in the overall performance, that is outcomes of their services, by most members. First and foremost, the notion of performance is genuinely difficult and elusive in the case of most of the services in our study. [. . .] The relationship between inputs and outcomes is often difficult to discern, which might explain the traditional preoccupation of members with their accountability for inputs only; the contribution of any particular service is often difficult to isolate from the wider social environment. All this is self-evidently so in the case of health, the police, education, and social services. In the one instance where there is a clearly defined concept of performance, that of the water authority, the members had indeed a confident sense of knowing where they were going and how to check the achievement against objectives.

The second set of reasons stem from the complexity of the concept of accountability itself. This has [. . .] a number of different dimensions. If accountability for achieving goals is not possible, it may still be possible to be accountable for process: the way in which services are run as judged by the competence of individual actions. But process is [. . .] largely the domain of the service providers. It is they who claim to determine the language of evaluating the process of service delivery, be they surgeons, police or teachers. Where members of the authorities in our study did not perceive their accountability as responsibility for the performance of their services, seen in terms of process, they were only being realistic. They were, in fact, largely excluded from this domain by the service-providers.

The point is brought out by the two services in our studies where, if for very different reasons, the members *did* see themselves as accountable for process. In the case of the water authority, this was because the criteria for assessing process directly followed from those defining objectives: a failure in process could be deduced from a failure to achieve such objectives as an adequate supply of water or of the efficient disposal of water. There was no doubt about causality. More interesting, because more unexpected, the members of the social services not only saw themselves as accountable for process but also appeared to be reasonably confident that they were successfully carrying out their role. They were the only members responsible for labour-intensive services (as distinct from those delivered by pipes) who seemed remarkably free from doubts about their own ability to know what is going on in their service. Nor is this surprising, perhaps, given that social services are different [. . .] in that the service-providers have failed fully to assert their claim to the language of evaluation: witness the ability of the members of the social service committee to review and reverse the decisions of service-providers (to underline the uniqueness of this, only imagine a health authority telling a surgeon what operations he or she should carry out or an education committee telling a headteacher how to score examination papers).

The third reason why members lack interest in outcomes is that they tend to be suspicious of managerial tools and techniques for assessing perform-ance with the exception, as always, of the water authority. Across services they are, as we have seen, at best agnostic about the use of comparative information or performance indicators. [. . .] The pattern is not entirely consistent, and there were once again signs of a generational divide. The sense of being manipulated by the gatekeepers of information and data was particularly strong among members of the health and education committees who both complained about the lack of relevant information. It was less evident in the case of the police and social services. The differences seem to reflect less variations in the adequacy or quality of the information being supplied (on reading some of the interview material, officers of the council concerned commented indignantly that members had all the information they wanted) than variations in the degree of trust between members and their chief officers. The paradox would seem to be that if a chief officer is not trusted, he or she will be asked for ever more information – yet never satisfy her or his audience. Conversely, if he or she is trusted, his or her rendering of accounts – in terms of the information provided – is likely to be accepted. [. . .]

It is this wariness towards official information, and particularly statistical data, which helps to explain the lack of the use made by the members in our study of the kind of comparative analyses of performance provided by the Audit Commission or by inspectorates. Independent managerial account-ability and political accountability do not appear to mesh: the former, contrary to our own expectations, and that of the policy-makers, does not link with and reinforce the latter. Partly this may reflect the timing of our study: when the members were interviewed, the system of audit and inspection was only beginning to get off the ground. Partly, however, it also reflects an underlying antipathy towards technical tools of accountability (qualified by generational differences, once more). Our interviews sug-gested considerable suspicion of a value-for-money approach as somehow being incompatible with services dedicated to the public good and perhaps also threatening qualitative and professional objectives. Matthew Arnold's hostility to a 'mechanistic' approach to evaluating education is clearly shared by many members responsible for delivering human services. [. . .]

The example of the social services committee brings out a further dimension of accountability. The members of this committee [. . .] were able to review decisions taken by service providers; many of them, furthermore, saw themselves as responding to individual needs and problems – on a case-by-case basis – rather than providing a coherent, planned service. They stressed, therefore, a dimension of accountability which can all too easily be overlooked when the emphasis is on the efficiency and effectiveness of the overall performance of a service. That is account-ability in the traditional sense of being answerable for the individual actions of service providers. Thus it may be argued that the performance of a service is no more than the sum of the actions performed, and if these are done conscientiously and competently, then all is well with the service as a whole. Conversely dissatisfaction with individual actions can be seen as evidence of inadequacy or failure. Indeed, this view seemed to underlie the emphasis put by many of the authority members on using individual complaints or cases as their criterion for evaluating the performance of services: if there were no such complaints or problems, they often seemed to assume, then there was no cause to worry about the performance of the service. Accountability, on this interpretation, revolves around the ability to call service-providers retrospectively to account for their actions, and good performance can be deduced from the absence of noise.

This view of accountability presents some difficulties. First, individual competence is no guarantee of collective competence. If the wrong service is being provided to the wrong people, then the ability to call individual service-providers to account will do nothing to ensure that they are meeting the appropriate objectives of the service. In other words, accountability for individual actions cannot substitute for, only complement, accountability for setting the appropriate objectives, that is for the framework within which individual decisions are taken, and which provides the criteria for justifying those decisions. Second [. . .], accountability is problematic precisely because of the assertion by many service-providers that only they can define and evaluate competence. The social services committee is unique [. . .] among our services precisely because members do not concede this monopoly of evaluation to the service providers, just as the water authority is unique in that competence can be deduced from outcomes because the service providers are pipes, to exaggerate only a little: that is, it is about the meeting of specific objectives, with little uncertainty about the relationship between inputs and outputs. In other words, even if the ability to make service-providers answerable for their actions is an important dimension of accountability, albeit only one dimension, it is one which the members of many authorities cannot, in practice, exercise. [. . .] To make this point is to turn to our next puzzle, which is the extent to which the success of service-providers in appropriating the language of evaluation depends on their professional status.

Members, Experts and Professionals

One clear conclusion emerges from our evidence. This is that professional status, in the strict sense, has nothing to do with the occupational power of service-providers to determine the language of evaluation. The argument that the problems of accountability in the NHS, and the consequent frustrations of authority members, stem from the professional status of doctors, does not survive our comparative approach. Many of the same problems, and many of the same frustrations, were evident in the case of the police authority, despite the fact that the police lack all the attributes of a profession as traditionally derived from the medical model. So, whatever the reasons why a particular occupation manages to appropriate the language of evaluation, they would appear to have little to do with high social status, esoteric knowledge, and the other characteristics of the medical profession which are usually invoked to explain its power.

Nor does the explanation lie in the fact that members of authorities perceive their service-providers as professionals even when the latter lack such defining characteristics; that is their subjective definitions differ from textbook definitions. Despite the rhetoric of professionalism adopted by the police [. . .] the authority members were not at all inclined to subscribe to it. On the contrary, they were assertively sceptical about such claims, as they were to a lesser extent in the case of teachers and social workers. Equally, they tended to be doubtful about the degree of 'expertise' of the service-providers: emphatically so in the case of social workers, but hardly less so in the case of teachers and the police. This scepticism was shared by elected and non-elected members and cut across political parties. [. . .]

The reasons why some occupations manage to assert their ability to define the language of evaluation, while others don't, seem to be complex. A possible explanation might run along the following lines. First, this ability seems to reflect the differential capacity of service-providers to make their own activities invisible. Thus, our interviews suggest that many service-providers were seen not as professionals or experts but rather as members of a 'mystery' in the dual sense of that word: that is as belonging to a guild or engaged in secret, enigmatic rituals (*Oxford English Dictionary*). In turn, this would indicate that the service characteristics, the environment in which work is carried out, may be as important as producer characteristics. For example, in the health services, authority members found the activities of ancillary workers as mysterious (in the sense of being difficult to control, assess and get to grips with) as those of doctors. Second, this ability also seems to reflect service characteristics in one key respect. If the service ranks high on certainty, as in the case of the water authority, then members may impute a high degree of expertise or professionalism to the service managers, and yet feel that they are in command of the language of evaluation: this is because, to return to a point already made, there are clearly defined objectives and the effective and efficient performance of the service can be assessed in terms of outputs.

While these explanations help to make sense of our findings, they still leave some puzzles. In particular, there remains the contrast between social workers, on the one hand, and teachers and the police on the other. In terms of both service and producer characteristics, social workers do not seem to be so very different from the other two groups. They are relatively low-status, would-be professional. They all work in services with a high degree of uncertainty and complexity [. . .]. Yet social workers are very much the exception among the three occupational groups when it comes to being held accountable by authority members for their actions. One reason may be [. . .] that social services, unlike the other two, rank high on heterogeneity: that is social workers are only a minority of the total labour force. In short, we may be getting a hint that where a particular occupational group dominates a service, its ability to appropriate the language of evaluation may derive from its power as an organized interest group or trade union: the one common element shared by teachers and the police. And where a particular occupational group is only one of many contributing to the productions of service, its power may (as in the case of the medical profession) reflect either status or a key role in that service, that is the ability to bring it to a standstill. [. . .]

These explanations are necessarily tentative and perhaps incomplete. It may be that a historical dimension would help to solve our puzzle: for example the peculiar experience of social work may reflect the fact that the managerial structure for delivering services (the poor law system) evolved before the occupation itself gained an identity – precisely the opposite of what happened in the case of the medical profession. However, while our findings may not yield a full explanation, they do generate some firm if negative conclusions. In summary, these are: first, that the problems of accountability cut across elected and nominated authorities; second, that professional status as such does not provide an adequate explanation of the differences and similarities found across services; third, that the way in which authority members perceive their accountability role does not fit neatly with the current policy emphasis on managerial accountability for the efficient and effective performance of services. It is to the implications of these findings for policy and ways of thinking about accountability to which we turn in our final section.

Thinking about Accountability

[. . .] The first, and perhaps strongest, conclusion generated by our study is that the widespread assumption that direct election can somehow be equated with the effective practice of accountability does not hold water. If member accountability to the public (or to a secretary of state) logically entails the ability of members to call service deliverers to account, then the education committee in our study is a 'Black Swan'. While members saw themselves as accountable, they also complained about their inability to control the service. Conversely the equally widespread assumption that nominated bodies can be equated with the absence of effective accountability is not sustained by our evidence. If members' perceptions of accountability are largely shaped by internalized feelings of a duty and an ability to explain and justify, as suggested by our evidence, election is not a necessary condition for bringing this about. Nor is election a sufficient condition for ensuring control. This finding should come as no surprise; it is in line with much of the literature on local government [. . .] which suggests that members often feel frustrated in their role and by their inability to get a grip on their services. What should come as a surprise is the persistence and durability of the myth that elected status equals accountability: a myth which seems to ignore what is actually involved in the practice of accountability.

The first implication of this conclusion is that problems of accountability in services like the NHS, now run by nominated authorities, would not disappear if these were to be put under the control of elected members. This would introduce 'democracy' only in a formal sense, if it is conceded that accountability in the full sense depends on the ability to establish control over the service concerned. The second implication is that, whatever one's view of the desirability or otherwise of having services run by elected bodies, if the purpose is to bring about effective accountability to the public, then it is crucial to bring about effective control over the service concerned. This is the missing link, and the necessary condition for completing the circle of accountability.

If the negative conclusion is strong, the positive implications are less clear. If, as our findings indicate, the problems of control reflect service characteristics – and, in particular, the ability of service-providers either to appropriate the language of evaluation or to make their activities invisible (and perhaps both)– then the problems of asserting effective accountability are deep-rooted. Developing tools for assessing the performance of service-providers not only is a conceptually difficult, though not impossible, task, but also is likely to encounter resistance from organized service-providers who will, quite rightly, see any such attempt as a challenge to their autonomy. Developing such tools is an intellectual challenge; introducing them is a political challenge – as the recent case of the teachers has demonstrated. [. . .]

Our findings also suggest strongly the need to bring together managerial and political concepts of accountability. To discuss accountability in terms of setting objectives, and monitoring progress towards them, is to adopt a managerial approach. Our finding that, with the exception of the water authority where such an approach is appropriate, members see such managerial techniques as inadequate or inapplicable, suggests that yet another link in the chain of accountability is missing. This is the link between members and technicians in the design of tools of accountability. The suspicion of members may reflect, with some reason, the fear that technical tools are usurping their own function: that auditors and inspectors are either explicitly or implicitly setting their objectives and standards which should be generated by political debate. Similarly, and with equal reason, members may feel that these objectives and standards are an incomplete and partial way of looking at performance: that the result may be to introduce hidden biases and, for example, tilt performance towards cutting costs rather than achieving quality as defined by members or professionals. The example of performance indicators, such as those used in the NHS, is a case in point. Ostensibly these are neutral, technical exercises: the objective products of experts. Yet implicit in them is a set of values or assumptions about what counts as good performance, and what therefore the language of evaluation should be. The fact that 'good performance' is itself a contestable notion tends, all too easily, to be overlooked. Even in services like water, where the notion of 'good performance' is largely unproblematic at present, this may

change if there is increased conflict over competing priorities. Accountability for following a set of *rules* (whether devised by accountants,
economists or lawyers) is only one dimension of accountability; it cannot be
divorced from the wider context of accountability for *conduct* (which
includes the way in which rules are devised and applied).

This would in turn imply that the process of producing technical tools of
accountability needs to be 'politicized' if such tools are not to be seen as a
threat or irrelevance by authority members. In other words, the production
of such tools should be seen for what it is: not just as a neutral exercise in the
application of objective expertise but as an argument about what should
count as good performance. [. . .] If definitions of efficiency and effectiveness are seen to be imposed by the technicians of accountability then, as
our evidence confirms, they are also likely to be rejected; if, however, they
are seen as the product of a joint debate, they may be accepted and used.

For accountability depends [. . .] on an agreed framework of meaning. If
there is no such framework, if information about actions or statistical data is
meaningless to one or other of the actors in the accountability arena
(whether as citizens, authority members or service-providers) then the
result will be a dialogue of the deaf. Information, the life-blood of
accountability, will be literally meaningless; of no significance in judging
actions or performance. This, indeed, is precisely what seems to have
happened. [. . .] Government policy has been to promote accountability
through greater visibility for the public services by the requirement to
publish information about performance. There is, however, little evidence
that either authority members or the public at large respond to or use such
information. The only thing which has been made more visible is ambiguity,
in the absence of agreement as to what meaning (if any) should be attached
to the information that is published. Again, the need would seem to be for
the construction of an agreed and common vocabulary, both between
central and local government, and between authority members and
service-providers through engagement in argument.

The need to move to an agreed vocabulary is reinforced by the fact that, in
local government, in contrast to central government, the machinery of audit
is seen not as the servant of the elected representatives but as a check on
them. In the case of central government (because of the division of
responsibility between the executive and the legislature), auditors and
ombudsmen are accountable to parliament: in the case of local government,
there is no such link – logically enough, given the fact that councillors have
both executive and representative roles. So, for example, auditors are
responsible for enforcing the law about what local authorities may or may
not do: they are the critics, not the servants of councillors. [. . .] It is
therefore not surprising that the technicians of accountability may be viewed
with suspicion by local authority members, instead of being seen as an
essential part of the practice of accountability. And further compounding
the difficulties, different instruments of accountability may use different
criteria. Thus, while the Audit Commission may be arguing that the

inadequate management of falling rolls by local authorities is wasting resources, HM Inspectorate may be drawing attention to the effects of inadequate or poor professional practices: the managerial and professional approaches may be appearing to pull in opposite directions and giving very different signals.

From this perspective, accountability is brought about not only by institutions or techniques but also by dialogue. The question to put about institutions is whether or not they promote the process of argument about what should be the criteria of judgement and about the relationship between them: it is political deliberation – 'the medium wherein men make sense of their common situation in discourse with one another – which is at the heart of accountability. It was precisely this realization which [. . .] lay at the root of the Athenian concept of democracy that still tends to shape our ways of thinking about accountability. The point emerges clearly from Aristotle's discussion of the relationship between the people and the experts.[1] On the one hand, Aristotle conceded, it may well be that:

> the function of judging whether medical attendance has been properly given should belong to those whose profession it is to attend patients and cure the complaints from which they suffer – in a word, to members of the medical profession. The same may be held to be true of all other professions and arts; and just as doctors should have their conduct examined before a body of doctors, so too should those who follow other professions have theirs examined before a body of their own profession.

On the other hand he argued:

> In the first place . . . each individual may, indeed be a worse judge than the experts; but all, when they meet together, are either better than experts or at any rate no worse. In the second place, there are a number of arts in which the creative artist is not the only, or even the best, judge. These are the arts whose *products* [our emphasis] can be understood and judged, even by those who do not possess any skill in the art. A house, for instance, is something which can be understood by others besides the builder; indeed, the user of a house – or in other words, the householder – will judge it even better than he does.

In short, to translate Aristotle's point into the context of the modern debate about accountability, while experts may indeed be the best judges of the technical process of service delivery, they can – and indeed should – be called to account for the end-product or outputs. If accountability is seen exclusively in terms of process, then the experts' language of service evaluation is likely to prevail (whether it is the expertise of the service-providers themselves or that of the technicians of accountability). If, however, accountability is seen in terms of being responsible for outputs, then the language of service evaluation will be that of political argument.

To draw this conclusion is to suggest a criterion for assessing institutional arrangements for service delivery rather than to indicate a particular form. To argue for seeing accountability in terms of political *argument* is not to argue, necessarily, for political *control* in the sense of making directly elected bodies or members responsible for service delivery. The irony would seem to be, as our findings hint, that the fact of election may have the paradoxical effect of weakening the pressure on members to justify their actions in terms of the service performance, seen as the achievement of desired objectives or outputs, rather than strengthening it. [. . .]

It is also possible to draw out a number of more specific, though conflicting, implications for institutional design from our analysis of accountability. One of the problems complicating the practice of accountability stems [. . .] from the difficulty of assigning responsibility for outputs or outcomes to any single service. The converse of the contemporary emphasis on the interrelationship between different services and social factors is to blur the focus of accountability. This has given new meaning to Mill's phrase [. . .] that 'responsibility is null when nobody knows who is responsible'. The logic of this would argue for moving towards all-purpose local authorities, responsible for *all* the services whose activities bear on each other. But such an approach generates as many problems as it promises to solve. It does not encompass responsibility for the social and economic environment which influences all services; if we were to take a 'holistic' view of accountability, we would be driven to ever-increasing centralization (the model would be not elected local authorities, but central government agencies like health authorities). Equally all-embracing accountability might all too easily become meaningless accountability. If our analysis is at all correct in stressing that the problems of accountability reflect the heterogeneity, complexity and uncertainty about the relationship between means and ends within individual services, then they would be compounded if the focus of accountability were to become the end-product of the sum of the performance of different services. The result might be to make the notion of performance even more vacuous and the process of service delivery even less permeable. To quote the conclusions of a study of Swedish local government:

> The ideal of representative democracy with an open and direct interplay between voters and elected representatives is replaced by a process of negotiation which is difficult to penetrate and in which responsibility for the final outcome is often unclear.[2]

This is not only an apt summary of the contemporary problems of accountability, but also a reminder that these problems stem not from the particular nature of British institutions (although they may be aggravated by them) but from the nature of modern services and that they appear to persist even in systems, like Sweden's, where elected authorities control services which are the responsibility of central government agencies [in the UK].

The alternative implication to be drawn is that the direction of change should be towards unpackaging, rather than aggregating, individual services: in particular, towards unpackaging them geographically in order to recreate the circumstances in which an Athenian-type face-to-face accountability becomes possible. This would chime with the growing emphasis, remarkably consistent across the services in our study, on downward accountability (and, indeed, with the personal perceptions of the members in our survey who overwhelmingly saw themselves as being downwardly accountable to the community and who tended to use their hands-on experience of the services concerned as their language of evaluation). It would suggest that the direction of movement should be toward strengthening local forums in which service-providers would be directly answerable for their conduct to the community being served. Again, some possible difficulties must be noted. The first is that a particular definition of accountability is implicit in such developments. It is accountability seen as explanation or justification, but without formal sanctions. But what happens if an explanation or justification fails to satisfy or, indeed, what leverage is there to compel a full rendering of accounts? It may be that informal social sanctions exercised in a face-to-face setting can be as strong (or possibly even stronger) than formal political or legal sanctions exercised in a larger context. The second is that it may be difficult to reconcile downward accountability, even if only in a restricted sense, with hierarchical upward accountability; or to put it somewhat differently, accountability for the performance of a service in a particular locality with the overall performance of the service in a wider geographical setting. Different forums may generate different criteria, or evaluative languages. While it may be argued that multiple criteria should indeed be generated, since services inevitably have multiple objectives, the result could be a Babel of evaluative languages: the problem of reconciliation or agreeing on a shared vocabulary of authoritative judgement would remain.

Yet a different set of implications follows if the problems of accountability are seen to derive not from institutional design, or lack of opportunity for engaging in argument, but from the organizational power of service deliverers, whether these claim to be professionals or not. If this power is taken as a given, if it is argued that service-providers will inevitably subvert any attempt at setting criteria for the outputs of services, then two very different approaches might be advocated. The first might be to substitute market provision for public services: to make service-providers responsive (or accountable) to consumers by marketing their goods. But creating a true market may be politically impossible. Even if it were feasible, however, this model would not fit those services like the police and parts of the social services whose function is social control. Also, this approach fails to address the problems of asymmetry of knowledge between providers and consumers, that is precisely the problem which stalks the whole discussion of accountability. The second, alternative approach would be to strengthen the internal mechanisms of accountability within the professions or bodies of service deliverers. If peer judgement is the inevitable coinage of accountability, given the nature of particular services and the power of the providers, then let it be an effective coinage. In other words, this is an argument for opening up and making more visible both the mechanisms of, and the criteria used in, peer accountability: forcing, as it were, the service-providers to explain how they police their performance. Even if this were feasible, this approach still implies a particular – and restricted – definition of accountability: it is accountability seen in terms of the quality of the processes involved in delivering services. It fails to deal with the question of whether a good overall performance can be deduced from the technical quality of individual actions. [. . .]

Notes

1 Aristotle (1948) *The Politics*, trans. Sir Ernest Barker. Oxford: Clarendon Press pp. 145–7.
2 L. Stromberg and J. Westerstahl (1984) *The New Swedish Communes*. Göteborg: Department of Political Science, University of Göteborg.

14

Performance Indicators:'backseat driving' or 'hands off' control?

Neil Carter

[. . .] The Conservative government of Mrs Thatcher [. . .] made a great play of its intention to transform the delivery of public sector services by improving economy, efficiency and effectiveness in the bureaucracy. A central plank of this strategy was the decentralization of service delivery which has been a feature of all the recent civil service initiatives. Thus the Rayner scrutinies inspired a new organizational structure in the Department of Environment involving 120 cost centres, each possessing its own budget to cover running costs. All departments now possess a Top Management Information System (MINIS) that encourages management at all levels to set strategic objectives that can then be translated down the line into personal objectives for individuals. The Financial Management Initiative (FMI) was introduced by Barney Hayhoe, then Minister for the Civil Service, as 'a push to greater decentralization and delegation down the line, which will represent a highly significant change in the culture of the Civil Service'. More radically, the Ibbs Report planned to hive off departments as agencies managed by a chief executive possessing 'delegated authority from their Minister for operations of the agencies within the framework of policy directives and resource allocation prescribed by the Minister' (Efficiency Unit, 1988: 17).

Nevertheless the decentralization strategy within central government has met only limited success, illustrated by the findings of the government's own Efficiency Unit, which concludes that it is still true that 'the freedom of an individual manager to manage effectively and responsibly in the Civil Service is severely circumscribed' (1988: 5). Moreover, during the 1980s the balance of power between central and local government has swung even more in favour of the former: the reduction in local authority block grants, the imposition of cash limits and the policy of ratecapping have all further eroded local government autonomy.

The decentralizing plans of the government have partly foundered on the familiar bureaucratic paradox that it is necessary to centralize in order to decentralize (Perrow, 1977). The logic is straightforward: if the government

From *Policy and Politics*, 1989, 17(2): 131–8 (abridged).

is to retain control and accountability then the centre must be able to state explicitly the form, quantity and quality of inputs, outputs and outcomes that it expects the decentralized service to provide. The problem was that when the government came to implement decentralization it discovered the inadequacy of the existing information and measurement systems; quite simply, it was often impossible to ascertain what departments were actually doing.

One means of squaring the circle was to emphasize the importance of performance evaluation, hence the FMI contains the explicit objective that managers at all levels should have 'a clear view of objectives; and the means to assess, and wherever possible measure, outputs or performance in relation to those objectives' (Cmnd 9058, 1983: 1). Enter the 'performance indicator', which has become increasingly fashionable because, in theory, it provides the opportunity for government to retain firm control over departments by exercising a strategy of 'hands off' rather than 'hands on' control.

However, this chapter argues that despite the proliferation of perform-ance indicators across the public sector during the 1980s, progress has been tardy, and the performance indicator remains an imperfect, often ineffective instrument of control. So the Ibbs Report, coming some five years after the introduction of the FMI, still found it necessary to emphasize the 'need to ensure that indicators of effective performance are developed and used for regular monitoring' (Efficiency Unit, 1988: 11). One explanation is that performance measurement raises profound conceptual, technical and organizational problems. Some of these problems can be discovered in government publications evaluating the implementation of the FMI (re-viewed in Carter, 1988a) and in recent academic work (Flynn, 1986). This chapter examines the main issues arising from the strategy of using performance indicators as a 'hands off' instrument of control: the difficulty in assessing units that do not 'own' some or all of their performance (a concept to which we will return), the lack of clear organizational objectives, the implications for management style, the inadequacy of information systems, the relationship between the centre and the periphery, and that between the bureaucrat and the professional service-provider.

The chapter draws on the findings of a research project at the University of Bath that made a comparative cross-sector study of current practices used by public sector services to evaluate their own performance. These organiz-ations included the National Health Service (NHS), social security, police, prisons, the Lord Chancellor's department, schools, universities and water authorities. All the services were selected, on the one hand, for their similarity in comparing the control of a large number of sub-agencies or branches and, on the other hand, for the many different problems of control that each organization encounters.

The Wave of Interest in Performance Indicators

There has been an unprecedented wave of interest in performance indicators in the public sector during the 1980s. Since the FMI there has been a rapid expansion in the number of performance indicators published in the annual Public Expenditure White Papers, output measurement schemes have evolved in some 31 government departments (HM Treasury, 1986, 1987) and there is a proliferation of schemes in public sector services such as the water authorities and the nationalized industries (Woodward, 1986). Indirect pressure from the centre through the Audit Commission (1986) provided a further inducement to local government to follow the example of councils like the London Borough of Bexley (1985) in adopting performance indicators to evaluate the delivery of local services.

Progress in the development of performance indicators varies between the organizations under study. Early arrivals included the social security, where a system of target-linked performance indicators was introduced in the early 1970s during the brief enthusiasm in government circles for implementing Management By Objectives (MBO) schemes (Garrett, 1980), and the water authorities which have used 'level of service' indicators since the late 1970s (Committee of Public Accounts, 1985). Following trenchant criticisms of its monitoring systems by the Public Accounts Committee and the Social Services Committee the NHS introduced a set of indicators in 1983 which was updated in 1985 with a huge package numbering some 420 indicators [. . .]. This contrasts with the parsimonious efforts of the police and prison departments which, with a few exceptions, have only recently developed a series of performance indicators (Carter, 1988b). The educational field has long dabbled with performance measures such as staff/student ratios and examination results, but there are few established performance indicators for schools and only since the Jarrett Report (1985) have universities attempted to outline a comprehensive set of performance indicators (Committee of Vice-Chancellors and Principals, 1986, 1987). The Lord Chancellor's department is primarily responsible for the administration in England and Wales of all courts of law (above magistrates' courts), the operation of the Legal Aid system and the appointment of the judiciary. To evaluate the first of these functions, the department formulated a series of performance indicators when it constructed its Circuit Objectives in the mid-1980s.

Despite their differences most of these services share certain characteristics: to summarize, there are usually several input measures (the resources required to provide a service), but no, or very few, final outputs (the service provided by the organization), or outcome measures (the impact of the service on the consumer). The shortage of output measures makes it difficult to measure efficiency and effectiveness because there is no indicator of the impact of performance. Departments attempt to compensate for these omissions by including a mixture of throughput and intermediate output measures. Thus the NHS measures a host of activities and processes such as patients treated, length of stay and patient turnover. The police measure notified crime levels and clear-up rates, and local education authorities measure examination results. The Lord Chancellor's department measures the average waiting time for Crown Courts between committal for trial and the trial itself; waiting time being a reasonable proxy for effectiveness because, as an administrative department, its main task is to get cases to trial as quickly as possible. The social security shares this same consideration in its measurement of clearance times and error rates which assess speed and accuracy in the payment of benefits. However, much depends on the validity of these performance indicators as proxies of output; unless they are recognized and accepted as measuring something meaningful, by all levels of an organization, then performance indicators will not increase management control.

Ownership of Performance

A major limitation on the usefulness of performance indicators as a means of extending managerial control is that branches or sub-units do not fully 'own' their performance. That is, in important respects the success of an organization will depend on central decisions and the coordination of different streams of activity, as well as their local execution. Consequently, the validity of performance indicators will depend on the distribution of performance ownership at different levels of the organization; put simply, who can be held responsible for each dimension or element of performance? Two aspects of this issue are taken up below.

The first involves the degree to which performance is affected by 'environmental' factors outside the control of the organization. For example, when the Metropolitan Police announced a large increase in crime levels in London during 1986, Sir Kenneth Newman explained it on television in this way: 'Figures that are supposed to be performance measures of the police are in fact a performance measure of society as a whole.' In other words, the figures reflect the propensity to commit crime rather than the ability of the police to prevent crime; indeed the implication is that the police can do nothing about crime despite crime prevention being one of their main objectives! Similarly the performance of schoolchildren is largely dependent on factors outside the ambit of the classroom. A performance indicator of the exam results of local education authorities will be most useful if it takes into account measures of social advantage (such as a middle-class background) as well as social disadvantage (heads of the households who are engaged in skilled or unskilled manual labour, from a non-white ethnic group or single parent family), along the lines of Gray and Jesson's regression analysis (1987). The ability of the water authorities to provide water to all their consumers will depend on weather conditions; a very cold spell or a drought may lead to a breakdown in supply.

The second aspect is the extent to which performance is constrained by the interdependence of different units, services or activities within an organization. The NHS is characterized by a particularly complex set of working relationships, so that the throughput of patients in a hospital may be dependent on radiologists, anaesthetists and surgeons as well as the social workers responsible for finding somewhere for the patient to go. The two aspects often combine: the Crown Court listings officer seeking to reduce waiting times is hampered by external factors, like the crime and clear-up rates and the number of guilty pleas, and intra-organizational factors such as the pace at which barristers and solicitors work, the length of the judges' day and the personal idiosyncrasies of the judiciary. The ability of the NHS to improve the health of the nation depends as much on the quality of housing provision as on the quality of health care. Clearly, any credible system of performance indicators must resolve the complex conceptual problem of apportioning who owns performance if it is to prove a useful tool of managerial control.

Objectives

There is great uncertainty in many service organizations because objectives are by no means self-evident. Firstly, objectives are often absent, ambiguous or phrased in a very general, imprecise way. Second, organizations have multiple objectives. The police are involved in several functions, including crime prevention, traffic duties, community relations and maintaining law and order. The objectives of these activities are not necessarily compatible: a drugs raid in a sensitive inner city area may prevent crime but at the cost of damaging community relations. The NHS has a variety of objectives including preventive medicine, providing equal and free access to health services, a broad range of services and responsiveness to local needs. This eclectic array of objectives may conflict and certainly requires policy trade-offs. Third, it is often conceptually difficult to establish the relationship between the activities of a service and its impact. For example, the NHS objectives may be defined in terms of activities (numbers of patients treated every year) or outcomes (impact on the health of the nation). In the latter case, 'the relationship between the production of health services and the state of the nation's health is extremely uncertain' (Day and Klein, 1987); hence the difficulty in developing effectiveness measures for the NHS.

Dials v Tin-openers: Implications for Management Style

It is helpful to think of performance indicators as being used either as dials or as tin-openers. Implicit in the use of performance indicators as dials is the assumption that standards of performance are unambiguous; implicit in the use of performance indicators as tin-openers is the assumption that performance is a contestable notion.

Obviously, from the point of view of controlling service delivery, the ideal performance indicator operates like a dial, providing a precise measure of outputs and outcomes and where there is a clear understanding of what is good and bad performance. This would enable indicators to be linked prescriptively to specific objectives or targets and used to monitor progress towards achieving those targets.

Yet public sector organizations have very few precise measures; perhaps only the water authorities possess a set of indicators that can measure performance exactly, against an explicit normative standard such as the quality of water. Elsewhere, departments have increasingly adopted a target-setting approach: in recent years the White Paper has included overall targets such as the achievement of a specified number of hip, cataract or bypass operations, or the removal of a specified number of surplus school places. As Lord Young (1988) observed, the advantage of target performance indicators like '10 per cent of teachers by 1990 to spend some time in industry each year' is that they are at least measurable, if less precise than a normative measure of water quality.

However, the majority of indicators are tin-openers rather than dials: by opening up a 'can of worms' they do not give answers but prompt interrogation and inquiry, and by themselves provide an incomplete and inaccurate picture. For example, in the NHS the overall reduction in the length of patient stay in recent years is no guarantee of quality of care and may mean that patients are discharged before they are fully recovered. A performance indicator may be value-laden but not directly prescriptive; it may include a presumption that a movement in a particular direction, such as towards lower unit costs or lower error rates, is desirable without setting a specific target. Here the emphasis is on travelling along a particular route rather than arriving at a specified destination; it is about comparing *relative* performance – either over time or of different units – rather than performance against normative standards or precise targets.

These different types of performance indicators have important implications for managerial styles. The prescriptive indicator is a top-down management tool that lends itself to a command style of management, but the difficulty in measuring outputs has constrained the use of this form of indicator in the public sector. Indeed, the technical constraints on measurement stem partly from the consequences of the important objections to the top-down approach highlighted in the implementation literature. [. . .] In particular, there is widespread criticism of the assumption that a clear-cut distinction exists between policy and implementation; that is, that 'goals' are set at the top, the policy is handed down at different levels of the organization to be enacted and that evaluation involves a straightforward process of constructing measures of outcome. Instead, writers like Ham and Hill (1984) point to advantages in a 'bottom-up' approach where policy is viewed as a continuous process of change arising from the interaction of different interest groups within organizations, and from the impact of environmental factors.

Quite clearly, prescriptive performance indicators are closely linked to the much criticized top-down model. However, the descriptive tin-opener suggests the need for a more persuasive style of management; far from being a simple top-down exercise, performance measurement instead necessarily involves a contestable and complex process of negotiation at and between different levels of management and activity.

Information

The devolution of responsibility envisaged by the FMI requires the centre of the department to possess regular information about the use of resources and the effectiveness of activities, hence the new emphasis on performance indicators. But performance indicators need to be based on robust data which is frequently unavailable in public sector services. Consequently there has been a drive to improve data systems. It is recognized that the flow of information is vital and that new technology can now make possible what was impossible before. However, the attempts by many departments to construct performance indicators are hampered by inadequate information. For example, the Lord Chancellor's department is still dependent on outdated manual recording systems. The police department admits that its new matrix of indicators consists of a large number of statistics that are 'dressed-up data' rather than performance measures, but it does at least bring together information that has long lain unused. Even where there are apparently long-established, useful performance indicators, like the social security clearance rates, the department recognizes that the information upon which they are based is highly suspect, and that they have only a limited use as a management tool.

It is an important characteristic of the public sector that most performance indicator packages are 'data driven', which brings their appropriateness into question: that is, they are based on existing information and are therefore easier to develop if not always reliable or useful, rather than consisting of data gathered for the specific purpose of constructing a relevant measure. The NHS package is a good example of a set of data-driven performance indicators, illustrating the problems with the slow recording of data. Consequently, most performance indicators are developed months after the event, which negates their applicability as a practical management tool and makes the indicators susceptible to rejection as being misleading by the people involved in using them. In contrast, the new Governor's 'Weekly monitoring system' is an interesting attempt by the prison department to collect new information on a daily basis that can be used at all levels of the organization. Perhaps it is the potential short-term explosiveness of the prison service that has encouraged the department to construct a weekly monitoring system whereas the NHS does not operate under the same urgent pressures.

The quality of information will influence the use of the *negative* or proscriptive indicator – specifying not targets or ends, but things that simply should not happen in a well-run organization – a concept that is insufficiently developed in the literature. Providing the organization possesses a sophisticated information system that provides accurate data quickly and frequently, then the negative indicator can be a useful managerial tool for controlling the organization at different levels on a day-to-day basis. For example, the water authorities monitor the presence of daphnae and shrimps in water, the number of flooded sewers and the number of homes without water. The prison services' Governor's 'Weekly monitoring system' produces several negative indicators: the failure to fulfil a checklist of basic routines such as weekly bathing, the distribution of mail and access to visitors, is a good sign that trouble may be brewing. Indeed, negative indicators are also one way of measuring service quality; examples include social security clearance and error rates, and the regular monitoring of consumer complaints is another. On a longer time-span, the NHS has recently adopted a measure of 'avoidable deaths' of patients dying from specific, treatable disorders such as appendicitis and cervical cancer.

Centre and Periphery

Another problem with performance indicators is that the institutional structure of public sector organizations is often characterized by indirect lines of responsibility and accountability. For example, local education authorities (LEAs) operate an arm's-length relationship with the Department of Education and Science (DES) because of the strong local control over education. Thus the main intermediate output measure in use, the number of pupils passing five or more O-levels, is not obviously used by the DES as a means of influencing the policies of LEAs, other than through the Inspectorate of Schools. Indeed, the DES published performance indicator is further limited because it is an average measure for the whole LEA and fails to distinguish variation in performance between schools.

Police forces possess a unique form of constitutional autonomy, as set out in the 1964 Police Act. Police authorities are separate from county councils and set the police budget. Chief constables exercise control in their own right and have considerable scope to set their own objectives and deploy resources in their preferred way. However, the Home Secretary has important powers over both the chief constable and the police authority, notably the power to dispense the police grant which covers 51 per cent of each force, and a further quarter of the local police budget through the block grant. Moreover, as Morgan argues, central control has increased to the point that policing can no longer be regarded as a local service but as 'a national service which is administered locally' (1987: 75).

The performance of the police service provides a *prima facie* case for close scrutiny because it has benefited from an increase in budget of 36 per cent in real terms since 1979 and a massive rise in salaries, and yet crime levels continue to rise and clear-up rates fail to improve. However, the Home Office has proceeded cautiously when applying the principles of FMI to the police. The key Home Office circular 114/83 maintains the central role of the Inspectorate in monitoring police performance by giving it a new duty to examine value for money in the financial management of resources. A new matrix of indicators which utilizes police statistics by categorizing them in functional areas such as drugs and crime and delineating easily measurable indicators, is for the inspectors' use alone; it is not expected to be published or available for wider scrutiny. There are several explanations for this relatively slow progress. The first one is political, namely the reluctance of the government to pursue a policy that might generate criticism of the police, particularly as the huge increases in police numbers since 1979 do not seem to have had any impact on crime levels. The second is the institutional constraints that prevent the Home Office from attempting to impose a national performance indicator package on the 46 quasi-autonomous police forces. The third is the self-defined professional status of the police force which allows them to set the agenda and control the vocabulary of police actions and accountability. It is to the power of the professionals that we now turn.

Professionals and Administrators

The relationship between professionals and administrators is of fundamental importance in holding services accountable for their performance (Day and Klein, 1987). Central to the notion of professionalism is the assertion that what defines a professional is precisely the fact that he or she is accountable only to his or her peers. It is the professional body that sets the objectives and rules that govern the performance of the individual and it is the profession that defines what is satisfactory performance. Critical to the ability of the government to exercise control over service delivery is the independence of professional accountability from the processes of managerial and political accountability. This independence, combined with the professional mystification that their expertise is incomprehensible to the outsider, makes it difficult for management to impose performance indicators on service deliverers.

The medical profession is the classic example of a state-recognized monopoly that has proven resistant to any form of hierarchical control over matters that it regards as the sole domain of the profession, despite the fact that the NHS has a formal line of accountability to the centre. Doctors are not answerable to administrators for the public resources at their disposal, and they can only be dismissed by peer review. To illustrate, the hospital manager has great difficulty planning the use of the operating theatre because doctors take different lengths of time to perform similar operations, or reducing the length of stay in hospital because this is ultimately a medical decision.

The court listings officer, seeking to reduce the length of waiting time for trial, must plan the use of the courtroom wary of the complete professional independence exercised by the judge – to call evidence, adjourn at whim and generally exercise autonomy over the length of the hearing. University lecturers, like judges and consultants, until recently had contracts providing considerable autonomy from the administration because of tenure. Perhaps more important, the manager only exercises control over the 'timetabled' part of the contract – the hours spent in the lecture theatre, operating theatre or courtroom; the remaining time is nominally for practices like personal research but, in practice, the professional chooses how this time is spent. The police brook no interference in setting manning levels for specific tasks or employing strategies to deal with particular tasks. A strongly-unionized group of workers, such as prison officers, can offer similar resistance to managerial encroachment on their work practices. Above all, these groups try to dictate the meaning of performance indicators by asserting that only they can properly interpret performance indicators, precisely because the meaning of these findings is, in reality, often ambiguous.

Conclusion

It is argued that performance indicators are an instrument for exercising central control over services while pursuing a policy of decentralization. The attraction of performance indicators is that they offer a means of 'hands off' control to a Conservative administration committed to the principle of reducing the role of central government, yet confronted by the paradox that decentralization of services requires tighter central control. However, both the design and use of performance indicators is highly problematic. This chapter has analysed some of the main conceptual and practical difficulties that mediate the use of indicators as an instrument of control. These factors include the measurement of outputs and outcomes, the need to isolate the ownership of performance, the uncertainty about service objectives, the need for sophisticated information systems and the complex relationships between centre and periphery and between administrators and professionals. Quite simply, the chapter argues that performance indicators are still an imperfect instrument of control; in particular, they involve a much-resented degree of unwanted 'backseat driving' on the part of the government without, as yet, providing a greater degree of central control over services.

And yet it is ironical that a government dedicated to a belief in the market has adopted the techniques first devised in the 1960s by exponents of rational planning! Indeed, the contemporary enthusiasm for performance indicators in many ways represents no more than a resurrection of the tradition of 'new managerialism' advocated by the Fulton and Maud reports 20 years ago. Consequently, it is no accident that many of the same thorny issues that dogged early reforms reappear to haunt contemporary exponents of the genre!

However, the political context is different in the 1980s. Firstly, the Thatcher government has provided sustained and powerful support for the current initiative, unlike the earlier Wilson and Heath administrations. Secondly, the computer technology for making general use of performance indicators is now available. Consequently, the urgency of the quest for more and better performance indicators in government departments that was inspired by the FMI shows no sign of abating, as illustrated by the recent review of NHS indicators and the aforementioned developments in the police and prison departments. Moreover, the creation of agencies following the implementation of the Ibbs Report will undermine many of the traditional constitutional means of holding services accountable to parliament; undoubtedly the generation of yet more performance indicators will help fill this accountability vacuum.

Nevertheless the government faces one particularly difficult and familiar obstacle: the power of the professionals. What started as a series of conceptual and technical problems about designing and using performance indicators may ultimately become a political question about the nature of Thatcherism. Put simply, to what extent is the Thatcher government radical enough and brave enough to tackle the vested professional interests of service deliverers like doctors and the police? Performance indicators are potentially an instrument for holding service deliverers accountable to the centre whilst continuing a policy of decentralization, but to do so the government must provide the political commitment and muscle to overcome resistance. It is questionable whether Mrs Thatcher has the will, quite apart from the ability, to take on this task.

References

Audit Commission (1986) *Performance Control in Local Government*. London: HMSO.
Carter, N. (1988a) 'Measuring government performance', *Political Quarterly*, 59(3): 369–75.
Carter, N. (1988b) 'Performance indicators in the Criminal Justice system', in *Crime UK 1988*. Newbury: Policy Journals.
Carter, N., Day, P. and Klein, R. (1987) 'Private experience, public performance: a comparative essay on the use of performance indicators in the public and private sectors'. Paper presented at the Public Administration Committee Conference, York, September.
Cmnd 9058 (1983) *Financial Management in Government Departments*. London: HMSO.
Committee of Public Accounts (1985) *Monitoring and Control of the Water Authorities*. London: HMSO.

Committee of the Vice-Chancellors and Principals of the Universities of the United Kingdom (1986) *Performance Indicators in Universities*. Report of Working Group, London.

Committee of the Vice-Chancellors and Principals of the Universities of the United Kingdom (1987) *University Management Statistics and Performance Indicators*. London.

Day, P. and Klein, R. (1987) *Accountability*. London: Tavistock.

Efficiency Unit (1988) *Improving Management in Government: the Next Steps*. Report to the Prime Minister (The Ibbs Report). London: HMSO.

Flynn, N. (1986) 'Performance measurement in public sector services', *Policy and Politics*, 14(3): 389–404.

Garrett, J. (1980) *Managing the Civil Service*. London: Heinemann.

Gray, J. and Jesson, D. (1987) 'Exam results and local authority league tables', in *Education and Training UK 1987*. Newbury: Policy Journals.

Ham, C. and Hill, M. (1984) *The Policy Process in the Modern Capitalist State*. Brighton: Wheatsheaf.

H.M. Treasury (1986) *Output and Performance Measurement in Central Government: Progress in Departments*. Working Paper No. 38 (ed. S. Lewis), London.

H.M. Treasury (1987) *Output and Performance Measurement in Central Government: Some Practical Achievements*. Working Paper No. 45 (ed. P. Durham). London.

Home Office (1983) *Circular No. 114/1983: Manpower, Effectiveness and Efficiency in the Police Service*. London.

Jarrett Report (1985) *Inquiry into University Efficiency*. London: HMSO.

London Borough of Bexley (1985) *Action Plan 1984/85*.

Morgan, R. (1987) 'Police', in M. Parkinson (ed.) *Reshaping Local Government*. Newbury: Policy Journals. pp. 59–76.

Perrow, C. (1977) 'The bureaucratic paradox: the efficient organization centralizes in order to decentralize', *Organizational Dynamics*, Spring: 3–14.

Woodward, S. (1986) 'Performance indicators and management performance in nationalized industries', *Public Administration*, 64 (Autumn): 303–17.

Young, Lord (1988) in *The Independent*, 7 March.

15

Doing Well While Doing Good: dilemmas of performance measurement in nonprofit organizations and the need for a multiple-constituency approach

Rosabeth Moss Kanter and David V. Summers

We know, for instance, that we have to measure results. We also know that with the exception of business, we do not know how to measure results in most organizations. (Peter Drucker, *The Age of Discontinuity*, 1968)

An important part of the strategic management process is assessing performance. Managers, employees, and others need to gauge whether an organization is doing well or poorly with respect to its standards for performance.

Although the measurement of performance is not a simple matter in any kind of organization (a task force at a major auto company recently identified over a hundred measures of organizational performance currently in use in the company), it is even more complicated for nonprofit organizations. Financial measures are central in for-profit organizations not only because profits can be measured easily but also because they are a good test of both market-need satisfaction and the capacity of the organization to run itself efficiently. But the 'test' in nonprofits is different: these organizations have defined themselves not around their financial returns but around their mission, or the services they offer. And services, of course, are notoriously intangible and difficult to measure. The clients receiving them and the professionals delivering them may make very different judgments about their quality, and donors may hold still another standard. And 'doing good' is a matter of societal values about which there may be little or no consensus. It is this factor – the centrality of social values over financial values – that complicates measurement for nonprofit organizations.

Profit-making organizations are more flexible with respect to the deployment and redeployment of resources in any number of areas, as long as bottom-line criteria of financial performance are satisfied. But the centrality

---

From W. W. Powell (ed.), *The Non-Profit Sector: A Research Handbook*. New Haven, CT: Yale University Press, 1987, pp. 98–110 (abridged).

of mission for nonprofit organizations places limitations on their flexibility of action. Money can be obtained in a number of ways; social values cannot. Therefore, an organization that establishes itself to make a profit via providing health care (financial goals first, mission second) has more flexibility to change fields, move across systems, or deflect resources from one set of activities to another than an organization in which financial goals are subordinated to mission.

The apparent freedom of major for-profit corporations to redefine their missions as making money rather than making widgets, thereby permitting themselves to move in and out of businesses at will, has been decried by business critics. But nonprofit organizations have no such apparent freedom. Without their mission, the organizations' reason for being collapses. Indeed, one critical test for whether an organization can attain nonprofit status is whether it claims to be 'doing good' in one of the areas that society, or some segment of it, recognizes as valuable.

Admittedly, the lines dividing for-profit and not-for-profit organizations with respect to performance measurement are blurring. For-profit organizations are coming to stress social mission and values as a result of a new awareness of the role of values in highly successful corporations (Ouchi, 1981; Peters and Waterman, 1982; Kanter, 1983). At the same time, nonprofits are increasingly setting more stringent financial goals, reporting 'operating income' as though it were 'profit', discussing strategic planning, 'repositioning' themselves to take advantage of 'market niches', and considering such market tests of performance as revenues from clients/customers as more important than the raising of nonmarket funds from donors. We have observed this dual evolution in major profit-making corporations, on the one hand, and in nonprofit health care systems in Virginia, Illinois, and North Dakota, on the other.

Still, if there is a distinction left, issues of performance measurement for nonprofit organizations are complicated by the absence of an overarching measure like financial performance and by the mission-directedness of the organization. The nonprofit organization, then, faces these dilemmas: (1) knowing when it is doing well, and (2) being able to make changes, or to redirect resources, when members of the organization suspect it is *not* doing well with respect to its 'market', but can still attract resources by nonmarket means from nostalgic or believing donors.

We argue further that nonprofit organizations also have organizational rigidities – owing to the difficulty of effectiveness measurement and the varying standards of clients, donors, and others – that make it difficult for them to innovate or change. The question of values is always a politicized one, and the larger the number of groups claiming to define values for a nonprofit organization the more difficult measurement and making needed adjustments become.

In this chapter we will indicate why performance measures are important and what functions they serve. We will see the many constituencies involved in defining organizational performance – constituencies that actively prefer different measures because of their own reasons for participating in the organization and their own uses for the data. Behind this argument is a view of organizations not as impersonal instruments guided by managers but as temporary alliances of separate groups, each interpreting the organization's purpose a little differently.

We will review the common ways in which organizational performance can be measured and then argue that, because of the existence of multiple constituencies or stakeholders, no one of these alone can guide an organization. Rather than present a way out of the dilemma of performance measurement for nonprofit organizations, we propose instead that acknowledgment of the realities of multiple constituencies and explicit attempts to develop multiple measures is the only sensible course. [. . .]

Why an Issue Exists: Problems with Measuring Goal Accomplishment

It would seem, on the surface, that measurement of organizational performance should be a simple matter: determine the organization's objectives, and then assess whether they have been attained. But the social science literature, particularly that related to nonprofit organizations, makes clear why this is difficult to do.

A long tradition in organization research defines effectiveness in terms of outputs and goal accomplishment (for example, Georgopolous and Tannenbaum, 1957; Etzioni, 1964; Price, 1968; Campbell, 1977; Hall, 1978). But another long tradition criticizes this approach – most recently, and perhaps most important, on the grounds that because organizations are complex entities, the specification of their goals is itself problematic. Organizations may have many goals, and they can be inconsistent, contradictory, or incoherent; it is often unclear even at what level or with respect to what units the attainment of goals should be measured. As one author claims, goals may even be a mystification (Perrow, 1981). This is one reason simple financial tests like 'profits' are so appealing, and it is so often hard to get consensus on goals beyond this broad one.

The multiplicity of goals is fairly well recognized by analysts in the field, who define *effectiveness* as the 'balanced attainment of many goals' (Kirchoff, 1977), which they then seek to catalog and weigh. In the behavioral objectives model, for example, effectiveness is measured by getting 'experts' in the organization to specify (1) a catalog of concrete observable organizational objectives; (2) the conditions under which the organization should be able to achieve them; and (3) the degree to which each objective should be satisfied (Campbell, 1977). Pennings and Goodman (1977) define *effectiveness* similarly; but they do not explain how goals are to be identified, nor do they treat the complex issues that arise when there is more than a single ultimate criterion. Complexity is aggravated by the fact that some goals may be incoherent, unstated, or defined *post hoc* by the organization to justify its actions.

Organizations differ in their complexity, of course, as well as in the degree of coherence among subunits. Relatively autonomous subunits in their turn are likely to pursue multiple and sometimes inconsistent objectives. Such 'loosely coupled systems' are especially prevalent in nonprofit, governmental, and service organizations, such as a state university system, which has been described as an 'organized anarchy' (March and Olsen 1976). Hospitals, too, are multiproduct organizations serving many purposes, only one of which is patient care, so that, as Scott and his colleagues have pointed out (1978), effectiveness with respect to one set of objectives (such as intensive care) might not generalize to others (say, teaching), and structural features of various segments of the organization may not correspond.

Thus goals exist at a variety of levels and may be differentially pursued by various parts of the organization. As Kirchoff (1977) notes, 'Operational definitions have failed to clarify distinctions between organizational effectiveness, managerial effectiveness, and manager and subordinate behaviors and attitudes.' Which units, then, are to be measured? Should one examine individual performance, behaviors, and satisfaction (Argyris 1962; Lawler *et al.*, 1974); contribution of and coordination among subunits (Pennings and Goodman 1977); or subunit goal attainment, treating each as an autonomous 'profit center' (Manns and March 1978, for academic departments in universities)? Which cut through an organization is most appropriate for the measurement of effectiveness? Regarding human service organizations, Herzlinger (1979) notes the choice that must be made whether to generate cost data by *organizational unit* or by *program*, when the latter might cut across many functional, geographic, or client-defined divisions.

Finally, there is the related question of whether to measure outcomes in terms of holistic-categorical or aggregated-individual data. For some analysts, for example, the effectiveness of higher education is measured by its impact on individual consumers (Astin 1968, 1971, 1977; Feldman and Newcomb 1969; Bower 1977), just as that of hospitals can be measured by outcomes for individual patients. It can also be argued, however, that more global goals such as 'education' or 'health' are insufficiently measured by aggregated individual experiences.

When goals are vague or ill defined, effectiveness criteria may themselves become substitutes for goals, particularly when they are more precise and suggest concrete actions. This is one of the central issues generated by the necessity to operationalize goals in order to measure performance. For example, when the effectiveness of police departments is defined as 'production rates' – the number of tickets written, or the percentage of arrests resulting in convictions – the measures may create informal quota systems (Marx, 1976). Without regard to their larger mission, police workers may gear their activities to improving rates. Although organizations need criteria in order to achieve consensus about what constitutes effective individual and joint effort, they must beware of letting a measurement system define the organization's purpose (Epstein *et al.*, 1977; Farris, 1975). Otherwise, specific goals can become the minimally acceptable standards, with performance dropping to that level.

Drucker has offered incisive comments on this point:

> It may sound plausible to measure the effectiveness of a mental hospital by how well its beds – a scarce and expensive commodity – are utilized. Yet a study of the mental hospitals of the Veterans' Administration brought out that this yardstick leads to mental patients being kept in the hospital – which, therapeutically, is about the worst thing that can be done to them. Clearly, however, lack of utilization, that is, empty beds, would also not be the right yardstick. How then does one measure whether a mental hospital is doing a good job within the wretched limits of our knowledge of mental disease?
>
> And how does one measure whether a university is doing a good job? By the jobs and salaries its students get twenty years after graduation? By that elusive myth, the 'reputation' of this or that faculty which, only too often, is nothing but self-praise and good academic propaganda? By the number of Ph.D.s or scientific prizes the alumni have earned? Or by the donations they make to their alma mater? Each such yardstick bespeaks a value judgment regarding the purpose of the university – and a very narrow one at that. Even if these were the right objectives, such yardsticks measure performance just as dubiously as the count of bed utilization measures performance in mental hospitals. (1968: 196–7)

When immediate effectiveness measures set the standards for the organization, a tendency can arise to favor the short term over the long term – to maximize the score on indicators of today's performance. But very different criteria may be appropriate to the short, intermediate, and long runs – for example, short term: production, efficiency, satisfaction; intermediate term: adaptiveness, development; long term: survival (Gibson *et al.*, 1973). When effectiveness is defined in terms of adaptability it is sometimes clear how short-term and long-term measures can conflict. If short-term efficiency and production-oriented measures tend to produce ritualistic behavior geared toward quantity rather than quality, then the 'random, deviant' behavior that enhances an organization's ability to be 'creative [and] flexible' (Weick, 1977) may be lost.

Task-effectiveness or goal-attainment criteria may vary with an organization's life stage (Scott, 1977) because every stage brings different key problems. Thus, when we measure effectiveness, we must include an assessment of how well an organization handles the critical issues of each period. Kimberly (1979) defines three stages of development of a new medical school: initiation, innovation, and institutionalization. Initially the school's problem is to carve out a niche; later, to survive and grow. Kimberly notes the paradoxical nature of success: 'Success by later standards may undermine the very activities that have made the organization effective.' Moreover, over time, goals are displaced (Thompson and McEwen, 1958).

The problems of operationalization lead to a meaning/measurement dilemma for any organization whose output is not easily quantifiable (Warner, 1967). On the one hand, efforts designed to meet standards of objectivity (for example use of quantitative indicators such as number of grants, or mortality rates after surgery) are vulnerable to skepticism about their intrinsic meaning. On the other hand, efforts designed to convey high levels of meanings (such as grantors' assessments of the impact of projects, or physicians' judgments about community health) may be criticized for their subjectivity (Epstein *et al.*, 1977: 72).

Such a dilemma appears when we consider efficiency measures in higher education – costs per student, student/faculty ratios, costs per faculty member, or costs per square foot (Bowen and Douglas, 1971; O'Neill, 1971; Meeth, 1974; Hartmark, 1975). Such measures – which of course seem more important in times of financial stringency – can be challenged as not capturing anything meaningful about the quality of education or the experience of students. Campbell (1977) argues that effectiveness measures should always be subjective and based on the views of organizational members (which raises the question of 'which members').

But measures of quality or experience are subjective and intangible. This is one of the reasons agreement among those who rank organizations or their units on effectiveness tends to be low. The criteria used to make meaningful subjective assessments of effectiveness tend to be uncorrelated or negatively correlated. Furthermore, supposedly 'hard' objective measures sometimes turn out to be 'soft' and subjective – for example survey data, derived from judgments of organizational participants, translated into scalar terms. In short, it may be inadvisable to search for universal, objective, operational performance criteria centering around goal attainment because they tend to (1) replace larger goals and become the standard that motivates organizational behavior; (2) favor shorter-term over longer-term criteria; and (3) decrease the meaningfulness of the assessment process.

Another major problem with the goal-attainment tradition is one of substance, not measurement. Some writers argue that outcome measures of effectiveness are never pure indicators of performance quality because other factors enter in, the most notable being the characteristics of the materials or objects on which the organization performs, the available technology (Mahoney and Frost, 1974), and a variety of environmental factors beyond the organization's control. For organization-design experts, effectiveness in accomplishing objectives can be affected by (1) theoretical bottlenecks – people don't know how to do it; (2) resource bottlenecks – people don't have the resources the job requires; and (3) organizational bottlenecks – people cannot put the resources together (Galbraith, 1977). Whereas the latter two can perhaps be said to constitute indications of ineffectiveness, the first is often beyond the control of the organization.

Furthermore, desirable outcomes are often achieved not by aspects of the organization itself but by client characteristics (Lefton, 1975). Outcome measurements for hospitals, for example, are affected both by medical knowledge and by patients' prior states. Hospitals that attract patients who possess features associated with greater health (such as high income or occupational status) may appear to be more effective in turning out healthier patients (may register lower mortality rates, for example, or shorter illnesses) (Scott *et al.*, 1978). This factor may explain why elite universities turn out better students – they select the better students in the first place. Thus, it is often difficult to draw conclusions about comparative effectiveness unless a variety of other factors are controlled.

These contingency factors affecting goal attainment have led to two different perspectives on the measurement of effectiveness. According to one, effectiveness measures should be confined to accomplishments directly under the organization's control (Campbell, 1977). According to the other, measures should factor in the favorability of technological knowledge, environmental support, and raw-material quality, thus taking these extra-organizational issues into account.

Frustrated by the problems of measuring effectiveness outlined above, some analysts (for example, the population ecologists such as Hannan and Freeman, 1977; Aldrich, 1979) have suggested that organizational survival be the ultimate criterion. At least, they implicitly argue, survival is as concrete an issue as profits, it can be measured easily, and it indicates *ipso facto* an organization's success on such critical effectiveness dimensions as resource attraction and internal organization.

Adaptation to the environment seems particularly critical to many researchers in the organization-environment tradition. First, characteristics of the environment strongly influence what kinds of organizations will be effective and which internal structures and processes are likely to fit their environment (Burns and Stalker, 1960; Lawrence and Lorsch, 1967; Thompson, 1967; Osborn and Hunt, 1974; Leifer and Delbecq 1978; Aldrich, 1979). Second, for some organizations effectiveness may be a matter of convincing dominant actors in their environment that they *are* effective so that they can attract resources (for example, Yuchtman and Seashore, 1967). In this view, measures of performance used to win such confidence may be decoupled from measures of the organization's achievement of more abstractly defined goals (Meyer and Rowan, 1977). The organization's own actions, then, may have little to do with its apparent 'successes'. It may simply be located in a favorable environment (Aldrich, 1979). Thus, survival is a sign of adaptive capacity (though it might also signify the power to hold on even if no longer adaptive in an objective sense).

In the domain of nonprofit organizations, survival can indeed be an appropriate effectiveness standard. In alternative, or utopian communities (residential and economic arrangements owned cooperatively by and for the benefit of members), a survival measure – longevity – can be a success criterion (Kanter, 1972). In this case longevity appears to cover other effectiveness dimensions because (1) the communities' overriding goal was to exist (goal attainment); (2) longevity was an indicator that the communities were satisfying their members since members continued to support them (morale, and perhaps appropriate structure/process); and (3) longevity suggested that they had weathered crises (flexibility, adaptation) and earned sufficient income (resource attraction). Of course, longevity does not tell us whether the communities did as well as they could have, only that they did well enough to continue operating.

There are some obvious limitations on the use of survival as a measure. First, it is highly skewed since there is a general 'liability of newness' for virtually all organizations (Stinchcombe, 1965; Freeman *et al.*, 1983). Second, it provides no guide to short-term decision-making by either managers or other constituencies. Third, survival is sometimes artificial: organizations may survive because a benefactor or owner is willing to support them despite their ineffectiveness. Finally, to the extent that organizations act as though survival were their ultimate goal (as many do), they may lose sight of other purposes, including their reasons for existing in the first place. Public service organizations are often accused of responding not to public needs but to the demands (real and imagined) of funding agencies and budget allocators (Herzlinger, 1979).

Survival may also be unrelated or even negatively related to impact, another ultimate criterion. *Impact* can be defined more broadly than goal attainment (although they might be connected) as a long-term influence on the state of the environment surrounding the organization. Many of the utopian communities that were successful in surviving had little or no impact on their environments in terms of such measures as their ability to effect changes in adverse laws or to encourage others to form or join similar alternative communities (Kanter, 1972).

Impact may even threaten survival. The impact of the March of Dimes – eradication of polio, the disease for which it raised funds – might have killed the organization; but members had sufficient stake in its continuation that they adopted a new mission to keep it alive (Sills, 1957). Impact can also threaten the survival of organizations with avowedly political goals. The more they take a low profile and reduce their impact, the more they may be able to protect themselves; but they may elicit opposition to the extent that they start having impact (Marx, 1974).

Behind Goals: Measures for Whom and Why?

The significant questions about performance measurement are thus not technical but conceptual: not *how* to measure effectiveness or productivity but *what* to measure and how definitions and techniques are chosen and are linked to other aspects of an organization's structure, functioning, and environmental relations. Problems plaguing this field are not mere annoyances to be brushed aside as soon as better measurement techniques are invented; instead, they are fundamental aspects of modern organizations – profit-making as well as nonprofit.

Recent models of organizations have moved away from rationalistic and voluntaristic assumptions about goal consensus, unity of purpose, and the possibility of discovering universal performance standards. The new models emphasize instead more political views, in which multiple stakeholders both inside and outside compete to use an organization for their purposes and to set performance standards that will advance their interests to make their jobs easier (Kanter, 1980). Furthermore, political models make it clear that organizations may not control all the factors that influence how their effectiveness is defined and whether they meet effectiveness standards (Mintzberg, 1983; Pfeffer, 1981; Pfeffer and Salancik, 1977); the older, voluntaristic models were more likely to see the organization as controlling all variables. Thus, the search for objective standards has declined. Multiple constituencies and multiple environments require multiple measures.

Constituency interests play a role in definitions of effectiveness via the uses to which various groups wish to put the data. Actors in and around an organization may require different kinds of effectiveness measures for different kinds of decisions and purposes. No single indicator will suffice.

Classic definitions of organizational effectiveness and models of measurement often favored, implicitly if not explicitly, some constituencies over others. Certainly profit (though supposedly an objective market measure of effectiveness, based on the efficiency with which input could be transformed into output) makes the interest of owners or shareholders paramount. Those analysts who define effectiveness as the ability of an organization to adapt to, manipulate, or fulfill expectations of the external environment (such as Bidwell and Kasarda, 1975; Hirsch, 1975; Katz and Kahn, 1978) use the 'supersystem' as the judge, thus making paramount the interests of supporters, sponsors, clients, regulators, and so on. Those who consider the satisfaction of customers (Gartner and Riessman, 1974) or participants (Cummings and Molloy, 1977) to be the central criterion similarly emphasize one set of interests over others.

A multiple-constituency or multiple-stakeholder approach to effectiveness is thus warranted (Bluedorn, 1980; Connolly *et al.*, 1980). But simply to acknowledge the existence of many passive points of view is not enough. Different constituencies *actively* prefer different kinds of effectiveness measures. For example, managers might prefer structural measures of organizational characteristics because they have control over such factors; the rank and file might prefer process measures of activities because they control their own performance; and clients and customers prefer outcome measures because they want results, not promises or mere effort (Scott *et al.*, 1978). Inside organizations, too, standards – and therefore measures – differ by field and function. Mahoney and Weitzel (1969) show that managers of research and development units in corporations apply models of effectiveness differently than do managers of more general business operations, perhaps because of differences in their perceptions of the production process and their more technological environments. Perrow (1977) states it simply: power affects the definition of effectiveness. In short, the interests involved are based not only on position but also on politics.

While acknowledging the existence of numerous interests and perspectives, some analysts still argue that a single standard of effectiveness can be developed based on the definition held by the organization's 'dominant coalition' (Yuchtman and Seashore, 1967; Gross, 1968; Price, 1968; Pennings and Goodman, 1977). Buried in the notion of a dominant coalition is the idea that the various constituencies have already engaged in a bargaining process that has given them input into the organization's goal statement. Indeed, in the conflict-and-bargaining model of effectiveness, definitions of dominant coalition members prevail. Effective organizations are those that achieve the purposes established by the winning actors in the bargaining process (Elmore, 1978). (The problem with this definition is its subjectivity. An individual's view of the organization's success or failure is determined by his or her position in the bargaining process.)

Organizational development models go even further in tying effectiveness to the achievement of consensus in the bargaining process (see Cunningham's reviews: 1977, 1978). Here the effective organization is one that 'can build consensus between policymakers and implementors so as to create joint commitment to the goals of the organization'; thus better decisions occur with better relationships between constituencies (Elmore, 1978). Research confirms that inside and outside constituencies (such as branch bank employees and customers) can agree on standards, especially when the inside group occupies a boundary-spanning role (Schneider *et al.*, 1980).

Even those who reject the view that the dominant coalition's definition of organizational effectiveness should prevail still consider the coalition the most appropriate source of operational information about some dimensions of effectiveness. For example, Cameron (1978) argued that if one measures effectiveness by organizational characteristics, the dominant coalition (meaning the official, titled leaders) comprises the appropriate informants, since they have organization-wide information. But even though this is a statement about data sources rather than effectiveness definitions, if one follows this line of reasoning, it is likely that dominant coalition interests would be most strongly represented in the measurement process.

In contrast, another strong school of thought holds that the existence of multiple interests must be acknowledged in both the definitional and the data collection stages. Scott (1977) argued that criteria for evaluating organizational effectiveness and the data collected to assess it must be chosen from a variety of sources. This contemporary multiple-goal model (Scott, 1978) sees organizations as composed of shifting coalitions of subgroups, both inside and outside, with differing views of what the organization should produce. Extending this view, Cummings (1977) defined effectiveness as the degree to which the organization is instrumental for both its inside and outside constituencies, since organizations are instruments of outcomes. This approach is limited by Cummings's identification of the individual rather than the organization as the appropriate unit of analysis.

This review leads us to several important conclusions. In general, organizational performance measures serve three kinds of functions, reflecting different aspects of an organization:

1. *Institutional Functions*

Measures to provide evidence that the organization is meeting standards or engaging in activities that confer legitimacy upon it; and to provide indicators of 'progress' or 'improvement' to instill pride in the organization's key constituencies, thus reaffirming their decision to support the organization and encouraging others to join them. The primary institutional functions of measuring performance thus revolve around *legitimacy renewal* and *resource attraction*. The constituencies served involve those linking the organization to its environment. In nonprofit organizations these might be boards, volunteers, and donors.

2. *Managerial Functions*

Measures to provide information to enable adjustment of activities to better meet standards; to provide knowledge of progress toward desired states; to spot trouble or potential trouble so that corrective action can be taken; and to allocate resources (budgets) and rewards among organizational participants and units. The primary managerial functions thus revolve around *structure and process corrections* and *internal allocation*. The constituencies served are the various levels and types of managers and professionals. In nonprofit organizations the managers may want different information for different reasons than the professionals, and the two may split into conflicting constituencies.

3. *Technical Functions*

Measures to provide information on the efficiency or quality with which the organization delivers its basic products or services. The constituencies served are the customers or clients.

The contradictions between some of these measurement purposes and the gap between the constituencies create problems for all organizations. For nonprofits, these problems are exaggerated because of two kinds of loose coupling: between *sources of legitimacy* and *standards of management* and between those *providing resources* (donors of funds or time) and those *receiving services* (clients). In between are the managers and professionals, who have their own view of what the organization should be doing. [. . .]

Dilemmas of Nonprofit Performance Measurement

[. . .] Generally, nonprofit organizations tend to provide services rather than manufacture goods, but service is often intangible and hard to measure (Thompson and McEwen, 1958; Newman and Wallender, 1978). Indeed, outcomes in some cases may be inherently unknowable (Drucker, 1968). This issue is, of course, shared with for-profit service organizations as well (and there are those who argue that *all* organizations are at root providing services, even if they do it via selling goods).

But the intangibility of the measurement of services is compounded in not-for-profit organizations by the weaker influence clients – the recipients of services – have on their operations compared to the customers of profit-making organizations. Since the income of nonprofit organizations depends only partially (if at all) on fees for services, then marketlike measures of performance oriented around client- or customer-related measures tend to be rejected outright or to play a nondominant role. The needs of donors (of money or time) may play a much bigger role. Although it is often argued that the performance of service organizations should be a function of consumer involvement and satisfaction (Gartner and Riessman, 1974), some nonprofits face little competition, and the market is virtually unlimited. With little competition, recipients of services do not tend to provide feedback (Selby, 1978). A nonprofit [. . .] may receive feedback only during periods of growth, when efforts are made to build new facilities in communities not served by any hospital. At such times there may be two or three competing health care organizations, but the competition is framed in terms of *promises* for services, since nothing can be delivered until one organization is selected and begins its operations. Of course, as nonprofits and for-profits start to compete head-on, as is happening in health care in some communities, we can expect the two kinds of organization to begin to converge in their performance measures.

Second, goal conflicts interfere with rational planning [. . .]. Because of the existence of divergent goals and objectives, owing to the many constituencies involved and particularly to the dependence on donations unrelated to services, management may refrain from stating the organization's goals in anything but broad terms for fear of alienating major donors. There is no clear market check, and the influence of clients is reduced because clients may not be the organization's major source of funds. These two factors permit goal ambiguity and diversity of values to persist. But without clear specific statements of intended results, it is difficult to assess performance. In general, goal accomplishment is difficult when feedback from the environment is relatively fuzzy and signals indicating unacceptable goals are less effective and take longer to come (Thompson and McEwen, 1958).

Third, the focus in nonprofit organizations is likely to shift away from output to input. Rather than focus on results (delivery of services, attainment of goals), these organizations are likely to concentrate on resource attraction. Since nonprofit organizations tend to provide services that are hard to measure, there is rarely a new bottom line. Thus, planning becomes more concerned with fund-raising or resource inputs than with service, in part because of the greater ease of measuring the former. Although the success of nonprofits rests in part on resource attraction, products or specific benefits do not tend to be available to donors (Shapiro, 1973), and therefore performance criteria for resource allocation (service delivery) might be unrelated to criteria for resource attraction. In profit-making organizations, generating profits is an end in itself, with less interest in their allocation, but in nonprofits generating funds is only a step, and allocating them is key.

As a consequence, a fourth characteristic develops. The existence of ambiguous operating objectives creates opportunities for internal politics and goal displacement, for loose coupling between official or stated mission and operative goals. Because objectives are stated vaguely and planning concentrates on resource acquisition, managers inside the organization gain considerable leeway in their activities, opening up the possibility for political maneuvering or for ignoring the needs of clients while trying to please powerful donors – or for playing one constituency off against another.

In any nonprofit organization with a wide gap in the incentives, personnel, and procedures available for resource allocation (or service delivery), we can expect either a high degree of conflict (reflected in arguments about performance measures) or attempts to insulate donors or funders from allocators or deliverers (reflected in statements about professionalism and the need for independence), either of which tends to reduce the willingness to have performance measured at all.

Fifth, in nonprofit organizations [. . .] where professionals play important roles, professional standards create rigidities and interfere with new responses to changing constituency needs. Where professionals hold power, as many sociologists have pointed out, they often operate to maintain a monopoly on delivery of particular services by restricting entry, requiring that preexisting standards be met that reinforce repetition of past behavior, and erecting legal barriers to clients seeking services elsewhere. Professional power of this kind flourishes in nonprofit organizations because of the absence of direct market tests of client satisfaction and because of the willingness of donors to encourage organizations to repeat behaviors and activities even when the clients appear to be less than satisfied. Witness the desire of university alumni donors to maintain the university as they remember it, whether or not it meets today's student needs; this desire reinforces the power of the faculty to declare that they know better than the students what the students need (although faculty standards may also conflict with alumni desires).

Furthermore, the worthiness of a nonprofit's activities may tend to be assumed, so that its mere existence is seen as indicative of 'good works' or 'social-moral contributions' and there is no need to show returns and results (Drucker, 1968). Whereas financially weak for-profit organizations might find greater difficulty raising capital for continuing operations because of financial problems, financially weak nonprofit organizations might use that circumstance as an occasion for rallying donors to contribute additional funds to shore up operations – simply because of the belief in the worthiness of the organization. Indeed, to some donors the organization's very difficulties might provide confirmation of the need for its existence – and the more problems it encounters fulfilling its mission because of the new wrinkles in goal attainment, then the more vigorously its efforts should be pursued. Since nonprofits tend to believe in their own functioning, failure to achieve goals is taken not as a sign of weakness in the organization but as a sign that efforts should be intensified.

The existence of this impressive set of dilemmas may account for the virtual absence of control systems in human service organizations – even the separate elements of control, such as measuring effectiveness and efficiency or monitoring and evaluating performance (Herzlinger, 1979). But the difficulty of assessing performance should not deter managers and boards of nonprofit organizations from trying to set objectives and assess results – to determine if they are indeed 'doing well while doing good'.

The ideal performance assessment system in a nonprofit organization would acknowledge the existence of multiple constituencies and build measures around all of them. It would acknowledge the gap between grand mission and operative goals and develop objectives for both the short term and the long term. It would guard against falling into any of the traps outlined in this chapter by developing an explicit but complex array of tests of performance that balance clients and donors, board and professionals, groups of managers, and any of the other constituencies with a stake in the organization.

A balanced approach would provide the data to help the organization know whether it is 'doing well' on any of the dimensions of performance with which an active constituency might be concerned. Conflicts between measures can be better adjudicated when the data are clear. The ultimate test of performance for a nonprofit organization is, of course, whether those representatives of society that allowed it to join the category of 'do-good' organizations (starting with the Internal Revenue Service) continue to feel it deserves this status. The test lies beyond the scope of management science and in the realm of social values.

Note

We would like to thank Woody Powell for his comments and editorial suggestions.

References

Aldrich, H. (1979) *Organizations and Environments*. Englewood Cliffs, NJ: Prentice-Hall.

Argyris, Chris (1962) *Interpersonal Competence and Organizational Effectiveness*. Homewood, Ill.: Irwin.

Astin, Alexander W. (1968) *The College Environment*. Washington, DC: American Council on Education.

Astin, Alexander W. (1971) *Predicting Academic Performance in College*. Riverside, NJ: Free Press.

Astin, Alexander W. (1977) *Four Critical Years*. San Francisco: Jossey-Bass.

Bidwell, Charles E. and Kasarda, John D. (1975) 'School district organization and student achievement', *American Sociological Review*, 40: 55–70.

Bluedorn, A. C. (1980) 'Cutting the Gordian knot: a critique of the effectiveness tradition in organizational research', *Sociol. Soc. Res.* (July): 64.

Bowen, Howard R. and Douglas, Gordon K. (1971) *Efficiency in Liberal Education: A Study of Comparative Instructional Costs for Different Ways of Organizing Teaching-Learning in a Liberal Arts College*. New York: McGraw-Hill.

Bower, Joseph L. (1977) 'Effective Public Management', *Harvard Business Review*, March–April. (Available in *HBR* reprint series, Management of Nonprofit Organizations, Part 2.)

Burns, T. and Stalker, G. M. (1960) *The Management of Innovation*. London: Tavistock.

Cameron, Kim (1978) 'Measuring organizational effectiveness in institutions of higher education', *Administrative Science Quarterly*, 23 (December): 604–32.

Campbell, John P. (1977) 'On the nature of organizational effectiveness', in Paul S. Goodman and Johannes M. Pennings (eds), *New Perspectives on Organizational Effectiveness*. San Francisco: Jossey-Bass. pp. 13–55.

Connolly, T. E., Conlon, J. and Deutsch, S. J. (1980) 'Organizational effectiveness: a multiple-constituency approach', *Academy of Management Review*, 5: 211–17.

Cummings, Larry L. (1977) 'Emergence of the instrumental organization', in Paul S. Goodman and Johannes M. Pennings (eds), *New Perspectives on Organizational Effectiveness*. San Francisco: Jossey-Bass. pp. 56–72.

Cummings, Thomas G. and Molloy, Edmond C. (1977) *Improving Productivity and the Quality of Work Life*. New York: Praeger.

Cunningham, J. Barton (1977) 'Approaches to the evaluation of organizational effectiveness', *Academy of Management Review*, 2(3) (July): 463–74.

Cunningham, J. Barton (1978) 'A systems-resource approach for evaluating organizational effectiveness', *Human Relations*, 31: 631–56.

Drucker, Peter (1968) *The Age of Discontinuity*. New York: Harper & Row.

Elmore, Richard F. (1978) 'Organizational models of social program implementation', *Public Policy*, 26(2) (Spring): 185–229.

Epstein, Marc J., Flamholtz, Eric G. and McDonough, John J. (1977) *Corporate Social Performance: The Measurement of Product and Service Contributions*. New York: National Association of Accountants.

Etzioni, Amitai (1964) *Modern Organizations*. Englewood Cliffs, NJ: Prentice-Hall.

Farris, George F. (1975) 'Chicken, eggs and productivity in organizations', *Organizational Dynamics*, 3(4) (Spring): 2–16.

Feldman, Kenneth A. and Newcomb, Theodore M. (1969) *The Impact of College on Students*. San Francisco: Jossey-Bass.

Freeman, John, Carroll, Glenn R. and Hannan, Michael T. (1983) 'The liability of newness: age dependence in organizational death rates', *American Sociological Review*, 48: 692–710.

Galbraith, Jay R. (1977) *Organization Design*. Reading, Mass.: Addison-Wesley.

Gartner, Alan and Riessman, Frank (1974) *The Service Society and the Consumer Vanguard*. New York: Harper & Row.

Georgopolous, Basil S. and Tannenbaum, Arnold S. (1957) 'The study of organizational effectiveness', *American Sociological Review*, 22: 534–40.

Gibson, James L., Ivanevich, John M. and Donnelly, James H. Jr. (1973) *Organizations: Structure, Process, Behavior*. Dallas: BPI.

Gross, Edwards (1968) 'Universities as organizations: a research approach', *American Sociological Review*, 33: 518–44.

Hall, Richard P. (1978) 'Conceptual, methodological, and moral issues in the study of organizational effectiveness', Working Paper, Department of Sociology, SUNY-Albany.

Hannan, Michael T. and Freeman, John (1977) 'Obstacles to comparative studies', in Paul S. Goodman and Johannes M. Pennings (eds), *New Perspectives on Organizational Effectiveness*. San Francisco: Jossey-Bass. pp. 101–31.

Hartmark, Lief (1975) *Accountability, Efficiency, and Effectiveness in the State University of New York*. SUNY-Albany: Comparative Development Studies Center.

Herzlinger, R. E. (1979) 'Management control systems in human service organizations'. Paper delivered at Conference on Human Service Organization and Organization Theory, Center for Advanced Study in the Behavioral Sciences, Stanford, Calif., 2–3 March.

Hirsch, Paul M. (1975) 'Organizational effectiveness and the institutional environment', *Administrative Science Quarterly*, 20: 327–44.

Kanter, Rosabeth Moss (1972) *Commitment and Community: Communes and Utopias in Sociological Perspective*. Cambridge, Mass.: Harvard University Press.

Kanter, Rosabeth Moss (1980) 'Power and change in organizations: setting intellectual directions for organizational analysis'. Paper presented at the Plenary Session of the American Sociological Association Annual Meeting, New York.

Kanter, Rosabeth Moss (1983) *The Change Masters*. New York: Simon & Schuster.

Kanter, Rosabeth Moss and Stein, Barry A. (eds) (1979) 'Growing pains', in *Life in Organizations: Workplaces as People Experience Them*. New York: Basic Books.

Katz, Daniel and Kahn, Robert L. (1978) *The Social Psychology of Organizations*. New York: Wiley.

Kimberly, J. (1979) 'Issues in the creation of organizations: initiation, innovation and institutionalization', *Academic Management Journal*, 22: 437–67.

Kirchoff, Bruce A. (1977) 'Organizational effectiveness measurement and policy research', *Academy of Management Review*, 2(3) (July): 347–55.

Lawler, Edward E., Hall, Douglas T. and Oldham, Greg R. (1974) 'Organizational climate: relationship to organizational structure, process, and performance', *Organizational Behavior and Human Performance*, 11(1) (February): 139–55.

Lawrence, P. R. and Lorsch, J. W. (1967) *Organization and Environment*. Boston: Harvard Business School Div. Res.

Lefton, M. (1975) 'Client characteristics and organizational functioning: an interorganizational focus', in A. R. Negandhi (ed.), *Interorganization Theory*. Kent, Ohio: Comparative Administration Research Institute. pp. 128–41.

Leifer, R. and Delbecq, A. (1978) 'Organizational/environmental interchange: a model of boundary-spanning activity', *Academic Management Review*, 3(1): 40–51.

Mahoney, T. A. and Frost, P. J. (1974) 'The role of technology in models of organizational effectiveness', *Organizational Behavior and Human Performance*, 11(1): 122–39.

Mahoney, Thomas A. and Weitzel, William (1969) 'Managerial models of organizational effectiveness', *Administrative Science Quarterly*, 14: 357–65.

Manns, Curtis L. and March, James G. (1978) 'Financial adversity, internal competition, and curriculum change in a university', *Administrative Science Quarterly*, 23 (December): 541–52.

March, J. G. and Olsen, G. P. (1976) *Ambiguity and Choice in Organizations*. Bergen, Norway: Bergen Universitetsforlaget.

Marx, Gary T. (1974) 'Ironies of social control: authorities as possible contributors to deviance through non-enforcement, covert facilitation, and escalation'. Paper presented at meeting of the International Sociological Association, Toronto.

Marx, Gary T. (1976) 'Alternative measures of police performance', in E. Viant (ed.), *Criminal Justice Research*. Lexington, Mass.: Heath. pp. 179–93.

Meeth, R. L. (1974) *Quality Education for Less Money*. San Francisco: Jossey-Bass.

Meyer, John W. and Rowan, Brian (1977) 'Institutionalized organizations: formal structure as myth and ceremony', *American Journal of Sociology*, 83(2): 340–63.

Mintzberg, Henry (1983) *Power In and Around Organizations*. Englewood Cliffs, NJ: Prentice-Hall.

Newman, William H. and Wallender, III, Harvey W. (1978) 'Managing not-for-profit enterprises', *Academy of Management Review*, 3(1) (January): 24–32.

O'Neill, June (1971) *Resource Use in Higher Education: Trends in Outputs and Inputs*. New York: McGraw Hill.

Osborn, R. N. and Hunt, J. D. (1974) 'Environment and organizational effectiveness', *Administrative Science Quarterly*, 19: 231–46.

Ouchi, William (1981) *Theory Z*. Reading, Mass.: Addison-Wesley.

Pennings, Johannes M. and Goodman, Paul S. (1977) 'Toward a workable framework', in Paul S. Goodman and Johannes M. Pennings (eds), *New Perspectives on Organizational Effectiveness*. San Francisco: Jossey-Bass. pp. 146–84.

Perrow, Charles (1977) 'Three types of effectiveness studies', in Paul S. Goodman and Johannes M. Pennings (eds), *New Perspectives on Organizational Effectiveness*. San Francisco: Jossey-Bass. pp. 96–105.

Perrow, Charles (1981) 'Disintegrating social sciences', *New York University Education Quarterly*, 12(2) (Winter): 2–9.

Peters, Thomas J. and Waterman, Robert (1982) *In Search of Excellence*. New York: Harper & Row.

Pfeffer, Jeffrey (1981) *Power in Organizations*. Boston: Pitman.

Pfeffer, Jeffrey and Salancik, Gerald R. (1977) 'Organization design: the case for a coalitional model of organizations', *Organization Dynamics*, Autumn: 15–29.

Price, James L. (1968) *Organizational Effectiveness: An Inventory of Propositions*. Homewood, Ill.: Irwin.

Schneider, B., Parkington, J. J. and Buxton, V. M. (1980) 'Employee and customer perceptions of service in banks', *Administrative Science Quarterly*, 25: 252–67.

Scott, W. Richard (1977) 'Effectiveness of organizational effectiveness studies', in Paul S. Goodman and Johannes M. Pennings (eds), *New Perspectives on Organizational Effectiveness*. San Francisco: Jossey-Bass. pp. 63–95.

Scott, W. Richard (1978) 'Measuring output in hospitals', Stanford University, Background paper for Panel to Review Productivity Measures, May.

Scott, W. Richard, Flood, Ann Barry, Ewy, Wayne and Forrest, William H. Jr. (1978) 'Organizational effectiveness: studying the quality of surgical care in hospitals', in M. Meyer and Associates, *Environments and Organization*. San Francisco: Jossey-Bass.

Seashore, Stanley E. (1977) 'The measurement of organizational effectiveness'. Paper presented at the University of Minnesota, Minneapolis (cited in Campbell, 1977).

Selby, Cecily Cannan (1978) 'Better performance from "non-profits"', *Harvard Business Review*, 56 (September–October): 92–8.

Shapiro, Benson P. (1973) 'Marketing for nonprofit organizations', *Harvard Business Review*, September–October. (Available in *HBR* reprint series. Management of Nonprofit Organizations.)

Sills, David (1957) *The Volunteers*. Glencoe, Ill.: Free Press.

Stinchcombe, Arthur L. (1965) 'Social structure and organizations', in James G. March (ed.), *Handbook of Organizations*. Chicago: Rand-McNally. pp. 142–93.

Thompson, James D. (1967) *Organizations in Action*. New York: McGraw-Hill.

Thompson, James D. and McEwen, William J. (1958) 'Organizational goals and environment', *American Sociological Review*, 23: 23–31.

Warner, W. Keith (1967) 'Problems in measuring the goal attainment of voluntary organizations', *Adult Education*, 19(1) (Fall): 3–15.

Weick, Karl E. (1977) 'Re-punctuating the problem', in Paul S. Goodman and Johannes M. Pennings (eds), *New Perspectives on Organizational Effectiveness*. San Francisco: Jossey-Bass. pp. 193–225.

Yuchtman, Ephraim and Seashore, Stanley E. (1967) 'A system resource approach to organizational effectiveness', *American Sociological Review*, 32: 891–903.

16

The Welfare State, the Professions and Citizens

Margareta Bertilsson

What is the relation between the welfare state and the professions? This question is not sufficiently explored in the contemporary theories of the professions. Here sociological attention primarily shows the monopoly of knowledge practices which the modern professions occupy and the various strategies that they pursue. [. . .] In this chapter I advance the thesis that the modern professions have a crucial role in the administration of the welfare state, especially within the frame of administering *citizens' rights*. One important collective actor in the modern nation-state is the *body of citizens* as it has become embodied in the policies of the welfare state. [. . .] I am thus seeking to develop the theory once formulated by Talcott Parsons, where he stated the following: 'Comparative study of the social structures of the most important civilizations shows that the professions occupy a position of importance in our society which is, in any comparable degree of development, unique in history.'[1]

In one respect I extend and develop Parsons's view much further than he himself did. His insistence on the essential role of the 'client' in understanding the 'professional complex' in modern society is in this chapter extended to cover the role of the (universal) citizen. This shift of attention permits us to locate the discussion of the modern professions in the midst of the social and political theory of the welfare state. [. . .]

The Liberal State and the Welfare State

The distinction between the liberal state and the welfare state, seen here as ideal-typical models, has economic, political and legal consequences not only for how we view citizens but also for how we view the role of the modern professions. In the one (liberal) case we speak of professions regulating the market, and in turn being regulated by the market; and in the other

From R. Torstendhal and M. Burrage (eds), *The Formation of the Professions: Knowledge, State and Strategy*. London: Sage, 1990, pp. 114–33 (abridged).

(welfare) case we speak of professions regulating the law, and in turn being regulated by the law. In the first case, an important device to allocate social goods is by means of the supply and demand of the market, and in the other case by means of law. One could speak of these two mechanisms as *monetarization* and *juridification* respectively. Modern societies of course make use of *both* types of goods allocation. [. . .] In a liberal state the realm of action freedom left to the professions presumably is much wider than in the 'juridified' welfare state. The 'free professions' are corollaries of the liberal state. But the welfare state to a very considerable extent depends on the professional judgements which it, paradoxically, seeks to control politically.

In the liberal state there is a set of elementary rights guarding the 'civil sphere' of individuals. The rise of the modern individual coincides with the rise of the liberal state itself. The maturation of the liberal state occurs when civil rights (freedom to hold and sell property, freedom of assembly and expression) are *universalized* and offered to all societal members (of a certain age and mental capacity). In the USA the liberal state came to fruition in the 1960s when the civil rights movement extended citizenship to black people.

The welfare state differs from the liberal state in its expansion of the claims of rights of individuals. This means at the same time an expanded public sector financed by means of taxation. Individuals in the welfare state are citizens endowed with legally guaranteed social rights (with regard to health, pensions, child subsidies and so on) rather than customers/clients purchasing these goods on the market from diverse professional practitioners. The role of the professions is important in both types of structural goods allocation, but it differs considerably between them. The following examples from legal theory should reveal some poignant differences:

In the liberal state the typical structure of law takes the form of 'pure' legal propositions of the following type: 'if (x), then (y)' or if the owner has acquired the merchandise through a lawful transaction (for example, a sale, gift or bequest), then he or she can dispose of it at will lawfully. Such a legal system offers a set of institutionally guaranteed rights to individuals, and gives them citizen status. These are negative rights; individuals are guaranteed freedom from state intervention. [. . .]

The negative rights are prototypical for the classical liberal state. They are expressed legally as imperatives directed to the individuals themselves. We speak in this case of a direct relation between the state and the individuals, although in real life there are of course mediating links in terms of administrative organs of various kinds. Schematically it looks as shown in Figure 16.1. [. . .]

In political and legal language the classical rights of the liberal state are *formal* rights. They grant, as Anatole France once put it, the same right to both the rich and the poor to sleep under the bridges.

The welfare state has as its primary aim to *materialize* the formal rights of the classical period and extend them to cover a minimum material standard

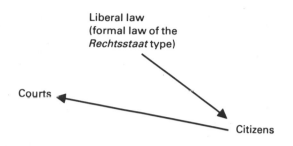

Figure 16.1   *The classical liberal state model*

of well-being for all citizens (and not only those who can pay). New sets of rights are proposed which in the Swedish case include the old-age pension, sick-leave pension, maternity and parental leaves and allowances, and child allowances. More recently claims of rights have been extended to 'consumers' rights', 'workers' rights', and 'patients' rights'.

In the liberal state claims of rights are achieved by the market mechanism, and may as such be equally extensive as citizens' rights in the welfare state, whereas in the welfare state they are achieved by means of law. The role of the professions differs in each case: in the liberal state professional services are offered on the market; in the welfare state a set of 'material laws' make them available to the body of citizens. This distinction clarifies the difference between private customers/clients and citizens endowed with rights. [. . .]

The schematized structure of material welfare laws differs from the classic liberal ones as shown in Figure 16.2. Welfare laws are of a 'compensatory' kind, and directly implicated in the redistribution of social resources. They are positive rights; the state interferes with the lives of citizens in order to restitute their social life-chances. As administrators of welfare legislation, professional experts become the mediators between the state and the citizens. As seen in the schema, the relation between the state (polity) and the citizens is no longer of the direct (liberal) type. Some welfare rights, such as pensions rights, are offered directly to individuals once they fulfil certain criteria of age, pregnancy, ill-health and so on, but professionals decide on the matter of candidacy. Other welfare rights embodied in general clauses are weak from a legal viewpoint: to offer an individual 'a right to gainful work, to clean air, to good health' lacks (legal) precision as to what constitutes 'gainful work', 'clean air', 'good health' and to whose duty it is to honour these rights in practice. Such promissory rights are seen rather as important social political directives, and form what T. H. Marshall has referred to as 'the legitimate expectations' of modern man. The welfare state is directly dependent on the competencies of various professionals to administer its wide extensions of rights. It is important for the credibility of a modern welfare polity to have access to professional expertise both in issuing and in executing rights.

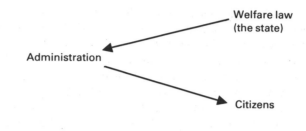

Figure 16.2   *Welfare state model*

Professions are crucial in the running of both types of society, but their roles differ. A most challenging task for a theory of the professions must be to delineate differences and similarities in the structure of professional services between the two (ideal-typical) forms of modern societies. In the liberal society, the professions are client-constitutive, and in the other they are citizen-constitutive. In the welfare type of society professional practices are intimately woven into the political warp, and there is a 'politicization' of the professions, at the same time as political practice is being 'professional-ized'. In the one (liberal) type professional practices can help solidify the private well-being of (some) individuals, and thus put at risk the universal status of citizenry; and in the other type, professional practice can help strengthen state-administration, and thus 'colonize' the life-world of individuals and reduce their citizenships into mere state dependencies. But in either case, the future of the individual as endowed with either client- or citizen-status is dependent on the extension and orientation of professional practices.

My theme in this chapter differs from many modern theories on the professions in that I suggest a constitutive link between the extension of professional services and the claims of the modern individual to possess either a client- or a citizen-status. Indeed, I think it is possible to extend this link to include even that of the individual; without professional services constructing 'needs' of individuals (often by means of an academic symbol system), they would be impoverished and pre-modern creatures, lacking subjectivity and individuality. The modern professional practitioners are constitutive of modern society and its individuals. It is this link between modern society, the individual and the professions which is at the centre of attention here. [. . .]

A Professional Interest Theory and the Evolution of Citizenship

In *Citizenship and Social Class* (1950), Marshall advances a developmental view of the modern citizenry and states (implicitly) the role of the modern professions in enabling citizenship. The welfare state, he says, 'collectivizes the professions and professionalizes social services'. In the course of the evolution of the modern welfare state the once-free liberal professions lose their gentle social status and enter the middle of the social-political arena. Their services are becoming crucial political devices, and hence the professions themselves undergo a process of 'collectivization' (or socialization). New professions are being created in the process of expanding social services. In the following I shall explicate what a collectivization view of the modern professions means in more detail, especially in constituting modern citizenry. In developing T. H. Marshall's view of the rise of citizenship, I should like to stress the intrinsic, or what I call 'constitutive', relation between the various stages of citizenry and types of professional practices.

Marshall distinguishes three phases in the evolution of citizenship: (1) the civil citizenship starting to evolve in the eighteenth century; (2) the suffrage, or the political citizenship, evolving in the nineteenth century and coming to full fruition in our own century; and finally (3) the rise of the social citizenry clearly related to the emergence of the modern welfare state in our own century. [. . .]

Civil Citizenship

As already suggested in the previous section on the liberal state, it is possible to trace the origin of modern society to the birth of the legal individual who can own and dispose of property, enter into contracts and express *his* own personal will (women had no legal status at the time). Locke's *Two Treatises of Government* (1689) stands out in the history of political philosophy as perhaps the first modern treatise. A civil space is carved out for the individual now given 'inalienable' natural rights. These rights include 'liberty of the person, freedom of speech, thought and faith, the right to own property and to conclude valid contracts'. The civil space carved out for man meant an 'equal right to justice' for the bourgeois and the nobleman alike, and was in this sense a revolution of social forms (although most of the population without property were excluded from social participation). The emergence of the market and the nation-state demanded abstract social relations. The notion of citizen as an 'abstract individual' broke the boundaries of family, kinship and community. Social belongings were no longer decided by concrete and visible devices known to all concerned but by means of an abstract symbol system requiring verbal skills. Because of this structural transformation of social life, new professional groups trained in abstract thought became central to social administration. Previously the theologians had excelled in an abstract symbolic language, although in the service of the sacred rather than the profane.

According to the line of thought that I am following here, the legal profession was the first *modern* profession. Civil citizenship could come about only as a function of there coming into existence an independent order of courts free from the demands of both the church and the king. Max Weber saw in the rise of an independent law profession trained academically (at the new European universities) an important carrier of both formal and substantial rationalization of the social order. A new abstract language of statehood and citizenship was needed to terminate the powers of the feudal lords. The king (at least if he was enlightened enough) needed citizens, initially only as his subjects, and he needed from them not only tax money but also their 'acceptance' of his rule. The legal profession was essential in the promulgation and articulation of the new social and political order, as only its members could generate the discursive base needed to legitimize the new rule.

There are different theories to account for the emergence of both citizens and their 'rights'. [. . .] Professionals are powerful social actors in the wider structural articulation of human rights and human needs typical of the modern world order. The system of abstract symbols may very well conceal the subjective and particular interests of social groups. Nevertheless, it is the wider and perhaps unintended consequences of such a subjective interest theory that is of concern here.

The linkage of interests and rights was to become powerful in modern history. For trade and industry to flourish subjective interests and individual rights were needed as 'motives' of action. The link between subjective interests and abstract rights turned out to be especially powerful when the interests of two collective actors could merge into a common destiny. The interests of the bourgeoisie coincided with those of an emergent law profession. The latter profession gave, on the discursive level, and in a formal-rational manner, expression to the action interests of the bourgeoisie. The affinity of interests between the bourgeoisie and the law profession led to an important structural, and perhaps pivotal, dimension in the formation of the new market society.

The emergence of a professional sphere with its own strong interests helped the new bourgeois class to state its interests *legally*. This is an important consideration, as it incorporated the birth of a new professional labour force trained academically, who were to formulate their interests around such 'universal' notions as 'citizen', 'mankind' and 'humanity'. The modern professions were important means of humanization of a secular social order.

It is important to point out the shift in the loyalties of professions that occurred with the rise of the modern nation-state. Before the rise of the citizen-state professional practitioners were the servants of kings and masters, whose orders they had to obey. In the new industrialist society the rule shifted representational forms. The majestic appearances of the king as shown by spectacular displays of weapons and of armies were replaced by the (verbal) power of citizens-individuals: instead of spectacular physical displays the new forms of power took the shape of a neutral and abstract symbol system mediated by academically trained specialists. The professions – initially represented by the legal profession – were citizen-constitutive, for without the discourse that their members alone could offer no abstract citizen rights could have occurred. The power of the citizens had no other institutional backing than the one guaranteed by the 'power of speech'; for example an abstract discourse, preserved 'legally' as the embedded interests of a special law profession. In the case of the imperial or feudal rules, the power was given by God often in combination with the army and preserved by extended family and kinship relations. It is a general characteristic of modern professions, however, that their role as 'power containers' resides primarily in a neutral and abstract symbol system, though often guarded by various ceremonial rituals. [. . .]

The civil citizenship among men was soon to pave the road for even more radical demands: the rights of men to elect their own representatives of local and national government.

Political Citizenship

In the nineteenth century the process of individualization in the legal and the economic orders perforated the organs of political power as well. As Marshall has put it, men demanded a 'right to participate in the exercise of political power', to be 'a member of a body invested with political authorities' and to become an 'elector of the members of such a body'. The struggle for political rights, above all universal suffrage, resulted in the institutionalization of parliaments on a national level, and of community councils on a local level. [. . .]

The institutional anchorage of the newly emergent political rights of the nineteenth century lay in the rise of a parliament with the diversity of political interests now represented as party politics. As a consequence of party politics and representative democracy, a new class of professionals entered the historical arena; the 'professional politicians'. But as a rule politicians, whether they are laymen or professionals, did not (and still do not) speak in 'universal' categories. On the contrary, they have particular (party) interests to represent in parliament. In order to follow our line of thought we need to find new professional groups capable of expressing 'universal' interests. The question is which professional interests at the time were to further the political rights of men in the same way as the legal profession had helped in furthering the interests of the bourgeois?

Among the newly emergent professions of the nineteenth century were the educators and the journalists; namely, those encouraging man's mental capacity to reach above mental slavery. The reformers and the educators of the nineteenth century made up its vanguard strata. They nourished the hope that education could free man from his ancient tutelage. Certainly, these wide circles of educators and reformers could count as the (not yet specialized) forerunners of the modern social service professionals. The existence of these widely dispersed early 'professionals', whose mission it was to educate the masses (not least to avoid the communist menace), were sociological preconditions for the realization of political rights and political citizenship. [. . .]

I am therefore suggesting that the widely dispersed educators and the reformers of the nineteenth century – such as teachers, ministers and journalists – took the same fostering role as had the legal profession in the previous century in strengthening and consolidating citizenship among the people. Thanks to their constitutive endeavours, both on the political and the symbolic level, an enlightened public could emerge where the germ of participatory democracy had taken hold. Nevertheless, the newly achieved formal rights of men could not long conceal the glaring inequalities inherent in the structure of social life itself.

Social Citizenship

[. . .] The social aspects of citizenship emerged in the twentieth century. The formal claim of equality among legal and political citizens revealed the social inequalities of men and women. Guarantees had to be made to eradicate these inequalities. This was (and is) a controversial stage as it required a redistribution of social resources, either by means of law (juridification) or the market (monetarization) or more often by a combination of the two. This required new institutional settings, either publicly or privately run. In any case extensive use of professional service was needed. The 'professionalization' of the social order formed the social structural context in terms of which the articulation of 'social rights' was made possible. The constitutive link between professional practice and citizen rights emerged in a new and politically explosive light.

The interference in men's natural-communal relations in order to redistribute social resources is a double-edged process. It offers freedom to men and women in general (not only to those with property) but on the condition that they are severed from old traditions. This, as Adorno gloomily warns, is the rise of '*die verwaltete Welt*'. Old communal relations are replaced by social-administrative bonds requiring new types of abstract solidarities among men and women. This is also a process of extensive scientification of social life. In the realization of the modern welfare state political parties are dependent on modern social and economic science as mediated by the social service professions. The making of the welfare state draws upon intensified professional skills and practices. I think that it is indeed possible to claim that the welfare state is as much a professional as it is a political achievement. The social extension of citizenship requires the abstract reasoning and calculation of the modern professions trained scientifically in universal rather than particular categories.

[. . .] What I want to stress is the fact that the professional action complex, as it specifically comes to emerge in modern society as a growing sector of its labour force, becomes the prime collective actor in the administration and legitimation of social rights and social citizenry. Whether ruled by left- or right-wing parties, the modern welfare state is anchored institutionally in the 'professional complex'. Hence, it is possible to claim that its stability resides in the strength of the professional ventures. The primacy of modern professional actors in reproducing the social rights of individuals is due to the fact that their diverse occupational *interests* are themselves at stake!

Let me illustrate some such social rights in the case of Sweden. This is not a complete list, but includes some of the more salient ones. In order to safeguard the individual from crises occurring both in his or her own individual life-cycle as well as those emanating from social life and the workplace, social citizenry includes: old-age pensions; illness and disability pensions; paid maternity and parental leave; childhood allowances; student allowances and student loans both for the young and the adults who want to improve their professional lot; 'decent pay for decent work'; improvement in workers' participation in the running of the work setting; a better workplace, equipment and environment; unemployment and work disability compensations; allowances for retraining and compensation for expenses in connection with occupational moves; and so on. It is part and parcel of both union and political-economic life to improve and extend this list continuously and to advise on possible means to effectuate and strengthen these diffuse and often controversial rights. Once rights have been achieved politically and codified legally and semi-legally, they become exceedingly difficult to abolish! Strategic social interests are at stake.

Nevertheless, unless these rights can become grounded in particular professional interests, they are likely to fade away from the public view. Professional agents administer these rights in daily practice; doctors, psychologists and social workers decide on the criteria of physical, mental and environmental health and whether a person can become a candidate for various types of allowances. The workers' rights to participate in the running of the workplace (and not to interfere with the rights of any other); whether this or that clause is applicable in any particular case; or whether or not the correct procedures have been used, are decided by lawyers or by other professional representatives. [. . .]

What I have been saying in the case of the welfare state and the role of the professions is of course equally applicable in the liberal state with its 'customers/clients'. The claims of the latter need professional representation, and professional interests need an expanding market of audiences.

Impact on Professional Life

In the process of this structural transformation of the social, political and economic life due to the rise of the welfare society, or in the case of the modern liberal state the rise of various customer–client organizations, the old professions of (for example) medicine and of law have changed considerably. They could hardly any longer be recognized as 'free, liberal professions' as they have become central agents in the administration of the modern state. The following quote from Michael Walzer's *Spheres of Justice* nicely illustrates what Marshall calls the 'collectivization' of the professions in today's society:

> In Europe during the Middle Ages, the cure of souls was public, the cure of bodies private. Today . . . the situation is reversed . . . . Among medieval Christians, eternity was a socially recognized need, and every effort was made to see that it was widely and equally distributed, that every Christian had an equal chance at salvation and eternal life: hence, a church in every parish, regular services, catechism for the young, compulsory communion, and so on. Among modern citizens, longevity is a socially recognized need; and increasingly every effort is made to see that it is widely and equally distributed, that every citizen has an equal chance at a long and healthy life: hence doctors and hospitals in every district, regular check-ups, health education for the young, compulsory vaccination, and so on.
>   Parallel to the shift in attitudes, and following naturally from it, was a shift in institutions: from the church to the clinic and the hospital. . . . The licencing of physicians, the establishment of state medical schools and urban clinics, the filtering of tax money into the great voluntary hospitals: these measures involved, perhaps, only marginal interference with the profession – some of them, in fact, reinforced its guildlike character: but they already represent an important public commitment. Indeed, they represent a commitment that ultimately can be fulfilled only by turning physicians, or some substantial number of them, into public physicians . . . and by abolishing or constraining the market in medical care.[2]

[. . .] In the case of Sweden (as I suppose elsewhere) numerous examples could be provided of how the old gentleman-doctor or gentleman-judge became merely salaried, bureaucratized, state officials paid in accordance with union contracts with the state. This structural transformation was not won, and is not yet won, without resistance from the old professions, not even in an otherwise levelled-out society like Sweden. The medical profession certainly mobilized organized resistance against the attempts of the state to limit private practices among medical doctors in order to equalize medical practices across the country. Claims for equality of the various regions in Sweden demanded a much more controlled supply of medical practices. The state – that is, the association of abstract citizens – had at its disposal sanctions against the obstructions of an old and status-clad medical profession; no subsidies were provided from the state insurance, making consultation with a doctor a considerable expense. Such sanctions were and are efficient in the hands of the state (now representing citizens and thus abstract justice) to control the obstructions of private professions. [. . .]

It is not only the old professions in medicine and in law that have changed in character and identity in the course of the development of the modern welfare state. Most revealing in the changing structural profile of the modern professions is the explosion of new, so-called 'semi-professions'. The following statistics from Sweden (compiled according to union figures and therefore not complete) reveal the changing structural profile among the professions. A comparison across various academic professions reveals that the social workers have grown from *c.* 3,000 in 1960 to an estimated but quite uncertain number of about 25,000 in 1987; the number of psychologists is today estimated at *c.* 5,900, in 1960 they were *c.* 260; the estimated number of professional economists in Sweden presently ranges somewhere in between 30,000 and 35,000, in 1960 a rough estimation of the economists amounts to *c.* 5,000; the academic engineers are presently numbered at 49,500, whereas in 1950 they were no more than 5,000. In the period 1950–87, the legal profession has grown 2.5 times; the number of engineers has in the same period grown 10 times. From 1960 to 1987 the social workers have grown at least 7 times; and the psychologists almost 23 times over!

The structure of growth among the Swedish professions over the last couple of decades certainly illustrates the growth of industry and of production, but also the expansion and institutionalization of 'social rights' socially and politically. An important question in this context is whether or not history can be turned back and if the welfare state is reversible. To the extent to which these professions, particularly those administering social and political life, have collective interests to defend and maintain against interferences from yet other group interests, one could expect the continuation of the welfare rights among modern citizens, even if there were to be a drastic change in governmental policies. Realistically speaking, any politically elected government must show restraint in dealing with well-organized professional (and corporate) interests. It would be costly, both economically and politically, to lay professionals off the labour market, and provide them with no substitute! [. . .]

The Problem of Professional Representation

In many current writings on professionalism, there exists a clear tendency to view professional power from a cynical point of view, as 'symbolic capital', as 'monopolization of cultural resources', as 'credential politics' or the rise of the 'sinecure society'. [. . .] The credential system in modern society bestowing upon the professions their 'sinecural locations' allows them also to speak in universal categories, and thus make possible discursively the rise of universal men and women. Perhaps these practices are the unanticipated consequences of modern professional power, but a theory of the professions should also comprise such consequences. The correlate of the citizen allows us to take a different view of professional power and its accountability: to whom are the modern professionals accountable? Whose interests do they represent? [. . .] The asymmetry in (for instance) the relation between a doctor and patients with regard to the possession of medical knowledge seems to rule out the concept of 'representation'. In the case of a lawyer, however, we speak of 'legal representation' as there is a supposed client prior to the representative act. The decisive question is thus whether or not there is a person prior to the act of representation capable of controlling its proceedings. In the context of professional powers it has been questioned whether there are prior wills to hold practitioners accountable because of the asymmetry in the relationships. Traditionally, the professional relationships were characterized as 'trust-relations'. What other choices do we really have but to trust the competency of a doctor when he or she presents us with the diagnosis that we suffer from cancer, and that we are in need of a particular kind of therapy?

The traditional asymmetry with regard to the possession of knowledge between a professional practitioner and a client/patient certainly could mould professional power into the merely symbolic and representational kind. It is my belief, however, that modern society, whether in its welfare or liberal version, has gradually closed the gap in status and power that the old professions used to possess. Professions are today held accountable either by means of state control or by means of organizations of customers or clients, in particular by powerful insurance organizations in pursuit of malpractice. [. . .]

Whatever the future will be regarding the current moves on 'accountability' of both scientific and professional practices, the bases of professional powers are certainly coming under increasing attack due to the rise of various citizens' organizations and social movements. The results of these moves among groups of citizens and clients are likely to change the previous asymmetry and (unquestioned) trust that earlier characterized relations between professional practitioners and clients/patients. It is unlikely that professional representation would turn descriptive in the classical sense, but such powers will most likely have to deal with more or less organized 'interests' ready to question the mere symbolic content of professional power in the future, the justificatory bases of which are discursive; professional practitioners of various sorts will have to provide us with 'good reasons' for their diagnoses and treatments.

[. . .] The point is that individuals as clients or as citizens are allowed to question the bases of expert power and seek to distinguish whether it is based on justificatory reasons or not. Professional representation can thus be seen from within the framework of the wider discursive culture which the professions themselves have helped to foster. The success of the professionalized society results paradoxically in the 'de-professionalization' of modern society; organizations among citizens and clients will force upon professional practitioners the necessity to review their own actions from the point of view of the larger citizenry and even of humanity as such.

In a society with a complex division of labour we need professional specialization and representation. It is not a practical and efficient state of affairs to let each individual be his or her own doctor, lawyer, accountant and so on. The point is not to let increasing specialization in knowledge and in practice lead to a state of affairs of ignorance and passivity, and thus alienation, among the citizenry at large. On the contrary, the promise of a modern, enlightened, professional culture lies in its discursive and justificatory bases of power. The menaces that confront us today are not the professions and their claim to power but blind faith, whatever its form of manifestation.

Conclusion

In this chapter I have stressed the intrinsic relationship between professional power and citizens' rights as constitutive of one another. I have not considered the controversial issue as to whether such links are best served by means of juridification or monetarization, by means of the welfare state or the liberal state with its market mechanisms. I have no answer to this question.

Instead, I focused on the strategic role of the professions in both types of social economies; in modern society they have become both client- and citizen-constitutive. But there is a contradiction inherent in the structural position of the modern professional, and perhaps the contradiction is more apparent in the case of the welfare state. In the (pure) liberal state a professional practitioner can perhaps claim that he or she *represents* the client only, rather than the abstract citizen body. Such a loyalty becomes more difficult in the welfare state where the medical doctor has to mediate between the concern for the patient and the abstract citizen body. What is good for all is not necessarily best for the individual. This is what I mean by the duality of the modern professional practice finding itself torn between the body-citizen (the state) and the individual person. The fusion of universal and particular interests, of state and individual representation, is likely to elicit role conflicts in the professional practitioner. [. . .] There is a cleavage in the 'legitimate expectations' (to use Marshall's term) of an individual and that which can be provided by state means. It is this kind of crisis symptoms that perhaps torment the modern (welfare) professions. It is not easy to be an executor of legitimate power and at the same time serve those who are the subjects of that same power.

Our social citizenship and the rights that it bestows upon us are said to be much more resilient and perhaps negotiable than the more consolidated civil rights of an earlier epoch. To work out the negotiable status of our social citizenship by means of an interest theory of the professions would be the ultimate theoretical *and* political test of the thesis that I have suggested in this chapter. There is no room, however, to develop that theme here.

Notes

1 Parsons, Talcott (1949) *Essays in Sociological Theory, Pure and Applied.* New York: The Free Press of Glencoe. p. 34.
2 Walzer, Michael (1983) *Spheres of Justice.* New York. pp. 212–13.

17

Consumerism and the Public Sector: how well does the coat fit?

Jenny Potter

In a paper on performance measurement and the consumer, Pollitt noted that performance assessment can now fairly be described as a bandwagon, and that in many of the public services rushing in – or being pushed – to look critically at their performance:

> 'consumerism' has . . . become an officially-approved fashion. In hospitals, schools, housing schemes, advice and information services and many other aspects of public administration managers are being exhorted to pay more attention to consumer wishes, offer consumers wider choice, and develop techniques for 'marketing' their particular service. (1987: 43)

But how successfully have the basic principles of consumerism been absorbed by public sector managers? Is consumerism as currently applied in the public sector little more than a second-hand coat, to be discarded when fashions change once more, or can it be tailor-made to suit the particular requirements of the public sector? To answer these questions we need first to examine the relevance and adequacy of consumerism's basic principles, and then to look at how these are currently put into practice.

The Theory of Consumerism

Consumer theorists argue that there is an imbalance of power between those who provide goods and services, and those for whom they are provided. The former possess all the advantages of corporate power and organization, resources, and political influence. The latter, in the market-place at least, have the choice of buying or not buying a product or service, and – where competitive markets exist – of choosing according to their own preferences. They carry weight, therefore, only as the sum of their individual choices.

To shift the balance of power in favour of consumers, those representing their interests have isolated five key factors which provide a structural underpinning of consumerism. These are the principles of access, choice,

From *Public Administration*, 66 (Summer 1988): 149–64 (abridged).

information, redress and representation. People must first of all have access to the benefits offered by a product or service (without access, they cannot 'get in'). Their choice of products and services must be as wide as possible to establish some measure of consumer sovereignty, and they need as much information as possible, both to enable them to make sensible choices, and to make the fullest possible use of whatever it is they are seeking. They will also need some means of communicating their grievances when things go wrong, and receiving adequate redress. Finally, they need some means of making sure that their interests are adequately represented to those who take decisions affecting their welfare.

These five tenets were first developed in relation to goods and services sold in the market-place. Consumer choice plays a key role here. People have different requirements and preferences, differing ability to pay, and different views on what constitutes value for money. Where choice exists, individuals can influence the profits and (one assumes) the behaviour of producers by selecting goods and services with the right mix – for them – of price and quality. The existence of competition tends to work in favour of consumers by operating to keep prices down and quality up for each mix that is produced.

Applying Consumer Principles to Public Services

[. . .] Most public services are provided because they are considered to be in the public interest, and working for the public good. They are broadly of two kinds: those designed to give people access to services they would not otherwise be able to enjoy, and those concerned with some form of social control. At the same time, the resources of the public sector are finite and limited, and distributed as an act of political will. This creates an immediate dilemma for the pure application of consumer principles. On the one hand, the nature of public services suggests they are of the utmost importance to those consumers who want to use them; on the other hand, the interests of individual consumers must constantly be juggled against the interests of the community as a whole, and of other groups who make up that community. Although Stewart and Clarke (Local Government Training Board, 1987) are right to stress, in their development of the public service orientation for local government, that the primary purpose of public services has to be service for the public, deciding what is meant by the 'public' in each particular case presents an immediate problem.

Access

Because those who pay for public services and those who benefit from them are not necessarily the same people, the cardinal consumer principle of access cannot be translated into an automatic consumer right. Deciding *who* shall have access to *what* is a political responsibility, and one that in local government is clearly the province of elected members. (How these decisions are made in the health service is much less clear, and only now creeping on to the political agenda.)

Consumerist contributions to the debate about access are generally of two kinds. On the one hand, they call for the definition of clear and explicit criteria on which to base these vitally important decisions about how services should be rationed. They insist that these criteria are brought into the open, because only in this way can the decisions be understood and challenged. The value of this approach can be illustrated in relation to council house allocation policies. Unless you know the criteria an authority applies, you cannot effectively press your case as a prospective tenant, nor can you argue for different, perhaps more equitable, rules.

The other approach is to encourage access more in the sense of accessibility. Public services are large, bureaucratic, enclosed organizations, structured and run according to their own rules, and often for their own convenience. To an outsider they present the impenetrable facade of a walled city. [. . .] And the general move to decentralize services and authorities will usually have better access as an aim, although not necessarily the sole or most important one.

Choice

Consumer choice is another principle that cannot, in the public sector, be translated into an absolute right. Of course choices exist within many parts of the public sector, and the range is being extended all the time, most recently and dramatically by the creation of city technological colleges as an alternative to schools provided by local education authorities. But because the provision of public services usually involves redistributing costs and benefits within society, individual consumer choice cannot be the sole driving force that dictates who benefits, and who pays. Indeed, it is plainly not relevant to some services at all. The parent whose child is being taken into care, for example, would probably 'choose' not to have the service at all. [. . .]

The consumerist argument is that where consumers cannot express their preferences directly through exercising their choices, other mechanisms must be found to make sure their interests are taken into account by decision-makers. One of the routes favoured by, among others, the National Consumer Council, has been the development of performance measure-ment in a way that can incorporate consumers' views (1986). This route applies many of the lessons learned from classic management and marketing theory. It involves identifying consumers' preferences, defining clear and measurable political objectives that state what services should achieve for their intended beneficiaries (individual service users and the wider community), developing criteria for evaluating aspects of service that matter to consumers, and bringing this kind of performance information into the public domain.

A 'consumer' approach to performance measurement differs from that practised in most public services in its insistence that consumers' interests – and those of the wider public – should be brought into the heart of the evaluative process. The argument goes that if the ultimate purpose of public services is to serve the public, measures of consumer and community benefits are the most important measures of all. They confer meaning on all the others, and provide a context within which it is possible to consider questions of efficiency and economy.

Performance measurement of this kind can be applied to most services provided by the public sector. It offers a useful substitute for consumer choice, as long as consumers' interests and preferences are properly identified and taken into account. For some services, however, particularly those provided for vulnerable groups such as mentally ill people and children in care, the absence of choice must be tackled on a more individual level. When people cannot make choices for themselves (either because they are considered incapable, or because society has taken away their ability to make choices) it is very easy to overlook their interests.

The response has been to develop the notion of individual rights. *Clients' Rights*, the influential report produced by a working party of the National Council for Voluntary Organizations (1984), was concerned not so much with enunciating rights for clients of social services departments – as this could be achieved only on a very abstract level – but with practical ways of giving clients some dignity in essentially subservient situations and making sure they were able to express their point of view. This approach is also relevant to the health service. The King's Fund Centre's work (1986) on priority care groups starts by expressing key principles which emphasize the value, needs and rights of the individual, and then attempts to translate these principles into examples of good practice.

The point is that choice is a crucial consideration in relation to the public sector. Where individuals have the power to choose (and an appropriate range of options to choose from), services can become sensitive to their real needs and preferences. But because of the redistributive nature of the public sector, consumer choice cannot be the sole mechanism for reconciling competing claims on the public purse. Where individuals are not able to make choices directly, other mechanisms must be developed to ensure that their interests are taken into account.

Information

The case for the third consumer principle, information, is more easily made. Indeed, information takes on an even greater importance in the public sector, because the services at stake are likely to be crucial to consumers' welfare, and because the imbalance in the amount of information possessed by providers and consumers is often so wide.

As in the private sector, individual consumers of public services need information to enable them to make the best choices about the services they want to use, and how to derive maximum benefit from them. They also need more general information if they – or their representatives – are to have any real say in the way public services are run.

They need information about goals and objectives; about the standards of service authorities aim to provide, and the standards achieved; about their rights to a service, and their responsibilities in using them; about the way authorities are structured and the decision-making processes; about why decisions are taken, and about what those decisions actually are. Information of this kind can confer real power, if by power one means the ability to influence change. Without it, consumers are merely whistling in the dark.

Redress

Redress, the fourth consumer principle, also takes on major importance in the public sector. Individuals have an obvious need for mechanisms to settle their grievances quickly, simply and fairly. But the existence of redress mechanisms can bring wider benefits, by acting as a check on the actions of service providers, and by constituting a form of quality control that allows services to identify and put right any underlying problems in their management systems, policies and practices.

The report on complaints procedures in local government, produced by the University of Sheffield (Lewis *et al.*, 1987), provides a fairly dismal record of how responsive authorities are to the principle of redress. Less than half the authorities surveyed even claimed to have authority-wide procedures for handling complaints and of these, only a small proportion gave any publicity to their procedures. (Many claims about having a complaints procedure were in any case suspect.) Just over a third of authorities claimed to have adopted the code of practice on complaints procedures produced by their own local authority associations and the Commissioner for Local Administration in England. Some insisted they had never heard of it. Few authorities used complaints as a form of quality control, and few undertook any form of statistical analysis. Social services departments had the best record here, but only some one in five analysed their complaints. The authors found evidence to suggest the existence of a 'submerged body of complaints which administrative cultures help to suppress'.

Although the report was largely concerned with practice, something about officers' attitudes towards complaints and complainants emerged as well, most starkly in the belief of some officers that complaints to the

Ombudsman were made largely by 'malcontents and misfits who have problems other than the one complained of'.

Representation

Representation is one of the more problematic of the five consumer principles. Taken literally, it means simply that the views of consumers should be adequately represented to decision-makers at all points in the system where decisions are taken concerning their interests.

As a principle, it must be reasonably uncontroversial on an individual level. It can be seen in action in the development of forms of advocacy for particularly vulnerable individuals such as people with mental handicaps. It is also generally accepted within public services that are run at arm's length from politicians, such as the publicly run utilities, and the National Health Service. Because consumers of these services are generally unorganized and lack resources of their own, official recognition of the need for representation has been institutionalized in bodies established to represent consumers' interests, paid for out of public funds. [. . .]

The principle becomes much more difficult to apply to services provided by local government, because a formalized and democratic system of representation already exists. Elected members can bang their fists on the ballot box as proof of their legitimacy and claim quite reasonably to represent the interests of the constituents, to right their wrongs and put forward their point of view. [. . .]

The traditional consumer response has been to argue that while members are elected to take decisions on behalf of individuals and the community, they cannot possibly hope to know everything about consumers' preferences. These need to be identified and represented to them, so that they can base their political decisions on facts rather than untested assumptions. The current crop of opinion surveys carried out among local government residents and service users, and patients in the health service, can be seen as a form of representation by research. [. . .]

It is here that the traditional consumer movement, and the five principles it has put forward, are in danger of being overtaken by the development of forms of participatory democracy in which users, and local communities, are given the opportunity not just to put forward their point of view, but to assume responsibility for the decisions themselves. It takes only a small, logical step to progress from the principle of representation to that of participation, but it marks a giant leap in the way most public services are currently run.

Is Consumerism Enough?

Having set out the five consumer principles, and examined their application to services provided by local government and the National Health Service, it is now time to consider whether consumerism provides an adequate basis for helping public services redefine their relationship with users and the public.

The first point to make concerns a somewhat surprising gap in the principles themselves. Because they are concerned with the relationship between providers and consumers, and particularly with the redistribution of power between the two parties, they do not address the critical question of what sort of services should be provided. The implication is that once the relationship has become more evenly balanced, the parameters of what constitutes a good-quality service will emerge, or at least that consumers in any particular place, or consumers of any particular service, will be able to express their own preferences, needs, expectations and satisfactions. The first principle of any genuinely 'consumer-responsive' authority or service must therefore be to establish the concerns of its intended beneficiaries. [. . .]

Perhaps a little more didacticism is required, especially as quality of service remains fairly low on the agenda of most local authorities. Maxwell's definition of the six key dimensions of quality (1984), developed in relation to health services, provides a good starting point. Adapting his definition to incorporate the consumer's perspective suggests that services should be: *appropriate* and *relevant* (to meet individual and community preferences, wishes and needs); *available* and *accessible* (to everyone, or to those groups/individuals given explicit priority); *equitable* (that is, fair in the treatment of individuals or groups of people in similar circumstances); *acceptable* in terms of the quality of service provided, and the manner in which it is provided (this criterion incorporates a number of others, including whether services are approachable, convenient, pleasant to use, reliable, timely, prompt, responsive and humane); *economic* and *efficient* (from the viewpoint of service users, those who pay for services through rates and taxes, and the community as a whole); and *effective* in terms of the benefits they bring to users and the community.

In spite of this gap in the principles themselves, consumerism has a lot to offer public services. If one accepts that an imbalance of power exists between those who provide public services, and those for whom they are provided, and if one also accepts that the primary purpose of public services is to serve the public, then a careful application of the five principles can be enormously helpful in suggesting how public services can do their job better. In this sense, those who run public services, and those pressing for the adoption of a consumerist approach, belong to the same 'side'. They are both, after all, working for the same ends, although consumerism aims to stack the cards a little more fairly in the hands of consumers themselves.

But is consumerism enough radically to redefine the relationship between public services and their public? The first problem posed by this chapter was that of defining just what is meant by 'the public'. Individuals have all sorts of relationships with public services, especially those provided by local government: they may be customers or users in the traditional sense, or potential users, or they may be affected indirectly or directly by services. They may pay for services through their rates and taxes, and vote (or choose not to vote) in local and national elections. They are also citizens in the widest sense. Relationships in the health service are a little less complicated (perhaps because lines of political accountability are less obviously drawn) but individuals may still be users, potential users (either now or in the future), affected by services provided to others, or taxpayers. [. . .]

Rhodes has argued convincingly (1987) that the public service orientation – an attempt to translate Peters and Waterman's *In Search of Excellence* to the public sector – must be set within a broader perspective than that of service delivery. Instead, he suggests that the PSO should be defined as the three Cs of consumerism, caring, and citizenship, and 'the greatest of these is citizenship'.

By citizenship, he refers back to the Greek concept in which citizens shared in decision and office:

> In other words, the concept of citizen is active, involving both rights and duties through:
>
> > . . . membership in a political unit, involving cooperation in public decisions as a right and sharing of public burdens . . . as a duty.
>
> And this emphasis is most succinctly captured in Wildavsky's definition of citizenship as 'moral development' or 'enhancing capacity to make choices that take account of other people's preferences'. (Rhodes, 1987: 66)

The apolitical nature of consumerism, and the fact that it is grounded in economic theory, means that it is not equipped itself to develop this kind of sharing or swapping of roles between the governors and the governed, the administrators and the administrated. Consumerism's primary concern is to place consumers' preferences on the agenda, rather than encourage consumers to take account of the preferences of others.

Perhaps this explains why consumerist principles stop at representation instead of moving on to embrace participation. Of course there are instances where consumers themselves have made this step, especially when they are readily identified as a group, sharing common interests. The tenants' movement provides one such example, and the idea of tenant participation in management is becoming increasingly accepted. [. . .]

Consumerism can help authorities to advance from considering individual members of their public as passive clients or recipients of services – who get what they are given for which they must be thankful – to thinking of them as customers with legitimate rights and preferences as well as responsibilities. But it will rarely be enough to turn members of the public into partners, actively involved in shaping public services. For this to take place, the arguments must be shifted to the political arena, and some attempt made to develop the ideal of citizenship to which Rhodes refers. Consumerism is fine as far as it goes, but it does not go far enough to effect a radical shift in the distribution of power.

Consumerism in Action

Having set out the principles of consumerism it is now time to look at the extent to which they have been put into practice. [. . .]

Central government, with its emphasis on value for money (a classic consumer demand), competition and consumer choice, gets much of the credit for shaking the public sector out of the complacency and inertia that bedevil large bureaucracies, even if its motives were largely to control public expenditure and clamp down on the activities of certain left-wing authorities. It has also created a climate in which public services are looking to the best of the private sector for inspiration. Other forces at work include:

- the Local Government Training Board's development of the public service orientation, with its core value of service for the public, and its emphasis on quality of service, putting value on the public as customers and citizens, and a high level of responsiveness to the public;
- the Griffiths Report on NHS management (1983) which stressed the importance of quality of patient care and determining patient satisfaction:

  It is central to the approach of management in planning and delivering services . . . to ascertain how well the service is being delivered at local level by obtaining the experience and perceptions of patients and the community;

- following Griffiths, the adoption within health authorities of a range of quality assurance programmes. Stemming originally from manufacturing industries, QA involves two key stages: first, designing a specification for a product or service, which involves defining quality in terms of the fitness for purpose of that product or service, and its ability to satisfy a given need; and second, testing whether the product or service matches up to the specification. The application of QA to service planning, delivery and evaluation calls, therefore, for clarity in defining what quality means. And the definition of quality (fitness for purpose and ability to satisfy a given need) places the game very firmly at the consumer's end of the court, because it is presumably his or her purpose that the service should be trying to meet (and those of other consumers, and potential consumers, and future consumers as well, of course);
- the Audit Commission's gradual progression (in theory at least) from an accountant's concern with economy and efficiency, to a manager's wider responsibility for service effectiveness. Howard Davies, Controller of Audit, has suggested that there are four levels at which one can conduct the debate about local authority performance: inputs, outputs, output quality and, most importantly of all, outcomes, 'whether what the authority set out to achieve has indeed been accomplished' (Davies, 1987).

But to what extent have these forces brought about any real change in the way public services operate, and how they treat their consumers and citizens? It should be said immediately that a small number of local authorities, and health authorities, appear to have taken fully on board the notion of service for the public, and developed strategies for (a) finding out what their customers (and communities) want, like, and think about the services provided; and (b) perhaps the more difficult stage, incorporating this information into the planning and review process. Examples of innovative practice can be drawn from all shades of the political spectrum. The radical right and the radical left appear at times to have gone full circle. The efforts of each are often designed to help ordinary people take control over their lives. [. . .]

An authority with a particularly well-developed policy of consumer-centred management is the London Borough of Richmond upon Thames (Alliance). The policy has led to action on six fronts: organizational change; the development of regular public consultation meetings and specific rates consultation meetings; the adoption of a five-year corporate communications strategy; a growing recognition of the need to involve staff in customer-centred initiatives; a market research programme combining regular attitude surveys among residents with individual exercises conducted by (or for) service departments; and changes in management practice. Each year, service departments prepare management reports which must state, among other things, how the department has tapped the views of its customers.

Other authorities have attempted structural reforms as a means of gearing the organization to serve its public rather than the other way round. Arun District Council (Conservative) accomplished a remarkable restructuring within just four years. [. . .]

Under a Labour administration, the Metropolitan Borough of Walsall 'went local' (the Walsall version of decentralization) by considering what consumers want from its services. Lewis and Bovaird (1986) included the following statement under the new objectives of the authority:

> Service should be personal and informal. People relate to people so the public should know the officers they are dealing with and officers should begin to 'own' the problems of the neighbourhood and to identify with the people they serve. Developing from this, users of services should become to be always referred to as consumers, to show the new relationship they should enjoy with the local authority and to illustrate their ability and power to influence service delivery.

The health service, too, has responded positively to the challenge posed by Griffiths. Many authorities within England and Wales have appointed quality assurance managers. In the early days their remit was often unclear (and they were usually existing staff such as chief nursing officers given another hat) but the meetings of the Quality Assurance Interest Group attest to a growing expertise and genuine concern to define and evaluate patient care.

Some health authorities stand out for their willingness to bring consumers' concerns into the heart of service planning. Wessex Regional Health Authority, for example, has developed a model for performance standards review. Its aim is to develop a statement of the characteristics of good service from the viewpoint of service provision (input), service operation (process), and service effectiveness (outcome), and to specify indicators that measure the level of attainment. The statement is intended to be informed by views from three different groups: hospital-based professionals, general practitioners, and clients/users of the service (whose views are to be established by a survey of client expectations and attitudes).

The National Consumer Council is currently working with two district health authorities – Paddington and North Kensington, and East Dorset, with the active collaboration of Wessex Region – to assess consumers' experiences of the NHS. The focus is on a neglected client group – elderly people suffering from dementia and their informal carers (NCC, 1987). After establishing consumers' concerns through interviews and group discussions, the work will define client-oriented goals for the service in association with all those who have a stake in it: clients, families, informal carers, service staff, managers, planners, medical and allied practitioners, and voluntary organizations. Only when goals are established can the parameters of performance be defined.

If the good stands out within local government and the health service, what about the rest? One depressing conclusion is that most current initiatives in the health service have concentrated on its hotel aspects – what one district general manager referred to as the quality of the custard (Templeton College, 1987) – rather than what must be the NHS's prime function: to improve people's health. Perhaps this concentration reflects a narrow interpretation of what consumers are actually concerned about. More probably, it stems from the still unassailable power of the medical profession. It would be a brave authority indeed that seeks patients' views on the quality of medical care provided by clinicians.

More positively, there is certainly interest in the ideas of consumerism, though whether this interest is genuine or fanned by the prevailing climate is difficult to determine. As government pushes forward its privatization programme, and extends consumer choice, public services will be forced to take note of what sort of services people actually want. At the same time, however, financial controls are tying the services' hands. Of the handful of innovative authorities interviewed for the LGTB, at least three had been or were facing the prospect of rate-capping. And no one concerned with patient care can condone the closing of hospital wards and operating theatres (presumably under the banner of efficiency) while waiting lists lengthen. The government's insistence on extending consumer choice, laudable in itself, may result in increased choice for some consumers to the very real disadvantage of others. There is no doubt, for example, that many council tenants want to buy their homes, but the options open to those who are unable to buy are diminishing all the time.

Furthermore, in spite of the current interest in consumerism, it is possible to detect an undercurrent of defensiveness, even hostility, towards those who are trying to get consumers' concerns placed on the agenda. This can be explained partly by the natural defensiveness of any group which feels threatened by the comments (sometimes critical) of 'outsiders'. It is compounded by the old belief that because consumers – and their representatives – are, by definition, not 'experts', they are rarely worth listening to, whether as speakers at conferences or as individual members of the public. Professionals have in this sense the most to lose from the new consumer orientation, as their judgements no longer hold automatic sway. Many are unwilling to lay themselves open to what they consider un-informed and unfair comment from the public.

Many authorities also appear to be experiencing great difficulty in putting consumerism's ideas into practice. Some fall at the first hurdle, which is defining just who their customers are. This confusion is reflected in discussions about what to call people: consumers, customers, users, clients, citizens, patients, 'the public' and so on. (In the health service, there have been apparently serious attempts to coin a new word combining 'clients' and 'patients', ending up with 'clipats'.) It is necessary to recognize that people have different relationships with public services, and that different people want or need different things. [. . .]

Another common failing is to mistake the means for the end. Public opinion surveys are currently fashionable among local authorities, as are patient satisfaction surveys in hospitals. The motto seems to be: if in doubt, carry out a survey. The particular advantage of surveys is that they seek the views of a representative sample of people, rather than simply of those who are determined and articulate enough to volunteer their opinions. But many questions can never be fully explored through structured questionnaires. And sometimes surveys are carried out without the necessary skills, and without a commitment to act on the results. [. . .]

Authorities face real problems in developing systems and procedures to cope with all the new information they are getting from their customers and publics. To an outsider, it seems extraordinary that major public services have not developed sophisticated systems to monitor and analyse com-plaints; they need this information simply to manage their businesses, let alone to keep their customers happy. Some authorities with quite sophisti-cated information-gathering systems do not always know what to do with the results. It is as if there is a policy vacuum which cannot be filled with isolated bits and pieces of information.

While it would be churlish to deride the very real progress being made, the most significant developments are taking place in the field of customer relations (the necessary veneer of consumerism), and in developing forms of managerial responsiveness to consumers' views. Real attempts to give power to consumers are rare, though they do exist. Oxford City Council, for example, has involved prospective tenants in all decisions about the design of a new housing estate, from the site layout to the colour of the bricks and the choice of fittings. Middlesbrough Borough Council has introduced community councils for a number of areas, each with control of its own (small) community budget – currently £3,000.

More generally, however, authorities are improving their performance according to the five consumer principles outlined in this chapter both because it helps them to do a better job, and because they have recognized that paying more attention to their customers and public offers a way of re-kindling public support. This is not just a question of improving their public image. There are votes to be won as well, at a time when local government needs all the support it can get if it is to maintain its franchises. But most authorities which are improving public information do so under the banner of public relations rather than because they have recognized that information can alter the balance of power.

Issues to Face

Consumerism involves more than being nice to consumers, though even this simple idea could be put into practice a little more effectively. [. . .] It demands a searching review of the relationship between providers and those for whom services are provided, and it suggests a fundamental shift in perspective that places the interests of consumers and the wider public at the heart of the way services are planned, delivered and evaluated. Allowing consumers a real input to the process of setting objectives is one way this could be put into practice. Developing forms of performance evaluation that look at aspects of service that matter to consumers, and at their actual experiences, is another. Giving people the power to make their own choices, either as individual service users or as local communities, is a third.

If faced up to politically, consumerism can also pave the way to a more radical sharing out of roles between the governors and the governed, even if it will not achieve this of its own accord. The question then becomes not just whether the coat fits, but what sort of coat one wants. First, however, there are a number of issues which must be faced by public service managers, both professionally and politically.

At the outset, what *value* do such managers place on users, citizens, and members of the public? It is easy to categorize consumers as ignorant, ill-informed, overly demanding, volatile, apathetic, inconsistent, and so on. It requires an imaginative leap to consider consumers as equals in a three-cornered exchange with politicians (who possess the power) and professionals (who possess the skills and the expertise, and any delegated or assumed power as well).

The question of value affects every aspect of the way an authority, or service, is run. It has an obvious bearing on the contact between staff and public at the front line. It spills over into questions of organization, where the time and convenience of staff are valued far more highly than those of users and potential users. It marks the difference between an authority that is ready to hear what its public has to say, and one that is willing actually to learn from what it hears. And it is reflected in organizational cultures, which give a sense of purpose and cohesion to all an authority's actions.

The second issue concerns the extent to which public services are willing to accept consumers as *judges*, both of what they should be doing, and of whether they are doing it well. Consumers will not always want – or be able to appropriate – the last word. The patient on the operating table will not always be the best judge of whether the operation was a success, or whether it was the right operation in the first place (though it is dangerous to assume that the patient will not have a valid point of view). But performance cannot be examined properly without putting many of the questions to consumers themselves. How do you judge, for example, whether a service is relevant to individuals without reference to what they might want or like? You might, as a politician, decide to impose your own political solutions on the matter – that is your right and your responsibility. And you might, as a professional, argue that your expertise and experience must at times overrule the judgements and preferences your consumers are putting forward. But you need, as a politician or a professional, constantly to test your assumptions against the views and experiences of those whose interests you are in business to serve. And this process must be brought into the public domain. It is not enough to conduct your reviews and evaluations behind closed doors.

The final and most crucial issue concerns *power*. How far do you *want* to redress the imbalance of power that exists between providers and users or citizens? The institutions of representative democracy provide a cast-iron excuse for defending the status quo, with perhaps some minor changes at the margins to restore a human face to public services. But is this enough to translate service for the public from an ideal to a reality?

References

Arun District Council (1987) *Strategy Papers*. Littlehampton: ADC.

Davies, Howard (1987) *Performance Measurement in Local Government*. Paper presented to a conference on performance measurement and the consumer organized by the National Consumer Council in association with the Chartered Institute of Public Finance and Accountancy and the Public Finance Foundation. London: National Consumer Council.

Griffiths, E. R. (1983) *NHS Management Inquiry* (letter to Secretary of State for Social Services). London: Department of Health and Social Services.

King's Fund Centre (1986) *Living Well into Old Age: Applying Principles of Good Practice to Services for People with Dementia*. London: King's Fund Publishing Office.

Lewis, C. D. and Bovaird, A. G. (1986) *Going Local: IT for Front-line Consumer Services*. Luton: Local Government Training Board.

Lewis, N., Seneviratne, M. and Cracknell, S. (1987) *Complaints Procedures in Local Government*. Sheffield: University of Sheffield Centre for Criminological and Socio-legal Studies.

Local Government Training Board (1987) *Getting Closer to the Public*. Luton: LGTB.

Maxwell, R. J. (1984) 'Quality assessment in health', *British Medical Journal*, 288, 12 May.

National Consumer Council (1986) *Measuring Up: Consumer Assessment of Local Authority Services – a Guideline Study*. London: NCC.

National Consumer Council (1987) *Assessing Consumers' Experiences of the National Health Service: Outline of Work to be Conducted by the NCC with Reference to Services for Elderly People Suffering from Dementia*. London: NCC.

National Council for Voluntary Organizations (1984) *Clients' Rights: Report of an NCVO Working Party*. London: Bedford Square Press.

Pollitt, Christopher (1987) *Performance Measurement and the Consumer*. London: National Consumer Council.

Rhodes, R. A. W. (1987) 'Developing the public service orientation, or let's add a soupçon of political theory', *Local Government Studies* May/June: 63–73.

Templeton College (1987) *Managing for Better Health* (Templeton series on District General Managers, No. 2: DGMs and quality improvement). Oxford: Templeton College.

18

Organizational Culture: origins and weaknesses

V. Lynn Meek

The study of organizational culture – the proposition that organizations create myths and legends, engage in rites and rituals, and are governed through shared symbols and customs – is much in vogue. Although the reasons for this are not entirely clear, two issues deserve mention: (1) the effect of political, ideological and socioeconomic factors on social theory; (2) the related issue of the scholarly and ideological implications of the selective borrowing of key concepts from one discipline by other fields of study.

The present preoccupation with organizational culture is probably related to socioeconomic factors in Western society. Most Western countries have experienced a dramatic downturn in their economies. This, in turn, has helped to emphasize the structural inequalities inherent in these societies and has placed the structure of Western capitalism under severe pressure. It is probably no accident that many scholars are emphasizing cultural problems – particularly where cultural problems are naively operationalized in terms of 'people problems' – at a time when the structures of many Western institutions are under strain.

Some social theorists use the term 'culture' to embrace all that is human within the organization. They emphasize culture, either consciously or unconsciously, in such a way as to blur or hide problems and contradictions inherent in the social structure. Of course, both an organization's culture and its structure are socially created; but that is not what is at issue here. The problem with some studies of organizational culture is that they appear to presume that there exists in a real and tangible sense a collective organizational culture that can be created, measured and manipulated in order to enhance organizational effectiveness. The link between 'culture' and 'effectiveness' has become, recently, quite pronounced, and studies incorporating in their title such phrases as the 'culture of school effectiveness', or the 'culture of corporate effectiveness' abound. It is implied that an ineffective organization can be made effective – a school can produce the 'model citizen', that is, one who can find employment, and the

From *Organization Studies*, 9(4) (1988): 453–73 (abridged).

corporation can enhance its profit margin – if an unhealthy organizational culture can be supplanted with a healthy one. The problem is one of changing people's values, norms and attitudes so that they make the 'right' and necessary contribution to the healthy collective 'culture' despite (or in ignorance of) any inherent conflict of individual and group interest or the way in which power, authority and control are structured in the organization.

Areas of study, such as the study of complex organizations – including educational and corporate administration, management studies, and human relations and interpersonal dynamics – are influenced by concepts that filter down into the ranks of their practitioners from older, well-founded disciplines. The idea of culture in organizations is a concept borrowed mostly from anthropology, although some sociologists, such as Durkheim, have also been influential.

There is nothing wrong with one discipline borrowing concepts from another discipline; this process has resulted in important theoretical innovations. However, there is a danger that, when one area of study borrows key concepts from other disciplines, the concepts become either stereotyped or distorted in the transfer. Also, when concepts are borrowed from other disciplines, they may not be borrowed *in toto*: that is, rather than accepting an entire 'package' – which may include the historical debates surrounding the 'proper' uses of the concepts – people only select aspects of the concepts that suit their interests and thinking at a particular time. This may result either in a slanted and biased application of the concepts or a dilution of their original analytical power.

The concept of organizational culture can be a powerful analytical tool in the analysis and interpretation of human action within complex organizations. Alternatively, it can be misused to reify the social reality of organizational life. It may be timely to have a close look at some of the ways in which the concept of 'culture' has been used in organizational research, paying particular attention to questions concerning what aspects of the concept of culture have been borrowed from anthropology and, to a lesser extent, sociology. It seems that much of the use of culture as a unitary concept expressing, on the one hand, social cohesion and integration, and on the other, organizational effectiveness, is the result of the transfer of the concept of culture to organizational analysis from a particular anthropological and sociological theoretical tradition, i.e., the 'structural–functional' theoretical paradigm.

[. . .] There is a growing body of literature that critically assesses the study of organizational culture, and it is likely that the debate surrounding the 'proper' use of the concept of culture in organizational analysis will continue for some time (see, in particular, Allaire and Firsirotu, 1984; Gregory, 1983; Smircich, 1983). This chapter contributes to the debate in three limited ways. First, it briefly reviews a few of the consequences of the selective borrowing of the concept of culture. The purpose here is not to debunk past studies of organizational culture, but to attempt to illustrate some of the political and ideological as well as the scholarly effects of viewing culture from a particular theoretical perspective. The chapter then attempts to disentangle the subtle difference between an organization's culture and its social structure, concluding with a brief discussion of some 'sub-concepts' that comprise the idea of culture. Culture, as a total concept, is too all-embracing. It needs to be dissected into manageable proportions so that it can be used in the interpretation of observed behaviour.

The Concept Borrowed

Some recent studies of organizational or corporate culture have been undertaken by what Turner (1986), drawing on Ott's (1984) terminology, calls 'pop cultural magicians', 'tricksters' who make their living by convincing North American and European corporate executives that they can equal the productivity of Japanese industry through the mechanical manipulation of organizational symbols, myths and customs. Such studies are not much concerned with theory of any sort, but seize upon fads in the realm of ideas. However, many 'honest grapplers' (Turner, 1986) in their approach to corporate culture have produced studies that also seem unduly linked to the interest of management and which promulgate the idea that 'culture' is the collective consciousness of the organization, 'owned' by management and available to management for manipulation. An attempt will be made to illustrate the effects of these weaknesses on the study of corporate culture, not by questioning the integrity of individual researchers, but through examining the theoretical basis on which the idea of corporate culture rests. The argument will explore three interrelated themes:

1 Organizational theorists – particularly, though not exclusively, those belonging to the human relations and related schools – have not considered the multiplicity of theories of culture, but have borrowed the concept of culture from only one anthropological tradition: structural–functionalism.
2 Although theories of organizational or corporate culture have their 'roots' in structural–functionalism, they have also 'mutated' in the process of application.
3 The equating of corporate culture with a 'natural' force for social integration within the organization – with a unitary organizational collective consciousness that can both be measured and manipulated – seems to flow from the structural–functional tradition from which the concept is borrowed.

[. . .] The purpose of this chapter is not to ground contemporary criticisms of corporate culture studies in past criticisms of structural–functionalism. Rather, the intention is to illustrate how studies of corporate culture, because of the structural–functional theoretical legacy, tend to ignore or gloss over inherent conflicts and important structural features of the organization, particularly the structure of power and conflict, structured inequality and the significance of the structure of 'class cultures' (see Turner, 1986). Later in the chapter an attempt will be made to build the concept of structure and conflict back into a theory of corporate culture.

The structural–functional theoretical framework has had a profound influence on all aspects of the study of complex organizations. Its influence on the concept of organizational culture is particularly notable, which is not surprising since 'structural–functional' theory has its roots in the development of British social anthropology in the 1920s, 1930s and 1940s (Kuper, 1973). While Talcott Parsons transported structural–functionalism across the Atlantic, the British social anthropologists – themselves influenced by the French sociologist Emile Durkheim – gave birth to the theory. Out of the many conceptualizations of culture available, social theorists have been prone to seize – sometimes somewhat uncritically – upon Durkheim's idea of the collective consciousness and upon Radcliffe-Brown's notion that 'cultural patterns are crystallized in social structure "as institutionalized and standardized modes of behaviour and thought whose normal forms are socially recognized in the explicit or implicit rules to which members of a society tend to conform"' (Keesing, 1974: 83). Several studies of organizational culture seem to assume that 'culture' is a unifying force within the organization, that there exists a universal homogeneous culture, and that the task for the researcher is to discover it. A few examples will help illustrate the point.

Kilmann (1982: 11) refers to culture as 'the collective will of members'; it is 'what the corporation *really wants* or what *really counts* in order to get ahead'. According to Schwartz and Davis (1981: 33) culture is 'a pattern of beliefs and expectations shared by the organization's members' that create 'norms that powerfully shape the behaviour of individuals and groups in the organization'. Kilmann *et al.* (1985a: 2) claim that their edited book *Gaining Control of the Corporate Culture* represents the '"state of the art" of corporate culture' and that the contributors are 'those who are at the leading edge of this topic'. In chapter after chapter, definitions of culture are provided that stress the internalization of norms, social integration and stability, that link culture firmly with the interests of management, and that treat culture as the collective will or consciousness of the organization. [. . .]

Gaining Control of the Corporate Culture contains interesting and valuable information on aspects of the operation of various corporations, but except for one or two chapters, the theories of culture used by the contributors rest on the premise that the norms, values and beliefs of organizational members are factors that create consensus, predict behaviour and create unity. This leads to conclusions that are little more than statements about managements' responsibility to reward positive behaviour and attitudes, to foster the self-esteem and self-confidence of organizations' members, to encourage allegiance to organizational goals and missions, to inform members of the need for change when it arises, and to create a feeling of *esprit de corps* within the organization. If the book represents the 'state of the art' of corporate culture studies, then it is a state of the art based on a very narrow conceptualization of the idea of culture. The degree to which norms, for example, are internalized and create integrated and stable structures is, first of all, an empirical question, not something to be assumed through theory. Culture, if it is to have any meaning, needs to be related to the total organization, not regarded as phenomena solely vested in the hands of management. The idea that culture is the collective will of the organization – its personality, an invisible force or the organization's soul – is a metaphysical explanation of behaviour and events that are impossible to observe. Any theory which assumes that culture is the internalization of dominant norms and values must also assume that all members must hold to the dominant value system or else be 'outside culture'. Of course, such a stance flies in the face of reality, particularly when we consider organizations where management tends to belong to one social class and workers to another. In such organizations, values, norms and social meanings are structured by 'class cultures' and are a constant potential source for dispute, with strikes only one example where such disputes become overt conflicts. For example, it would be difficult to explain the 1984 strike of the British coal miners either in terms of the collective will of the corporation or in terms of the internalization of dominant norms and values. As will be discussed later, norms and values have as much potential for creating conflict within organizations as they do for creating social cohesion.

It should be noted that just because organizational theorists may have borrowed the concept of culture from a certain social anthropological tradition, it does not necessarily mean that organizational theorists use the concept of culture in exactly the same way as would social anthropologists. For example, while Radcliffe-Brown and other social anthropologists have treated culture as an integral feature of the structure and function of all societies – relating specific cultures to particular social outcomes – some organizational theorists have been inclined to treat culture as either exotic or 'irrational' behaviour (Kanter, 1977). More importantly, several studies of organizational culture have moved the concept of culture beyond that of a unifying and regulatory mechanism towards it being a form of social control created and manipulated by management. Baker (1980), for example, writes about 'managing organizational culture' and Allen and Kraft (1982) attempt to illustrate 'how to create the corporate culture you want and need'. Schein (1985: 2) maintains that 'organizational cultures are created by leaders, and one of the most decisive functions of leadership may well be the creation, the management, and – if and when that may become necessary – the destruction of culture'. According to Schein (1985: 2) 'we must recognize the centrality of this culture management function in the leadership concept'. [. . .]

It has often been noted that one of the crucial weaknesses of structural–functional theory is its reliance on a biological metaphor (see, in particular, Nisbet, 1969). In accordance with the metaphor, the theory assumes that an organization can be understood as either a huge organism or a 'superindividual'; hence, 'culture' is transferred from the individual actors who create and reproduce it to the organization as a whole. Since it is the organic organization that has 'culture', culture, including members' norms, values and beliefs, is necessarily a mechanism that creates organizational unity; the parts of a healthy organism do not work against themselves. [. . .]

The use of organic simile and the idea that culture can be regarded as the collective consciousness of the group are mostly derived from the theories of Durkheim. Although these theories remain in vogue, it is important to note past criticisms:

> The metaphysical concepts of a group mind, collective sensorium or consciousness are due to an apparent antinomy of sociological reality: the psychological nature of human culture on the one hand and on the other the fact that culture transcends the individual. The fallacious solution of this antinomy is the theory that human minds combine or integrate and form a superindividual and yet essentially spiritual being. . . . [S]uch concepts as consciousness of kind or the inevitability of collective imitation, account for the psychological yet superindividual nature of social reality by introducing some theoretical metaphysical short cut. (Malinowski, 1930: 623)

In incorporating the idea of collective consciousness into that of organizational culture many theorists have failed to also incorporate the historical cricitisms attached to the original notion.

Individuals create and reproduce culture, but obviously they do not do so in a vacuum. The resources the individual has to draw upon in creating culture are not manufactured by the individual. Language is the classic example: no one person creates language, but we all use language creatively (Giddens, 1982). This point will be examined in more detail below.

The human relations school of 'scientific' management deserves special mention for it was the first body of theorists to explore informal social relations in organizations and to take the concept of organizational culture seriously (see Perrow, 1979 for a review of the history of the human relations school), but the human relations theorists have approached organizational culture mainly from a behaviourist-oriented psychological framework. The language used by human relations theorists is based on a medical/biological metaphor: they speak of healthy and unhealthy organizational culture or climate and talk about organizational hygiene. Human relations theorists regard culture as something which an organization has and which can be manipulated to serve the ends of management. In summarizing past research efforts of the human relations school, Gregory (1983: 361) argues that the school's 'promanagement position resulted in biased research that studied the "irrational" behaviour of lower ranking personnel and supported unquestioningly the "rational manager" model'. Moreover:

> The current corporate culture studies are not substantially different from earlier Human Relations research, in that the goal is still to illustrate the impact of 'irrational' human factors on 'rational' corporate objectives. 'Rational' corporate objectives correspond to management's goals for the organization. Researchers in

both areas sought to provide managers with tools to assess and control the organizational culture of their subordinates. (Gregory, 1983: 361)

Despite such criticisms, practitioners, as well as academic researchers, have been intent upon discovering what creates 'healthy' and 'unhealthy' organizational culture. Managers of large corporations have come to think that economic success is somehow linked with the type of organizational culture or climate that they create. The idea of corporate culture has been pursued in such popular forms as *Business Week* 1980 and *Fortune Magazine* 1982. Ouchi's (1981) work, and the development of 'Theory Z' linking successful and unsuccessful organizational performance to the type of culture created by American and Japanese companies, has gained great popularity. Corporate managers seem to believe that a unifying organizational culture can be created and manipulated, and are prepared to pay good money to back their beliefs: 'the marketing of "corporate culture" is largely underway' (Smircich, 1983: 346).

Those intent upon creating a 'healthy' and 'successful' corporate climate are often blind to 'what is' by their pursuit of 'what should be' (Gregory, 1983; Smircich, 1983; Allaire and Firsirotu, 1984). Corporate success, particularly economic success, is dependent far more upon external environmental influences and the vagaries of the market-place than on internal interpersonal dynamics. More importantly, the assumption that a corporate culture can be created so as to unite members for the effective and efficient attainment of corporate goals flies in the face of almost everyone's experience of organizational life. Organizations are often arenas for dispute and conflict, and one of the main items under dispute is often values. Organizations are not one homogeneous culture, but are 'multicultural', and culture can be a source of conflict (Gregory, 1983). Cultural conflict is most obvious in professional organizations – large teaching hospitals, research laboratories, tertiary education institutions. C. P. Snow's thesis of two cultures manifests itself month after month in every meeting of a university's academic board. Several studies have shown that academics may tend to give greater allegiance to their profession than to their college or university, which may produce conflict between the interest of the individual academic and the interests of those who manage the institution. Unity within organizational subcultures (academic departments, for example) can be a source of conflict as the various subcultures compete for both scarce resources and prestige.

Nonetheless, human relations and related fields of study, and their preoccupation with the idea of a healthy or successful corporate culture, need to be taken seriously for two reasons. First, there are successful and not-so-successful organizations, and there is something about the successful organization that goes beyond explanations based on superior technology, efficient management and an advantageous position in the market-place. There is a certain 'feel' about the successful school, university or large corporation, and the phenomenon, whatever it is and whatever 'success' may mean, deserves investigation.

Second, while organizations may be regarded as forums for conflict and dispute, they also wield power in modern society through what Galbraith (1983) terms their ability to *condition* their own members and the public at large. Organizations have access to the three primary instruments of power: condign power (physical), compensatory power (economic) and conditioned power (belief). According to Galbraith, conditioned power is the most important in modern industrial society, and organization is the locus of conditioned power. It is through 'persuasion, education, or the social commitment to what seems natural, proper or right' that the corporation, educational institution, church and the state 'cause the individual to submit to the will of another or of others' (Galbraith, 1983: 23). Organizations may also enforce their will through the use of physical or economic power. In the past, the church was particularly prone to exercise its power through such means, but conditioned power is central 'to the functioning of the modern economy and polity, and in capitalist and socialist countries alike' (Galbraith, 1983: 23). Thus, it is imperative that we understand the beliefs, symbols, myths, ideologies and folklores – the 'culture' – of the modern organization as a form of social control. It is not a form of social control created and manipulated by management, but a process in which management, workers and the community at large participate alike.

Furthermore, Galbraith (1983) argues that there is a symmetric relationship between how power is exercised and how it is challenged: condign power is met with violence, compensatory power is met with the regulation of the market-place, and conditioned power is met with countervailing beliefs and ideologies. Consumer and environmental action groups represent a good example of a symmetric challenge to the conditioned power of modern corporations. In this respect, organizational culture is not a force for social integration, but a phenomenon likely to breed 'counter-cultures'.

An adequate theory of culture needs to be divorced from the direct interests of management and the naive assumption that a 'successful corporate culture' is either 'naturally good and stabilizing' or can be 'consciously manipulated'. Just because group interaction within an organization is based on norms and symbols, it does not necessarily follow that consensus and cohesion, based on shared and internalized value systems, are the result. Hopefully, the structural–functional theoretical assumptions on which the biomorphic, cohesive, integrative and stabilizing characteristics of organizational studies of corporate culture rest have been adequately demonstrated and critiqued, and the need for a theory of culture that more adequately takes account of the contextual richness of social life within the organization as a whole has been illustrated. Before suggesting alternative ways of viewing corporate culture, a few additional words need to be said about the manipulation of culture.

While it is maintained that culture *as a whole* cannot be consciously manipulated by management or any other group, culture is not necessarily static: cultures do change within organizations, and management does have more direct control than other organizational members over certain aspects of the corporate cultures, such as control over logos and officially stated missions and ethos. In this regard, some scholars have expressed concern that certain organizations can foster an allegiance to a corporate ethos that borders on religious fervour, while the ethos itself is of questionable social value (Turner, 1986). The way in which management attempts to intervene in the culture of an organization should be a research priority, particularly in relation to the potential 'conditioned power' of organization. However, empirically assessing the power and ability of management to intervene in the culture of an organization and assuming through theory that management creates, changes and imposes 'culture' on a passive and uncritical membership – that management creates a cultural milieu in which rank-and-file staff are immersed and have no choice but to internalize its embedded norms and values – are quite separate considerations.

If culture emerges from the social interaction of all organizational members (as is argued here), then the way in which management may attempt to manipulate organizational symbols, myths, customs, etc., must be interpreted in relation to the *total* organizational culture of which management itself is only one part. Hitler did not create Nazi Germany by himself. It may be the case that some organizations are more prone to accept executive control, including control over organizational symbols and meanings, than are other organizations, but again, this is, first of all, an empirical question, not something that can be assumed through theory. Also, power, as Weber maintained, is exercised not merely through its acceptance by others, but rests on having the resources – which flow, at least in part, from one's position in the social structure – to impose one's will on others despite opposition.

While, in practice, questions of power, conflict and culture in the modern organization cannot be divorced, the symbiotic relationship between the phenomena may be more adequately understood if a conceptual distinction is drawn between culture and social structure. We will now look at what consequences such a distinction may have for a theory of organizational or corporate culture.

Towards a Theory of Culture

While the idea of organizational culture has been approached in a variety of ways, the various theories, basically, fall into two camps or schools (Smircich, 1983). First, as was argued above, there are those who treat organizational culture as a variable: it is something that an organization has (see Cummings and Schmidt, 1972; Schwartz and Davis, 1981; Deal and Kennedy, 1982; Peters and Waterman, 1982). Second, there is the view that 'culture is something an organization is' (Smircich, 1983: 347; and see Harris and Cronen, 1979; Weick, 1979; Morgan, 1980; Wacker, 1981). The second approach is much more closely aligned to the way in which anthropologists treat culture. Rather than regarding culture as something imported into an organization from the broader society, or as something created by management, these theorists believe that culture is the product of negotiated and shared symbols and meanings; it emerges from social interaction. In this approach to culture, the researcher is not analysing some 'irrational' or exotic aspect of organizational life. The interpretation of organizational culture must be deeply embedded in the contextual richness of the total social life of organizational members. Culture cannot be treated as being incidental, or outside of, the 'true purpose' of the organization (Gregory, 1983).

Treating culture as emerging from social interaction – treating it as something that the organization 'is', rather than treating it as a variable that can be manipulated by management – has obvious research implications. It also has political implications. If culture is regarded as embedded in social interaction, that is, as something that is socially produced and reproduced over time, influencing people's behaviour in relation to the use of language, technology, rules and laws, and knowledge and ideas (including ideas about legitimate authority and leadership), then it cannot be discovered or mechanically manipulated; it can only be described and interpreted. The researcher adopting the social emergent view of culture cannot suggest how it can be created or destroyed; the researcher can only attempt to record and examine how culture may be altered in the process of social reproduction. People do not just passively absorb meanings and symbols; they produce and reproduce culture, and in the process of reproducing it, they may transform it. The social emergent approach to culture also moves the researcher away from the political and ideological interests of management, towards those of the organizational community as a whole. [. . .]

For the purposes of analysis and interpretation, it seems necessary to distinguish between culture and social structure, but in so doing, two factors must be kept firmly in mind. First, culture and structure are two sides of the same coin: they are parallel and complementary and constantly interacting with one another:

> One of the more useful ways – but far from the only one – of distinguishing between culture and social system is to see the former as an ordered system of meaning and of symbols, in terms of which social interaction takes place; and to see the latter as the pattern of social interaction itself. (Geertz, 1973: 144)

Second, both culture and structure are abstractions, not tangible entities:

> The difference between the two concepts is not that one is an abstraction and the other a concrete, observable unit of behaviour, for both are abstractions of regularities from observations of actual behaviour, whether these regularities are implicit and unconscious or explicit and verbalized. (Singer, 1968: 533)

The task for the researcher in the field is not to observe culture or structure, but to observe the concrete behaviour of individual actors. Culture and social structure are not concrete entities; rather they are abstract concepts that are to be used to interpret behaviour. Geertz's (1973: 5) definition of

culture clearly focuses the attention of the researcher on concrete behaviour: 'Believing, with Max Weber, that man is an animal suspended in
webs of significance he himself has spun, I take culture to be those webs, and
the analysis of it to be therefore not an experimental science in search of law
but an interpretive one in search of meaning.' [. . .]

The Dissection of Culture

[. . .] Symbol is the most inclusive of the various cultural derivatives, 'not
only because language, ritual, and myth are forms of symbolism but because
symbolic analysis is a form of reference, a style of analysis in its own right'
(Pettigrew, 1979: 575). Symbols are shared codes of meaning and include a
variety of things – words, stories, icons, organizational logos or national
flags – that provide 'meanings, evoke emotions, and impel men [and women]
to action' (Cohen, 1974: 23). Language is a representation, a symbol, of the
real thing. Organizations may be distinguished by the language their
members use: academics use jargon to mystify knowledge and computer
programmers use a language that mystifies everyone but themselves. The
guard tower is a symbol of both the concentration camp and the modern
prison, impelling individuals to a form of negative action. Religious icons
may, on the one hand, unite the faithful, and on the other, lead them to
scourge the infidel.

Organization has itself been defined as being nothing more or less than
patterns of symbolic discourse. Within the phenomenology, symbolic
interactionism and ethnomethodology schools:

> organizations become *figments of participants' interpretation of their organiz-
> ational experience*; they have no external reality but are merely social creations and
> construction *emerging* from actors making sense out of ongoing streams of actions
> and interactions. In what Burrell and Morgan (1979: 260) call their *interpretive
> paradigm*, 'organizations simply do not exist'. (Allaire and Firsirotu, 1984: 208)

This approach to organizational analysis is in danger of collapsing the social
organizational and cultural components of social life into one unitary
concept. As argued above, there is a need to maintain a conceptual
distinction between culture and social structure, particularly for the
purposes of investigating change and conflict. When the sociostructural
pattern of human organization is collapsed into being solely a pattern of
symbolic discourse, 'the dynamic elements in social change which arise from
the failure of cultural patterns to be perfectly congruent with forms of social
organization are largely incapable of formation' (Geertz, 1957: 992)

An organization is, of course, a structured association of individuals, and
it is individuals who create meanings and symbols. Organization cannot be
reduced to the individual, for to do so misinterprets the significance, and the

power, of organization. MacIntyre puts the case in relation to the military organization thus:

> You cannot characterise an army by referring to the soldiers who belong to it. For to do that you have to identify them as soliders; and to do that is already to bring in the concept of an army. For a soldier just is an individual who belongs to an army. Thus we see that the characterisation of individuals and of classes [or organizations] has to go together. Essentially these are not two separate tasks. (quoted in Thompson, 1978: 30)

Certainly, symbols are worthy of the researcher's attention. If the symbolic mode of interpretation is to consider the dynamics of change and conflict, then it seems that symbols need to be analysed in terms of a 'dialogue' between actors' sets of meanings and other social organizational aspects of the institution.

Closely related to the idea of culture as patterns of symbolic discourse is the notion of culture as ideational or cognitive systems, i.e. cultures seen as systems of knowledge (Keesing, 1974). One of the main proponents of this stance in anthropology is Goodenough:

> A society's culture consists of whatever it is one has to know or believe in order to operate in a manner acceptable to its members. Culture is not a material phenomenon; it does not consist of things, people, behavior, or emotions. It is rather an organization of these things. It is the form of things that people have in mind, their models for perceiving, relating, and otherwise interpreting them. (quoted in Keesing, 1974: 77)

Obviously, men and women must share some knowledge in common in order to act in concert: organized work would be impossible if people did not share some meanings, knowledge systems and symbols. 'Most occupations . . . operate on the premise that the people who work in them know certain procedures and certain ways of thinking about and responding to typical situations and problems' (Becker, 1982: 522). However, like symbolic interactionism, the ideational or cognitive theory of organizational culture fails when it is elevated to a universal theory that attempts to explain all social organizational phenomena. 'Analyses of cultures as cognitive systems have not progressed very far beyond a mapping of limited and neatly bonded semantic domains' (Keesing, 1974: 78). Organizational culture is too rich and diverse to be amenable to a comprehensive interpretation through ideational codes, however sophisticated their elaboration.

However, the investigation of cognitive systems can be a powerful analytical tool so long as the interpretation of ideas and knowledge is related to, but kept separate from, social structural issues. It is here that the concept of ideology may play an important role. Ideology is not only 'a set of beliefs about the social world and how it operates', but also contains ethical statements 'about the rightness of certain social arrangements' (Wilson, 1973: 91). An ideology may be congruent with the social structure, or it may be expressly divergent from the pattern of social interaction within the organization. Also, an organization may contain a number of ideologies, with ideological groupings in competition with one another over such issues as power and legitimate authority. These are, of course, empirical questions that can be answered only through research.

Contrary to the popular lay definition, myth is not regarded by anthropologists as an erroneous story. Rather, 'a myth is a narrative of events; the narrative has a sacred quality; the sacred communication is made in symbolic form; at least some of the events and objects which occur in the myth neither occur nor exist in the world other than that of myth itself; and the narrative refers in dramatic form to origins or transformations' (Cohen, 1969: 337). Organizational myths or stories certainly do not constitute all that is 'cultural' in an organization, but the interpretation of organization members' myths and folklores is one angle of attack on the problem of organizational culture that has proved to be fruitful. Creation myths are usually thought of as something belonging to traditional societies, but members of modern organizations also have their stories about how the organization came into being and how it developed over time. Clark terms such folk stories or myths 'organizational sagas':

> Saga . . . has come to mean a narrative of heroic exploits, of a unique development that has deeply stirred the emotions of participants and descendants. Thus, a saga is not simply a story but a story that at some time has had a particular base of believers. (Clark, 1972: 178–9)

The notion of an organizational saga is a useful theoretical tool for the study of certain aspects of symbolic behaviour. As a concept it gives importance to publicly expressed stories about group uniqueness; it is an explanation of what makes an organization unique and distinctive in the eyes of its members. In theory, these stories or 'folk histories' may function as symbolic justifications for members' actions in concrete situations.

Martin *et al.* (1983: 439), while recognizing the emphasis on uniqueness in organizational stories and sagas, maintain that there are also 'similarities in content and structure' in all such stories: 'a culture's claim to uniqueness is expressed through cultural manifestations that are not in fact unique. This is the uniqueness paradox.' Anthropologists, such as Malinowski, Lévi-Strauss, and others, have also looked at the creation myths of different traditional societies in order to discover similarities in content and structure.

It also needs to be recognized that myths, folklores and sagas may be a source of conflict, particularly in the context of rapid social change. There is evidence to suggest that at least one organization's saga, while appropriate to the development of the institution during a particular historical period, became quite inappropriate and caused disunity, following dramatic changes in the institution's external political environment (Meek, 1982). In another study (Meek, 1984), it was argued that the organization had developed two sets of shared beliefs and ideologies that were in competition with one another: a saga and a counter-saga.

All organizations have forms of ritualized behaviour. A university, for example, would not be a university without the ritual and symbols that surround such events as graduation ceremonies and inaugural lectures. The ritual is as old as the idea of the university itself. At graduation, academics and graduands clothe themselves in medieval garb and speak in foreign tongues – Latin. The procession preceding an inaugural lecture is led by the bearer of arms carrying a mace. Except for historians, most members of the university organization have long forgotten the origin and function of such cultural artifacts as the academic gown and mace, but they all know that these artifacts symbolize the university, and they share a feeling of belonging to an academic community whenever the artifacts are displayed and the ritual is performed.

According to Benedict (1934: 396), ritual simply is the 'prescribed formal behaviour for occasions not given over to technological routine'. This definition is attractive in its simplicity, although it leaves the question of how rituals are to be interpreted unanswered. Anthropologists (Beattie, 1966) and organizational theorists (Pettigrew, 1979) often maintain that what is important is what rituals 'say' not what they 'do'. In this sense, Harrison (1951) maintained that 'ritual is a dramatization of myth'. However, Leach (1968: 524) argues that 'ritual may "do things" as well as "say things". The most obvious examples are healing rituals which form a vast class and have a world-wide distribution.' Ritualized physical exercise in Japanese industries is both an expression of corporate allegiance and a mechanism for maintaining the health of the workforce.

It is often assumed that rituals legitimize established authority, and 'provide a shared experience of belonging and express and reinforce what is valued' (Pettigrew, 1979: 576). However, as Gluckman (1962) has shown, 'rituals of rebellion' may have the opposite function: they allow people to act out hostilities that may not be expressed in normal everyday social relations.

The interpretation of ritual is just as complicated as any other aspect of cultural behaviour. However, research into the ritualization of behaviour should not assume from the outset that ritual expresses and sanctifies the established social order. It may do this, but ritual may also be a mechanism for maintaining one group in power despite the will of others, or it may be a dramatized expression of rebellion of one group against others. Once again, these are empirical questions, not something that can be assumed through theory.

Summary

There has been a tendency for some researchers to treat organizational culture as a 'variable' that can be controlled and manipulated like any other organizational variable. Culture *as a whole* cannot be manipulated, turned on and off, although it needs to be recognized that some are in a better position than others to attempt to intentionally influence aspects of it. The tendency to assume otherwise results, at least in part, from the selective way in which the concept of culture has been borrowed from anthropology and sociology. The basis of the argument presented in this chapter is that culture should be regarded as something that an organization 'is', not as something that an organization 'has': it is not an independent variable, nor can it be created, discovered or destroyed by the whims of management. Nonetheless, it seems necessary for the purposes of the interpretation of actors' behaviour, that a conceptual distinction be made between 'culture' and 'social structure'. It must be kept in mind, though, that both culture and structure are abstractions, and have use only in relation to the interpretation of observed concrete behaviour. This chapter, however, does not advance any one elaborate or steadfast theoretical model of cultural interpretation; for 'it is going to take more than one kind of theoretical model to do justice to the variety, complexity, and richness of human culture' (Singer, 1968: 541).

References

Allaire, Yvan, and Firsirotu, Mihaela E. (1984) 'Theories of organizational culture', *Organization Studies*, 5(3): 193–226.

Allen, F. R. and Kraft, C. (1982) *The Organizational Unconscious: How to Create the Corporate Culture You Want and Need*. Englewood Cliffs, NJ: Prentice-Hall.

Baker, E. L. (1980) 'Managing organizational culture', *Management Review*, July: 8–13.

Beattie, John (1966) 'Ritual and social change', *Man*, 1: 60–74.

Becker, Howard S. (1982) 'Culture: a sociological view', *Yale Review*, 71: 513–27.

Benedict, Ruth (1934) 'Ritual', *International Encyclopaedia of the Social Sciences*, 13: 396–7.

Burrell, Gibson and Morgan, Gareth (1979) *Sociological Paradigms and Organizational Analysis*. London: Heinemann.

Cohen, Abner (1974) *Two-dimensional Man: an Essay on the Anthropology of Power and Symbolism in Complex Society*. London: Routledge & Kegan Paul.

Cohen, Percy S. (1969) 'Theories of myth', *Man*, 4: 337–53.

Cummings, L. L. and Schmidt, Stuart M. (1972) 'Managerial attitudes of Greeks: the roles of culture and industrialization', *Administrative Science Quarterly*, 17: 265–72.

Deal, Terence E. and Kennedy, Allan A. (1982) *Corporate Cultures: the Rites and Rituals of Corporate Life*. Reading, Mass.: Addison-Wesley.

Galbraith, John Kenneth (1983) *The Anatomy of Power*. London: Corgi Books.

Geertz, Clifford (1957) 'Ritual and social change: a Javanese example', *American Anthropologist*, 59: 991–1012.

Geertz, Clifford (1973) *The Interpretation of Culture*. London: Hutchinson.

Giddens, Anthony (1982) *Sociology: a Brief but Critical Introduction*. London: Macmillan.

Gluckman, Max (1962) 'Les rites de passage', in M. Gluckman (ed.), *Essays on the Ritual of Social Relations*. Manchester: Manchester University Press. pp. 1–52.

Gregory, Kathleen L. (1983) 'Native view paradigms; multiple cultures and culture conflicts in organizations', *Administrative Science Quarterly*, 28: 359–77.

Harris, Linda and Cronen, Vernon (1979) 'A rules-based model for the analysis and evaluation of organizational communication', *Communication Quarterly*, Winter: 12–18.

Harrison, Jane E. (1951) *Ancient Art and Ritual* (1913). New York: Oxford University Press.

Kanter, R. M. (1977) *Men and Women of the Corporation*. New York: Basic Books.

Keesing, Roger M. (1974) 'Theories of culture', *Annual Review of Anthropology*, 3: 73–97.

Kilmann, Ralph H. (1982) 'Getting control of the corporate culture', *Managing*, 3: 11–17.

Kilmann, Ralph H. (1985) 'Five steps for closing culture-gaps', in R. H. Kilmann, M. J. Saxton and R. Serpa (eds), *Gaining Control of the Corporate Culture*. San Francisco: Jossey-Bass. pp. 351–69.

Kilmann, Ralph H., Saxton, Mary J. and Serpa, Roy (eds) (1985a) *Gaining Control of the Corporate Culture*. San Francisco: Jossey-Bass.

Kilmann, Ralph H., Saxton, Mary J. and Serpa, Roy (1985b) 'Conclusion: why culture is not just a fad', in *Gaining Control of the Corporate Culture*. San Francisco: Jossey-Bass. pp. 421–33.

Kuper, Adam (1973) *Anthropologists and Anthropology: the British School 1922–72*. London: Penguin.

Leach, Edmund R. (1968) 'Ritual', *International Encyclopaedia of the Social Sciences*, 13: 520–6.

Martin, Joanne, Fieldman, Martha S., Hatch, Mary Jo and Sitkin, Sim B. (1983) 'The uniqueness paradox in organizational stories', *Administrative Science Quarterly*, 28: 438–53.

Meek, V. Lynn (1982) *The University of Papua New Guinea: a Case Study in the Sociology of Higher Education*. St Lucia: University of Queensland Press.

Meek, V. Lynn (1984) *Brown Coal or Plato?* Hawthorn: Australian Council for Educational Research.

Morgan, Gareth (1980) 'Paradigms, metaphors and puzzle solving in organizational theory', *Administrative Science Quarterly*, 25: 605–22.

Nisbet, R. A. (1969) *Social Change and History*. New York: Oxford University Press.

Ott, K. K. (1984) 'Two problems that threaten organizational culture research . . .'. Paper presented at the first international conference on 'Organizational Symbolism and Corporate Culture', Lund, Sweden, 26–30 June.

Ouchi, W. (1981) *Theory Z*. Reading, Mass.: Addison-Wesley.

Perrow, C. (1979) *Complex Organizations: a Critical Essay*, 2nd edn. Glenview, Ill.: Scott-Foresman.

Peters, Thomas J. and Waterman, Robert H. (1982) *In Search of Excellence*. New York: Harper & Row.

Pettigrew, Andrew M. (1979) 'On studying organizational cultures', *Administrative Science Quarterly*, 24: 570–81.

Schein, Edgar H. (1985) *Organizational Culture and Leadership*. San Francisco: Jossey-Bass.

Schwartz, H. M. and Davis, S. M. (1981) 'Matching corporate culture and business strategy', *Organizational Dynamics*, Summer: 30–48.

Singer, Milton (1968) 'Culture: the concept of culture', *International Encyclopaedia of the Social Sciences*, 3: 527–41.

Smircich, Linda (1983) 'Concepts of culture and organizational analysis', *Administrative Science Quarterly*, 28: 339–59.

Thompson, E. P. (1978) *The Poverty of Theory*. London: Merlin.

Turner, Barry A. (1986) 'Sociological aspects of organizational symbolism', *Organization Studies*, 7(2): 101–15.

Wacker, Gerald (1981) 'Towards cognitive methodology of organizational assessment', *Journal of Applied Behavioral Science*, 17: 114–29.

Weick, Karl E. (1979) *The Social Psychology of Organizing*. Reading, Mass.: Addison-Wesley.

Wilson, John (1973) *Introduction to Social Movement*. New York: Basic Books.

19

Personnel and Public Management

Hans Weggemans

In the last few decades, personnel management (PM) has undergone a number of important developments: changes that are closely connected with social changes. First, we can draw attention to some important *social movements*, such as the democratization in the 1960s and the emancipation of women in the 1970s. The humanization of labour can be mentioned in this connection, too. These social movements have clearly influenced the contents of PM, through government measures, pressure by trade unions, or through initiatives of the management of the organization itself. Issues such as affirmative action, participation, health and safety have won a fixed position in the activities of personnel departments. Parallel to these factors, a process of *professionalization* of the personnel function began, one result of which was that specialists with a specific training derived legitimacy for their attitude and activities from their professional group – personnel managers. This professionalization has had great influence on the position and role of PM within the organization, particularly regarding the ideological basis.

In this chapter we shall discuss in short two themes of a more general nature related to personnel management: the position and role of the personnel function and the often conflicting values in which this function has to be managed. These themes will be highlighted with a few examples from the Netherlands and the chapter ends with some reflections on future developments especially in the public sector.

Public Personnel Management: Some Themes

Role and Position

An important theme when considering personnel management is the issue of the role and position of the personnel function and the power and influence of personnel management (Legge, 1978; Watson, 1977).

From J. Kooiman and K. A. Eliassen (eds), *Managing Public Organizations*, London: Sage, 1987, pp. 158–72 (abridged).

The personnel function in organizations is potentially situated in a field of tension. Contradictory and conflicting expectations are often expressed to personnel functionaries. On the one hand the management of the organization expects a positive contribution to the attainment of the goals of the organization, mostly at the lowest possible cost, and on the other hand individual employees expect the personnel functionary to defend their interests to the management of the organization. The two expectations may conflict and lead to an ambiguous task conception for the personnel manager. This is not necessarily the case, however, for sometimes the two interests or expectations coincide. How personnel management solves this 'man-in-the-middle problem' depends on several factors, such as the role conception of the individual personnel functionaries, the prevailing ideology or culture in the organization, the existing position of personnel management and so on. Another influencing factor is the professionalization of the personnel function, in the sense of developing specific expertise and forming a professional group.

In general, the professionalization of the personnel function in Western Europe has had the result that personnel policy has grown to be an independent task implemented by specialists. Its institutionalization has led to separate employment departments. In the 1960s and 1970s the emphasis – certainly in the Netherlands – came to lie on increasing the well-being of the individual employee. In the public sector this was even more so. 'Fairness' and 'justice' were key words. Thomason calls this the 'welfare stream' which is to be distinguished from the 'procurement stream', which is more efficiency-oriented and takes the organization's interests as a starting point (Thomason, 1978: 15–16). Both streams, which are to be seen as extremes on a continuum, have their representatives in public management, too, although the number of supporters varies over time.

During the last few years the opinion that PM is a part of the general management function and that every line manager has responsibilities concerning human resources has won ground. Decentralization of the personnel function is a logical consequence of this (Legge, 1978: 65). Integration of personnel management with the other management tasks took place when it was realized that personnel management had no say in important matters such as policy formulation and implementation; this was caused in general by its not very strategic approach and by the 'welfare-orientation'. Legge's opinion is that the personnel function ought to make its contribution to the organization's success clearly visible, but she also finds that there is a vicious circle: 'Yet, to obtain adequate resources to undertake these tasks, a personnel department requires power which, at present in many organizations it lacks, precisely because of its inability to convince those who do control resources of its potential contribution' (Legge, 1978: 136).

Watson (1977) stresses the structural conflict of interests between employers and employees, anchored in social relative power. He thinks that PM will have to identify itself with the general management and the goals of the organization in order to be able to exercise any influence: 'The influence of the personnel specialist is dependent on the help he can provide to the dominant coalition of the organization in its achieving of its objectives' (Watson, 1977: 201).

If we consider the role problems of the personnel functionary from the viewpoint of the power of the personnel function, we can conclude that these problems can be solved for the greater part by an unambiguous choice for and identification with the organization's general management. Of course, such a conclusion does not impede the fact that many individual interests coincide with organizational interests, because of the relation between motivation and work satisfaction on the one hand and productivity and effectiveness on the other.

For the government there is a number of extra factors, such as certain standards and values that are translated politically: a just distribution of income, right to work, abatement of unemployment, protection of the weak, and so on. Such starting points complicate the personnel functionary's task. Apart from individual and organization interests, a contribution must be made to the attainment of political goals with regard to the personnel policy. These political goals – for example positive discrimination on behalf of ethnic minorities – can have strained relations with other goals, such as recruiting and maintaining the best possible expertise.

In other words, the role and position of the personnel manager are determined to an important extent by the interaction of three facets: individual rights (legal position, pay and conditions), organization interests (efficiency and effectiveness) and political interests (to require external support). [. . .]

Conflicting Values

Personnel management is involved in the utilization of human resources. The task of the personnel specialist has advisory, service and guidance aspects. We have to develop, implement and evaluate personnel policies, to design certain procedures, methods and programmes, all related to the individual in the organization (see Miner and Miner, 1977: 4).

In the well-known textbooks all the facets of the tasks of personnel management have been enumerated carefully and illustrated with examples. It is usually not made clear, however, how these different functions and activities fit together. Klingner and Nalbandian (1985) have attempted to fill this gap. They see PM not only as a collection of techniques, but also as an 'interaction of four dominant values'. These values are: social equity; political responsiveness; administrative efficiency; and individual rights.

These values are said to generate mutually conflicting expectations about the goals and methods of managing people (Klingner and Nalbandian, 1985: 15). The mutual priority of these values define – in the context of the situation – the interaction between certain aspects of the personnel function.

Next, these four values are related to the core-functions in the organization.

> The core-functions are those which public agencies must perform in order to permit public employees to work competently under satisfying conditions: to *procure* employees, to *allocate* work and rewards among them, to *develop* their skills, and to develop and maintain (*sanction*) the terms of the employment relationship. (Klingner and Nalbandian, 1985: 15).

The influence of values on the core-functions in an organization is filtered by environmental factors such as economic, political, social and technological.

The way in which such marginal conditions influence the execution of the functions will have to be *examined* by each organization. Moreover, an organization will have to make sure that PM 'will adapt to changing environmental conditions when necessary' (ibid.: 16). To attain this, methods such as regulation, procedures and techniques are used.

What is especially valuable in this approach to theory formation is the fact that Klingner and Nalbandian assume a relation between the environment, the organization and the personnel function in the organization. The second important aspect of this framework of analysis is the fact that they make the political dimension in public personnel management explicit. The idea that the interaction of conflicting values determines the role and contents of personnel management to a great extent seems to be relevant for the situation within government.

Comparability of Public and Private Sectors

[. . .] Studying public personnel management requires its own specific framework of analysis in order to be able to express the influence of the political dimension in governmental organizations. Rosenbloom's (1982) opinion is that for a long time it was tried to manage government personnel in accordance with values and notions derived from the private sector. However, his opinion is that 'there are essential sources of the "publicness" of public personnel administration . . . the values that pervade public personnel management flow from the unique constitutional and political concerns found in the public sector' (Rosenbloom, 1982: 246). He mentions four factors: the constitution, the market, sovereignty and the public interest. His conclusion is that they have no genuine counterpart in the private sector. 'In addition public personnel policy is complicated by fragmentation of authority and competition among values' (p. 253).

Thomson and Beaumont are also of the opinion that the public sector distinguishes itself from the private sector on three points: economic structure, ways of decision-making and industrial relations (Thomson and Beaumont, 1978: 6–18). Of all these factors one seems to be of particular importance: the nature of industrial relations within the two sectors.

For example, the extent of being organized differs generally. In England the private sector is less highly organized, the consultations on working conditions are less centralized and the pay system is more differentiated than it is in the public sector. In the Netherlands there is a similar situation.

Another difference concerns the formal framework within which PM is to work (Klingner and Nalbandian, 1985: 291). One important aspect of this refers to the fact that the government is [the] political authority as well as employer. In the next section we shall return to this. The right to strike may also differ. In general, actions of employees in the public sector are restricted by more regulations than those of employees in the private sector.

In spite of these differences the two sectors have many similarities, especially as regards the contents of their tasks. Activities such as pay and conditions, recruitment and selection, motivation, are not substantially different in the two sectors. The instruments of personnel management resemble each other to a great extent, too. Besides, the two sectors are strongly dependent on one another. For example, they meet constantly in the labour market, which causes the reward relations between certain professions in the two sectors to be under continuous scrutiny.

As for the way payment is effected, the government is in a special position. The extent of the influence of the market on the pay system is an important variable with the government. For some categories this influence is only small, for example with respect to professions which do not exist in the private sector, such as the police and teachers. For other categories the influence of the market is great, since the government is involved in open competition with organizations in the private sector. Often we see a reference moment contained in the pay system. In one way or another a comparison between rewards in the private sector and the government is attempted. This often results in different commissions, rates and procedures ('independent fact-finding'). [. . .]

How far the noted differences work in the salary policy with the government depends strongly on the level of pay and conditions. In times of retrenchment many governments wish to reduce public expenditure, which will put pressure on the salaries of officials. In other words, the political authority wishes to have an influence on the employer–employee negotiations with the government.

When determining the working conditions of its own personnel the government sometimes uses working conditions in the private sector as a point of reference; sometimes it consciously deviates from them for political reasons and sometimes it does not know any comparable categories. Besides, the question remains whether the government ought to follow trade and industry, or ought to be a trendsetter by indirectly influencing salaries in the private sector via its own salary policy. [. . .]

Interaction of Roles: Employer and Politician

The theory of employment relations usually distinguishes three parties: employees, employers and the government. The position of the 'labour' factor in the organization and in society is determined by means of processes of interaction between these parties. What is special in the public sector is that the government holds two positions: employer of government personnel and political authority. [. . .]

This construction may lead to role obscurity, ambiguity and conflicts, depending on the way in which the two roles are given their contents and whether they are conducted separately in practice (for example by different ministers). This situation is unknown in the private sector. There the government is an external factor for PM, whose actions are taken as restrictive marginal conditions.

It is striking that in the literature on PM within government, insufficient attention has been paid to this fundamental difference. Unjustly so, for being able to conduct both roles at the same time is in many cases an important source of power and influence, for example with respect to influencing the negotiations on working conditions between employers and employees in the private sector, as described above. The government can be a trendsetter, should it wish to be, and should the proper authorities agree. Because of this structural property the interactions between employers, employees and the government gain a special character which is worthy of separate study. How does it use both responsibilities in the negotiations with the other governmental employers, with the trade unions and with representatives of the private sector? Do the elected representatives of the people supervise the employer or the political authority? Is it necessary to separate the two roles in decision-making or not? Will this double role lead to a power increase for the employer with the government? These are research questions that are worth studying with the help of the specific framework advocated earlier. The double role might be seen as the institutionalization of conflicting values like 'political responsiveness' and 'administrative efficiency' from the value-framework of Klingner and Nalbandian (1985).

Decision-making and Coordination

The decision-making about working conditions with the government is fragmented. Different political authorities determine the legal position and confer with the trade unions. The way in which the 'places of decision-making' are related to each other vary from country to country in general, and within a country often by sector. Sometimes there is agreement on a national level, sometimes it is in the hands of individual organizations. This may also vary according to subject.

Therefore, managing human resources in public management can be divided into at least three levels:

1 personnel management on the central level: the public personnel as a whole;
2 personnel management on one level (central or local government) or in one sector (health service, police, fire brigade);
3 personnel management in one single organization (department, municipality).

Generally, employers, employees and the government are striving after a certain degree of coordination. For doing so there can be different motives such as: a certain sense of justice ('equal task and effort: equal pay'); striving for uniformity in certain fields; acting as a unity in the negotiations; in order to prevent competition between employers (for example in the labour market).

In the last few years (characterized by stringent retrenchment policy in the public sector) different governments have had their interests served by a certain degree of guidance and supervision of the expenditure on public employees. Mutual arrangements have thus become of political or social-economic interest. This need to control is often at variance with the need of individual organizations to have [. . .] a certain degree of autonomy. This is deemed necessary because they need to be able to express local political choices, to try and make use of specific circumstances, to operate alertly in the labour market and to pursue a flexible working conditions policy.

This tension in the system of decision-making and coordination between the management levels is fed by the double role of, in this case, the central authority: political authority and coordinating employer for the whole public sector.

It seems to be important to find a balance between the aforementioned two important principles in managing the whole public sector (striving after coherence and an equal legal position) and the necessity of policy discretion on the level of individual organizations. This is an important issue in the public personnel management system.

In this section we have reflected on five relevant themes from literature and our own empirical research. In the next section we shall give an illustration of the practice of these themes using the developments in public personnel management in the Netherlands.

Developments in Dutch Public Personnel Management

In this section we shall describe important developments in personnel management in the Netherlands during the last few years, and the factors and conditions which influenced those developments. Of course, this description is of necessity limited, and so we shall pay most attention to the themes outlined in the first section. First, however, we shall consider a very important contextual factor for public personnel management in the organization, namely the retrenchment policy of government since 1979; a factor that can be marked down as an important catalyst for certain processes in public personnel management.

Retrenchment and Employment

Since the turn of the century the number of government tasks has risen sharply, due to the building of the welfare state. Because of the increasing number of government tasks the government's share in employment compared with the market sector has also risen. In the period from 1960 to 1984 the government's share increased from 12 per cent (1960) to 16 per cent (1984). It should be noted, however, that the subsidized sector is included in the market sector in these figures (such as sanitation, welfare, Dutch railways). Should we include them in the government sector, this share would have risen even more sharply. Particularly in the period since 1970, the government has increased compared with the market sector. In those years the government thought that economic growth could be furthered particularly via creating jobs in the collective sector, and scientific reports supported this idea.

By 1980 the understanding had developed that fighting unemployment should be done mainly through an improvement in the market sector. Government expenditure had grown too high and needed to be curbed. 'Retrenchment' became the motto of successive cabinets.

On the one hand collective expenditures have been constantly cut down in the last few years, so that many government organizations have been forced to dispose of jobs because of the relatively high figure spent on pay and extra costs. On the other hand, measures are taken that are aimed at promoting employment, such as refilling vacancies, using part of the retrenchment on price compensation for creating new jobs (refilling appropriations). Various measures in due course have not failed to have an effect on the employment development with the government. In the period from 1982 to 1986 we saw a decline in the number of jobs in some sectors (municipalities, ministries), whereas a certain stabilization took place in other sectors. As already noted, retrenchment policy worked as an important catalyst for the character and contents of personnel management with the government. Discussion of role and position is thus given a new lease of life. We shall discuss this further in the next section.

Managerialism and Rationalism

In the Netherlands the term 'personnel management' has been in use for only a short time. An understanding that human resources ought to be managed has existed for only the last few years. Formerly, the stress was on the implementation of laws and regulations, and on the legal position of the employee. In the 1970s this changed. Under the influence of organization-technical ideas (human resources school) and the political desire to socialize personnel policy the stress is now more on policy development. Goals and means had to be explicated and as much as possible needed to be done in order to improve motivation, participation and the well-being of the individual. The reactive approach made way for the active approach of the personnel function.

Parallel to this development – or promoted by it – there was a relatively strong professionalization of the personnel function. [. . .] The result was an approach that can be characterized by and large as 'individual-oriented', fed mainly by moral and ideological considerations.

From an independent position the personnel function had to try and bring about a synthesis between individual interest and organizational interest, with the stress on the former. Often personnel departments became more independent, in order to express the independent position. The term 'personnel management' was not used. The term 'personnel *policy*' was used. In the past this greater independence meant that the personnel function in the Netherlands often had the character of an oppositional power against management (Bolweg, 1982: 49).

In the 1980s, discussion of the role and position of the personnel function had a new lease of life from the retrenchment policy of different government organizations. Far-reaching measures concerning working conditions and employment were often taken without PM being involved. Their power and influence in the policy process were small, also because of the fact that they often held a position far from the management. The implementation of measures, however, is mostly a task for the personnel departments. Particularly, negotiations with the trade unions play a crucial part in the implementation process. Personnel management has responsibilities it hardly had when the policy was brought about. This results in conflicts and puts the personnel functionary in a very difficult position.

In the last few years a shift in orientation could be observed. The activities have changed from employees' participation, emancipation, job evaluation, etc. to more efficiency-aimed activities such as flexibility, reorganization, and developing good management instruments (such as personnel infor-mation systems).

Guidance and control of organization processes have become an import-ant goal of PM. Individual interests are not actually the starting point, but they are related to organizational interests and, if necessary, they are made subordinate to them. In fact, we can speak of a rationalization of PM and of a growing identification with other management tasks (McGowen and Poister, 1983).

Some people have the impression that this has caused the power and influence of PM to grow. One indication is the perceptible growth in interest on the part of politicians. The 'personnel' task has become an important political task, especially in the large cities.

Public and Private Sectors

Public personnel in the Netherlands still have a special legal status. Pay and conditions are unilaterally determined although there is some consultation between the unions on the one hand and the minister or local councillors on the other hand; there is no system of collective bargaining. Second, public personnel are not entitled to strike in order to further their claims in a labour dispute. And third, their legal position and status have been laid down in a special act: the Public Servants Act of 1929.

This special legal status was legitimized by the notion that public personnel are the state's servants and should therefore have special rights and duties. In return, the pay and conditions should generally be better than those of employees in the private sector.

Because of the growing number of government activities and so the growing number of employees, most public personnel are performing similar jobs and activities to their counterparts in the private sector. Therefore there is hardly any reason to maintain their special status.

There is another reason why the special legal status is questioned: that is, the policies of the present Dutch government. One of the most important objectives of the current government is the strengthening of the private sector at the expense of the public sector, both on economic and political grounds (inasmuch as these are to be distinguished). During the last four years the labour costs in the two sectors have increasingly approached each other. The most important feature of this process concerns the pay levels. Till 1981 the pay and conditions of public personnel automatically followed the pay and conditions of the private sector, by means of the trend mechanism (based on an average of about 40 collective agreements in the private sector). This trend mechanism, however, was totally undifferentiated. As a consequence this mechanism was criticized more and more. In 1981 the necessity of cutting back public spending was the direct cause for abandoning the connection between private and public sector wages. From this moment onwards, the changes in wages have become the subject of political discussion and budgetary decisions. The government and parliament determine the pay and conditions of employees, in their role as political authority and not in their role as employer. It is clear that the unions in particular objected strongly to this change of course. At the present moment, the government is looking for alternative ways of pay settlement.

Because of the government's retrenchment policy, pay and conditions in the public sector have approached those of employees in the private sector. In the meantime, the Dutch government is still looking for a good replacement for the trend mechanism for wage development in the public sector. Eventually, the choice may again be in favour of a trend mechanism, but more differentiated; in combination with a certain degree of decentralization, in order to implement a more market-like wage policy.

Industrial relations in the public sector in the Netherlands are characterized by the non-existence of a system of collective bargaining. In its role as political authority and employer, the government negotiates with representatives of the unions of public personnel, but if they do not reach an agreement, the central or local authority can decide unilaterally about pay and other conditions. Recently, this situation was firmly criticized. Both parliament and the unions want to create a system in which both partners are considered to be equal. When the economy was prosperous and there were no financial constraints, this fundamental issue did not come to the fore. In times of retrenchment this system of combined roles becomes problematic and will generate conflicts. In this period parliament (or the local politicians) takes the role of employer, being more interested in budget motives than in trying to develop a good personnel policy.

Besides, the unions do not even have the right to strike. The Netherlands signed the European Social Covenant in 1961, which legitimized strikes of public personnel, but this has never been implemented by formal law. Since 1961 discussion has been going on concerning the ways in which the right to strike should be implemented. The question of which categories of employees should not be allowed a right of strike was a particular issue of debate. At this moment there is no consensus on this subject. Neverthless, there have been strikes in the Netherlands but there are more juridical constraints than in the private sector.

Conclusion

Personnel management in the public sector will have to concentrate these coming years mainly on the following external and internal tasks.

Strategic Approach

Personnel problems and social problems require a strategic approach in the next few years. [. . .]

Essential here is the extent of the links between the organization and its environment. This means that PM will have to anticipate or change socially and will have to translate up-to-date issues into personnel policy, such as women's emancipation; the rights of ethnic minorities; fighting youth unemployment; and humanization of labour.

Decentralization

In many organizations personnel management has developed into a professional, independent function. This has caused the implementation of the task to be too far away from line-management. Moreover, implementing tasks from a central staff department is inefficient and ineffective. De-centralization to the line-management seems advisable, together with the specialists. In fact, each manager is a personnel manager.

Instrumentation and Evaluation

It is important for PM to have the disposal of good instruments which, together, make it possible to work towards results. Instruments such as recruitment and selection, training, reward systems, etc. should also be measurable, in the sense that their effects are made clear and as to how far their contribution to the goals of personnel management and the goal-attainment of the organization are evaluated. In general, there is little talk of evaluable goals in personnel management. Strategies and goals need to be operationalized and evaluated in course of time. That way PM will be able to explain its contribution to the organization's functioning.

Pay System

As we said before, a typical problem for government organizations is the reward system. In the public sector it is necessary to develop instruments, procedures and methods in order to be comparable with working conditions in the private sector. Because the two sectors are interwoven, for example as to their activities in the labour market, this is of the greatest importance. It will be necessary to strive after a political stance that is as independent as possible. From the viewpoint of industrial relations (equal negotiations between employer and employee) it is important for an independent organ to collect accurate information to aid the negotiations.

Difference between Political and Employer Roles

The roles of political authority and employer cannot be separated; both central (government) and decentral (local authorities). From the viewpoint of industrial relations it is advisable for politics as much as possible to keep aloof from the negotiations between employer and employee. An entang-ling of the two interests would affect the legitimacy of acting with regard to the trade unions. At most, politics should set marginal conditions or a rough framework for negotiating. The collective bargaining system will have to give guarantees for the methods and procedures.

Intergovernmental Relations

The employer side is fragmented. On the one hand the general idea prevails that the various working conditions for different categories of civil servants should be coordinated, because of the idea that equal work under comparable circumstances should be met with comparable means. This means that a coordination system will have to be developed, which formalizes both the horizontal (between organizations at the same management level) and the vertical (between levels) relations and which regulates mutual communication and information exchange.

This external task for personnel management is very important for the position in the negotiations with the unions and for its own strategic stance within personnel management.

Finally, one remark of a more theoretical nature. In many points personnel policy in the public sector has similarities with the private sector, particularly in role and position and contents of the task. In the matter of decision-making and industrial relations, however, there are substantial differences. The double role of political authority and employer is very important there. This fact justifies a separate and specific theoretical approach to personnel management with the government. The starting point of a conflicting value system seems to be a possible fruitful framework of analysis for the studying of the dynamic in public personnel management. In my opinion, the interactions between values such as political responsiveness, social equity, organization efficiency and effectiveness and individual right, combined with the interaction between the roles of politician and employer, account for a significant part of the developments and processes in public personnel management. Much theoretical and empirical work will have to be done, however, to give this pronouncement empirical validity.

References

Bolweg, J. F. (1982) 'Personeelsbeleid: deprofessionalisering door openingen naar management en organisatie', in *Professionalisering van het personeelsbeleid*. Kluwer.

Klingner, D. E. and Nalbandian, J. (1985) *Public Personnel Management, Contexts and Strategies*. Englewood Cliffs, NJ: Prentice-Hall.

Legge, K. (1978) *Power, Innovation and Problem-solving in Personnel Management*. London: McGraw-Hill.

McGowen, R. P. and Poister, T. H. (1983) 'Personnel-related management tools in municipal administration', *Review of Public Administration*, 4(1): 78–96.

Miner, J. B. and Miner, M. G. (1977) *Personnel and Industrial Relations*, 3rd edn. London: Macmillan.

Rosenbloom, D. H. (1982) 'Emphasizing the public in public personnel administration', *Policy Studies Journal*, 11 (Dec): 245–55.

Thomason, G. (1978) *A Textbook of Personnel Management*, 3rd edn. London: IPM.

Thomson, A. W. J. and Beaumont, P. B. (1978) *Public Sector Bargaining: A Study of Relative Gain*. Aldershot: Saxon House.

Watson, T. J. (1977) *The Personnel Managers*. London: Routledge & Kegan Paul.

Index